The Best American
Sports Writing
2009

GUEST EDITORS OF
THE BEST AMERICAN SPORTS WRITING

THE BEST AMERICAN SPORTS WRITING™ 2009

Edited and with an Introduction
by Leigh Montville

Glenn Stout, *Series Editor*

A Mariner Original
HOUGHTON MIFFLIN HARCOURT
BOSTON • NEW YORK 2009

www.hmhbooks.com.

ISSN 1056-8034
ISBN 978-0-547-06971-5

Printed in the United States of America

DOC 10 9 8 7 6 5 4 3 2 1

Contents

Foreword

A FEW YEARS AGO I was invited to speak on a panel at a literary festival. It was my good fortune to share the stage with the series editor for another Best American title. We had never met before. In fact, I had never met any of the other series editors. We don't share cubicles in some gleaming office building but are scattered across the country, each in his or her rabbit warren, oblivious to the daily activities of each other, uniting only in the fall when our books are displayed together next to the checkout line at the local mega-bookstore. Before the program began we chatted a bit and shared some of our experiences. To no one's surprise, despite the subject difference of our books, they were not dissimilar.

At the end of the program we took some questions from the crowd, and one of the aspiring writers in attendance asked my colleague what was the most difficult task involved in editing one of these books. I imagine the writer expected to hear that it was reading so much material, or dealing with writers who lobby to appear in the book, or adapting to the yearly change in guest editors.

But as the question sank in, my colleague slowly turned my way. When our gaze met I experienced that same glimmer of recognition Magic Johnson's teammates must have felt across the court when Johnson was able to telegraph the impending arrival of a perfect, blind cross-court pass with nothing but a glance. In that brief instant my colleague and I shared the kind of secret knowledge that can only be gained by a decade or more of staring into the same abyss. He knew that I knew, and I knew that he knew.

No, the most daunting task we face as series editor of one of these collections is not the endless mountain of reading material, the plaintive letters of introduction and pleas that sometimes accompany submissions, our relationship with the guest editor, or anything else any reader could ever imagine.

It is the annual writing of this, the foreword.

As most writers worth anything will tell you, writing anything at all is rarely easy, but when one must write essentially the same portion of the same book year after year after year, one hazards turning out the literary equivalent of sitting on a recombinant stationary bicycle and pedaling like mad. The first few times the experience is not all that bad, but after a week or so one starts to avoid the basement, where the bicycle now sits gaining a slow cover of dust, a reminder of drudgery and sloth.

So too can be the foreword. At least that is my fear.

This is my nineteenth foray into these first pages of *The Best American Sports Writing,* and although I understand and empathize with those readers who skip past these words to get to the good parts, I nevertheless feel a responsibility to do a bit more than pen some pro forma version of the same thing I wrote last year or some preview of what I will write next year.

The writers who share the pages that follow know what I mean. Each time they confront the computer screen they face a similar experience. We've all been here before. Most of us are professionals, and after only a few years the experiences we confront and report on are not all that different. This is sports, after all, and in some form every story we write or witness is basically the same — there is some kind of conflict or competition, a winner and a loser, a victim and a victor, a beginning and an end. The challenge, of course, is each time to look inside that framework and see, not what is the same, but what is unique and different and tells us something unexpected.

Yet the difference between what I have to do as I confront the task of writing this foreword each year and what the other writers of this book do is also pronounced. I have now written a foreword to the same book some nineteen times. This is nothing. Most of the writers featured in these pages confront the same challenge each and every day.

Even after nineteen years I am often in awe of their efforts. Year in and year out I continue to be amazed at their creativity and commitment, their seemingly endless variety of approaches, and their capacity to astonish me in new and surprising ways. There is a reason, after all, why not all genres of journalism and writing result in collections as successful as this one, and that is that those writers have failed this essential test — to continually find the new within the old and to make us care.

And we do care. As many readers know, this is supposed to be a "bad" time for journalists and writers, and for newspapers, magazines, and publishing companies, and even, presumably, for the alphabet itself. And if one's measuring stick is a pile of money or credit card debt, as layoffs and downsizing and uncertainty have recently taken their toll, it is a bad time. But those are hardly the only measures. The work continues regardless, and for many of us, no matter how much we may complain, the only way we could ever really stop writing is if someone amputated our hands. Even then I suspect most of us would still manage to scratch out something with our bloodied stumps. Because at times like this you don't stop writing — you write *more*. Desperation can and does inspire. What follows will be better than what has come before. Of this I have no doubt.

I am under no illusions about the literary genre of the foreword. It is the equivalent of that piece of parsley that garnishes the plate before a meal and is usually still there, hiding under the napkin, at the end. No one, after all, is ever going to publish *The Best American Forewords*. Still, I try to use this space as a test, an exercise in writing something else, my chance to inspire and acknowledge and leave the reader looking forward to what comes next.

Speaking of which — next year's volume marks the twentieth edition of this series. And by then I think I might really have an idea about something to write for the foreword.

Every season I read every issue of hundreds of general interest and sports magazines in search of writing that might merit inclusion in *The Best American Sports Writing*. I also survey the Internet and contact the sports editors of some three hundred newspapers and hundreds of magazine editors and request their submissions. These sources of good sports stories are, of course, overwhelming and insufficient, so everyone reading this is encouraged to send me stories they've written or read in the past year that they would like to see reprinted in this volume. Writers, readers, and all other interested parties should feel free to alert me to either your own work or that of someone else for consideration in *The Best American Sports Writing 2010* according to the following criteria. Each story:

- must be column-length or longer;
- must have been published in 2009;
- must not be a reprint or a book excerpt;
- must have been published in the United States or Canada; and
- must be received by February 1, 2010.

All submissions must include the name of the author, the date of publication, and the publication name and address. Photocopies, tear sheets, or clean copies are fine. Readable reductions to 8½×11 are preferred. Submissions from online publications must be made in hard copy, and those who submit stories from newspapers should submit the story in hard copy as published. Since newsprint generally suffers in transit, newspaper stories are best copied and then mounted on 8½×11 paper; if the story also appeared online, attach the appropriate URL. There is no limit to the number of submissions either an individual or a publication may make, but please use common sense. Because of the volume of material I receive, no submission can be returned or acknowledged. I also believe it is inappropriate for me to comment on or critique any individual submission. Publications that want to be absolutely certain their contributions are considered are advised to provide a complimentary subscription to the address listed below. Those that already do so should make sure to extend the subscription.

No electronic submissions will be accepted, although stories that only appeared online are eligible. Please send all submissions by U.S. mail — midwinter weather conditions here at *BASW* headquarters often prevent me from receiving UPS or FedEx submissions — and please try to hit the deadline. I detest telling people in March that the deadline was February 1. I cannot overstate the obvious but will try to do so again — a story cannot be considered for this volume if it does not find its way to me. Don't be shy about submitting your own material.

Please submit either an original or a clear paper copy of each story, including publication name, author, and date the story appeared, to:

Glenn Stout
PO Box 549
Alburgh, VT 05440

Those with questions or comments may contact me at
basweditor@yahoo.com. Copies of previous editions of this book
can be ordered through most bookstores or online book dealers.
An index of stories that have appeared in this series can be found at
my website, glennstout.net. For updated information, readers and
writers are also encouraged to join the *Best American Sports Writing*
group on Facebook.

Thanks again go out to all at Houghton Mifflin Harcourt, particularly my editor, Susan Canavan, and Meagan Stacey and
Elizabeth Lee. Thanks also to Leigh Montville for his conscientious and enthusiastic participation. I again thank the website
sportsjournalists.com for posting submission guidelines, and my
thanks go also to Siobhan and Saorla. Like me, they live with this
book each year, sometimes tripping over it in the corner, and they
help me keep the pile straight, usually with grace and good humor.
But most of all, I once again give thanks to the writers for delivering me here each year.

All things considered, I rather like this abyss.

GLENN STOUT
Alburgh, Vermont

Introduction

THE VOICE FROM BEYOND one wall of my little office cubicle came from Will McDonough. He was the ever-intrepid reporter, the best in the business, working through his Rolodex of famous names, bartering rumor for facts on the telephone, tit for latest tat, wringing out the daily truth of what was happening on the Boston sports scene. The voice from beyond a second wall came from Peter Hotton. He was the *Boston Globe*'s resident handyman, answering reader hotline questions about household dilemmas ranging from carpenter ants to mildew to the pros and cons of aluminum siding.

I worked between these voices every day. Stereo. I was a sports columnist. The voices from the other sides of the walls were part of the challenge of the job.

"Tell me what the Patriots are going to do with the number-one draft choice," McDonough would say to the famous name of the moment. "They're not going to keep it, are they? They're not that crazy . . ."

"Sounds like a problem with the grout," Hotton would say to the reader. "You have to scrape out the old stuff, replace it with new. No, no, you can do it yourself . . ."

I could hear everything.

I would try to concentrate on the subject at hand, my quasi-literary effort of the moment. There were thoughts I wanted to put down, first on paper, back when everyone used typewriters, then later on the screen of the fat computer that blinked in front of me, the same size as an unopened case of beer, but sometimes the words would disappear on the country road from my imagination to my fingers. The other words, the outside words, would be too interesting.

"Larry Bird . . ."

"Septic tanks . . ."

"Jim Plunkett . . ."

"Mulch!"

The possibilities for further distraction were everywhere in the sports department of a big-city newspaper. At least they were in this one. If I stepped from my swivel chair, walked no more than ten feet, I could visit other desks, other people, other opinions. Baseball writer Peter Gammons might be back from Fenway Park, stuffed full of so much information it burst from the pores of his body. Bob Ryan, basketball, might be back from the Boston Garden, fresh from watching the Celtics practice. Bud Collins might be stopping in, back from Wimbledon, but packed for the next tennis tournament in Mauritania or wherever it was. Someone always was back from somewhere with news, anecdotes, opinions.

Neil Singelais, a formidable and myopic character who was the schoolboy editor, was a sports department anchor, engaged in loud and constant arguments with local coaches who thought their young athletes had been disrespected in public print. The conversations usually ended with a slammed phone at one end or the other . . . A man named Sully, no one knew him by anything else, would appear with his picks for the next night's dog races. He picked the winners under five or six aliases like Clocker Red or Top Dog, the choices spread across a chart in the paper, each pick running against his five other picks. He would boast how many winners he had selected on a previous night. No one ever pointed out his statistical advantage . . . An intern, a nighthawk, would yell from a desk of nighthawks answering phones, "Does anyone know if Derek Sanderson is married? A woman wants to know."

Someone might produce a Wiffle bat. A game would begin. Someone might drop a lit cigarette into a wastebasket. A fire would begin. A television would play constantly over the copy desk if any sporting event was in progress. Four-letter words would fly through the air, foul and happy lightning bugs. The boss, at any moment, could call you into his separate office and say you had to go to Milwaukee tomorrow.

"Yaz says . . ."

"I'd prop that up with a wooden dowel . . ."

"Andre Tippett . . ."

"Do you have a generator?"

The trick was to shut everything out. This sometimes was a very hard trick.

I was a sportswriter at the *Globe* from 1968 through 1989. I say I have been a sportswriter for all of my adult life — three years at a newspaper in New Haven before I reached Boston, twelve years at *Sports Illustrated* after I left, and now I write sports books — but the real time was at the *Globe*. That was when I was a real sportswriter.

The clock was always running when the real sportswriters worked at a newspaper. Impediments always stood in the way. Travel to an event and you sat in a press box line with other poor souls, everyone crammed together, stat sheets and Diet Cokes edging into someone else's space, everybody typing, eighteen minutes to deadline, seventeen, sixteen. Strangers on the way out of the event read over your shoulder, commented on your rapid judgments. Have a little time and decide to work in the office and you were in the everyday chaos.

Was this the way Updike or Philip Roth did it? Probably not, but this was the way Grantland Rice and Red Smith and Jim Murray and Damon Runyon did it. A. J. Liebling and W. C. Heinz covered fights at ringside. Good enough. You were part of a continuum.

"I can write faster than anyone who writes better," McDonough always said. "I can write better than anyone who writes faster."

That seemed to be a fine goal for everyone in the business, a golden rule of composition. Metaphors were snatched from the air, slapped on the printed page. Maybe they applied. Maybe they didn't. Anecdotes were shoved into any place possible. Sometimes they even were appropriate. Clichés were blotted out by some inner mechanism, some cliché spotter that sometimes worked and sometimes didn't. The theme of a story, a column, whatever, had to be decided early, then hammered through to the end. I remember — and this happened often — reaching the final paragraphs in a story and realizing that this point, this view, was what I should have used for the entire construction. Too late. I remember reading stories in the morning, nine-hundred-word efforts that had been blasted into life in, say, a twenty-minute time span, created with more adrenaline than wit or style during the preceding night. It felt like I was reading something written by someone else.

"It's in English," I would say. "That's good. The score is in there. That's good."

All work was done with this sense of urgency. The newspaper was the main delivery system for sports news. Television had changed the game, made the sportswriter climb further behind the scenes, find explanations for what many viewers already had seen take place on the field or court or hockey rink, but the newspaper still was the voice that delivered the true story. Television left a lot of holes. "The *Globe*'s Here!" billboards around the city proclaimed. Everyone knew what that meant. Everyone bought the *Globe*.

"I check the front-page headline to see if we're at war," Clutch Glendon, a sports fan from Dorchester, once told me. "If we're not, I throw away the whole front of the paper. Then I read every word in the sports. Devour it."

Clutch Glendon was the public we serviced. The sports department was one of the *Globe*'s most solid assets. The editor, Tom Winship, always claimed that sports was what kept the paper solvent during the agitated times of forced busing in Boston in the seventies. While a large number of consumers balked at the *Globe*'s pro-busing position — bullets fired at the building on Morrissey Boulevard, delivery trucks pushed into the Fort Point Channel — the same consumers wanted to know what was happening with the Red Sox, the Bruins, the Celts. They continued to buy the paper.

Management responded by spending big money on sports. The *Globe* covered all possible events. Four and five and six people would cover spring training in Florida. A battalion of writers would cover the Super Bowl. Two, maybe three writers would cover the Celtics and Bruins on the road. More if the teams were in the playoffs. The many local colleges were covered, home and away. The crew covering the Olympics grew larger every four years. (The *Globe* rented an entire house when the Winter Games were in Lake Placid in 1980.) Assorted writers wrote "takeouts" — long, magazine-length stories, profiles, and deeper explorations of problems or trends. A takeout ran almost every day. The sports section itself ran for pages and pages.

The mandate was to find out everything, interview everyone. (I once wrote a story about the food the Red Sox ate in their locker room after games during a winning streak. I copied down the items in my notebook as I walked around the buffet spread, and Vinnie Orlando, the clubhouse attendant, screamed, "Jesus Christ, now they're interviewing the food!") The job was to beat the *Boston Herald,* to beat the Boston television stations, to beat the national competition, to beat everyone, to beat the world.

"Covering the Red Sox was harder than covering the war," Steve Fainaru, a baseball beat writer at the *Globe* in the eighties, now a war correspondent for the *Washington Post,* said last year after he won the Pulitzer Prize for his work in Iraq. "There was the danger, the worry that you could be killed in Iraq, but take that away and the stories were yours. It was easy. You talked to people and worked on a story, and you didn't have to worry if someone else would scoop you in the morning. That's *all* you would worry about when you were covering the Red Sox. You'd watch the news in terror every night. You'd be afraid to pick up the *Herald* in the morning. The pressure never left."

This was exactly the job I wanted. I loved it. I loved it all. I loved the energy. I loved the games. I loved the writing. When I was ten years old, I had decided I wanted to do this. I delivered the local New Haven newspaper every morning, and when I was finished, I flipped open the paper to the sports page, and a man named Frank Birmingham had his picture in the top left corner at the beginning of his column. He would be in Louisville for the Kentucky Derby, in Sarasota at spring training, in New York for the World Series. Someone paid him to do this! I couldn't imagine a better job in the world.

Nothing at the *Globe* changed my mind. I went to all the places Frank Birmingham went. I went to more. I went to Australia for the America's Cup. I went to London to watch Marvin Hagler win a world boxing title. I went to the Fabulous Forum and Madison Square Garden and Yankee Stadium and Dodger Stadium and Augusta National and Seoul, Korea, for the Olympics and to Waltham, Massachusetts, for the annual Thanksgiving Day football game against Brockton High School. I talked with all of the legends of the time, found them where I found them and talked. I talked with Yaz and Larry and Bobby. I talked with Joe Namath once in a shower. He was undressed, soaping himself up. I was fully clothed. I talked with Muhammad Ali once while Redd Foxx told him dirty jokes. I talked with rookies and old-timers. I talked with Bronco Nagurski. I talked with Gordie Howe, Bobby Hull, Jean Beliveau. I talked with everyone.

On one summer day, I went to Salem, New Hampshire, and talked with Duffy Lewis in his condo. He had been the left fielder for the Red Sox years ago when Tris Speaker played center and Harry Hooper played right. This was the stuff of baseball history books. He was an old man now, retired, pleasant and quiet until his wife announced she was going downstairs to collect the mail. The moment she was gone he hurried to the closet.

"You want a quick one?" he asked, pulling out a bottle of Wild Turkey and two glasses. The time was eleven o'clock in the morning.

I remember that I hurried back to the office with this little anecdote. I added it to the pile, added it to the noise. Duffy Lewis and me! Wild Turkey! Eleven in the morning! Someone else, no doubt, told a story about another athlete and alcohol at an odd time. Someone else added another. And another.

Every day was a package to be unwrapped. Gammons would write chain-of-consciousness note columns for Sunday filled with fact, with opinion, with names from everywhere, sports and politics, rock 'n' roll, wackiness of all dimensions. The columns were so long they filled an entire page, and he would have written more if he had been given another page. Ryan explained picks and rolls and the deficiencies of, say, the Los Angeles Lakers with the depth of a Talmudic scholar. McDonough would declare that this was what the facts were in any given situation, believe me or be a fool. He once wound up rolling on the floor with a copy editor in a dispute about an adjective. Collins would dramatize tennis matches as if they were heavyweight championship bouts, bloody battles. The phones would ring. The clock would click toward deadline. Someone would ask if you wanted a sandwich from the cafeteria.

"Did you hear what Jim Rice did?"

"Try a little spackle . . ."

Wonderful.

The change in the scene already had begun, of course, when I left for *SI* in 1989, which now is twenty years ago. The advent and development of the personal computer had shrunk the communal gathering considerably as writers were able to work from home, typing out their stories in solitude and their underwear. Nobody went to the office. Television had begun to have a larger and larger effect. McDonough worked in television. Collins was there. Gammons. Ryan had taken a whirl as a local sportscaster. Everybody seemed to talk on some radio show. The perception that the newspaper was the important and final word on sports had begun to disappear.

The stories had become harder and harder to do. As the athletes made money, more money, staggering amounts of money, they became more insulated. The press conference became a daily fact of life, replacing the conversation at the locker stall. Everyone pretty much heard the same words, spoken in front of some curtain covered with an advertising message for prime exposure. Television clambered to the front, cameras and lights, the sound bite more important than the anecdote. "How do you feel?" replaced "Do you own a dog? What'd your father do for a living? Why do you make the sign of the cross in the dirt when you step to the plate?"

The technology that was supposed to make the sportswriter's job easier with later deadlines, with easier access to resources, instead became a fat, sucking beast in the corner. With every advance, with the arrival of the Internet, which captured hearts and minds in a dazzlingly short stretch of time, with the constant advance to e-mails to blogs to YouTube videos, to who knows what might come next, the value of the word on the newspaper page became less and less. The *Globe*'s here? No, I read it already online.

"What a great job you have," people would say in the long ago. "I'd do that for nothing."

Now they can. Now they do.

On the day I write this essay, a half-dozen newspapers filed for bankruptcy. By the time you read it, I'm sure the list will be much larger. I still get the *Globe* every day, but it shrinks in front of my eyes. The advertising is pretty much gone. The editorial mandate to go out and kill the world, the swagger, is gone. The paper is on life support, part of a business on life support. Swagger is hard to find with the sick.

I was interested, when I became the guest editor of the book you have in your hands, to see how many stories I would read from newspapers. The *Best American Sports Writing* series always has been tough territory for the real sportswriters to crack. They have been short-order cooks going up against French chefs. The constraints of time and speed always have worked against them, favoring the measured and polished efforts of writers from magazines. The stories from newspapers that made the book routinely have been the takeouts, the magazine-type pieces that were executed over a longer stretch of time. Oddly, the stories that didn't make the book were the ones you read first on the day they were published, bursts of fact and opinion that covered a game, a moment, a flash of the day. The flash of the day, alas, soon becomes dated, replaced by the next flash of tomorrow.

Glenn Stout, the true editor of this series, sent me eighty stories from the past year in a taped-together Nike shoebox. From this I was supposed to cut the field to the twenty-four entries that appear in this book. Eight of the eighty stories came from American daily newspapers. One, "Searching for Answers to a Painful Question" by Mike Wise of the *Washington Post,* made the book. That was it. A story from a blog made the book. One from a literary magazine at the University of Virginia made the book. The rest were from familiar magazine sources: *Sports Illustrated, ESPN, Texas Monthly, Outside, Backpacker, Esquire, Play,* etc. The newspapers — and the one story by Wise was a grand takeout about the murder of a Baylor basketball player by his former teammate — were at the back of the pack.

Was I surprised?

No.

Was I saddened?

A little.

Was I also, in a curious way, heartened?

Yes. Very much.

The writing in all of the stories in this book is terrific. The stories are terrific. From Jon Wertheim's tale of a mixed martial arts expert who became an alleged participant in the largest bank robbery in British history (*SI*) to Alan Prendergast's account of senseless death on a mountain (*Outside*) to Wright Thompson's very different close-up look at an aging Jack Nicklaus (ESPN.com) to Tracy Ross's hike with her father, the man who molested her as a child (*Backpacker*), the reader is brought to places that surprise, delight, amuse, sadden, touch one emotion after another.

Bruce Barcott, in "Life and Limb," first published in *Runner's World,* writes one of the great lead sentences of all time: "On the day he decided to pay a man to cut off his leg with a power saw, Tom White woke up with a powerful yearning to run." If you don't read the sentence after that, check your pulse because you might be dead. Bestselling author Michael Lewis explains Cuba and baseball and the siren call of capitalist dollars in "Commie Ball" in ways that no one ever has (*Vanity Fair*). John Spong in *Texas Monthly* takes an easy handout of a story — fifty-nine-year-old man returns to play college football — steps behind the fast interview, and finds in "Untitled Mike Flynt Project" a character and tale far darker than everyone else suspected.

The list continues. Read the stories for yourself. Amazing stuff.

Not only would I put this book on the same shelf with any of its predecessors, I could make a book, two books, out of the stories that didn't make the cut and put them on the shelf. There has been great intramural debate about the future of sports writing as newspapers decline, as emphasis shifts further and further to the home computer screen, as the next steps are formulated in the gathering of news. Who will pay the reporters? How will it all work? What form will it take? I would suggest that this book is at least one comforting light in the window of the future.

There will be great stories written about sports as long as sports exist. There always will be a market. There always will be people who can do the job. The pen can describe thoughts, emotions, go to places the television cameras never can find, never will find, no matter what technology is developed. No, the stories might not come out of the clanging newsroom that I knew. No, they might not land as part of a thud on the doorstep in the morning. No, the picture of the man who went to the places and games might not be at the top of the printed page. There still will be stories. There still will be writers. There still will be great sports writing.

Will there be sportswriters?

Ah, now that is a different question.

I root very hard for the survivors left in that place where I once lived. Their numbers are down, and their workload has increased. The job has become a twenty-four-hour grind, responsibilities stretched to cover all news all the time, instant reports to be filed on the website, competition coming from a thousand different directions. The Southeast Expressway goes past the *Globe*, and every now and then as I hurtle along, sixty miles per hour, and look at the building, I confess that I mostly think about the fun from the past. I have trouble thinking about fun in there at the present.

We shall see what we shall see.

(An addendum: Peter Gammons is now a venerable talking head on ESPN baseball coverage and in 2005 was inducted into the media wing of the Baseball Hall of Fame. Bob Ryan still writes a column in the *Globe* and is a member of the Basketball Hall of Fame. Both Will McDonough, who passed away in 2003, and Bud Collins, who continues to cover tennis for ESPN and an assortment of outlets, are members of the National Sportscasters and Sportswriters Hall of Fame. Peter Hotton still answers reader questions about household problems for the *Globe,* but now he does it in an online chat. Myself? I took assorted breaks to scuttle around the Internet while I wrote these words and sometimes listened to a television program or a CD playing in another room. Habits die hard.)

LEIGH MONTVILLE

BRUCE BARCOTT

Life and Limb

FROM RUNNER'S WORLD

ON THE DAY he decided to pay a man to cut off his leg with a power saw, Tom White woke up with a powerful yearning to run. It was last October, early morning. The girls were still asleep. White rolled over and found an empty bed. His wife, Tammy, had already pulled on her shoes and set off on a five-mile run on the streets of Buena Vista, Colorado. Without him. Again.

The Whites are well-known in Buena Vista, a farm town on the sunny central Colorado plain between the Arkansas River and the 14,000-foot Collegiate Peaks. Tom, a forty-seven-year-old country doctor, has delivered many of the kids in town. He's a trim, compact fellow with an unflaggingly sunny outlook — kind of a one-man optimist's club. It's not uncommon for a woman to stop him in the produce section of the City Market, put his hand on her pregnant belly, and ask, "Is that a contraction?" Tammy, forty-six, is a physical therapist whose patients sometimes drop by the family's house on Main Street for treatment right there in the living room. The sight of Tom and Tammy running together was a part of daily life in Buena Vista. Tom had been a nationally ranked cross-country runner in college, and Tammy completed a marathon about once a month. For ten years they'd paced each other along the river trails and up the high ridges outside of town. But by early 2007, the townsfolk didn't see Dr. Tom running so much anymore. A degenerative condition in his left leg, the result of a motorcycle accident in his twenties, was giving him pain. That summer the pain worsened. By autumn, Tammy was running alone. For Tom, the injury was more than a disappointment. It was maddening.

Running was an integral part of his life, his identity, it was how he moved when he felt most completely himself. And it had been taken away from him once before, after the crash. He'd spent years teaching himself how to run on a badly wounded leg. Now he was losing it all over again.

It was a school day, so he had to get the show on the road. He showered, dressed, and woke the girls. Eight-year-old Whitney and her four-year-old sister, Jasmine, both wearing Hannah Montana T-shirts, picked their way through matching bowls of Kix cereal. "Jassy, you want some oatmeal?" Tom asked. She made a face and shook her head. He mixed some Spanish coffee — hot milk, instant coffee, two teaspoons of sugar — and handed Tammy a mug as she came in the back door, flushed and damp with sweat.

Tammy drove Jasmine to preschool, and Tom walked Whitney a mile down the road to Avery-Parsons Elementary. This was their morning custom. Whitney kicked a soccer ball as she and her dad chatted about possible Halloween costumes. Tom quietly endured the pain shooting through his leg. On the walk home, he wrestled with his frustrations.

The previous weekend he'd taken the Buena Vista Demons to the state cross-country championships. In their spare time, Tom and Tammy coached the high school girls cross-country team, and it was a tradition for them to join the runners on a 5-K warm-up. But last weekend, the pain was too much to bear.

"Coach!" the girls called. "You running with us?"

Tom's heart sank. "I can't," he said. "You go on without me."

He watched his squad head off. *Next year,* he thought, *I'm going to be telling my own daughters I can't walk to school with them.*

Over the years he'd joked about getting his gimpy leg cut off. "When this thing doesn't serve me anymore," he'd tell Tammy, "I'm going to get it amputated. Get a prosthesis."

Now it didn't seem like such a joke. Three years earlier, at the New York City Marathon, he heard about the Achilles Track Club's Freedom Team, a group of disabled Iraq and Afghanistan war veterans racing on prostheses. At that race, he met Sarah Reinertsen, a triathlete who runs on a hydraulic knee and a Flex-Run foot, a variation of the carbon-fiber Cheetah foot used by Paralympic athletes. Reinertsen had lost a leg to a congenital condition and still outpaced many able-bodied runners.

Back at home, White slipped into the garage to get his bike. He walked past a corkboard pinned with finishing medals and a rack of running shoes custom-designed for his unorthodox gait. Because it didn't pound his leg, bicycling was one activity he could still enjoy without pain. He rode the mile to his office, where Rhoda Boucher, his nurse, handed him a full schedule of patients. Tom saw a little bit of everything at Mountain Medical Clinic, the practice he ran with two partners: broken bones, newborn checkups, injured river guides, obese patients with heart failure. His oldest patient was ninety-five; his youngest born last night.

The work took his mind off his own decision for a few hours. As a medical procedure, amputation goes back 2,500 years, but the human fear of limb loss hearkens back even further, to something primal. It's a horror-movie cliché, and for good reason. The psychological toll — the self ripped apart, the disfigurement, the revulsion in the eyes of others — arguably dwarfs the pain. Amputation has always been an act forced upon a body. It's the last resort, the corner where gangrene traps the limb.

For Tom White it was a different story. The choice he faced wasn't life or death. It was life or better life. With his natural leg, he faced a future without running or hiking — the pursuits that animated his physical self. He felt fully alive, he *was who he was,* when his heart was pumping and his lungs were bellowing. Now he was considering cutting off a part of himself to retain that core identity. For Tom, amputation didn't look like a loss. It looked like a life regained — if everything went well.

That afternoon, he went through a stack of charts, dealt with prescription refills, and locked up the office. As he rode home, he recalled hitting a rut a few days earlier, and how it made his shin creak. Now a dull, familiar pain crept up his leg. *Aw, man,* he thought. *Even the bike's giving me trouble now.*

That night, lying in bed next to Tammy, he let his thoughts slip across the pillow. "You know," he said, "I think it's time to amputate my left foot."

Tammy's eyes freaked. *Holy cow! I can't believe he's telling me this right when we're falling asleep,* she thought.

Her reaction surprised him. "Cool!" she said. She missed him as a running partner. But more than that, Tammy wanted to grow old with Tom — *with* him. So much of their joy in life came from running and hiking. Vicarious pleasure sucked. She wanted Tom to feel the endorphin rush too.

The next morning she chased Tom around the kitchen with a date book. "Let's schedule it next month," she said.

"Whoa!" he said. Second thoughts kicked in. He was still talking theory. She was pressing for fact.

Hours later, the 2007 *Runner's World* "Heroes of Running" issue came in the mail. Tammy flipped open a piece on Amy Palmiero-Winters. She'd run a 3:04 in the Chicago Marathon on a prosthesis. "Tom!" Tammy called. "Do you believe in fate? Look at her."

She held out a photo of Palmiero-Winters, looking powerful and confident on her mechanical setup. Tom took a good long gaze. He didn't see a disabled person. He saw an elite marathoner pushing to qualify for the Olympic Trials. He smiled.

"That's it," he told Tammy. "That's what I want."

Tom White decided to cut off his leg at a time when there had never been a better time to do such a thing. In the past few years, a profound change has swept through American society and the global sports culture. Seemingly overnight, amputees have morphed from pity magnets to competitors. What once was handicapped is now bionic. A generation ago, disabled activists fought to pass the Americans with Disabilities Act. Today the International Association of Athletics Federations (IAAF), track and field's world governing body, wrestles with the implications of South African sprinter Oscar Pistorius, who uses prosthetic legs, beating able-bodied runners in elite competition.

New technology has certainly made an impact. Devices like the Cheetah foot and the C-leg (a biomechanical prosthesis that uses a computer chip to run a hydraulic knee) allow amputees a more natural range of motion. But the gear — which has been widely available for nearly a decade — is only part of the story.

The real change has come in public awareness and attitude. It has something to do with Iraq War amputees proudly wearing prostheses emblazoned with Harley-Davidson logos and American flags. It has something to do with athletes like Pistorius making a leap from Paralympic champion to Olympic hopeful. It has something to do with amputees like Reinertsen flashing her high-tech leg in glossy ads for Lincoln sedans. These athletes raise the visibility of prostheses at a time when the melding of man and machine seems not only possible but inevitable. Tech fanatics are talking about mobile-phone implants. Skin-deep microchips help owners locate lost pets. Pistorius and Reinertsen are no longer human tragedies. They're the future. And they look damn cool.

In fact, the perception of athletes using prosthetic limbs has changed so quickly that some are now howling about the perceived advantage of prostheses users. Lawyers spent much of the past year dueling over Pistorius's right to run in the Beijing Olympics. (When Pistorius failed to post a qualifying time, he ended the controversy over Beijing. But the issue — whether prostheses give him an unfair advantage — is far from settled.)

Last fall, as the issue of prosthetics in sports made headlines around the world, Tom White chose to undergo one of the most radical transformations any runner will ever face: from two-legged to one. Tom's choice raised profound questions about identity, athletics, and the human body. How far would you go to sustain your running life? Would you sacrifice money, career opportunities, relationships? Would you give up your left leg?

I followed Tom through the entire process, from decision to surgery and on through months of grueling rehabilitation. Though Oscar Pistorius and Sarah Reinertsen make it look easy, running on a prosthetic limb — heck, *walking* on one — is hardly easy. It's a struggle. It takes grit and determination. When you lose a leg, it's a long, hard road back to running.

A week after making his decision, Tom sat in the exam room of Dr. David Hahn, a Denver orthopedic surgeon. Dr. Hahn, fifty-nine, had seen a lot of legs in his career. White's was a piece of medical history. Twenty-five years earlier a motorcycle accident had nearly severed the limb four inches above the ankle. Reattachment surgery, pioneering for its time, saved the lower leg and foot. It was heroic work back then, but the bone had never fully healed. Now it was cracked beyond repair. For twenty-five years, Tom had run on the human equivalent of a patched tire. He'd finally worn it out.

"You know, my first job is usually to tell people all the ways they can keep their leg," Dr. Hahn told Tom. "But it looks like you've already done that."

Three weeks later, on November 27, Tom and Tammy and the

girls made the two-hour drive from Buena Vista to Denver's Presby-terian/St. Luke's Medical Center. Along the way they tallied moun-tains Tom's foot had climbed. "Mount Princeton! Mount Yale!" A few days earlier, Tom and Tammy had told the girls what was going to happen. "My foot hurts me, and once the doctors take it off, it won't hurt me anymore," Tom said.

Whitney began to cry. Tammy wondered if the amputation scared her. But that wasn't it. "I'm sad because Daddy was hurting and we didn't know," Whitney said.

That afternoon, Tom sat in a hospital gown on a gurney, prepped for surgery. A saline drip line draped from his right arm. For a man about to lose a limb, he looked calm. "I don't have any fear about the surgery," he said. "I'm excited to get this going." Asked what he planned to do with the foot, he answered, "You know, it would make great practical joke material." He laughed. "Tammy wants it cremated and spread someplace. But no. I think I'll just let them toss it out as medical waste."

Tom understood the risks. He'd seen men his age die in routine surgery. Things can happen — bleeding, infection, embolisms, hos-pital screwups. You didn't have to tell him that doctors and nurses were human. He also knew there was no guarantee he'd run again. If the amputated leg got infected, they'd have to cut again, above the knee. And who knew how he'd take to a mechanical leg? Chris Jones, the prosthetics expert he'd be working with, had warned him: "These things don't walk themselves."

He took those risks and fears and stuffed them in a locker in a far corner of his mind. If he was going to get through this, he had to stay up, focus on the positive. "I just need to get through rehab and then I'll be good," he said.

Late in the afternoon, a nurse wheeled him to the operating room. Tammy held his hand, told him she loved him, then let go. She turned and walked away. Once she was out of Tom's sight, she let herself wipe away a tear.

The anesthesiologist poked an epidural catheter into his spine. For years, Tom had advised pregnant patients not to fear the epi-dural. "It's just a little sting, like having blood drawn," he told them. But he never knew for sure. Now, as he nodded out, his last thought was this: *I'm happy I was telling them the truth . . .*

It took twenty-two minutes to lose the lower leg. Working behind a plastic face shield, Dr. Hahn used a scalpel to peel away muscle and tissue, exposing Tom's tibia (shinbone) and fibula, the beam-and-stud of the lower leg. The bones were small and thin, like the remnants of an order of pork ribs. A nurse handed Dr. Hahn a small reciprocating power saw, the kind of thing you'd use for small jobs around the house. Zip — tibia gone. Zip — fibula gone. Or rather, almost gone. In a maneuver known as an Ertl procedure, Dr. Hahn used a leftover bit of the fibula to form a bridge between the two bones, locking them in place with screws. The bridge would allow Tom to put more weight on the residual limb below the knee. With the bones secured, the surgeon clamped off Tom's blood vessels with tiny metal clips, then used flaps of skin hanging below the bone bridge to wrap the stump. (*Residual limb* is the medical term; *stump* is the word many amputees use.) Dr. Hahn sewed the works closed with surgical thread.

Then it was over. A nurse dressed the stump in bandages and wheeled Tom to a recovery room to let the anesthesia wear off.

The next morning, Tom sat up and stared at a spot ten inches below his bandaged stump. "Phantom pain is real," he told Tammy. "It feels like my left heel is sitting on the bed, like someone is pressing down on it. And there's a slight pain in my arch." There was, of course, no heel, no arch. Ninety percent of recent amputees get phantom sensations (not always pain) that are triggered by brain neurons wired to receive signals from nerves in the amputated limb. Over time those neurons reprogram themselves to respond to adjacent body regions, and the sensations subside.

A nurse stopped by. She had experience with fresh amputees. "That's nothing," she said. "Wait till your toes start itching."

Tom was in an ebullient mood, helped along by drugs that kept both his legs numb. Friends and family kept the phone jangling. "Listen, dude, I just dropped five pounds in surgery, and I'm back at my college weight," Tom told one caller. "I'm going to be kicking your butt soon enough." He hung up. "That was Tim Terrill," he said. "He's an old Vigilante. They put an item about my amputation up on the green line, and now all the old runners are calling me."

The green line was an e-mail list connecting alumni of the cross-country team at Adams State College, a small liberal arts school in

Alamosa, Colorado, about fifty miles north of the New Mexico border. They called themselves Vigilantes (pronounced *Vee-hill-an-tez*)
after their legendary coach Joe Vigil. Vigil is to cross-country running what John Wooden is to basketball. During his stint at Adams
State from 1965 to 1993, Vigil's teams won fifteen national titles.
He produced 425 All-Americans and 89 individual champions in
various running disciplines. Since then, he has coached Deena
Kastor, Meb Keflezighi, and other elites.

News of Tom's amputation set the green line abuzz. Of course,
over the years Vigil had produced runners who were faster than the
Buena Vista doctor, but none more beloved. The tales told about
White were passed down from generation to generation at Adams
State, part of a storied program's cultural lore. They were tales of
promise and misfortune, courage and fortitude. They were stories
of the time he lost his left leg — the first time.

As a teenager, Tom ran along lonely ribbons of road outside Albuquerque. A poster of Steve Prefontaine hung on his bedroom
wall. He was the only white kid on his high school cross-country
team. "We were half Navajo, half Hispanic, and me," he once recalled. The legacy of that team lives on in his hard-to-place accent.
When he speaks, what escapes his throat is the ghost of a studious
white boy navigating between the barrio and the rez.

Coach Vigil recruited him after Tom won the New Mexico cross-
country state championship in 1977. Despite Adams State's small
size and remote location, Vigil built a powerhouse program by
combining effective motivational techniques — the man has
world-class charm and magnetism — with cutting-edge scientific
training methods. "We ran a bold style," said Tom. "We went out
hard, got to the front, and stayed there. And if another team had a
strong runner, Coach Vigil would specifically assign a couple of our
guys to key on him. Didn't matter where they finished in the race;
they just had to beat their man."

His first year at Adams State, the team finished third at the NAIA
national championships. Tom took fifth in the individual race. The
next two years, Tom and his squad claimed the team title. By the
spring of his junior year, Tom had run a 4:02 mile and looked to vie
for the individual title in the national cross-country championships
the next fall.

Then came the accident. The summer before his senior season,
Tom and two teammates, Randy Cooper and Pat Porter, found

work as beekeepers in Rifle, Colorado, about 180 miles west of Denver. They lived in a tree house to save money. Porter would go on to dominate the U.S. cross-country scene in the 1980s, competing in two Olympics and posting a record eight straight national titles, but at that point he and Cooper and Tom were just three college kids trying to raise cash for tuition.

One night when Tom was making his way back to the tree house from Rifle, a drunk driver in a pickup swerved in front of Tom, who was riding a motorcycle. The truck's bumper caught Tom's left foot and tore it almost completely off his leg. He went down, skidded on the road, and came to a stop on his back. He lifted his left leg and watched his foot droop like a grotesque flag. All that kept it attached were his Achilles tendon and a flap of skin.

Thinking quickly, Tom applied his own tourniquet and then asked a passerby to compress a pressure point in his groin area, which prevented him from bleeding to death. A helicopter flew him to St. Mary's Hospital in Grand Junction, Colorado. When a doctor there saw him, Tom, still conscious, begged him not to amputate. "Doc, I'm a runner!" he said. "Save my foot. Please save my foot!"

As it happened, Dr. Richard Janson had just arrived at St. Mary's. Only two weeks before White's accident, Dr. Janson and a nurse wrote the hospital's first protocols for transporting amputated extremities. By coincidence, that nurse was on the chopper that flew Tom to St. Mary's. Dr. Janson hadn't been on call that day, but staffers called him anyway to see if he could help.

Dr. Janson reattached Tom's foot, but he didn't have enough skin to work with. After a temporary graft was performed by Dr. Janson five days later, White was flown to an Albuquerque hospital for a far more complex — and torturous — graft. Surgeons there peeled a patch from Tom's thigh and grafted it onto his leg. The skin wasn't just lifted and planted like a piece of sod. White's legs were pinned in a way that forced him to sit completely still for three weeks with his left leg bent cross-legged so it met his right thigh. Skin from the thigh was peeled back slowly, like the lid of a sardine tin, and grafted bit by bit to the left leg — while the skin was still attached to the right thigh. "You could tell he was in pain," recalled Vigil, who often visited White in the hospital. "His leg had atrophied to just skin and bones."

Though Dr. Janson saved Tom's foot, his racing days were over.

He joined Vigil's staff as an assistant to finish his senior year, but all the rehab in the world couldn't bring back a 4:02 mile. For two years he lived on crutches. When he finally set them down and walked again, the crutches bowed like wishbones.

For seven years, there was no running. Then Tom met Tammy. They fell in love and married. Tom went to the University of California, Davis, for med school. There in Davis, Tammy joined a running club called the Buffalo Chips. She'd leave on Saturday mornings and return with tales of runs through redwood groves, up the crest of the Sierra, or down to the Pacific. Tom felt like a hungry man hearing his wife describe a banquet.

He felt himself jonesing for a run. One day after watching Tammy finish a half-marathon, Tom acted on the impulse.

"Tammy, let's run to the car!" he said.

"What?"

"I want to run to the car!"

They ran to the car. "You couldn't really call it running," she later recalled. "It was a sorry sight. He looked like Quasimodo."

The next morning, Tom began teaching himself to run again. He made his way in a sort of stumble-hop around the block. The next morning he did a block and a half. Then two blocks. "It was ugly, but every day I went a little farther," he said. It took him a while to figure out how to adapt his gait. But eventually he started joining Tammy on her runs. His pronation was so extreme that he destroyed a new pair of running shoes every couple of months, until finally he found a custom shoemaker who designed an angled sole built to withstand his distinct pounding.

He started to enter races but encountered a unique problem. His limp was so pronounced that race officials would jump onto the course and pull him off. They thought he'd broken his leg. "Hey!" he'd shout. "I'm not done yet!"

The pain never went away. Every step hurt. But Tom trained himself to ignore it, to make it white noise. He built up his distance. One year he ran a marathon. Then a 50-K. He posted a 3:45 in the London Marathon. He tried the Leadville Trail 100 five times. He ran fifty miles several years, once making it to mile 72.

The race that made White a legend at Adams State wasn't a 100-miler, though. Every year a group of alumni return to Alamosa to challenge the current team in a five-mile race. It's not a typical

take-it-easy-on-the-old-guys match. Though the Grizzlies are peren-
nial national champion contenders, the alums often include Olym-
pic-caliber talent. In 1991, ten years after Tom's motorcycle accident, Tammy called up Joe Vigil. "Coach," she said, "don't tell
anyone, but Tom's coming to run the alumni meet." Pat Porter
won the race, but Tom White won the day. "He hobbled through
the entire five miles," recalled Vigil. "People were lined up and
down the last mile just to watch Tommy finish the race. Everybody
was cheering like crazy and crying."

Context is everything. When doctors warned him about the
tough rehab and psychological adjustments he'd face after amputation, White just smiled. "Usually an amputation is a trauma," he
said. "But I went through that trauma twenty-six years ago."

He was more concerned with the difficulties his daughters might
face in seeing a stump-legged father. "For children, a missing limb
is the most traumatic thing," he said. "You can't see diabetes or a
heart attack, but this you can see. It's a jarring sight."

But when Whitney and Jasmine visited him the day after surgery,
they seemed more spooked by the strangers in the hospital room
than by their dad's missing limb.

"My operation went real well," said Tom. "I don't hurt at all."

"Yay!" said Whitney.

"What did they do with the other part?" Jasmine asked.

"I told 'em to just get rid of it," Tom said. "I'm done with it."

The girls were also there a few days later when Dr. Hahn arrived
to unveil his handiwork. "Okay, girls, you know, it might look a little
different, but it's really okay," Tom said. When Dr. Hahn removed
the cast, he revealed what looked like a rounded slab of bacon — a
stump marbled white and red with skin and blood. Dr. Hahn liked
what he saw. When he left the room, Whitney and Jasmine brought
out a treat they'd saved for their father: gingerbread-man cookies.
The girls bit the left legs off their cookies and held them up.
"Daddy cookies!" they said.

When a limb is severed from the body, the vertebrates of the world
— creatures with spinal columns — face one of two fates. If they
are salamanders, their bodies will grow new limbs. For everyone
else, it's stumpville. Scientists are studying limb regeneration in salamanders, but until they come up with a way to transfer the am-

phibian's unique ability to other species, humans and others will have to be satisfied with a less-miraculous form of healing. After amputation, the sewed-up skin starts to form scar tissue to seal itself up. Broken capillaries near the amputation site leak blood and serum into surrounding tissue, causing the leg to swell. The ends of the tibia and fibula begin to grow new bone tissue that connects to the Ertl bridge, turning the saw-and-screw job into an organic structure.

For that biological process to happen, though, Tom White had to do one thing: rest. That was tough.

"I'm planning to head back to work on Tuesday," he told Dr. Hahn a few days after surgery. "I'll start slow, just a half-day." Dr. Hahn's eyes narrowed. He urged Tom to rest. "You know how easily a half-day can turn into a full day," the surgeon said.

Back in Buena Vista, Tom quickly slipped into a routine. He worked half-days at Mountain Medical, using crutches to move between exam rooms. His patients were happy to see him back. But at night, he had trouble sleeping. The phantom pain kept him up. Sometimes it was like getting hit with a charley horse. Other times his missing foot ached or burned. Sometimes it itched, or felt squeezed, or seemed like electric shocks were running through it. "One time I felt my left toes dragging on the floor, clear as day," he said. "I felt them move."

Tammy worried about Tom's schedule. "You're working too much," she told him.

He brushed her off. "Ahh, you don't know what you're talking about." He was a doctor. He could read his body's signals. Everything was a go. Tom felt so good, he made a pact with Andrew Miller, a bike-racing friend. They'd do the Leadville Trail 100 Race Across the Sky, a 100-mile mountain-bike race, later that summer. It seemed like a reasonable goal.

One month after the amputation, though, Dr. Hahn told White to knock it off. "You're working too much," he said, and it was affecting the recovery. Before Tom could get fitted for a prosthetic leg, the swelling in his stump had to subside. That wouldn't happen until he stopped hopping around the clinic every day.

So Tom cut back to three half-days a week. After lunch he'd come home and catch up on paperwork, or sit in a recliner and page through a prosthetics catalog, daydreaming about his shiny new leg. Through the living-room window he saw the snow pile up, and guiltily watched his wife deal with it. Tammy hated clearing snow. That was usually Tom's job. And, of course, this winter had to be the one with record dumps. "You stay in that chair and rest, mister," Tammy told him. "The faster you recover and get your new leg, the sooner you can get out there and shovel."

On a freezing January morning, two months after the amputation, White crutched his way into the clinic of Denver prosthetist Christopher Jones. It was time for his first leg fitting, and Tom was psyched. He wore running shorts and a "Vigilantes" T-shirt. He didn't really think he was going to tear into a 10-K that afternoon, but if it happened, he was damn sure going to be ready.

A prosthetist acts as a kind of pharmacist and physical therapist for amputees, designing and fabricating the right artificial limb, and then helping train patients to use the device. Jones was one of the best. His most famous patient, Captain David Rozelle, has become a powerful symbol of the Iraq War amputee. In 2003, Rozelle lost his right foot and lower leg to an antitank mine. Working with Jones, Rozelle got himself back up and running within months. Less than two years after his injury, Rozelle returned to active duty in Iraq, becoming the first amputee in recent military history to resume command in a combat zone.

Tom unwrapped his residual limb. "Looks like it's healed well," Jones said.

"Yeah, the swelling's gone and now it's atrophied," Tom said. "My left thigh is half the size of my right."

Jones wrapped the stump with a silicone liner, then layered wet plastered bandages on it to form a cast. From the cast, Jones would be able to make a socket for the prosthetic leg.

While the model hardened, Tom and Tammy wandered around Jones's office, which is part clinic, part woodworking shop, part museum. Today's new prostheses are high-tech wonders (with fancy price tags, between $15,000 and $35,000), but when it comes to the socket that binds them to the stump, there's old-fashioned drilling, grinding, filing, and sandpapering involved.

"Tom, did you see this?" Tammy said. She pointed to Jones's collection of antique prosthetic legs. They progressed from a wooden hand-whittled job, worn by a Civil War veteran, through World War

I models, 1950s-era legs, to today's cutting edge: the C-leg, a prosthesis for above-the-knee amputees that uses computer-controlled
hydraulics to mimic the actions of a biological knee.

Until recently, prosthetics was largely a mom-and-pop industry.
Innovations usually came from amputees who were so frustrated
with old equipment that they went into their garage and created
something better. But in the past twenty years, prosthetics has become a booming business. It's not because of war wounds. Too
many Americans are fat, out of shape, and smoking — and it's cost-
ing them their limbs. About 3,500 amputations are performed in
the United States every week. A little more than half result from
vascular disease (blood circulation problems, usually caused by diabetes or smoking). Trauma and cancer account for 46 percent of
amputations. The population of U.S. veterans of Iraq and Afghanistan requiring amputations tops 750, but they make up a small frac-
tion of the nation's estimated 1.7 million amputees. Analysts say
the market for prosthetic legs has been growing about 4 percent
annually, and industry officials expect Americans' unhealthy life-
styles to double the amputee population by 2050. "It's the baby
boom generation," says Jones. "As they age, vascular disease, diabetes, and smoking will lead to limb loss."

It's not just a demographic game, though. The increased visibility of Iraq War amputees has helped normalize the use of prostheses, and marketing has played a role. For nearly a century, the German company Otto Bock, founded to serve World War I amputees,
dominated the market. Bock was a staid, established institution
with little competition. Then about ten years ago Ossur, an Icelan-
dic upstart, began buying the mom-and-pop shops (including the
company that made the Cheetah) and ginned up an aggressive
marketing campaign. The company sponsored athletes like Oscar
Pistorius, Sarah Reinertsen, Brian Frasure, and Casey Tibbs on
"Team Ossur," picturing them in ads as bold risk-takers who embodied Ossur's motto, "Life without limitations." Ossur wanted to
make prosthetics cool — and it did. Today's prosthetics industry is
highly competitive, but it's still dominated by two players, with
Ossur playing Pepsi to Otto Bock's Coke.

"Let's give this a try," said Jones. He appeared from a back room
holding Tom's new foot, an Ossur carbon-fiber model called the
Talux. Attaching the hardware to the limb has always been tricky

with prostheses. Thirty years ago, an artificial leg was strapped on with buckles; today's designs use a ratcheting coupling, suspension sleeves, and various suction systems. Jones rolled a silicone-based sleeve, with a nonskid surface that felt like neoprene, over Tom's stump. Jones handed Tom the prosthesis. "Okay, now slowly fit yourself into the socket," Jones said.

Tom pushed his leg into the Talux. For the first time in months, he looked nervous.

"You hear that click?" said Jones. "That means you're connected. But you can get it tighter. If you can get to five or six clicks, you're solid. That's what you want."

Tom pushed harder. Four, five clicks. "That's it," Tom said.

"Take a few steps," said Jones.

Steps? Tom thought. *Heck, it's amazing to just stand up.* Instantly, he gained an inch of height. All those years of limping had induced a stoop. The new leg gave him perfect posture. For the first time in his life, he stood and looked at his wife eye to eye.

Tammy stepped back to give him space to move. Tom took three tentative steps across the room, turned, and walked back. His face drew into a rictus of concern and fear. *This isn't exactly the glove of comfort,* he thought. It was all wrong. He didn't feel like marathoner Sarah Reinertsen. He didn't feel like sprinter Oscar Pistorius. He felt like a man with a clunky hunk of metal on his leg. A hunk of metal that pinched and hurt. His head was aboil with misgiving. *Uh-oh,* he thought. *This may not go as planned.*

"Everything's going to feel heavy at first," Jones said. "Remember, you've been moving around for two months without any weight on that leg, and it used to have a five-pound foot attached to it." This prosthesis, a sort of training leg, weighed two and a half pounds. His final leg would weigh a little bit less.

"Yeah," Tom said. "Okay." He tried to put on a good face. He couldn't. His expression was that of a man whose doctor just told him he had cancer. "Let's adjust it, and I'll walk a little more."

Tom described where it pinched. Jones took the foot into his shop, where he used a router to grind away the socket. "Yeah, that's a little better," Tom said as he ambled, slowly, down the hall. Still, it wasn't great. He expected it to feel like his stump was hitting a cushy sofa. Instead he got a wooden chair.

For the better part of an hour, he worked with Tammy and the prosthetist, breaking down the mechanics of his new gait. He had to figure out the right hip motion and stride length. He had to learn how to strike the ground with his new carbon-fiber heel, roll and flex and push off without ankle muscles and tendons there to do the pushing. He had to find optimal mechanical efficiency in his gait, and he had to find it now. Any bad habits formed this early would be hard to break, and a slight flaw in his mechanics would waste huge amounts of energy. Researchers have found that below-the-knee amputees like Tom White require 20 to 25 percent more energy than non-amputees just to walk around. (Above-the-knee amputees use up to 60 percent more.) As a distance runner, Tom was used to training his body to move with exquisite efficiency, to think like a machine that turned calories into endurance and speed. Now he had to apply such thinking to every moment of his waking life.

The next day, Tom and Tammy drove back to Buena Vista with Tom's new leg. They went straight to their daughter Whitney's elementary school, where the teacher was expecting them. Whitney gave Tom a big hug, and the kids buzzed around his new leg. They made him take it off, put it on, take it off again. They passed it around, felt it, banged it on a desk, tried it on themselves.

"Is it made of titanium?" one boy asked.

"Yes," Tom said proudly. "Yes, it is."

By the end of the school day, word had spread through the playground grapevine. Whitney's dad had a robot leg. It wasn't weird or scary. It was cool.

He couldn't wear it all the time at first. He walked on the new leg in the mornings, then took it off in the afternoon and got around on crutches. His stump was sensitive, and putting pressure on it made it ache and swell a little. Every few days he'd call and check in with his old coach, Joe Vigil. They'd talk about life and running, coaching techniques, and Tom's progress.

"I had knee replacement, Tom, and I can tell you this: It's really going to affect your gait," Vigil told him.

"I know, Coach," Tom said. "It's like I'm learning to walk for the third time in my life. First as a baby, then after the accident, and now this. I'm going to get it right this time."

That was easier said than done. He worked at it, on his own and with Tammy. Had to perfect his leg swing. Get his hips balanced. Sometimes he'd walk past a store window on Main Street and watch what his right leg was doing, and then mimic the motion with his left. Tammy gave him feedback, but sometimes she bit her tongue. "It's great to live with a physical therapist," Tom said, laughing, "but sometimes it's hard too. They're always watching how you walk, and the professional in them wants to correct it."

For three months he worked on getting used to the leg. It was never easy. Sometimes the prosthesis pinched or his stump ached. One day at work, he had to take off the leg and use crutches. While standing in the hall between an elderly couple using walkers, looking at himself on crutches, he thought, *Oh my God. I'm in the lunch line at the nursing home.* Back in November, he'd set a goal. He wanted to be running on his prosthetic leg six months after surgery. Now that looked like a pipe dream. He couldn't imagine the carbon-fiber contraption ever feeling like a natural part of his body. "I don't see how I'm ever going to run on this," he told Tammy. The idea of riding the Leadville 100 seemed ludicrous. He had to call up his friend Andrew and back out of the race.

In the midst of his discouragement, he talked to Amy Palmiero-Winters. She knew what Tom was going through. Eleven years earlier, at age twenty-four, she lost her lower left leg (due to injuries suffered in a motorcycle accident that had occurred three years earlier). Now, at thirty-five, she lived the life of an elite athlete. PowerBar featured her in magazine ads. She had nearly broken three hours in the marathon on a prosthetic leg. Tom wanted to know if she was doing all that while suffering as much as he was. Maybe he just had to suck it up and get used to the pain.

"Amy, is your leg uncomfortable?" he asked. "Does it hurt at all?"

"No," she said. "It's comfortable. I wear it all day long."

"How long was it before it started to feel comfortable?"

Palmiero-Winters couldn't remember. Tom took that as a good sign. "At least it wasn't a horrible period that was burned into her memory," he said. She passed on a few tricks: Detach the leg when you're sitting down to take a little pressure off. Don't bend your knee all the way or the socket puts pressure behind your knee.

Not long after that, he achieved a tiny bit of success. Christopher Jones cast a new socket for him. Tom's muscles had atrophied so much that the old one made his stump feel like a clapper in a bell.

Then one day a stranger stopped him in a hallway. "Are you an amputee?" the man asked. Yes, said Tom, who was wearing pants. "I saw you earlier today, and I didn't even notice," said the stranger.

Yes! thought Tom. Finally he was walking well enough to fool somebody.

Despite the increased visibility of amputees, a certain amount of social stigma still comes with the territory. Even for Tom, who treated bodily deformities every day, it wasn't easy to endure the stares of strangers. Or the imagined stares. "Oh, get over it," Tammy told him. "Nobody's looking. Nobody cares." *Easy for her to say,* Tom thought. She wasn't the one shocking people every time she hiked up her pant leg.

Then Tom went to Boston and got schooled in the art of getting over it.

He and Tammy flew there in April for the marathon and the Women's Olympic Marathon Trials. Tammy planned to run in Monday's marathon, and daughter Whitney came to compete in the Newton Heartbreak Hill International Youth Race, a kids' fun run up the course's notorious rise. For Tom, it was a running reunion. He kept bumping into Adams State friends, including Coach Vigil. At the race expo the evening before the Olympic Trials, Tom finally met Amy Palmiero-Winters in person. She was walking around on her Flex-Run foot, a drink in one hand and a spare leg in the other.

"Wow, look at your leg!" Tom exclaimed.

"Have a look yourself," Palmiero-Winters said. She snapped the leg off, handed it to Tom, and stood on her remaining limb, perfectly balanced. "I give her back the leg," Tom said later in describing the scene, "and she just goes click-click and she's in. I'm cracking a sweat just putting my liner on!"

Officials at USA Track & Field had told Palmiero-Winters she could run in the Olympic Trials if she posted a qualifying time, but her personal best of 3:04 came up twenty-two minutes short. She came to the race anyway to cheer on the hopeful Olympians.

At the expo that night, she analyzed Tom's setup like a NASCAR mechanic working over an engine. "The first thing you need to do," she told him, "is get yourself a knee brace and pull it over the socket. There's a CVS around the corner. They're probably open late. Go."

Tom smiled and mumbled something about picking up the brace in the morning.

"No," she said. "Go now."

So he did. When he pulled the brace over his knee, the contraption seemed to pull together. His walking improved at once. "Holy Toledo!" he told Tammy. "I had no idea!"

The next day, Palmiero-Winters joined Tom, Tammy, and Whitney to watch the Olympic Trials. Unlike the point-to-point Boston Marathon course, the Trials layout featured a loop that the runners lapped four times. Tom's gang found a spot where they could watch Deena Kastor, Magdalena Lewy Boulet, and other front-runners pass by on one side of the course. Then, if they hustled, they could cross the Charles River and watch the runners pass on the other side of the loop. It was hot, sweaty work. Tom did his best to keep up, walking and jogging in a kind of gimpy hop. By the halfway point, sweat had turned his prosthetic liner into a sopping wet mess. His leg began to slip.

"You're not walking so well," observed Palmiero-Winters. "What's going on?"

"I sweat through my liner," he said. "I need to take it off and let it dry."

"Go ahead," she said.

Tom nervously eyed the crowd. Tens of thousands of people lined the course that day. "I'll wait until the crowd moves on, then I'll do it discreetly," he said. "A little bit of privacy, you know."

Tammy watched the whole thing go down. She often fought this battle with Tom and often lost. But Palmiero-Winters didn't back down. She'd been there, done that. If Tom was too shy to change his socket liner in public, at some point he would hurt himself — if not today, somewhere down the line. "Do it now," she told him.

Tom held firm. "I don't want to do it in front of all these people."

"Oh my God, just change it," she said. "Suck it up and do it!" She stood in front of him, hands on her hips, resolute. She wasn't going to let him off the hook.

"Arrgh!" Tom parked his butt on the grass and snapped off his leg. He unrolled the wet liners, let them dry, and then put them back on. Nobody in the crowd gave him a second glance. They were busy watching Kastor overtake Boulet for the lead.

At that moment, White realized that living with the leg was going to demand different kinds of courage. There was the courage to get up and walk on the thing — and eventually, maybe, run. And then there was the courage to snap it off at a party in a room full of strangers.

"Amy has this attitude like, 'Nothing wrong with *me*. I'm just gonna do my thing,'" he later said. "She taught me plenty of technical stuff, but nothing so important as that attitude. I don't have her command or her presence yet. But I'm working on it."

The end of spring drew closer, and with it the realization that nearly six months had passed since his amputation and Tom still seemed miles away from his two main goals. He hadn't yet walked Whitney to school, and he still couldn't run. Tom's frustration mounted.

"Well, of course you're not running on *that* thing!" Palmiero-Winters told him in Boston. White was still walking on his training leg, which wasn't really built for the pounding of roadwork. She pointed out her custom-made model, which had a socket that flared up higher near her knee to give her much better stability. So when he got back home to Colorado, Tom met with Chris Jones and designed a new leg based on Palmiero-Winters's model.

By the middle of May, the Colorado snowpack was fast disappearing. Sandbags were stacked around Buena Vista, ready to stave off the meltwater floods. Tom checked the mail every day, and then finally it arrived — his new leg, boxed and packed in Styrofoam peanuts. He threw off his old model and started snapping on the new one. He felt some trepidation. What if this one wasn't any better? But ohh, it felt good. Stable. Snug. He walked out the door, and the new leg felt better with every step.

The next day he walked Whitney to school. The whole family went, and they walked all the way: one mile to school, one mile back. Tom and Tammy talked about the upcoming cross-country season. They'd been trying to talk a friend into coaching a sixth-grade girls team. In the off-season Tom and Tammy organized a fitness and running club for elementary school kids, the Speed Demons, and recently Tom had begun coaching some local masters runners who met at the high school track Wednesday mornings at 5:00 A.M. The Whites were doing in Buena Vista what Joe Vigil had done at Adams State: building a running culture from the ground up. "Start them early, get them excited about it," Tom said.

"The main thing is to get them out there doing some physical activity they enjoy." As a doctor, the toughest patients for Tom, emotionally, were those with heart disease, diabetes, obesity, or other ailments that stemmed from inactivity. "That's part of the reason I'm doing this," he said. "So I can say to my patients, 'Hey, look at me, I've only got one good leg and I'm out there running, biking, staying active. You can do this.'"

"How's your leg feel?" Tammy asked on the way back home.

"Good," Tom said. "Like a combination stilt and pogo stick. It feels like I'm mastering a new sport. I have good steps and bad steps."

That Saturday, he tried something new. In between his daughters' soccer games, he snuck off to a quiet corner of the park, and he ran. Just for two minutes. But it wasn't walking. And it didn't hurt. And he couldn't keep the words from racing through his head: *I can run!*

He kept on running. He started at two minutes and added thirty seconds every day. "I'm realizing I need to get my ultra-runner's step back," he said. "It's kind of a slow shuffling gait, no high knees, stay low, conserve energy while moving forward." After several months of struggle, the path ahead was beginning to open up. Somewhere in the future he could see himself doing 10-Ks with his daughters, maybe even run a marathon with Tammy.

He smiled. "I feel like my third running life is just getting started."

The major advances in prosthetics have almost always been made by amputees themselves. Van Phillips, the engineer who created the Flex-Foot, lost his lower left leg in a waterskiing accident at age twenty-one. Hugh Herr, director of biomechatronics at MIT's Media Lab, is pushing prosthetics into the bionics age with joints that use microprocessors, integrated sensors, and advanced actuators to mimic natural motion. He lost both legs below the knee at age seventeen after being trapped in a blizzard on Mt. Washington.

There's a reason for this: it's almost impossible to know how a prosthesis works — or doesn't work — until you wear one yourself. As a doctor, Tom looked to medical professionals for advice in the early months of his recovery. After a while, he discovered that the best info often came from the amputee grapevine. Amy Palmiero-

Winters showed him how to brace his knee. A technician in Chris Jones's practice, an amputee himself, gave Tom crucial advice on cleaning his liner and minimizing sweat. ("Roll a little antiperspirant on your stump," the guy said — and he was right.) At a marathon in San Diego, Tom spent an hour talking with Sarah Reinertsen. She told him to give himself a break. "You've only been on your leg for a few months," she said. "It takes about a year before you really realize what you can do."

By mid-June, Tom was running for fourteen minutes at a stretch. Then, almost overnight, his stump lost a huge amount of sensitivity — as if his nerves had been set to volume 8, then turned down to 3. The hard wooden chair wasn't so hard anymore.

When Tom, Tammy, and the girls flew to France at the end of that month, Tom kept a secret notion in the back of his head. They were going over to watch Tammy run in the Marathon du Mont-Blanc, a spectacular race held in the streets of Chamonix and the foothills of the French Alps. When they arrived, Tom signed up for a 10-K held the day before the marathon. "I'll take it easy, see how far I can get," he told Tammy. "Run a kilometer, then walk, run, walk. See how it goes."

At the starting line, his leg caused no commotion at all. The other runners were preoccupied with their own prerace rituals. Anxiety crept into Tom's head just before the gun went off. *Man, maybe I should have signed up for the 5-K,* he thought.

A twelve-minute-mile pace put him at the back of the pack. At 2-K, he felt good. Maybe he'd stop at 5-K and take a rest. But then things started humming. He picked up the pace. Passed a few people. Then a few more. The course turned onto a hiking path and snaked into the hills. That worked to his advantage — Tom could really crank on the leg when he motored uphill. At the 5-K water stop, he didn't pause. Just kept on running.

By 7-K, sweat was soaking his liner. He could feel his stump sloshing. The voice of Amy Palmiero-Winters came into his head. *Do it now.* White stopped, snapped off his leg, wrung the sweat out of the liner, rolled it back on, and snapped on his leg. Right there in front of God and the Alps and the nation of France.

He continued on. His ears became his coach. Since he couldn't feel his foot strike the ground, Tom had to listen for the sound. When he tired, his footfall made a sliding sound. For the last three kilometers, he concentrated on making good strikes, good sounds. And that's when he felt it — a little bit of that old rhythm. When he was a kid, before the motorcycle accident, the rhythm of running was his biological clock. Back in those days, if he ran long enough, with proper mind frame and respect, he could slip into the rhythm and transform his body's movement into a mystical experience. It was like a scent from childhood, a sense-memory of which he caught just a trace up there among the edelweiss. That's what he missed the most, all those years. That's what he gave his left leg to get back again.

And then the finish was upon him. Tammy, Whitney, and Jasmine screamed his name. The girls dashed onto the course and ran the final fifty yards alongside him.

He hugged the girls and felt them crinkle his race bib. Around him, runners caught their breath and checked their times. Tammy offered a smile. He savored the world opening up around him and the feeling, once again, of being whole.

You wonder what you would do in Tom White's position. Would you have the courage, the energy to continue, the unflagging good disposition? You hope that you would, but fear otherwise.

CHRIS JONES

The Things We Forget

FROM ESPN: THE MAGAZINE

BEFORE THE LAST GAME at Yankee Stadium, Derek Jeter sat in his sock feet.

Teammates had filled the space in front of his locker with baseballs, jerseys, photographs, and lineup cards, and he was making treasures out of ordinary objects by writing his name on them. That night, even the heroes in the room had given themselves permission to believe in the things they used to believe in, to be kids again.

The first time I visited Yankee Stadium was on a family trip from Ontario. I was a kid, fourteen or so, and I don't remember much. My only genuine memory is of a food vendor; I wanted one of those big pretzels.

"I got one," the vendor said, "but it's not *hot* hot."

To me that meant it was warm, which was fine. I gave him my money. He gave me a frozen pretzel.

"I don't want this," I said.

"You touched it," he said. "It's yours."

That was the end of our negotiation. I sulked in my blue plastic seat and sucked on my pretzicle. It remains the single worst food item I've ever eaten, and I was pretty upset about it at the time. But that pretzel is the only reason I remember my first time at the Stadium. It's the only ticket stub I have from that night.

The last game at Yankee Stadium was different. Everyone who was there will keep some small part of Sunday, September 21, 2008, in their head or heart for the rest of their life. They might not remember the trivia of it: that the Yankees beat the Orioles 7–3; that

Jose Molina hit the park's final home run; that it was over when Brian Roberts grounded to first. But they'll remember how it felt to be there. They'll remember it the way we remember people and places that meant something to us but now are gone — as a collage of sights and sounds and smells that our brain has decided is worth keeping and that we have no power to edit or erase. The only universal truth about memories is that we're all younger in them than we are now. Memories *were*.

Before the game, the Yankees brought Yogi Berra to sit in front of reporters and share his stories. Yogi is eighty-three years old — Yankee Stadium was two when he was born — and he looked all of it. A yellowed, vintage uniform didn't help. "They say this was the kind of uniform we played in," he said, pinching the front of the baggy jersey between thick fingers. "I don't remember this one. We had wool uniforms, but nothing like this." Everybody laughed. Truth is, Berra doesn't remember himself in sepia. What we've seen in black-and-white, he remembers in color. "I think of all the teammates I had . . ." he said, leaving the thought unfinished because it could end only with those friends in the ground and Yankee Stadium — Yankee Stadium! — about to be trucked to a landfill.

"Sorry to see it go," Berra said, with one final Yogism. "I really do."

Sitting at my desk now, I remember how alive I felt that night, how in focus it all seemed. I remember the pregame ceremony that introduced the legends in attendance and those represented by their families. I remember especially Thurman Munson's son, Michael, wearing his father's uniform, standing at home and receiving a slap on the ass from Berra. I don't remember much about the game, but I do remember that Jeter gave a speech after and that I walked out onto the field. I remember what Yankee Stadium looked like from the grass, its grandstands impossibly tall, lights impossibly bright. I remember Mariano Rivera saying, "I'll miss this mound," and scooping up a jug of red earth. I remember a groundskeeper digging up home plate. I remember the sound the lights made when they went out for the final time, pops like flashbulbs in a gangster movie, and I remember what Yankee Stadium looked like when it was dark and empty — not like death, but like life, waiting to begin again.

But this is what I'll remember most: in the press box that night, everybody talked about the time Wade Boggs rode that cop's horse around the warning track after the Yankees won the Series in 1996. It made me wonder what happened to the horse. Nearly twelve years had passed; I figured the horse was dead.

After the game, I saw a long row of cops on horseback in right field. *Just maybe.* It was a long shot, but what's great about sports is that sometimes long shots come through. Caught up in the night's floodlit optimism, I asked the first cop in line if he knew what happened to Boggs's horse.

"You mean Beau," he replied.

My heart jumped. "Beau?"

"Yeah, Beau. He's retired. Living on a farm upstate."

"Really?"

"Yeah, he's lovin' life."

"Wow. What about the cop?"

"Lieutenant Jimmy Higgins," he said with a smirk. "He's retired too. Sorta."

"He's working security or something?"

"Nah, nothin' like that." The cop was quiet for a long time. "I think he's a nurse," he said. "But don't tell nobody."

A lot can happen in a year. A lot more can happen in twelve, or in eighty-five. On a night when it was so hard to tell the beginning from the end, I discovered that Beau the horse is living out his days in a New York pasture and Lieutenant Jimmy Higgins is a nurse.

I'll remember that.

Two thousand eight was a memorable year in sports, maybe the greatest ever. Giants-Patriots. Kansas-Memphis. Celtics-Lakers. Tiger-Rocco. Federer-Nadal. But because so much transpired, it can sometimes seem as if none of it did. Watching sports this year was looking at art in the Louvre: when you're overwhelmed, even the Mona Lisa begins to pale.

Yet out of so much magic emerged a gangly kid from Baltimore who ended up with eight gold medals around his neck, and even he doesn't know how it happened. In October, Michael Phelps sat on a backstage couch at MTV, thought back to Beijing and the 100 fly he won by one one-hundredth of a second, and said, "I've watched that race so many times, and I still can't figure it out. I can't see where I was better. Was it my start, was it my turn, was it my finish? I have no idea. It still blows my mind."

Normally, Olympic athletes enjoy two weeks in an intense, unyielding spotlight, then vanish. (I remember watching Apolo Ohno skate laps in an empty arena in 2005 as his coaches piped in crowd noise to remind him of the Olympics.) Phelps is different. Weeks after Beijing's torch had been snuffed out, he was still taking a nationwide victory lap. "East Coast, West Coast, East Coast, West Coast," he said. "It's been nuts."

On that October day, he was touring New York City on behalf of PureSport, a small sports-drink company that he was helping to turn into a giant simply by carrying around a bottle of the stuff. One of his stops was MTV's *Total Request Live* — about to join Yankee Stadium among the newly extinct — where he was surrounded by teenage girls who screamed for him to lift his shirt and show them the world's most famous twelve-pack. "I definitely don't have that now," Phelps said, letting them down softly. The abs were gone.

More than his stomach had changed since Beijing. The week before, I'd gone to Pete's Grille in Baltimore, home of the huge breakfast Phelps made famous: egg sandwiches, grits, waffles, omelets, eighty gallons of OJ. I asked the waitress if Phelps still came by now that he was rich and famous. "No," she said. "I don't think we'll be seeing him again for a long time." There had once been a shrine to Phelps behind the counter. Now, it had been scaled down and moved to the back wall. The way ex-lovers compete to be first over the breakup, Pete's Grille had decided to quit its former best customer. The life of a champion had taken its toll.

In more ways than one. "I've been back in the water twice," Phelps said at MTV. "It hasn't been pretty, and it hasn't been comfortable. January, February, when I really start to train, I'm just going to have to suck it up. The first three or four weeks are going to be brutal. All the fun will be gone by then." Even from that couch, Phelps was already turning his mind toward 2012. "That's how you have to think," he said. "That's how long it takes to prepare."

He had spent the previous four years thinking about winning eight gold medals. Would he have been disappointed with seven, had that one one-hundredth of a second gone the other way?

"Probably," Phelps said. "I wanted to be the first Michael Phelps, not the second Mark Spitz."

Phelps and Spitz talked after the record-tying seventh gold but not after the record-breaking eighth. By then, Spitz had disappeared altogether. There was radio silence between the two. What would the new king have said to him anyway? Neither wanted to acknowledge the hurt that comes with being erased. From now on, it was Phelps who would be made young again and again, remembered every four years as the best there ever was.

Sometimes, though, even the people who make history forget it. While Phelps was in Beijing, he studied the experience as though he were studying for a test. Athens, where he won six golds in 2004, was mostly lost to him, and he wanted to take home a clearer picture of 2008. "I tried to take it all in, more than I ever had before," he said. "Hanging out in the Olympic Village, we played these big games of Risk. I remember a lot of yelling and screaming after I would get knocked out of the game; I also remember a lot of yelling and screaming after I touched the wall. I remember, after my sixth race, I was just exhausted. But I told myself, *You've got two races left, the two shortest ones. You can get up for this.* I remember everything. I remember all of it."

He was quiet then, leaning his head onto the back of the couch. He looked exhausted again. "The thing is, my lifetime goal is accomplished. I wanted to be the first to do something. So this was the year I did what I've always wanted to do. Now I've got to find something else."

Later, on his way downstairs to a motorcade, photographers, and lines of police, Phelps stopped to check out the passport photos that lined the hallways, the rows of *TRL* guests who had agreed to look goofy in four tiny frames. Phelps pointed out Pink. "I got to hang out with her at a party a little while ago," he said. "She's a great girl." But the faces that jumped out at me were the ones who were no longer around. Here were Heath Ledger, Bernie Mac, Steve Irwin — in their primes not long ago, smiling for the pinhole camera, and then, in a blink, gone. One one-hundredth of a second really can make all the difference in the world.

Lance Armstrong stood on a stage in a hotel ballroom in Manhattan and clapped Bill Clinton on the back like an old friend. In front of them were more than fifty heads of state, countless diplomats in crisp white shirts, Bono, and Al Gore. But at that moment, the attention was on only these two different-seeming men and their efforts to change the world.

Armstrong told a story. "I'll never forget visiting the White House after my first Tour de France victory, in 1999," he said. "We were told we had seven minutes with the president, the president's busy. We're in the Rose Garden, and I stopped and said, 'Wow, look at that magnolia tree over there.' That seven-minute visit turned into a forty-five-minute visit because of this magnolia tree. I happen to be a real fan of magnolias, and it turns out, so was the president."

The pair have more in common than trees. They are legacy chasers. They care about the balance of judgment. Clinton, in his efforts to raise Africa out of abject poverty, seems driven by a desire to erase the sour, scandal-haunted note on which he finished his presidency. Somewhere in the mountains of France, Armstrong picked up the same itch. He doesn't want his story to be about something as ordinary as winning races. He wants to be remembered as the man who beat cancer in himself and then in everyone else.

He had just announced that he would be cycling competitively again, but it was clear that his return to the road had less to do with yellow jerseys than yellow bracelets. "It's the reason we're here today," he said of his LiveStrong Global Awareness campaign. "We have the medicine, we have the procedures, we have the technology to save lives on all of these continents. If we're not doing that, if we're not applying the medicine we have to the people who need it the most, then we are failing morally and ethically. That must change."

Success in that endeavor will mean Armstrong will live forever. Failure will mean he won the Tour de France seven times in a row.

Over the river in New Jersey, David Tyree sat at his locker, after another practice he was too injured to make. Unlike Armstrong's, the final — maybe only — chapter of Tyree's legacy has likely been written. "A lot of people tell me, 'You'll always be remembered for that catch.' It's the only thing they want to talk about after they find out who I am."

With his New York Giants trailing the still-perfect New England

Patriots late in the Super Bowl's fourth quarter, Tyree caught a thirty-two-yard desperation heave from Eli Manning, partly with his hands, mostly with the side of his helmet. Four plays later, Manning found Plaxico Burress in the end zone, and the Giants had started 2008 on an improbable, incredible note, with a 17–14 win over destiny.

Standing nearby, Manning said that now that the work to win another trophy had begun, he tried not to think about the first one much. "An athlete's memory has to be short. You have to train your mind to forget. That comes with experience. The more confidence you have, the shorter your memory gets. You always have to be thinking about the next play."

Tyree, however, couldn't get past his last. That was partly because "the Catch" was the last time he had touched a meaningful football. But it was also because people wouldn't let him forget. His locker was filled with fan mail, photographs, magazine covers, children's drawings — in each, he was making that catch. "That play was so much bigger than me," he said.

Tyree is no different than Clinton or Armstrong; he isn't satisfied with his legacy either. He wants to carve out something larger in the time he has left. "Don't get me wrong, it was a glorious moment," he said from his locker. "Seeing it fifteen or twenty years from now, watching it with my children, I'll remember it as something special. But I won't allow myself to be bottled up by it. People might remember me for that catch, but that catch isn't me. I'm not going to let one moment dictate the type of person I am or the kind of impact I can have on another person or society as a whole. There are a lot of things I have left in me."

In November, Giants coach Tom Coughlin announced that Tyree had been placed on injured reserve. He would not play a single down all season.

Most people, at some point in their life, wonder what it would be like to start over. Not long ago, I was driving through the desert into West Texas. In El Paso, I looked across the muddy river to Mexico. The bridge to the other side wasn't long, and the Mexicans hadn't bothered to occupy the tiny guard post. I walked across, and I was in a new country, gazing at a new horizon. I could have kept going, and nobody would have been able to find me. If Yankee Stadium could vanish, why couldn't I? I tried to imagine the strange brand of courage it would take to disappear.

In May, Annika Sorenstam announced that 2008 would be her last year on the LPGA Tour. One of the most dominant athletes of the past decade had decided to disappear. She had known she would retire since the previous winter, when she peeked at her watch on the driving range and wondered if it was time to go home. "I stopped and thought, *Wait a minute, I used to love this,*" she said. "All of a sudden, I'm watching the clock. That's when I knew this would be my last year."

She said this as she sat on the veranda of the Lake Nona Golf and Country Club in Orlando, overlooking empty fairways and a lake that turned white in the midday light. The night before, she had arrived home from a jet-lagged swing through Asia, where she won her fourth tournament of the year, the Suzhou Taihu Ladies Open in Suzhou, China. It was the eighty-ninth title of her career, seven more than Sam Snead's PGA Tour record.

She took a sip from a glass of water and said without smiling, "In comparison to a lot of other players, 2008 might have been a great year for me. But in comparison to some of my previous years, it's been pretty average. I've pushed myself into a corner where I have to win seven or eight times for it to be a good year. So not having the year I want, in my mind, justifies my decision. I have this battle with myself all the time: *Give yourself a break, you've had a great career.* But when I'm inside the ropes, I'm thinking, *Come on — you can hit this 5-iron to five feet, or you can make this ten-footer for birdie.* That has really hurt me, to know I just don't have it in me anymore. I wish I did, but I don't."

A deer appeared on the closest fairway. It stopped and waited. Two more appeared, and they all stood watching us watch them. "I wish I brought my camera," Sorenstam said.

The deer lightened something in her, and seeing her then was like watching her play this year, at least after she made public her impending departure. Fans took the opportunity to wash her in warm ovations each time she walked up the 18th fairway. "It's been amazing," she said. "I make a bogey, and I'm pissed off and I go to the next tee, and somebody says, 'Thank you for everything you've done.' How can I still be upset?"

Sorenstam talked about the life she's leaving and what she remembers of it. She talked about being compared with Nancy Lopez as a rookie; she talked about shooting 59, the only woman to reach golf's magic number; she talked about taking three LPGA Championships in a row, and she talked about being inducted into golf's Hall of Fame. Mostly, though, she talked about the two days in 2003 when she played with the men at the Colonial. It was the time when the focus on her was most intense. Her playing caused a great debate about men and women and equality and the sanctity of the game, but Sorenstam's decision sprang from a more private desire: to test herself, to see if she really had gone as far as she could go. And after it was over, after she missed the cut by four strokes and had spent Saturday recovering from the storm, she realized she was a long way from finished. There was more she could do.

"I got so much out of that experience," she said. "The end of that year and 2004 were probably my best time in the game, because of what I learned that week. I'm a perfectionist. I'm extremely hard on myself. But I was suddenly comfortable with who I was. Have I made mistakes in my career? Absolutely. Would I do anything different? Probably. But I gave it everything I have."

The three deer remained on the fairway. We watched until two more appeared. "I know I'm lucky," she continued. "I come from a little city in Sweden known for hockey, and here I am all these years later in Orlando, looking over a beautiful lake, watching deer cross a fairway."

"I'm very content," she said, finally. "I'm very happy."

She sounded as though she believed it. As the deer disappeared into the trees, Annika Sorenstam seemed ready to stop confusing the things she should remember with the things she should forget.

For Josh Hamilton, forgetting has never been an option. His tattooed arms tell his tale better than any archive could, gallons of ink drilled into his skin and laid bare for the world to see. With October's first chill cooling the Chapel Hill air outside, he sat in the storage room of a local bookstore, where he was doing a book signing, wearing only a T-shirt. He knew there was no point in trying to hide his backstory. He also knew 2008 will be remembered as the year his tattoos started to fade, the year people saw something other than that long period when he was lost. On July 14, Josh Hamilton was found.

Two years earlier, in 2006, not long before he was reinstated by

Major League Baseball after years of drug addiction and depression, Hamilton had a dream. In it he was being interviewed by a female TV reporter at a Home Run Derby at Yankee Stadium. He had a bat in his hands, but he didn't know how many home runs he had hit. He couldn't even tell what uniform he was wearing.

As events turned out, after he changed out of his street clothes in the Yankee clubhouse that July afternoon, his superhero costume was American League blue. Soon the rest would fall into place.

"The nerves don't hit you until you're actually there," he said, recounting the Derby as a line formed inside the bookstore. "I was the last guy to hit, so after the introductions, I went back inside the clubhouse and took off my shirt and unbuckled my pants and flopped down on a couch. The couches are so deep, people behind me didn't even know I was there. When the contest got to about the fifth guy, I popped up, and everybody was like, 'Aren't you in this thing?' That's when I started to get ready. That's when I started feeling it."

Hamilton stepped to the plate as Clay Counsil, his seventy-one-year-old friend and former youth coach, waited on the mound. "I felt just as if I was hitting on a high school field," he said. He hit the first pitch to the bleachers in right-center. Then he hit another one out, then another, then another, then even more. "The crowd — the more I hit, the more they got into it," he remembered. "When they started chanting my name, that was something I'll never forget. I had chills. And right after they started chanting my name, the very next pitch, I hit my farthest ball of the night." That one went 518 feet, high into the upper deck.

When the first round finally ended, Hamilton had hit twenty-eight home runs, a record. His closest competitors hit eight. But it wasn't the quantity of the performance that made the ground shake; it was its quality. During one stretch, Hamilton hit thirteen in a row. He hit them into the black batter's eye in deep center; he hit them off the mezzanine; he nearly hit one out of the Stadium altogether, through the slim gap in right that lets the trains see in.

And then he was interviewed by ESPN's Erin Andrews, and as he spoke with her — about God, about being saved, about the heights that can be reached even from life's lowest watermarks — Hamilton couldn't stop thinking about how the whole of his dream had come true. It was almost too much for him to take. He went back into the clubhouse to hide from the crowd noise, which still roared, and the magnitude of what he'd done. He decided to skip the semifinals to gather himself, but David Ortiz grabbed him and told him to get back out there, to stay warm. Before the final round, against Justin Morneau of the Twins, he retreated to the grass behind home plate. "If a camera had been on me, you would have thought I was crazy, because I was talking out loud," he said. "I said, 'Lord, if you want me to win this thing, I'll be happy to, but if not, we've already accomplished what we wanted to accomplish.'"

Hamilton couldn't recover from his own awe. Morneau won 5–3. But the trophy was a footnote. Morneau was the champion 2008 would most quickly forget, and Hamilton would forever be the personification of faith and redemption. Now he was traveling across the country selling the most appropriately titled book of the year, *Beyond Belief,* talking especially to people who looked a little too much like him. "Could God have used me had I stayed the clean-cut kid I was and made it straight out of high school like I was supposed to?" Hamilton asked in the back of the bookstore. "Probably. But when someone who looks like me and has been through the things I've been through talks about life, people see that no matter how far down you go, there's always a way back." It was a perfect closing note.

Then he said, "If I read your story and you haven't put God in there, I'm coming after you."

Hamilton got up and went out front to sit behind a table in the middle of the store. The first piles of books were placed in front of him. He signed, he shook hands, he posed for pictures, he held a baby. Hundreds had come to see him. Two boys carefully approached.

"Who's your favorite player?" Hamilton asked the younger one.

"You are," the boy said.

"Really?" Hamilton responded, sounding genuinely surprised. "I thought you were going to say Derek Jeter."

Afterward the boys beamed, holding their books as though they were made of glass. It was a sweet moment. They were brothers, fourteen-year-old Andrew and seven-year-old Alexander. I asked Alexander if Hamilton really was his favorite. He smiled and nodded. "At least for those thirty seconds," he said.

Just like that, I was back on the bridge to Mexico.

*

Of all the great stories of this year, the resurgence of Venus and
Serena Williams was the most overlooked. After their domination
at the All England Club — the first time they had met in a Grand
Slam final since 2003 and the fifth time Venus had won Wimbledon
— they snagged doubles gold together in Beijing. Serena then
went to New York and won the U.S. Open without losing a set.
(Her toughest opponent was Venus in the quarters.) After being
ranked as low as 140 two years ago, Serena was once again the best
women's player on the planet. In almost any other year, the Williams sisters might have basked in a long glow. Instead, even for
them, 2008 was a flash that was doused too soon.

"You know, it's funny," Serena said in September, lazing on a
Florida beach. "A few minutes after I won the U.S. Open, I was like,
Okay, I did that. I won. It's mine. But that was that. When I finally got
home that night, it was so late, I just went to sleep. The next morning, I woke up, and it was already over."

Venus, waiting for a flight to take her to Qatar for the season-
ending Sony Ericsson Championships, remembered the Olympics
the same way. "You really feel like you're in a moment in time that
will be over so fast, so I tried to take in as much as I could. We loved
Beijing — just being able to be there and to compete, then standing on the podium. We didn't want to leave. We didn't want it to be
over. But when that moment's gone, it's gone."

Worse, like Annika Sorenstam, neither sister seemed satisfied
with what she had accomplished — not in 2008, not in her career.
"I'm a little disappointed, to be honest," Venus said of winning her
fifth Wimbledon title. "I was hoping to have more by now. I was
thinking more like ten." Serena understood the sentiment. "I was
so disappointed not to win Wimbledon," she said, maybe forgetting
it was her sister who beat her. "And I felt even worse after I lost in
Paris. Going to New York, I felt like I really needed to win or else."

So why even bother to play? Why work so hard and give so much
if the reward in the end is neither happiness nor history? For Venus
and Serena, the answer was so obvious that the question had never
crossed their minds. Tennis is what they do and what they have
done since they were toddlers. It's what made them rich and famous, what allows them to travel the world, what earns them places
on podiums and magazine covers. Why bother playing? That was
like asking why they bothered to breathe.

"I love what I do," Venus said. "When I win, it's pure joy. It might only last a moment, but it's a great moment. And I could never hang up my racket knowing I had more in me. I'd never be able to forget that I had more left. I couldn't forgive myself."

Serena was more blunt. "They'll have to drag me out back and shoot me," she said.

Which reminds me of a story about a horse. Earlier this year, my favorite writer died. His name was W. C. Heinz. He wrote for newspapers and magazines mostly, about sports that people don't care much about anymore — boxing, the ponies. There was a memorial service one rainy night in New York City, at an old bar called Elaine's. In attendance were lots of old writers and a few young ones; what united us was our admiration of Heinz. We talked about how we wished we could write like him on his worst day. Then his daughter played a video of the man talking about his work and how much he hated everything he wrote, how it was never as perfect as he hoped it might be.

With one exception. He wrote a piece called "Death of a Racehorse" for the *New York Sun* in 1949. It was about a horse named Air Lift who broke down in his first race. In the rain beside the stables, with lightning streaking across the sky, they shot the animal, and Heinz watched. Then he wrote the most heartbreaking story about that afternoon. Heinz captured the moment with such beauty that Air Lift has lived forever.

And the writer knew what he had done. He knew it that afternoon at the track, and he knew it on the day he died. He knew how it felt to spend an entire life in pursuit of a feeling he got just that once. But it was a feeling so good, once was enough for him to never stop trying to find it again.

Venus and Serena Williams know the feeling too.

And now, so do the Celtics.

Chances are, if you've run into Kevin Garnett — if you've even caught a glimpse of Kevin Garnett from across an airport terminal or in a steak house — you remember him. You've probably had to remind yourself that you're both the same species.

A few days before the new season began, Garnett, Ray Allen, and Paul Pierce stood in the middle of a dimly lit room, above their practice gym in the Boston suburbs, in front of cameras and boom mikes. The Big Three were filming a series of spots for game broad-casts and the big scoreboard above the parquet floor. One of them was a pitch for a DVD called *Return to the Rafters,* a tribute to the sev-enteenth championship they won for Boston in six games over the Los Angeles Lakers in June.

"Can we get a copy of this?" Garnett asked, fake-pocketing the plastic jewel box and walking out of the room. He was told the DVDs weren't ready yet; all he had was an empty box. Then he was told he wasn't being effusive enough in his salesmanship. "You know, it would help if you gave me a copy!" he said.

It also would have helped if Paul Pierce hadn't come down with a sore throat that morning. His voice was raspy and thin. "Sweet," he croaked to open one of the takes. Just then, the boom mike ap-peared out of the darkness and bounced off the top of his head.

There were gasps and fear that the season was over before it had begun. Even after Pierce laughed it off, everyone stood in quiet corners of the room thinking about how much it takes to win and how little it takes to lose.

"We're about to whip the boom guy's ass," Garnett announced. "Everybody clear the room but the boom guy." Suddenly, it was the boom guy who'd lost his voice. Kevin Garnett standing in front of you glaring, even in jest, has that effect.

Later, Garnett spoke about the Celtics' run and how much it meant to him. He talked about watching Ray Allen take Pau Gasol to the hole in Game 4, finishing with a reverse lay-up that sealed one of the greatest comebacks in Finals history. (The Celtics rallied from twenty-four points down to win 97–91 and take a 3–1 series lead.) "That right there is when I thought, *We're going to win this,*" Garnett said. As he talked, he seemed to grow taller, as though the memory of triumph were enough to stretch him. It made it harder to ask the question I had to ask: "But how long will people remem-ber?"

Allen, the team's resident philosopher king, had thought about that one before. "I think it's something you guys talk about," he said. "There's a point at which you almost try to get a player to be-lieve he's gotta be remembered and that he's gotta do more and more so people will remember him. But really, all we can do is what we've done. People are going to decide who they want to remem-ber and who they don't. I think everyone — every fan, every player

— has his own little closet of history, and he puts whatever he wants in it. Maybe it's the Red Sox, maybe it's the Patriots, maybe it's us. Maybe it's Eddie House, maybe it's me. We have no say-so in that. It's not our closet."

The man knows his metaphors. A closet is a personal, intimate thing, cluttered and cleared out every now and then in a lifelong cycle that leaves only the stuff we could never part with — just like the space in our brain where we park memories.

"Listen," Garnett interrupted, leaning in closer, eyes narrowing. I was listening. "It's the one thing that connects me to this city and these guys forever," he said. "Ain't no one can take that away. It's like knowledge." He pointed to the side of his bald, shining head. "Once it's obtained, it's obtained."

The dude is six-eleven. Forget that crap about the closets.

Except there were rumors that coach Doc Rivers had forbidden his team from talking about the championship after that morning. With the official start of training camp, all any of them had accomplished was ordered into a plastic jewel box, never to be opened again, or at least not until these Celtics were a collection of very tall old men.

"We've definitely discussed how long we should live with last year," Rivers said. "No one's going to move out of our way because of what we did. If anything, it's going to make everybody play us harder. We have to do something different to win again. We have to be better than we were last year."

Pierce nodded. "It's hard not to think about it — every time I left my house this summer, people all over were saying congratulations. But not the people in Boston. In Boston, they said thank you." He swallowed to find what was left of his voice. "But all the great teams have won it more than once. So now we have to do it again. We have to forget what we did last year."

Downstairs in the gym, three walls were lined with championship banners, the old silks that had clung to the top of the Garden until it was knocked down. Hanging in a row, they looked like a massive teeth-whitening scale: the older the banner, the yellower it was. Early in the row is ironclad evidence of one of sport's all-time juggernauts, world champions from 1959 through 1966. Then comes a banner from 1968, which looks bloodstained. The banners start to bleach and thin, until there are decades-long gaps, culminating in the last space on the third wall, now occupied by a pristine white flag, so clean and new it looks like sunlight.

Pierce looked up at that banner and at the rest, the way he does every time he runs the court in practice. "Always, every day," he said, his voice finally failing him. He motioned to the gym's fourth wall, bare as an empty cupboard. "Look at that," he said. "I want to fill it all up. I want to fill it *all* up."

In the middle of working on this story, I learned I'd passed an online test that put me in the final round of auditions for *Jeopardy!* Along with thirty other potential contestants, I was summoned to a Toronto hotel for a written test and a make-believe game. Going into it, I liked my chances. But in the room, I was surrounded by people who knew more than I did, whose brains worked faster, who believed in their heart that they could play the game and win. *Jeopardy!* was their Super Bowl, and most of them were Mannings.

There was one guy especially: Anthony. Tall with a shaved head and glasses, he was a freelance editor, mostly of vanity-press books — books that their authors had to pay to get published, "books that probably shouldn't be books," Anthony said. He wanted badly to be a writer, but all he had to show for his ambition was three half-finished novels. He was, by most conventional measures, a failure, or at least not a success. In that room, though, maybe for the first time in his life, Anthony had his chance to be great. He stood out there the way Tiger Woods commands a driving range. Everybody knew he was the one.

If Rocco Mediate was known for anything before last summer, it was for being an affable guy with a bad back that had kept him from being what he might have been. He had made a good living and a lot of friends, but now, forty-five and nearing the end of his career, he had never been great. He had never actually found himself on a big enough stage to show that he was the one.

Then he teed up his ball at the U.S. Open at Torrey Pines, navigated through four rounds of near-perfect golf, and found himself the surprise leader in the clubhouse on Sunday afternoon, watching a small TV to see if a one-legged Tiger could sink a twelve-foot putt to catch him. "I wasn't thinking, *Miss it, miss it, miss it,*" Mediate said six months later. He was at home in Los Angeles, but Torrey Pines was still etched in his mind. "Of course I wanted to win. I played my ass off. But the kid is probably going to make the putt. Nothing he does surprises me."

The kid made the putt. Monday, it was.

In Sunday's gloaming, Mediate said out loud what we were all whispering: "You guys think I'm going to get my ass handed to me." But that night, alone in his hotel room, Mediate convinced himself that he could win — no, that he would win. "It was no fluke that I shot one-under that week," he said. "I thought if I shot par on Monday, it would probably do it."

He was sleepless that night, from excitement, not nerves. "I hate to wait for anything," Mediate said. "The worst hour is the hour before I get to play. I remember wishing for the sun to come up. I just wanted it to be light out."

Mediate watched the sun rise and pulled on a pair of black pants, a red shirt, and a black vest. Woods pulled on the same outfit. It was a sign of how close they would remain all day.

More than twelve thousand people lined the ropes at the first tee, the rest of the course mostly empty except for the two golfers. Mediate was exactly where he wanted to be: "I just kept telling myself, *This is the opportunity of a lifetime.* How many times do you get to play with the greatest player who's ever lived for the U.S. Open at Torrey Pines? It's amazing how everything stopped around us. I've heard so many stories from people who dropped whatever they were doing to watch us play golf."

Predictably, Woods took what seemed to be an insurmountable lead into the turn. But Mediate began to pull himself back into it, arising "from the depths of hell," as he put it. "Everybody expected me to get killed, and I loved that feeling. I loved everything about that day. Honest to God, I was just having so much f—ing fun."

Maybe because of that — because "it was just two guys having a blast and trying to beat each other's brains in" — eighteen extra holes weren't enough. Still tied, Woods and Mediate went back to number 7, the ninety-first hole of their tournament. Finally, Mediate tightened and cracked, his drive sailing left and into a bunker. "I would have loved to have played a hundred more holes, but that was the end."

In the ways that count the most, though, it still isn't over. Woods called the victory his best ever, then vanished for the rest of the year, his knee damaged beyond quick repair. ("Don't even joke about that," Mediate said when I asked whether he will be remembered as the man who broke Tiger. "I didn't break him. He was broken when he got there.") And Mediate has become our favorite ordinary man who found something extraordinary inside himself when it mattered most.

"Every day, people come up to me and want to talk about it," he said. "It just resonated for some reason. To be honest, I still sit up nights and think about it. *What if he misses that putt? What if I make that putt?* I'm still disappointed, but I'm not devastated. What Tiger did really was incredible. It was the greatest, most exhilarating time I've ever spent on a golf course. I could win three majors now, and it wouldn't be as good as that. These things just don't happen to guys like me."

But they do. Every so often — just often enough to believe that it might happen to us too — these things happen to guys like Rocco, to guys like Anthony. They are struck by lightning, and the rest of us feel the current run through us, a charge that comes with knowing what might be possible if only we show up on the right stage in the right light. In a year defined by the world's greatest athletes performing at the top of their game, what many of us will remember best is the one man who seems most like us, living out his dream as though it were ours.

Mediate wasn't the only unlikely highlight in a year that favored overdogs. Foundations of hope were laid in places that hadn't had much reason to cheer. Even cities like Pittsburgh saw their way out.

Until 2008, Sidney Crosby had always been the future. But after he, Evgeni Malkin, and the rest of the youthful Penguins — with the notable exception of 118-year-old Gary Roberts — reached the Stanley Cup Finals to face the Detroit Red Wings, Crosby became, even in defeat, something like the present. He found himself in a space he had never before occupied, one that sheltered him from questions about what would happen next. For seven blessed weeks, he didn't have to think beyond now. "When you're on a run like that, you don't have time to think about what you're doing," Crosby said. "You're in a bubble."

The ancient and toothless Red Wings put an end to his ride, and in the quiet that followed, Crosby allowed himself a few days to think about how close he had come: "It's weird how you remember just bits and pieces, but those bits and pieces definitely stick with you." He remembered the first game of the playoffs; he remembered when the Penguins scored a late goal to beat the Ottawa Senators; he remembered coming back from a 3–0 deficit against the New York Rangers; he remembered how good it felt to beat the Red Wings twice, once in the third overtime. "It was fun while it lasted," he said.

And now, inevitably, it had started all over again. After the shortest summer of his career, Crosby was back on the ice at the Igloo in October, skating circles beneath the giant banner that commemorated Mario Lemieux, his boss and mentor. On the day that the Red Wings went to the White House to accept the president's congratulations, Crosby and the Penguins were playing the Philadelphia Flyers. It was a close, hard-fought game. Once, Crosby slammed the door to the bench so hard, the echo sounded above the sold-out crowd. The Penguins lost an early lead, and the game went to overtime. Everybody was on their feet. It felt like spring, not fall. With seconds remaining, the Penguins scored. They filled the ice in celebration, Crosby at the center of it.

A few minutes later, in the cramped locker room, The Kid sat by his locker, soaked through and smiling. Up close, he seemed an unlikely man to carry the burdens foisted upon him. He still has pimples. But in 2008, he proved himself a worthy successor to Lemieux as he brought salvation closer than ever. "I think this team and this city have a great future," he said. It didn't seem like coincidence that, earlier that day, just across the street, the cornerstone for a new arena had been laid.

That final night in the Bronx, all I could think about was Thurman Munson's locker. It had sat empty in the clubhouse since his plane crashed in his hometown of Canton, Ohio, nearly thirty years ago. I was five when he died, and I can remember his death. I hadn't had a chance to meet Munson — to this day, I can only imagine what he would have looked like in the flesh, baboon-assed and glowering — but I felt as though I knew him, and I had believed he was immortal. When you're five, life is one long beginning; endings are reserved for adults.

I had stood in front of his locker on that September night, peering into the mirror that still hung on the back wall above the blue bench coated with a thin layer of white dust. I could see Munson in that mirror, and I could see myself as a boy. A few hours earlier, his son, Michael, had walked onto the field in his father's stead, in his father's pinstripes. I wanted to know what he remembered and whether he had once believed, the way we all did, that his father was immortal. So after the stadium lights had been extinguished, I pointed my car west into a driving rain, toward Canton.

Thurman Munson came up short of the runway while practicing takeoffs and landings at Canton-Akron Airport on August 2, 1979. He died instantly. At the spot, there is no commemoration, no cross or marker, just a field surrounded by a chain-link fence and a NO TRESPASSING sign. Air traffic control pylons whistle a little in the wind.

Some places are made sacred by the people and events that graced them. On that day in 1979, the worlds of many boys were rocked by the impact of a small plane crashing into a tree stump off Greensburg Road. But now the stump has been pulled, and there's nothing sacred about the place where Thurman Munson died. It's just forgettable grass.

Michael Munson is thirty-three years old. He owns a bar in town called Munson's Home Plate. He wasn't there when I sat down at the bar. "Death in the family," the bartender said. The walls were covered with photographs of Thurman. He was everywhere, including on the menu. The specialty of the house is a cheeseburger they call the Captain. It comes with a knife stuck in the top.

I had just finished mine when Michael walked in. He's a vending machine of a man, with close-cropped red hair and a goatee. A catcher like his father, he played four seasons in the minors for the Yankees and Giants. He looked as though he'd be hard to bowl over.

He dug a bottle of beer from behind his bar and sat down. I didn't mention my trip to the airport, but one of the first things he said was, "I don't want my father to be remembered for a plane crash." The sacred places, the son said, are the places his father lived.

One of them was Yankee Stadium. "The other night, when the announcer said, 'Representing his father, Thurman Munson . . .' I couldn't hear anything else," he said. "Someone had to push me to run to home plate." After the pregame ceremony, he changed out of his father's uniform and asked Ron Guidry, the former pitcher, to sneak him into the clubhouse. Michael wanted to see his dad's locker one last time.

Memories of his father are vague: a dark figure in the hallway, the outline of a smiling face, a shape against the wall. "It's almost like a shadow," he said. In that way, Michael was like all those other boys when his father died: Thurman Munson was an idea to him too.

Over time, he colored inside the lines. He tapped into the memories of his mother, his sisters, his father's teammates. "Their memories became my memories," he said. The picture became clearer still when he would visit his dad's locker and the circle of dirt around home plate. Eventually, he tried to summon his father's swing and the way he planted his feet when he threw to second. When he played baseball, Michael heard fans yell terrible things: *You're nothing like your dad,* or *Your father would be ashamed of you.* The insults hurt deeply, but in time he learned to turn them into tributes, like the way he wore number 51, his dad's number reversed.

Now the younger Munson stood in the stillness of the empty clubhouse, peering into the mirror, feeling like himself as a mop-topped little boy. He began to talk to his dad, and he heard his dad talk back. For fifteen minutes, they communed in that gooseflesh place, the long-dead father and his only son. "There were some things I had to say," Michael said. "It was now or never." Tears came then, because he was sad about a lot of things. But mostly he was sad that one of the last reminders of his father would be gone after that night, the locker moved to a museum across the street.

"I wish they didn't have to do it," Munson said. "It breaks my heart, to be honest." Closing Yankee Stadium meant his dad was no longer living history. He had been reduced to an artifact. It wouldn't be long before someone parked his car where Thurman Munson had once pulled on his uniform, before walking to a new stadium with new grass and new lockers and a new home plate. Michael Munson said goodbye to a locker that night, and he said goodbye to his dad. He dried his eyes and walked back out to the sound of more cheers. "Some of my memories of that night may fade," he said. "But those few minutes in front of his locker, that's burned into my mind. That night I felt as close to my father as I ever have."

I asked him if he took home a souvenir — if, like Rivera, he pocketed some dirt or blades of grass. "I don't need a jar of dirt to remember who my father was," he said. "I know who my father was."

We said goodbye. He had a baby daughter waiting at home. I imagined him telling her stories about her grandfather one day, and how in those stories, Thurman Munson would be great again.

Later that night I drove through West Virginia, and I thought about Michael Munson. I thought too about my own boys and how I hoped they would remember me. I did not think about Mexico. Normally, West Virginia at night is darker than the dark, but the rain had moved out, and there was a full moon, impossibly bright, and the mountains rose up beyond the shoulders, impossibly tall. I rounded a bend, and the road stretched in front of me, dark and empty — not like death, but like life, waiting to begin again.

The road ended in Philadelphia. Specifically, it ended in the bottom of the sixth inning in a cold, heavy rain.

Until the umpires waved their arms and the groundskeepers pulled a white tarp over the soggy infield, the Phillies and Tampa Bay Rays had been engaged in the least memorable World Series in recent history. Before the playoffs began, there were so many possible story lines. The Chicago Cubs could have played the Chicago White Sox; the Boston Red Sox could have played Manny Ramírez. Instead it was, Who is playing what?

Yes, the Rays had the potential to be a great story in their own right: worst to first, a fun young clubhouse led by a manager with a Mohawk. But they had been forgotten and invisible for so long, nobody could even pretend to have always loved them. And the Phillies . . . well, they had the misfortune of being from Philadelphia, which, in addition to being unseasonably cold and wet this fall, boasts a fan base that makes them just as impossible to love. There was an air of disbelief around the first four games, not because any of it was extraordinary, but because it seemed impossible that the last big championship of this amazing year would end on such a flat note.

Then came the fifth game, and then came the rain.

Cole Hamels pitched the Phillies to an early 2–1 lead. The fans were on their feet, waving white towels. It was cold, but the electric-ity of anticipation made it feel warmer than it was. The rain was light at first, looking like milk in the floodlights. The score remained the same through the top of the fifth as the game became official. The cheers grew louder, the rain grew heavier. Still they played. Somewhere below decks, commissioner Bud Selig needed the Rays to tie it up so he could suspend the game. The deep puddles on the infield reflected his dilemma. In the top of the sixth, B. J. Upton scored the tying run. Rounding third, he looked like a guy just learning how to roller-skate.

Game, Interrupted.

Selig called a press conference with an old rule book quivering in his hands, his vain stab at exuding authority. Someone told him to straighten his tie. "You're going on TV."

"Of all the things to worry about," he said.

The rain continued to fall, all night and into the next morning. By early Tuesday afternoon, the rest of the game, scheduled for that evening, had been postponed again. Finally, Wednesday night, exactly forty-six hours after Game 5 had been suspended, the fans returned to their seats, and the players returned to their places, like actors after an intermission. There we were, right back in the middle of it. It wasn't like déjà vu. It was more like how Josh Hamilton must have felt as he walked to the plate at Yankee Stadium, knowing he was about to learn the answers to all his questions.

The Phillies scored in the bottom of the sixth, but Rocco Baldelli — who, suffering from a rare illness, had begun the year feeling as though his muscles were melting — tied the game again with a solo shot in the next inning. After the seventh-inning stretch, J. P. Howell ran to the mound for the Rays. Pat Burrell, who was 0-for-13 in the Series, dug in. Howell threw his money pitch, a curveball outside, but Burrell was ready, diving out over the plate and poking the ball to deep center. Howell turned and watched it soar through the night, bouncing maybe a foot below the top of the wall. Burrell stopped at second and was replaced by a pinch runner named Eric Bruntlett, who soon scored what would be the winning run. After Brad Lidge struck out Eric Hinske on three pitches for the final out of the season, the Phillies piled on top of each other. It was as loud as I've ever heard a ballpark.

Out on the field, Jimmy Rollins sprayed a bottle of champagne into the surging crowd. Chase Utley handed out cigars. Jamie Moyer, forty-five years old, as old as Rocco Mediate, grabbed a shovel and began to dig up the pitching rubber — an object like an iceberg, with a deep, concrete-filled tube as its anchor. A bunch of people took turns helping Moyer excavate it. Once it was free, he hoisted it on his shoulder like a log and ran with it out onto the outfield grass. There he posed for pictures with his wife and seven children. His father was there too, and Moyer turned to him and said, "Congratulations," because he knows how it feels to see a son succeed.

I asked him how he thought he would feel about that night the next day, the day after, and the day after that. "The same way it feels right now," he said. "Pretty sweet."

In the Rays' clubhouse, J. P. Howell sat in his underwear at his locker, his back heaving with upset. He kept shaking his head and wiping away tears, and he stayed like that for a long time, until a reporter tapped him on the shoulder and asked if it would be all right to talk.

Howell stood up, just a skinny kid with a couple of tattoos wearing an old pair of boxers. He looked the most like me and the most like you. He turned around and swallowed. "Oh, man," he said, his eyes red and filling again. "I f—ed up."

James Shields, the pitcher who would have pitched Game 6, stood next to him. "J.P., man, go take a shower," he said.

"Take a shower?"

"Yeah. Take a shower."

"Okay," Howell said. "I'm going to take a shower."

There was something touching about the exchange, the shock of loss mixed with the bond of teammates.

"This is where we've wanted to be since we were little kids," Shields said in Howell's place. "J.P.'s upset right now, and he needs to go do his thing. But when we look back on this year, it'll be all smiles, man. All smiles."

Howell returned from his shower and pulled on a pair of jeans. The time off hadn't helped much. His eyes still betrayed him. "If I went fastball in, I could have beaten him," he said. "It's tough to have it come to an end, because this was one of the most fun years of my life. I can't be bitter, even though I am."

Then someone asked him about the Rays' famous thirty-minute rule: win or lose, thirty minutes after the game is over, it is over, gone like smoke along with everything else.

"Not tonight," Howell said. "I'm not going to cut if off. I'm going to let this eat me up for a while. We need to remember how this feels. This year we may be forgotten, but next year we've got another shot to be remembered." And in that instant, J. P. Howell became, for me, the story of the year.

He refused to leave his locker, as though the game might start again if he waited long enough; he forced himself to listen to the sound of the party still rollicking up the tunnel. Watching him, I thought about what Shields had said, about the Rays finding themselves where they had wanted to be since they were kids. Only not quite. Because kids don't think about losing, the way kids don't think about endings. Kids believe they will win.

Howell believed too. Even when he couldn't stop the tears, he believed that someday, maybe as soon as tomorrow, it would be him looking into the cameras and feeling the cold mist of champagne. He's believed in himself since he was five years old, the way we all once believed in ourselves. The difference is, Howell — like Michael Phelps, Lance Armstrong, and David Tyree; like Annika Sorenstam, Josh Hamilton, and Venus and Serena; like W. C. Heinz, Kevin Garnett, and Paul Pierce; like Rocco Mediate, Sidney Crosby, and Michael Munson; hell, even like Lieutenant Jimmy Higgins — never stopped believing. He and all the other athletes who made 2008 a year to remember never forgot what it feels like to be young and to believe in the possibility of it all. That's what makes them different, and that's what makes them great.

I'd been wrong all along. People who make history never worry about what they leave behind; their minds are always trained forward, dreaming of things to come. Memories were. The future will be. Watching Howell finally lift himself up and head for the back of the bus, I remembered how this journey began.

I remembered how I used to feel about Thurman Munson.

I remembered how I used to feel.

I remembered.

Halfway through the pile for The Best Sports Writing 2009 *I was worried because there weren't any stories about the major events of 2008. Chris Jones takes care of that in one deft swoop, hitting the top spots with a series of personal observations that add something new to the familiar. He should do this every year.*

GARY SMITH

Alive and Kicking

FROM SPORTS ILLUSTRATED

A BUS CAME OVER a rise the other day and halted at a busy inter-
section. It was a funny sort of bus, splashed with happy colors and
throbbing with noise. Inside were children of every human color,
brown and black and white and yellow. Maybe it was you it pulled
up alongside, but you were distracted, thinking of all you had to do
that day, and didn't even notice it.

It's a shame you missed it, because those were the Fugees, a team
that's much more than a team — a family cobbled from what was
left after the latest decade of men tearing each other apart. A
shame because you don't really learn everything you need to know
in kindergarten, as some people claim. But you just might've
learned it from that bus.

*Qendrim is the runt midfielder from Kosovo. The one whose town and home
went up in flames when the Serbs came ten years ago, and whose father
crossed mountains and forests to avoid the butchery and find his family in a
United Nations refugee camp.*

*When the Fugees arrived at their first out-of-state summer camp in Amer-
ica, Qendrim was astounded to find that each boy was assigned his own
room. By curfew that night all their mattresses had been dragged and
jammed into just a few rooms, and the boys were sleeping shoulder to shoulder. "One in a room," said Qendrim, "is just too lonely."*

Too bad your windows were up. The boys on the bus were sing-
ing their favorite song in the most astonishing assortment of accents. "Don't you want me, baby?" they crooned. "Don't you want

me — *ohhhhhh!*" It's the title verse from an '80s song by Human League, one you've probably heard, not a question you were expected to answer. Or was it?

They're war refugees from twenty-four countries, every nightmare on earth. Most had spoken no English when they arrived in America. They'd been placed in classrooms according to their age rather than their reading level and left to wither. Most of their families had been shattered, their fathers killed, imprisoned, or divorced because a single mother had a better chance to get a visa out of hell . . . and God knows what marauding armies had done to some of those mothers. Several Fugees had fought as child soldiers in Liberia. One had seen his father gunned down by soldiers, another had seen his dad's fingers sliced off. One had watched rebels give his brother a gun and a choice: kill yourself or your best friend. Then he'd watched his brother blow the friend away.

Resettlement agencies had covered their parents' rent and utilities during their first three months in America, along with providing some furniture, canned goods, and food stamps. Then they'd been left, with no car or education or language skills, to support families of five or six while earning the minimum wage as maids or just a little more as laborers in a chicken factory.

It wasn't paradise for their children either. Some were confined to their apartments, forbidden to go outside when their parents discovered that gang members and drug users sometimes made their new hometown — Clarkston, Georgia, on the outskirts of Atlanta — nearly as unsettling as their old one.

Until a woman holding a soccer ball stepped out of a little yellow car.

Munda is the squirt from Sierra Leone. It's one of the poorest countries on earth, a place where armies descended upon villages, chopped off the leaders' heads, and displayed them on stakes. But here, among the Fugees, one country and abomination blurred into the next, and at first the coach couldn't remember from which Munda hailed.

"I'm from South Africa," the ten-year-old boy declared. "Somalia," he told someone else. "Nigeria," he said when asked again. After all, Munda was a Fugee now, the tribe that was all tribes, and why did people have to cling to just one? Finally, when he admitted to the coach that he couldn't pronounce Sierra Leone, they settled on the word that sounded something like the one

that stumbled from his mouth when he tried. It's a homeland that makes him smile each morning when he enters the kitchen. Cereal, he tells people now. He's Munda, from Cereal.

The driver of that bus you missed, the woman wearing shorts and a T-shirt and a Smith College cap tugged over her short hair, leading the sing-along? "I was working as a waitress in a cocktail bar . . ."

It's true, she *was* working as a waitress, in a Cheesecake Factory in Atlanta. Imagine doing *that* while fasting for Ramadan! You see, no one or nothing on the funny bus is what you'd have guessed. She looks like the shortstop on your office softball team, Kathy from Erie, Pennsylvania — but no, she's Luma Mufleh from Amman, Jordan, a Muslim who grew up in a mansion as the daughter of a steel magnate named Hassan. She's the coach and founder of the Fugees, but she's a refugee too. A woman fleeing Cartier watches, Armani pantsuits, three maids, a chauffeur, a nanny, and a butler.

Luma was looking for a home just as hard as every one of those lost boys on the spring day in 2004 when the Fugees, by accident, began. She was depressed, to be honest, and running out of ways to justify to her large and wealthy extended family why she hadn't gone home for eight years, not for births or deaths or marriages. Her latest venture — a café just outside Atlanta into which she'd poured so much money, heart, and soul — had given her so little revenue or joy in return. She'd moved from western Massachusetts to Boston to North Carolina to Atlanta, been a waitress, a cook, a grocery stock clerk, an office worker for a charity, and a freelance website designer, none of it justifying her expensive Smith College degree, her anthropology major, or her father's big expectations of his gifted eldest daughter. Maybe a little comfort food, the kind that had nurtured her as a child in Amman, would help.

She followed directions she'd received to Talar's International Foods of the World in nearby Clarkston, made her purchases, and headed back toward her apartment. But in her fog of sadness she missed a turn, blinked a moment later, and found herself passing . . . Al-Momineen mosque? . . . a Buddhist temple? . . . black men in robes? . . . caramel-colored women in kaftans and burkas? . . . people *on foot* instead of in cars? Luma had a funny feeling she wasn't in Georgia anymore.

She took a left into an apartment complex, The Lakes, to turn around, and noticed ten children, all foreign-looking, playing soccer in the parking lot. Bare feet on asphalt, tattered ball bouncing off cars, two rocks for a goal, no adults in sight.

It was as if she were seeing exactly what her heart yearned for but her stubborn, lonely quest had forbidden her: *home*. All those days of playing pickup soccer with her siblings, cousins, and neighbors back in Jordan, laughing and arguing over every shot that hissed near their two-rock goal. She watched those ragtag kids from her yellow Volkswagen Beetle for an hour, then departed with a pang. She returned at the same time a few days later with a lovely white ball, stepped out of her car, and asked a bunch of kids, roughly a third her age, if she could play too.

They stared at her ball. *That's* what they really wanted. They conferred and turned to Luma. Okay. She was in.

She had a blast. She discovered that they were from Afghanistan and Sudan and were just a handful among several thousand war refugees who had been placed by relief agencies in Clarkston — a township that had been chosen because of its warm climate, its proximity to job opportunities in Atlanta, and a glut of underpopulated apartment complexes. Luma returned two days later at the same time, the mob of excited playmates larger, and soon it became a habit, the proprietor fleeing her oppressive café without telling her workers where or why she went.

It occurred to her one day: why not turn these refugee kids into a team . . . and become their coach? She had just resigned after four years as coach of a girls' YMCA team, weary of players and parents so fixated on playing time, winning, and scholarships that she barely recognized her childhood game.

She approached Roohullah, Zabiullah, and Noorullah, the three Afghan brothers whom she'd gotten to know best. "A team?" said Noorullah. "So we're going to be professionals and play on TV?"

Uhhhh . . . not exactly. And first she'd need their help rounding up enough kids. The three boys went to work, and Luma began trolling the neighborhood as well, posting flyers in English, Arabic, French, and Vietnamese, pulling up to bewildered refugee boys in her yellow Beetle and asking if they wanted *in*.

Twenty-three kids showed up for that first practice, none in cleats or soccer garb. They began pinballing across the field in bare feet or socks, in flip-flops, sandals, or old hiking boots, in blue jeans or tattered shorts; one flapped about in his boxers and a flannel shirt. They didn't know where to go, but they sure got there fast.

None had ever been coached. They'd learned the game on streets and in refugee camps. Luma didn't know whether to laugh or whoop or cover her eyes, but damn, the game was fun again.

It was strange, watching them. She'd become a chameleon, taking on the look, clothing, and easy slang of an American; she had to *convince* people that she was a Muslim from Jordan. But those kids . . . it was all right there on their skin and clothes, in their accents and mannerisms: the immigrant, the outsider, the otherness that she felt inside but kept hidden. She felt free around these kids.

She tried to get the attention of one carefree boy, his right foot bare and his left one clomping about in an oversized black sneaker, but she couldn't remember his name. "One Shoe," she heard his new teammates calling him, and when practice ended she watched him remove his sneaker, carefully wipe off the grime, return it to his backpack for the two-mile hike home, and say, "See you tomorrow, Coach."

How could she cut anyone? Why not coach *two* teams, she decided, an under-ten and an under-twelve in a local soccer league, enter a few weekend travel tournaments if she could scrape together enough money and move the two teams up to the next age brackets the following year if the idea worked.

She began harnessing the chaos. "She's a girl! She doesn't know what she's talking about," sneered a twelve-year-old from Sudan. At once Luma gathered her team — boys from countries where a woman wouldn't dream of telling a man what to do — placed the Sudanese boy in front of the goal, and lined up a penalty kick.

On all her youth and school teams — soccer, basketball, volleyball, softball, and tennis — she'd been the best and fiercest player. She'd scored a hat trick to lead her jayvee girls' soccer team to a 3–1 victory over the varsity boys, who — when they'd finished digesting their pride — presented to her a jersey with the words THE MAN across the back. "You're not going to wear that, are you?" her father had cried.

"Sure I am," she said, and did.

She took one step toward the ball, her right leg exploding like a karate chop — she'd taken that in high school too — and sent a

BB past the Sudanese boy and into the goal. "Anyone else?" asked Luma. Nope. Nobody else.

She stunned the kids again a few days later when they heard her speak in Arabic and French. She asked them to divide into groups of four for drills. When they split up by nationality or tribes, she shook her head no and reshuffled them. The East and West Africans sniped at one another. The northern Sudanese begrudged the southern. She made them run laps at the first whiff of old animosities. She outlawed all languages except English to smash any cliques.

But she wanted them to remember who they were. Maybe the name of the hot hip-hop band was floating around in the back of her head, but she never made that connection. Why not, she suggested, snip the *re* from *refugees* and call themselves the Fugees? Not the Fugees team. The Fugees *Family*. They liked that. She bought packs of white T-shirts from a roadside booth and etched their names and numbers in black marker. Now they had uniforms. When the kids heard a song on her radio a few weeks later, and the deejay credited the Fugees, they were outraged — that band had stolen their name!

She pulled up to the field at the Clarkston Community Center one day, a few weeks after practices had begun, and looked around. Where was her team? Finally she saw a half-dozen players cowering behind a dumpster and a building. "What's going on?" Luma asked.

"There's been a fight!" they said. "A bunch of kids jumped on Rooh! There was blood everywhere! He and his brothers ran home!"

Rooh, the fifth-grade Afghan Muslim who'd helped her form the team, was her leader. Suddenly Luma had a decision to make. Call off practice, hope Rooh was okay, and try again tomorrow? Or go find him? She jumped into her car and headed to his apartment complex, no idea which apartment was his. An Afghan boy led her to Rooh's. It was all happening so fast, she barely had time to consider the consequences of walking through that door.

Rooh, crying and bleeding, had locked himself in his bedroom. His father, who'd been captured by the Taliban years ago and escaped, had long since vanished so he wouldn't be snatched again. Rooh's older brother, having fled the Taliban too, was somewhere in Pakistan. His mother, Sheila, was in her bedroom, scrambling for a head scarf in case the visitor coming through their door was a male. Rooh's younger brothers, Zabi and Noor, were jabbering at the same time, trying to tell Luma what had happened. Some African American kids had jumped Rooh, they said, beat him, and slammed his skull against the asphalt.

"It is okay," the children called to their mother. She wouldn't need to cover her head; their guest was a woman, the one they'd told her about, their feisty new coach. The mother emerged from her room, saw the visitor from behind — short hair, soccer shoes, shorts — and blanched. "You said your coach was a woman!" she barked at her children. "You said she was a Muslim!"

The children fell to the floor laughing. Luma turned to face her. Okay . . . she *was* a woman. Sheila stabbed an accusing finger at Luma's bare legs. "No Muslim you!" she cried.

"Muslim yes!"

"No, no!"

Luma thought fast. "*'Ashhadu 'an la 'ilaha 'illa-Allah, wa 'ashhadu anna Muhammadan rasulu-Allah!*" she rattled off. It was the Shahadah, the Muslim declaration of belief, which translates, "I bear witness that there is no god but Allah and that Muhammad is His messenger."

Sheila blinked in surprise, eyes still glued to Luma's legs. Rooh emerged from his room. Luma cleaned his wounds. "I will take him and you to the emergency room," she told his mother. "I want to make sure his head injury is not serious."

Sheila looked at Luma. Ever since the Taliban had shorn her of her husband and eldest son, stampeding her and the rest of her family to Pakistan and then to America, she had been a camel, kneeling to take on one burden after another. "No," said Sheila. "You take him."

For a moment Luma absorbed the woman's reply. Then she led Rooh to her yellow Beetle and headed down the long, slippery slope.

Grace is the midfielder from Congo with the shaved head and the brilliant smile. When civil war began annihilating nearly four million of his people a decade ago, he fled with his mother and siblings on foot, confronting hunger so sharp that his mom had to sell her clothes to feed him, and passing mothers who hurled their babies into the river to save them from a fate even worse.

Now he and the Fugees were spending spring break at Camp Twin Lakes in rural Georgia, listening to a camp counselor explain the rules for an American game called egg toss. The children were going to use an egg . . . for a ball? Grace shrugged, paired off with a partner, and began tossing the egg, each taking one step away from the other with each successful catch, until . . . splat! Grace looked down as the yolk began to ooze through his fingers. His hands flew to his mouth, and he ate the egg.

How could Luma explain to all her bewildered relatives why she'd never returned home after college? Explain that wealth and status and a big family's embrace — all the things that her raggedy Fugees yearned for — could feel like jail? That roles were prisons too?

She had tried to bust out as a kid. She'd walked the streets of Aqaba, a Red Sea resort in Jordan, wearing shorts and the same breezy smile as her American friends from her international high school in Amman, the children of diplomats. She'd spun and cursed the Arab who'd grabbed her rear end, and then — when he'd justified the grab by hissing, "You shouldn't be dressing like American whores" — she'd punched him.

She'd tried to smuggle free speech from the dinner table of her American friends into her own house, loving how the Yanks argued over Bill Clinton and George Herbert Walker Bush. But all she'd get, when she introduced Jordanian politics at home, was a sudden hush.

She'd tried to breach the wall between rich and poor. She'd dropped off food at Palestinian refugee camps, gathered supplies for escapees who'd flooded Jordan after Iraq's invasion of Kuwait, and confronted her father when she discovered that her allowance was more than the salaries of their maids, cook, and chauffeur. She'd begun slipping the servants part of her monthly stipend and toys for their children, but she couldn't mingle or play with their kids, couldn't go anywhere that an educated, well-to-do young lady wasn't supposed to go without an army of aunts and uncles and cousins wagging their tongues.

Another wall went up after college. Luma's parents stopped speaking to her when they realized she wasn't coming home. Her financial support disappeared. Holidays became hell: if someone answered when she called . . . *click.* Now she *had* to make it in America, to prove her stubborn father wrong.

Which only turned the screws tighter as her careers floundered and she found herself, at twenty-nine, eating dinner on the floor with a poor Afghan family in Clarkston. Yes, she'd collapsed the wall between herself and poverty at last, but all the trouble and complexities behind that wall were crawling into her lap, demanding choices from her, decisions that could turn her into something so much more than a coach . . . yet so much less than the doctor or lawyer or tycoon her father expected.

Could she stand back and watch Rooh, struggling with English, fall perilously behind in school? No. She became his tutor. Could she tutor him without tutoring his brother Noor, or all the other failing Fugees? No. She paid someone else to do her laundry, put her personal life on ice, and scurried each evening from one apartment to the next.

"Coach!" the mothers called to her when she'd finished helping their children with homework. The women had no clue how to fill out forms for food stamps or green cards, how to compel the landlord to fix the oven or stop the mildew spreading across their walls. She became their advocate.

None of the players, back in their homelands, had had the luxury of worrying about grammar or manners, about deodorant or toothpaste. But without those things here, she knew, they'd be taunted or shunned. She became their grammar cop, their Miss Manners, their hygienist.

They didn't have soccer moms. The Fugees showed up late for practice because they had no rides, woke up late for school because their parents worked night shifts, or came home to empty apartments because it took their mothers an hour and a half to travel seventeen miles from work by train and bus. She became their chauffeur.

How many Fugees can fit in a yellow VW Beetle? Don't ask. She was about to drop off the last urchin one day after practice when he told her that his belly hurt from hunger. Fix a sandwich when you get home, she suggested. He shook his head. "This is the time of the month when our food runs out," he said. She began taking boys to Taco Bell — two tacos and a cup of ice water for $1.98 —

and to the store for a week's supply of groceries. She became their food bank.

She tried to help their mothers figure out a budget so they'd make it to the end of the month, but no math could stretch $5.75 an hour that far. She closed her café, started a company named Fresh Start, and offered the mothers ten bucks an hour to clean homes and offices. She became their employer.

She was exhausted. Mothers had begun calling her Sister and asking, "If anything happens to me, will you raise my children?" She knew she was getting in way too deep, but then . . . what she carved out of America had to be as deep and wide and rich as the life and family she'd given up in Jordan.

She awoke one morning to thirteen missed calls on her cell phone from Grace's mother, Paula. Paula's aunt, Mama Louise, had gone into labor and Coach was needed at the hospital on the double! No, not needed in the waiting room, but in the delivery room, clutching Mama Louise's hand and coaching her as if she too were a Fugee. Coach had never seen a birth, let alone coached one, but now she found herself sweating and barking, *"Poussez! Poussez!"* and chorusing a Catholic prayer with a forty-three-year-old Congolese woman who was hanging on to her hand for dear life. And now, *ohmygod,* the baby was coming out! And now — *what was that?* — the afterbirth?! The doctor and nurses saw the expression on Luma's face and howled. First one? they asked. Yep, she gulped. And now Mama Louise was telling Luma to cut the umbilical cord, and she was wincing and snipping. She grabbed her cell phone as she reeled out of the delivery room and began speed-dialing friends. "I just gave birth!" she blurted. Huh? How? What? To a baby girl, she spluttered. A baby girl named Aganze Luma Chishibanji.

The Fugees had never stayed in a hotel before. Even players whose mothers worked as chambermaids didn't quite understand the concept. Their coach braced as if for a tsunami as they raced with their plastic Kroger grocery bags stuffed with clothes and piled in, four to a room, on the eve of their first weekend road tournament.

A hotel, she explained to them, is a place where a traveler stays for a night or two, then moves on and some other traveler takes his place. But someone has to come in and clean the room so the next traveler has a nice place to sleep. Someone just like your moms.

Now they understood what staying in a hotel meant. It meant that the next two mornings, every one of their rooms was spotless, every towel folded and returned to its rack, every bed made without a wrinkle . . . because it might make life just a little easier for some exhausted immigrant women just like their mothers.

Oh, what joy the first time the Fugees won! They hugged, they hollered, they spread their arms like wings and swooped across the field, then swooned onto their backs.

They slept with their tournament medals and nailed them to their living-room walls so every guest could see them. It dawned on Luma: this meant more to them than she ever could've imagined. It dawned on Luma what that meant: she could demand from them even *more*.

The steel that her father manufactured hadn't *all* been trucked and sold across Jordan. One thick rod had gone into his eldest daughter. The former U.S. Marines who coached her youth teams in Jordan had tested it and found it formidable, then a blowtorch of a high school volleyball coach, an American named Rhonda Brown, had made it harder still. Even as a teenager Luma had begun channeling those coaches, ordering her eight-year-old sister and a half-dozen cousins out of the family Range Rover on a country road, demanding that they run to keep up with the SUV and reducing them to tears.

It shocked the Fugees, how the lady who wrapped an arm around them and listened to their woes, who understood just how it felt to start over in a faraway land, could stride onto the practice field and transform. If they tried to beg off running laps, claim their stomachs hurt, she'd bark, "Just fart!" If they tried to cut corners while doing sit-ups and push-ups, she'd explode. "If you're going to clown in practice, don't come! Go *home!* We don't want the quitters coming! Do you want to test me today? You'll run the hill for the rest of practice!"

Dead silent were the Fugees each time she summoned them to kneel around her on the field. Was Coach angry? They could never quite be sure; her unpredictability became her sword. Two Thursdays each month, she held a confessional. "Does anyone have something he'd like to tell us?" she'd ask. They knew she'd forged relationships with their parents, principals, and teachers. They had to assume she knew everything, to fear the double whammy if they stonewalled, and so they coughed up new indiscretions left and right.

After all, they'd signed the Fugee contract: no smoking, drugs, or alcohol — or no more Fugees. Miss a practice, miss a game. Miss two, goodbye! All progress reports and report cards went straight to Coach; C average minimum, or *see ya!* Five-absence limit per semester. Tutoring mandatory. No hair longer than Coach's. Curse and it's curtains.

I'll tell Coach. That's all their mothers need murmur to turn them to mush. They'd come to Luma from long, frustrating days at school, exhaust themselves in her grueling 1½-hour workouts, then pull their books from their backpacks for another hour and a half of tutoring, sometimes by flashlight on benches beside the field. Let all those relief-agency workers roll their eyes and tell her she was nuts to take on teenage refugee boys. Let others ache for them and give them excuses to fail. Not Luma. She'd show the depth of her respect for them by plumbing the depths of their resilience and character. She'd cut them no slack for the tragedy on their résumés, because she knew the world would not.

But she leavened all that misery with mirth. She planted rubber spiders on their food and tittered when they screeched. She made her ears wiggle. She turned them into ghouls and vampires and ferried them to wealthy neighborhoods to trick-or-treat. She'd cheer them on as a Fugee from Liberia named Josiah led them in a hilarious butt-rollicking dance routine to "It's Peanut Butter Jelly Time." Except for those one and a half hours on the practice field, Luma loved nothing more than to cram into one room with the kids on road trips as they yanked down the blinds and cranked up the heat, burrowing in their warm, safe Fugee cocoon. They didn't talk about their pain or pasts in that cocoon. It was the place where a Fugee could forget that he looked and talked and felt different, because everyone around him did as well.

They had no cheering section — their overwhelmed single parents had no time for children's games — so here, in the cocoon, they became their own audience, replaying every moment of each game, celebrating and mocking each other's every move. Josiah did the wickedest Luma impersonation, flinging a ball cap to the floor in disgust and screaming, "Spread out, Fugees! You clump like *bubble* bees! You play like *craps!*" They'd roll across each other laughing, and she'd marvel at the wonder of the world, at how an unmarried woman could find a family 6,500 miles from home in the unlikeliest ethnic stew, how a Jordanian could become the gateway to America for a jumble of Asian, Eastern European, and African kids.

Go back to Africa! Luma cringed when one team's parents shouted those words as the swiftly improving Fugees dismantled their sons. Some spectators mocked the Fugees' accents or snickered at names, such as Mohammadullah's. So painful grew the slurs in another game that a twelve-year-old Liberian player asked Luma if he could play with her Walkman earphones to blot them out. "How does it feel to coach a team of n—s?" an opposing player asked Luma.

Luma's unprintable reply broke her own team rule: smile at the slurs and walk away. One Fugee smiled so hard that an opposing coach snapped, "What are you looking at, boy? Turn your head, n—," and got the heave-ho from the ref.

Some Clarkston residents, not unlike those of any other town, recoiled from all the strangers. A town that was 90 percent white in 1980 had found itself, by 2007, with the highest concentration of African and European immigrants and the second-highest concentration of Asians among all towns in Georgia, with foreigners comprising roughly a third of its seven thousand residents.

Luma wondered why her team had to practice on a barren field behind an elementary school, electric wires dangling from poles, more broken glass and trash than grass poking from the dust. Adults quaffed beer and smoked weed in the surrounding woods. Young men strolled onto the field in midpractice. Tensions had begun to boil between refugee families and African Americans, some of whom called the immigrants "African booty scratchers." One gang, in packs of twenty and wielding bats, materialized at refugee-dominated apartment complexes, watched foreigners scatter, then plundered bicycles and TVs.

Firecrackers exploded one day near the practice field. A few Fugees had flashbacks and dove to the ground, panicking Luma and the rest of the team into following them. "What are we doing?" she asked when she finally lifted her head.

"They're coming to get us!" cried one boy. No, she convinced them, that's crazy. Or was it? Tito, a Liberian teenager who'd just joined the Fugees, was approaching that sorry field one day last year when a bullet ripped through his chin.

Luma rarely cried. She walked away when emotions were about to strangle her, lapsed into moody silence for a few days, or laced on boxing gloves and tore into the heavy bag at a gym. Then went right back to battle. She got permission from the town to practice on Armistead Field, adjacent to the municipal park, on a probationary basis rather than risk another day on that minefield. She scrounged up money for the players to be tutored in two classrooms at Atlanta Area School for the Deaf. She cleared out of her apartment five miles away and moved to Clarkston. Her home became Fugee Central, the team's hangout and sleepover pad on Friday nights. She drove the streets on weekday mornings scanning for Fugees late for school or wearing sagging pants. She moved Josiah and Prince, two Liberian teenagers whose single mothers were often away working, into her home for much of the year.

The doors of the school where she tutored her team burst open one evening just as homework was about to begin, and two Fugees raced in with four gang members on their heels. Luma felt her legs rush toward the gangbangers, heard her voice croak, "You need to leave now!" and saw her hand on the chest of a glowering young man nearly a foot taller than she.

"Do you know what we could do to you?" he asked.

Luma trembled as he turned and walked away.

The Fugees had never been to an all-you-can-eat restaurant. Their eyes grew wide as they approached their first buffet line, but not as wide as their coach's when she saw their plates: spaghetti piled atop fried chicken piled atop soft-serve ice cream piled atop grapes. "What are you doing?" she cried.

"But, Coach, we're hungry!"

It dawned on her that she'd failed to mention one critical fact. "You don't have to fit it all on one plate!" she said. "You can go back for more."

The boys looked at each other — God bless America! — and broke into cheers. They staggered onto the bus an hour later, and eventually they had another favorite sing-along. To the tune of the soccer anthem "Olé! Olé! Olé!" the Fugees sang, "Buffet! Buffet! Buffet!"

The last child in the yellow Volkswagen Beetle: that was the one who began to unnerve Luma. The final one to be dropped off after a practice or a weekend outing, when it was just she and he riding in the dark, and they couldn't look at each other. That was when the trauma found its way up from the cellar.

One night it was a boy from Sierra Leone. When he confided to her that sometimes his dad would grow angry and hit him, Luma replied, "My dad did the same sometimes when I was little."

The boy was quiet for a few seconds. Then, thinking he and his coach had found common ground, he said, "Oh. Did you see your dad's fingers get cut off?"

Luma gulped. "No," she said. "How?"

"Big knife."

"How big?"

"Machete."

Luma, for once, could think of nothing to say. She still can't.

Another night, at the end of her first year as Fugees coach, the last boy in her car was Jeremiah from Liberia. She was going away, she'd told the boys that day, to visit friends in Massachusetts, just for four days. But life had taught Jeremiah otherwise. Rebels had charged into his home during Liberia's civil war, when he was a toddler. The soldiers believed that his father, who held a modest job in the government's payroll office, had access to big money. When they discovered that he had none, they slaughtered him in the living room.

Jeremiah's eyes filled with tears just before he got out of Luma's car. "What's going to happen to the Fugees Family?" asked the nine-year-old boy.

"What do you mean?" asked Luma.

"You're leaving and never coming back, and we won't have soccer anymore."

"But I'll be back in a few days."

"But what if something happens . . . and you don't come back?"

Luma thought fast. "You know I never leave anywhere without my watch. Why don't you keep it for me until I come back?"

The boy stared at it after she left, realizing that it wasn't digital and he didn't know how to read it. *Yes!* How could she get angry at him if he called her each day she was away with a perfectly good question. "Coach!" he yelped each time she answered. "What time is it *now?*"

One night two years ago — two years after Luma had founded

the Fugees — she got a call from a friend. "Turn on the news," she was told. She did, just in time to see an apartment complex where three of her players lived going up in flames. She raced there, jumped out of her car, and blew past the police barricade, crying, "My kids are in there!"

She arrived to see firemen pulling out the dead bodies of the two younger sisters and brother of Christian, the fastest kid she'd ever seen, as six other Fugees watched in horror. Christian's mother, who had fled Liberia with her children, was sobbing, and a neighbor woman was screaming at fourteen-year-old Christian, demanding to know why he hadn't run back in and saved his siblings. Christian fled into the night, and Luma followed, driving up and down the streets of Clarkston in search of him.

Three days passed without a sign of him. Luma started a fundraising drive for his family and raised nearly $5,000. On the fourth day, she glanced over as the Fugees ran laps and saw Christian, shaggy and forlorn, hanging on to the fence. "I really want to play," he said.

"It's the same rules, no exceptions." She'd had to expel him from the team just before the fire for uttering obscenities.

She dug a spare pair of cleats out of her car and reinstated him. He was a model Fugee for the rest of that season, except during laps, when he'd slow to a walk after just a few, wincing in pain. "My heart hurts," he'd tell Luma, and she'd walk the rest of the laps with him, knowing it was the truest excuse that a Fugee had ever given her.

But then the season ended, summer came, and Luma — who spent half her waking hours trying to raise funds to keep her team afloat — couldn't afford to place the boys in summer camps or programs to keep them off the streets. Christian slipped through the cracks and never returned.

Luma tore at herself. Maybe if she'd worded something a little better on her website, fugeesfamily.org, or had made just one more appeal to one more group, she could've raised the money that would've kept him on the right path.

Sure, helping hands had emerged — wonderful volunteers such as Kevin and Susan Gordon who provided rides and supervision to the kids, and opposing teams that donated balls, cleats, and jerseys — and she was grateful. But each day brought a new family crisis, and it was becoming too much for one woman to coach, tutor, mother, raise funds, and remember that many birthdays.

Tracy saved her. Tracy Ediger, a woman who volunteered for Jubilee Partners, a Christian organization in Georgia that helped refugees get on their feet. "I can't do this on my own," Luma confided to her in 2006. Tracy joined the battle, and now the passionate visionary had the cool, rational, detail-doting partner that she needed.

Then Luma hit the lottery. A *New York Times* writer named Warren St. John, searching for a meaty refugee story, sent out a query to a relief-agency worker in the Atlanta area. Luma and the Fugees, he was told, were prime rib. The story appeared on the front page. A woman visited the Fugees after reading the article and asked what they needed. "A bus!" blurted a Fugee, and damned if the woman didn't write a $50,000 check to buy one. The Atlanta Falcons chipped in money, Nike sent cash, uniforms, and gear. "Look, Coach!" crowed Qendrim. "We went from Kroger bags to Nike bags!"

But no matter how much came in, it wasn't enough to keep up with Luma's dreams. In this, her fourth year, she expanded to five teams, including a girls' under-fourteen squad — nearly one hundred players in all. She hired a full-time teacher, rented a classroom from a private school, and initiated a full-day Fugees Academy so that six struggling boys could catch up on their reading, writing, and math. She watched their reading levels leap by two, three, four grades in just months and laid plans to expand the academy by one teacher and one class of six boys each year.

She turned reading books into a horse race, each book moving a Fugee one block forward on a chart, and grinned to see boys who'd been virtually illiterate a year or two earlier talking smack over who'd finish first and, as a prize, go with Coach on a mysterious summer road trip. She turned *them* into coaches, had them teach soccer to little kids in a weekly clinic at an elementary school, and into referees so they could officiate youth games. She had Tracy and three full-time Vista volunteers sizzling the phones to place the players in summer literacy and science camps. But her fondest pipe dream remained Fugeeville, a place in the woods with a big field, a building for classrooms, a computer lab, and cabins that sixty or seventy refugee families could move into, to heal their wounds and start anew.

Big dreams had a scent, and her kids began to sniff them. At a summer camp last year, when the Fugees were cut loose in a computer lab and asked to create a story, fourteen-year-old Al-Haji of Sierra Leone produced a video about the fragmentation of his homeland and concluded it with his dream. "I want to unite Africa," he declared. "If Coach Luma can do it with the Fugees, I can do it with Africa."

The Fugees had never been to college before. They gaped at the manicured lawns and ivy-covered walls when their coach's alma mater, Smith, in Northampton, Massachusetts, invited them last summer for a week. "It's like Harry Potter," *sighed Muamer, a fifteen-year-old Bosnian.*

"Why," asked Qendrim, from Kosovo, "would you ever leave this place?"

"Sometimes," said their coach, "you have to leave places you love and find other places you love," and they all knew that to be true.

They vowed to return to this magical place to attend college one day . . . and were crushed to learn that Smith admitted only women. Moma, a thirteen-year-old from Liberia, refused to surrender his dream.

"I'm coming here," he insisted. "They'll let me in, Coach. I'm gonna break the record!"

"It's not a record, Moma. It's a school policy."

"I don't care, Coach. I'm gonna break the record!"

A fifty-six-year-old Arab stepped off an airplane in Atlanta one day three summers ago. He'd never told his daughter this, but Hassan felt as if he'd aged ten years for each of the nine since Luma had left home. He watched, impressed, as she coached all those refugee boys and taught them the correct way to speak and write and carry themselves. But still he was confused, thinking this was just some sort of hobby, and he couldn't understand the stress he read on her face. "Why are you doing this?" he asked her. "For your career?"

"Don't tell me what to do with my life!" flared Luma. It felt as if nothing had changed.

She took him to Grace's apartment to eat dinner with the Congolese family. All his life Hassan had given alms to the poor, but from a distance. The four-year-old crawled all over him. The children called him Baba, Arabic for *father.* He watched their mother, Paula, serve fried fish, warning her children with a glare that no one was to eat a bite of it until Hassan and Luma had eaten all that they could, and then slap the hand of a child who reached for it. He watched them suck the bones when their turn came.

His eyes welled as he left the apartment. They had nothing, and they'd given him all. He turned to his daughter and hugged her. "I don't know how you do this," he said. "I can't do it. I'm really proud of you."

Luma didn't say a word. She couldn't. Maybe, she realized, each of them had underestimated the other.

When Hassan returned the following year, his daughter introduced him to Baby Luma, as Mama Louise's little girl had come to be known, the toddler she loved to bring to her home and dance with to "Livin' La Vida Loca." "This is the African Luma," she told her father.

He smiled. "I don't know how many Lumas there are going to be before you are through," he said.

Back in Jordan his walls and computer screen filled with pictures of Luma and the Fugees. "I was expecting much more from her," said Hassan, "and she turned out to be much more than I expected. How many Jordanians have been on the front page of the *New York Times?* Hussein, our old king. Abdullah, our new one. And *Luma.*

"What she's doing compensates for what I've lost. Not totally . . . but it's the way God wants. He willed that I not see my daughter, but that she would change the lives of many children. Who knows? Maybe one day one of my grandchildren will be president of the United States."

"He's in! One of my kids got in!" Huh? Who? What? It was Luma, speed-dialing her bewildered friends again last year. Shamsoun — a Sudanese boy who'd seen legs and arms severed when government planes bombed his village, who'd seen his father run for his life each time troops swarmed their mountain, who'd escaped to America only to lose his mother and two siblings in a car wreck en route to a Sudanese reunion in Tennessee — had just gotten a scholarship to play soccer at Pfeiffer University, outside Charlotte: Luma's first Fugee in a four-year college.

She'd gotten America wrong when she imagined it as a kid back in Jordan. It wasn't like the shiny steel rods that came out of her father's mill. It was like the piles of iron ore that went in, malleable enough so that if you really wanted to, if you had the heat, you could take a scoop of it and begin shaping it into what you wanted it to be. "It's not Utopia like it seemed in the movies and TV shows I'd seen growing up," she says. "But it's the only place in the world where this could happen. So many people here have stepped forward to help. I couldn't do this in any other country."

She put on her ball cap. She climbed back into the driver's seat on that bus. You know, the one you missed the other day. That's okay, because it'll come by again. It's America, that bus, just as colorful and loud and mixed up, always pulling away and coming back, giving us another chance to really see it . . . and jump on.

Can there be an edition of The Best American Sports Writing *without a contribution by Gary Smith? He is the best at what he does. Simple as that. Luma Mufleh, the woman with the bus, makes you want to get off the couch and do something, anything, worthwhile with your life.*

MATTHEW TEAGUE

Inside the Mind of a . . . Genius?

FROM PHILADELPHIA MAGAZINE

Sunrise was still an hour away, so Charlie Manuel flipped on a series of humming lights. A world of wire and net sprang into existence.

"Awright, awright," he said in his Appalachian accent. "You, um, you ready for this? Yeah. Awright. Are you sure?"

Yes, I'm ready for this, I thought. *I've known how to do this since I was three.*

Manuel dragged a bucket of balls to the middle of the batting cage, an insultingly short distance from the plate. Beyond the cage lay nothing but silence and blackness; we might as well have stood in outer space. "I'm just gonna throw you a few real soft ones, at first," he said.

For heaven's sake. I'm an American.

"Awright," he said. "Here it comes." He dipped his hand into the bucket and began the pitch, and I was immediately distracted by two elements of his wind-up.

First, he was doing it underhand. When a major league baseball manager offers you a hitting lesson and then proceeds in a style familiar to little girls everywhere, it's a clear sign of low expectation. Second, his face drew into a rictus of expression, lips pulled up and away from his teeth. He was *smiling.* Such joy is an almost unrecognizable feature on a big league manager.

Manuel's Phillies were a few days into spring training. Players arrived each morning and cantered into the clubhouse with a certain lift, a certain tilt, a certain swing. This year the Phillies start the season as division champions for the first time in a decade and a half. Last season was a sweaty, palpitating ride; the Phillies started by losing eleven of their first fifteen games, then had key players — stars Ryan Howard and Chase Utley — fall to injury. The team, which has lost more games in its history than any other team in any other professional sport, earned the dubious distinction of dropping its ten-thousandth as a franchise.

In those dark days, people across the city mocked the sixty-four-year-old manager. They mocked his congenial demeanor. They mocked his decisions. They mocked his accent, and called him names. "Moron." "Elmer Befuddled." "Idiot."

Then, against all prediction, the Phillies surged late in the season, winning thirteen of seventeen games and squeaking past the Mets to win their division and head to the playoffs for the first time since Czechoslovakia was a unified country.

And yet, in those bright days, people still mocked Manuel: the gentle moron. The kindly idiot. When it became clear that the Phillies would lose in the playoffs to Colorado, a *Daily News* columnist wrote, in what must have been a pass at Blue Ridge colloquial, "Sorry, Charlie. You've done laid all your eggs in one basket and all you have to do to cook an omelet with them is win three straight games against a team hot enough to melt a cast-iron frying pain [*sic*]."

Many people pined for the days of Larry Bowa, Manuel's fiery predecessor, who spent four years exploding all over his players. Granted, he never managed to frighten his team into success. But viewed from a distance, flying Bowa shrapnel did seem effective and satisfying. The guy embodied all the wrath pent up by Phillies fans, even as he caused it. He looked like we felt.

But now here stood Charlie Manuel, the bumbling ball coach, with a baseball in his hand: "Yeah, aw, awright, here we go . . ."

He lobbed the ball in my direction, and I hit a dribbler that bounced past him and his bucket. He glared at my bat, then strode to the plate to take it away. "Hitting a baseball is about balance, rhythm, and technique," he said. His stutter was gone.

"You need a sixty-forty balance to the rear," he said, "and you need to keep your hands above the ball, coming down to find your shortest distance to the ball."

He had transformed into a creature of perfect clarity. As he tossed pitches, I apologized for missing a couple, muttering about my church's softball league. He gave a quiet wave of his hand. A hand to say: enough of that.

Later I mentioned that my eyes weren't focusing properly, due to my contact lenses. "Bullcrap," he said, chuckling.

"I went to the eye doctor."

"Bullcrap." A dismissive wave. "Relax yer right hand."

Over a half-hour or so, he carved away all politeness, all embarrassment, all outside concerns and excuses, until nothing remained in my head but balance and hands and one downward angle. Everything else lay banished to the vacuum outside the cage, in the predawn black.

The almighty Yogi Berra, who has uttered more malapropisms than even tongue-tied Charlie Manuel, once said, "Think! How the hell are you gonna think and hit at the same time?" Philadelphians have long called Charlie Manuel empty-headed, and maybe in one sense they were right.

After a shocking number of pitches and much improvement, I stepped away from the plate and looked at my left hand. A rivulet of blood ran into my palm from under my wedding band. On any other day, in any other place, I would have stopped and searched for bandages. But Manuel's strange, quiescent manner had a propulsive quality; the calmer he became, the more I burned to knock the ball naked from its leather.

I pulled something from my finger and dropped it to the ground.

"That was a piece of my hand!" I said, grinning maniacally.

Manuel nodded. "That's a good boy."

I took up the bat again and thought, *There's more here than first appears.*

Entering a major league clubhouse is like stepping into the paddock before a Thoroughbred race: high-strung and expensive athletes stamp their hooves and snort, wound tight by pressure and competition. It's purposeful. Owners keep players, like horses, pushed to the nervous peak where performance meets breakdown. A manager must corral and focus that energy.

Phillies GM Pat Gillick says that's quite a trick. Players make enormous money now — more than their managers, often — and they can move on quickly. "These guys are almost independent contractors, making millions of dollars," he says. "There are only so many techniques you can use with them."

That was Larry Bowa's trouble, Gillick says. Bowa is a great coach, but a terrible manager. He's a genius with the hardware of baseball, the strategy, the numbers. And Manuel's been beaten up by fans and the Philly media for shakiness in those areas, for being a step behind with his in-game strategy. But people who understand the demands of managing debunk the idea that Charlie is, well, dumb.

"The average baseball manager — a C-minus or D-plus — is a better manager than most Fortune 500 CEOs," Jeff Angus told me recently. He's a baseball and business expert who wrote a book about both, *Management by Baseball*. "A baseball manager is making three hundred critical decisions per game. Most CEOs would melt down."

The notion that Charlie Manuel is an idiot — "Elmer Befuddled" — is ludicrous, Angus said: "With baseball, we have this illusion of certainty. And fans in Philadelphia are unusually sophisticated. But knowing the game and managing the game are not the same."

Anyway, those decisions — whom to play, when to remove a pitcher, and so forth — are endlessly debated but overrated. The most important part of managing baseball is the same as managing anything — dealing with people, in this case ridiculously well-paid entertainers who perform feats of athletic derring-do before millions of people. Derring-do that requires great focus and confidence. When Larry Bowa exploded in the dugout, which he frequently did, he spooked his players.

Bowa wasn't unique. When some major league baseball managers walk through their clubhouses, players visibly stiffen. But when Manuel walks through the Phillies clubhouse, the players do the opposite. They relax. He's got two children of his own — a son and daughter — but Manuel serves as a father figure to his whole roster of players. Among them, he almost looks like a bobble-head of himself, endlessly nodding and smiling.

"He is our leader," Ryan Howard told me. "Charlie keeps us loose."

Manuel's biggest liability — by all appearances, at least — might be his terrible communication skills. In press conferences, the bright lights seem to overexpose his thoughts, so that he ends up sputtering half-sentences and jumbled metaphors. Like the time a few years back when, asked about then–first baseman Jim Thome, he uncorked, "I think, I think that Jimmy, I think Jimmy, he's been here two years now, and I think that he also has to like, you gotta get to know him, and I think the more, the longer he's here and the fact that, you know, like, just once he feels like he's settled in and everything . . ." And so forth.

One of his more eloquent moments came when reporters asked him how a pitcher had managed to injure himself in his sleep. "I don't know," Manuel said. "I didn't sleep with him."

Yet his players hold a different view. Down at spring training, I asked pitcher Tom Gordon how Manuel ranks among the managers he's played for. "I'd say Charlie might be the best," Gordon replied. That's thunderous praise from someone who has, over two decades, played for almost a dozen managers, including Joe Torre at the Yankees. "He's that good."

Strangely enough, it's his plain speech that's Manuel's finest strength. "There's enough pressure in the major leagues as it is. There's enough pressure in Philadelphia as an athlete," catcher Chris Coste told me. "He has that rare ability to take as much pressure off you as possible." Manuel makes his guys laugh; he recently cut a commercial for the Phillies in which he stubs his "pinky toe" while berating players in the locker room. In February, during spring training, Manuel told pitcher Kyle Kendrick he'd been traded to a Japanese team, providing fudged paperwork to "prove" it. (Kendrick bought it.)

Manuel is more than just a locker-room jester, though. "He's a good communicator," Coste said.

I pictured Manuel, transfixed by flashbulbs. "People are going to laugh when they read that," I said.

Coste's eyes narrowed. "He's a good communicator with *us*."

I remembered Manuel's savant-like lucidity when he gave me a batting lesson: *sixty-forty balance to the rear, hands above the ball, find your shortest distance to the ball.* But that wasn't Coste's point. He meant that Manuel tells the truth, and sticks to the essence: When a player performs poorly, Manuel tells him so. When someone performs well, likewise. His straightforward manner, regardless of stuttering or grammatical errors, stops the churn of guesswork in a player's head. All those distractions go out — out into the black void — and all that remains is the game itself.

In his day, Bowa tried to reach that baseball Zen — literally. He took up Transcendental Meditation, striving for "enlightenment." And the meditation would help — until a batter made a crucial strikeout, or an outfielder fumbled a catch. Then Bowa would detonate again. Poses and mantras couldn't change Bowa because calmness wasn't in him. He couldn't graft inorganic placidity onto his nature.

As a young man, Manuel was like that too — quick fists and a loud mouth, a brawler from the backwoods of western Virginia. That wasn't his true nature, though. It would take a strange interlude halfway around the world to bring out the natural Zen of Charlie. First, however, he had to get out of Virginia.

Long day, his grandfather would say, stepping into the house. *Long day, so I'm goin' back to my room. No visitors.*

Then the familiar rhythm: *clump, clump, clackack:* boot, boot, door. The old man mined zinc and lead from the tilted earth of southwest Virginia, and he yielded more metal than conversation.

Charlie's own father preached at the local Holiness Church. It's a strict denomination that adheres to a rigid fundamentalist code, and the father believed in a lot of things. He disbelieved in many more, like sports. A waste of time, he said.

So after some number of minutes had passed, Charlie — who was just a boy — would rise and enter the grandfather's room. There the old man would be waiting, smiling. And together they would listen to baseball on the radio.

Charlie Manuel and his grandfather, sitting on the edge of a bed in the Virginia hills, listening to baseball on the radio in the middle of the twentieth century: they cut across space and time. Everything beyond the bedroom door fell away into the void of nonexistence — Charlie's father's opinions, especially — as they listened to Dizzy Dean drawl out the games. They ran the first-base line with young Mickey Mantle. Touched home plate with elegant Ted Williams, and tiny Yogi Berra. And stood with that fellow Jackie Robinson, as he ignored calls of "nigger" from the dugout of the hateable Philadelphia Phillies.

Nothing else mattered, because nothing else was. Baseball was the center of everything for Charlie — not only his escape, but his hope.

Charlie's father would never consent to a bat and ball, so the boy found rocks in the fields near his home, and practiced hitting them with a stick. *The Dodgers are down by three in the bottom of the ninth,* Dizzy might announce to the trees and hills. *And here comes Manuel to the plate. He's in fine form today.* The toss: a rock hanging in the air: the crack of wood on stone.

Charlie's grandfather took him to the mining company's store, where the employees spent their paychecks each Saturday. There was a black man there — a barber, remarkably, at the time — who started a county baseball league. At eleven, Charlie joined a team, scrambling to play with grown men. And then, in seventh grade, where sport wasn't a waste of time, Charlie joined another team, and then he was on his way — a power hitter, sending the cowhide rocks great distances, signed by the Minnesota Twins organization as an outfielder in 1963, right out of high school.

Manuel was a mustang of a young man, untamed, easily inflamed. He tended to fight, on and off the field. But he did hit well. So well that he made the Twins' big league team in 1969. That first year in the big time, though, an awkward slide into second base shattered his left ankle.

Manuel's hobbled major league career never quite stood up again. Finally, in 1976, he joined a new team, a team that wanted him around: the Yakult Swallows.

In Japan.

His airplane touched down first in Tokyo, where he stepped out to find a sea of Japanese fans and photographers. His handlers swept him into a hall where more people awaited the promised American, and he was presented with his new uniform.

Manuel was petrified. For all his swagger and spit — he still loved to fight, wherever — he felt lost in Japan. In Japan, the final aim in Taoist philosophy is emptiness, the state of "no mind," where thoughts only distract. This may explain baseball's popularity there; it's a game of stillness and quiet, until the singular moment when a batter swings at a ball. Deliberation and doubt only get in the way. There is no room for self-regard.

Manuel's first day on the island changed the way he saw the game, forever.

The night he arrived, he lay down about 3:00 A.M., on a bed made from cinder blocks and plywood. At 5:30, someone shook him: *Wake. Time to walk.*

Manuel staggered up and joined the other Swallows, who pulled on matching jumpsuits and walked for an hour, then did formation exercises, then enjoyed a breakfast of noodles, rice, and a warm, uncooked egg in its shell.

Then the team rode in a bus up a mountainside. Near the top, they disembarked and stood facing 169 steps. The Japanese players sprinted toward the top. Manuel huffed his way up 39 steps before he had to walk. At the top of the mountain, the team assembled for formation jogging. They practiced hitting, and Manuel hit the ball twice as far as the Japanese, pounding it clear off the mountaintop and into a forest. But then they formed up for more synchronized running, and he suffered.

At the end of the day, Manuel collapsed on his block-and-board bed, still wearing his clothes, more sore than he'd been in his life. He began to hatch a plan to escape from Japan, but realized he didn't even know where he was. And he couldn't move.

His translator — a Japanese man with the unexpected name of Luigi — entered his room. "You need to come take a bath," Luigi said.

Manuel resisted, but Luigi explained: "This is for you. This is very special."

Luigi and another player helped Manuel down some stairs, where he found a vast rippling bath with hot water pouring over a wall of rocks into a pool. The water steamed. Manuel felt too weak to protest, so he eased in, and the water seemed to boil the flesh off his bones. "Acchhhhhh," he cried, crawling into a corner of the bath to wait in solitude for a nude and waterlogged death. After a while, exhaustion won its battle with pain, so Manuel laid his head back and closed his eyes. In his half-sleep, he heard distinctly feminine giggling. He lifted his head to see forty or fifty naked Japanese women padding toward him.

Was this the "special" bath?

The women started playing with his reddish hair and muscular arms, laughing. Manuel lay there in a horror of paralysis, unable to lift even a hand. He thought, *You've got to be kidding me.*

And so life went in Japan: unendurable punishment followed by baffling exaltation. He gave in to it, partly because he had nowhere else to play baseball, partly because these Japanese clearly knew what they were doing. But it was more than that: Charlie was forced to stay focused, to move from moment to moment, because any intrusive thought — any self-regard — would have left him unbalanced. The Japanese taught Manuel a quiet sort of discipline, and he taught them to swing the bat like madmen. They taught him Japanese language — Manuel still speaks a little Japanese — and culture; he took his team to the Japanese World Series three times in six years, and smashed 189 home runs.

The Japanese surprised Manuel with what he calls, in his paradoxical way, "extraordinary common courtesy," outside and inside their baseball stadiums. A manager there would never publicly berate a player, for instance. "Not only did I learn a lot about myself," Manuel told me in spring training, "but I learned a lot about other people." And this, a simple yet surprisingly elusive skill: "I became a better listener."

Later, back in the United States, two dueling qualities — Manuel's passion, and his self-command — served him well as a batting coach, the kind whose charges would gladly work themselves until their hands bled. Manuel himself worked through a heart attack, cancer, and quadruple bypass surgery; while with the Indians, he managed for a time with a colostomy bag tucked under his uniform.

The wobbling arc of Charlie Manuel's career — from Virginia mine country, through adversity and injury, to the regimen of Japan — now gives him a peculiar view inside his ballplayers' heads. He can offer them perspective and calm.

"Philadelphia is known to be a tough place," Manuel says. "But it ain't nothing like where I come from."

Baseball is a slow game. It takes on a luxurious, almost velveteen pace: a pitch, a swing. A little pause. Another pitch, but no swing. Maybe a chat on the pitcher's mound. A moment for the fans to stand up and stretch. A little song. It's also this:

"Charlie. Charlie." Just his name. "Chaaarlieeeeee . . ."

In March, the Phillies played the Yankees in spring training, and Manuel faced a number of Phillies fans who were still a little unsteady with their heckling material. They threw out weird stuff. Insults about his . . . weight, maybe?

"Yo, Charlie! You want a hot dog?"

Manuel stood at the edge of the dugout, leaning on the fence with his forearms. Without moving any other part of his body, he chewed a wad of bubble gum in a slow rhythm, so otherwise unanimated that he looked for all the world as though he was working on a cud. Chew. Chew. Chew.

"Can I get you a HOT DOG, Charlie? A HOT DOG? CAN I GET YOU A FREAKIN' HOT DOG?"

It's something else a manager can do: Be a lightning rod. Take the abuse. Let it roll off you like, well, nothin' much, because there's a game on.

At midgame, Tom Gordon came onto the mound for his first appearance of the season. Gordon is forty years old, and each batter walked or hit given up seemed excruciating, because they weren't just "pitches"; they were "how he pitches now" — that is, can he? And when things aren't going well — and today, they weren't, as Manuel kept chewing his gum — there's no crueler game than baseball, because your failure unfolds at the game's slow pace.

As a battered Gordon walked off the field and into the dugout, Manuel reached over and gave him an encouraging slap on the haunch. Gordon responded with a small, summarizing nod, as though they had just wrapped up a discussion in what pitcher Jamie Moyer calls "baseball language."

In his office, after the 9–3 loss, Manuel shrugged off Gordon's trouble on the mound. He wavered a hand at his temple to indicate a squirrelly mental state. "The first time out for pitchers is always a little strange," he said. "And Tom always gets a slow start. It's fine."

That's what the tap to the butt told Gordon: *It's fine.* That's what the nod from Gordon gave back: *I know.* Baseball, especially early, in spring training, is a slow accretion, physically and mentally. Failure is expected. Failure has to be accounted for. How would Bowa, as a manager, have handled that moment with Gordon? The safe bet says that at best, he would have ignored him: *Pitchers. Their own breed. Let him figure it out.* But how, exactly, would that help Tom Gordon throw the ball better?

Manuel did lose control that one time.

In April of last year — the abyss of the Phillies' season, well before the late rise — Manuel met with the press after a humiliating 8–1 loss to the Mets. Radio talker Howard Eskin, who has led a years-long spitball campaign against Manuel, insinuated that the team was losing because he wasn't hard enough on his players: maybe Manuel didn't care enough to get angry.

Sure, Larry Bowa never won a championship. But at least he cared enough to pitch a fit.

"Why don't you drop by my office?" Manuel said. "I'll be waitin' on you."

When Eskin followed him, Manuel heaped whole bucketfuls of anger on the radioman's head. Eskin then made a circuit of media appearances to talk about Manuel and "his problem."

Manuel's problem, of course, was roundly misunderstood. Some people felt it was the manager's temper. The *New York Times* thought he might be sensitive about his Southern accent. Eskin, predictably, felt it was about Eskin. The problem wasn't any such thing. What had happened was that someone — anyone — had questioned the depth of Manuel's devotion to baseball, the game he had seen as "the only thing in the world to do" since he was a kid.

During spring training, one of Manuel's staff members told me, with affection, "Charlie has Forrest Gumped his way to the top. He's met, like, six U.S. presidents. Traveled around the world. Managed major league teams. Amazing."

That's not quite true. Happenstance didn't carry Charlie Manuel to the top of a major league baseball team. Even his knowledge — his unexpected articulation about the "balance, rhythm, and technique" of hitting — didn't carry him. Something else did.

Just before the Yankees game, I walked past their dugout and saw the stars there, lined up like broad-shouldered wax figures: Derek Jeter, Abreu, Rodriguez. And there, on a bench by himself, I saw a tiny, stooped figure. Yogi Berra.

In a quiet corner of the dugout, I asked Berra about Manuel's management style, and he smiled. "His players like him," he said, nodding. "He loves the game."

That affection is important, he said. Could it be the key to a ball club's success? Berra nodded again. "Well," he said with a grin. "Pitching helps you too."

Then I did something dumb: I asked Berra to sign a baseball for me. His face lit up, and he did so, in a cheerful blue ink. Then I turned to find a Yankees PR man staring at my ball. "I know you didn't just ask him for an autograph," he said, clearly angry. "I know you didn't."

"I did."

After receiving a lecture about the players' pregame focus, press credentials, and so forth, I was sent away. The sting of the encounter stayed with me throughout the game. Afterward, sitting in Manuel's office, I blurted out, "I did something unprofessional, when I talked to Yogi Berra."

He looked up from some paperwork. "What did you do?"

"I asked him to sign a ball."

Manuel considered this a moment. "Of course you did," he said. "It's *Yogi Berra*."

I realized then, with sudden clarity, that what sets Charlie Manuel apart from other managers — the quality that separates him from his predecessors — is humility. That's when I could see what his six years in Japan had given him. His childhood, his injuries, his discipline in an environment so different from home, all conspired to make him a humble man. He lives in a state of "no mind," seemingly without regard for himself at all.

It is this quality in Manuel — the fullness of his humility — that makes his team want to win for him. He is, as Yogi Berra once put it, an "overwhelming underdog." Baseball, it turns out, is a very simple game when you're in love with it.

I love stories that contradict stereotypes, especially when the stereotypes are formulated by talk-show buffoons and message-board bozos. The substance that obviously got Charlie Manuel hired in the first place is on display here. The story was written early in the 2008 season. Wonder how Charlie and the Phillies made out in the end. (Hah.)

WRIGHT THOMPSON

Father Bear

FROM ESPN.COM

WEST PALM BEACH, FLA. — For the past few days, Jack Nicklaus has been sick, listing a bit, even telling his oldest son he might need to lean on him. As he pulls his gold Lexus onto the tarmac of Signature Flight Service, he's still considering canceling this trip. He thinks of all the times he showed up when he didn't feel like it. He even kept an appointment after his grandson died; a devastated Jack believed a commitment should be honored. That's how his dad taught him to act. No, pushing seventy, he can't remember ever missing a business trip. He doesn't want to start now, so he's here, on muscle memory mostly, fighting a sinus infection and a hacking cough, parking his car next to the gleaming white Gulfstream V — tail number N1JN, affectionately called Air Bear — but even now, he isn't sure. It's not too late to turn around.

On board, his staff looks out the plane's large, oval windows. They didn't know until now whether he was making the two-hour flight down to the Dominican Republic. This is a simple trip. Two countries in about thirty-six hours, two golf courses to design, a few news conferences, a convoy of Range Rovers, a beachside villa or two, a handful of ministers and one ambassador to meet. He'd told everyone he was a game-time decision, and now he's headed toward the jet in shorts and an orange golf shirt. Just a minute before, communications director Scott Tolley sent someone down to get something from his car. Everyone is confronted by a potentially unpleasant start to the day: an ailing Bear, ready to get on with it, waiting on them. Jack doesn't like to wait. The men on the plane look at each other, clearly thinking the same thing.

"I told him to hurry," Tolley says.

Jack climbs the stairs, looking worn out. Sinatra plays on the jet's stereo; he is almost always playing on the jet's stereo, and Jack always notices if someone tries to slip in a different CD (a Motown disk made it one song). Jack says his good mornings, slumping into the big blue leather seat in the middle row.

"I'm still deciding on whether to go," he says.

The plane begins to roll forward, the pilot bringing the engines to life. Air Bear is cleared for takeoff. Jack leans back into his seat. He manages a smile.

"I guess it's too late to say no," he says.

Traveling at the Speed of Jack

He moves with a sense of urgency. Go, go, go. That's what people notice about him first. Decades removed from his golfing prime, Jack works more now than he did then, flying around the world, coming back to Southern Florida so he and his wife, Barbara — known to the little ones as Peepaw and Mimi — can watch their twenty-one grandchildren in sporting events, recitals, and plays. Then he's back on the road, visiting two dozen countries and as many states in the past year, a man with infinite dreams and a finite amount of time to make them come true. He is the head of Nicklaus Design and Nicklaus Companies, which employ all four of his sons and his son-in-law. Everyone depends on him, and he delivers, regularly running his staff, some of them half his age, into the ground. He doesn't want to talk about the glory days. Yesterday's boring. But today . . . today is full of wonder. Today is a blank canvas.

He takes care of himself. He's had one career undone by an aging body, and he doesn't want that to happen again. "I haven't had caffeine for thirty, thirty-five years," he says as the plane climbs to cruising altitude. "I haven't had a soft drink since the eighties. I haven't had a cigarette for close to thirty years — twenty-eight years, I guess. I don't drink. I haven't had a drink of hard liquor . . . that's not true. When I go to Mexico, I have a margarita. I have two or three margaritas a year. I'll occasionally go get a Wendy's."

Someone, the people close to him realize, should remind him

that he's almost seventy. "He didn't get the memo," his oldest son, Jack Nicklaus II, says.

Barbara says he never seems that old to her. Well, that's not exactly true. A sly smile comes to her face. "Yeah, if I ask him to go shopping. 'Oh, I can't walk on that cement.' 'You walk how many miles a day?' 'Yeah, but that's grass. That's on a golf course.'"

Even his kids see him as something of a superman, and this sinus infection is a subtle reminder that Jack Nicklaus cannot run hard forever. How long can he really do this? "I hope a lot longer," Jack II says. "Realistically, you have to imagine he's going to start slowing down. But honestly, I haven't seen it."

A few people who work with him have. He sometimes forgets a detail or two, and that never happened a decade ago. But the slips have been small, and day after day, Jack goes to work. He does it because he bores easily. He does it because he loves it. Mostly he does it for a deeper reason — to make sure that a business dependent on him can continue when he's gone.

"We've got to transcend me," he says.

Life at 47,000 Feet

Air Bear is not for the faint of heart. Not even Jack is immune to the ribbing. Like the time he signed an autograph for a well-endowed female fan, and when he got on the plane, his business partner Tim Kenny held up a cell phone with a picture on it of him signing and her in all her cleavaged glory, and Tim asked whether he should just go ahead and e-mail this to Barbara. Or when Tolley cracks on him for being so hoarse, saying the boss sounds like Louis Armstrong. Tolley, the king of imitations, goes down deep.

"I see trees of green," he sings.

Jack joins in, rumbling, "Red roses too."

Everyone laughs. The cabin of the plane is often filled with laughter, and, on this morning, as they get closer to the Dominican Republic, Jack begins to shake off some of the sickness. The idea of the afternoon's golf course work excites him, especially the holes on the front side that he needs to create from scratch. When he's feeling good, you can see it on the faces and hear it in the voices of the folks around him. When he's feeling good, he starts to needle

folks. Much of his humor is based on his awareness that the people
around him are intimidated: strangers by the legend of Jack, and
his staff by the perfection he demands of them and of himself.

He'll often wink before starting in. One afternoon, the CEO of a
company dealing with him caught a ride on Air Bear. Someone de-
liciously pointed out he was wearing a Polo brand shirt, not a
Nicklaus.

Jack smiled. Game on. "Polo," he said over the hum of the engines, his voice nasal. "You got a Polo shirt on?"

The CEO tried to dance. "No, I got a Nicklaus shirt. I spilled coffee on it."

Jack closed in. "When did you spill coffee on it? A month ago. In
1997? Why would you even own a Polo shirt?"

"They gave it to me for free."

"Who?"

"Our sales people."

"Why would they buy them knowing we have something of a relationship, which is hanging on by the thinnest of threads?"

A few minutes later, the CEO, worth untold amounts of money
and wildly successful in his own field, was wearing his stained Nicklaus shirt over the Polo. There is, of course, the tiniest chance that
Jack wasn't totally kidding.

Air Bear, the ultimate home-field advantage, closes in on its des-
tination.

DEFCON 1

The first stop of the day is the Punta Espada Golf Club in the Dominican, home to a Nicklaus course and this week's Champions
Tour event. Jack sits down in a room full of journalists, with a translator next to him. Even in Spanish, his talking points resonate.

He and his team are incredibly busy. Counting the Nicklaus
Signature courses that he does himself and the Nicklaus Design
courses done by his team, they are building in forty-five countries,
many of them just being introduced to the game. He tells the
crowd about the mayor of Moscow asking him to design some public courses, taking the sport to the people. All of that appeals to
Jack. He likes shaping the future of golf, likes being a founding fa-

ther, if you will, leaving his children all over the world: courses that will live long after he's gone. It pleases him to know that his family's name is on display in so many places. He thinks about that a lot.

In the middle of the news conference, Jack coughs, which sets off a chain reaction to which he is oblivious. A man watching from the back senses that the cough is somehow a sign that Jack isn't happy. This seems to happen often: people around Jack are so eager to please that they offer help he doesn't want or need. The man catches the attention of the moderator, pointing at a water bottle. The woman pours the water into a glass, then spends a minute or so trying to catch Jack's eye, discreetly at first but with increasing intensity, as if she wants to will the water into his hand. Finally, she gets his attention. He shakes off the glass.

He's not thirsty.

That's about the time the U.S. ambassador to the Dominican Republic shows up. He's brought his wife, and afterward, they inch forward for a picture. A crowd gathers. The tournament volunteers want autographs. Dignitaries want their thirty seconds.

Tolley tries to work Jack free. They've got to get out to the site of the new course. But Jack is surrounded. One time, an African tribe greeted his helicopter in traditional garb. Three generations of a Middle Eastern royal family once flew to meet him. They arrived in three planes: two 747s and a Gulfstream-IV. Today, it's the cognoscenti of this Caribbean island.

"At what point did I lose control?" Tolley asks dryly. "It's his world. We're just living in it."

A Private Answer to a Public Question

From the outside, his world seems perfect: more money than he can ever spend, a loving family, grandkids to dote on, a job he loves. But there are things that live inside Jack Nicklaus, hidden in the shadows, pushing and pulling him along. There is the memory of two people.

Almost forty years after Charlie Nicklaus died of pancreatic cancer, Jack can barely talk about him without crying. Everything Jack does is somehow connected in his mind to his father: the eighteen majors, the award-winning golf courses, the way he's always arranged his schedule around his children. "To this day," says long-time employee Andy O'Brien, "I still think he is trying to make his dad proud."

Charlie grew up the son of a boilermaker, who took him and his three brothers down to the hellish furnaces and told them, "This is why I want you to go to college." They listened, and all four boys earned degrees. Charlie became a pharmacist. Jack idolized his dad, who told him to take care of the good name he'd been given, and when Charlie died, at fifty-six, Jack was crushed. He never has totally recovered, and his dad is often on his mind. Jack wishes his father could see just one of his courses, to know how well his son has done. Charlie never had that chance; he got sick while Jack was completing his first project.

Over the years, Charlie has become a lodestar. When Jack makes a business deal, he always asks himself how it will affect his name before he asks about money. "What scares him?" O'Brien says. "My best guess is doing anything that would hurt the name his mom and dad entrusted him with."

Many people don't know it, but Jack has been in deep financial trouble twice in the past twenty-five years, both times due to entrusting his financial future — and the future of his family — to other people. Both times, he made good on the debts, starting over again. The first time, around his famous 1986 Masters victory, the man running his company made many risky investments, and Jack ended up responsible for more than $100 million. Almost broke, he avoided ruin by going to the banks, using that name as collateral. He swore he'd be more vigilant. The second time, two executives cooked the books and again he found himself staring at the possibility of losing everything he'd spent his whole life building. With time winding down, Jack cannot afford to let that happen again. So he stays involved, running like a man with something to prove, doing it to make Charlie proud, and to take care of those he'll leave behind. He sees himself as a protector, which brings us to another person he cannot speak about: Jake.

Jake was his grandson. Another child for him to dote on, another young man who'd grow up safe and sound because of his grandfather's hard work. Then Jack's cell phone rang. It never rings. He was on a golf course in California. On the other end was Barbara. She told him the horrible news: seventeen-month-old Jake had gotten away from the nanny and ended up in a hot tub. The doctors were losing the fight. His boy needed him at home. There was no laughter on the plane that day as it hurtled across the country.

That happened three years ago. He raises money in Jake's memory by auctioning charity rounds. It's almost the only golf he plays anymore. Once, he played for himself. Now, he plays for Jake. And still, he can barely say the little boy's name. Not long ago, he was in a board meeting for his children's charity, and he tried. The words stuck in his mouth, tears just behind those famous steely blue eyes. The words stuck in his throat, and they would not come out.

So when he goes out on the road and leaves his name on six continents, it's partly for him, for his own ego and satisfaction. But it's mostly for his family.

Man at Work

Jack walks out to the convoy of oversized off-road vehicles, filled with his designers, an agronomist, a landscape architect, investors, contractors, and a few people whose role there remains a mystery to him. He climbs into the driver's seat of the first vehicle, and he leads them out onto what will someday be the golf course at Las Iguanas, adjacent to Punta Espada, where the tournament is being played.

Everyone else follows, waiting for him to stop at each tee and green. When he does, about twenty men in golf shirts pour out, scurry up to him, and lean in. Sitting next to him is John Cope. He's the guy on the hot seat today, and he looks nervous. Jack has a lot of designers on staff, and Cope is the one assigned to help on the Las Iguanas project. The last time Jack was here, he sketched out the way he wanted the holes to look and to play. Cope then made his vision into a reality. At least, he hopes he did. Today is judgment day.

At each stop, Jack machine-guns advice: raise this, lower that, soften this, lose that bunker, make a lake, fill one in, bring in a cliff, put a waste area over there, move the turn point. The poor contractor has to figure out how to make it happen. "I need a hug," he says, laughing. Well, he's sort of laughing.

Then they come to number 7. This hole is a blank canvas, the first in a series where no real planning has been done. Jack stops his vehicle. All the others halt too. The golf-shirt entourage gathers. Cope slides his notebook into one of Jack's hands, a pencil into the other. Jack looks at both the tips and the members' tees. There is something funny about the Golden Bear imagining how a duffer would get around a course. As he has gotten older, and his own game has slipped, he's grown better at this. He doesn't just imagine a younger version of himself on the tee. He also imagines his grandson. "I've started to think like that," he says. "It's like trying to think in Spanish."

Today, the issue is how far Joe Golfer will be able to hit the ball in the air. Jack looks out from the tee. "That's not much of a carry," he says.

Senior designer Jim Lipe sits in the back. "It's a helluva carry for me," he says.

"You're a frigging old man," Jack says.

"I've got to hit it up the right side?"

"Here's what you've got, Jim," Jack says. "You've got 260 here. Members are gonna have 225. Ladies are gonna have 185 maybe, something like that, to get into that area. You play up here. You're an old man. That's where I play."

"Well, okay."

"Do you think that's right?" Jack asks. "If you don't like it, say so."

This is a critical moment. Sometimes, a staffer says, he really wants to know. Other times, he's thinking aloud and doesn't want anyone to talk him down. Or at least that's how some of the staff perceive it, especially the younger ones. So they try to listen to his voice and decipher the question behind the question.

Lipe, who has been with Jack for more than two decades, speaks freely. "I like it," he says.

They move on. In the second vehicle, designer Chris Cochran, who started a few months before Lipe, shakes his head. He's a world-class architect, helping to create some of the best courses on the planet. But even he's in awe watching Jack create golf holes so quickly. "I can't do this," he says. "I've got to sit in an office, plot, sketch, think about it."

A few minutes later, at the eighth, Jack's stumped. For the first time all day, he's quiet. A minute goes by. In his mind, the gray of the rock is turning an emerald green. That's what happens. Golf courses emerge fully formed from the ether of his mind. He puts his right hand over his mouth, makes a little thinking noise, folds his arms. He coughs. Synapses are firing, as he looks out at the gently sloping earth, figuring out the central problem he'll require golfers to solve. Nearby, Cochran watches. "Right now he's playing," he says. "He's got this imaginary course in his head."

Finally, Jack holds his right hand out. Cope once again slides a pencil in, and Jack begins to draw. Once, he heard an artist speak about the basic principles of his craft, and that's the first time Jack realized he'd unknowingly been following most of those principles. It's just the way he thinks, the product of a curious mind. He is always seeking information; folks jokingly call him "Carnac," and he is a bit of a know-it-all. But he never stops learning. In an airport security line, he'll ask what the x-ray machine will do to a person. He wants to know if that's a fig tree. And did you know Lake Como is the deepest lake in Europe? Do you know the ingredients in Diet Coke? Do you know what the land, and the owner, and the background dictate about this piece of property?

The hole comes quickly once he starts. He's talking quietly to himself. A cell phone rings in the entourage. He doesn't hear it. Barbara jokes that the house would burn down around him if it caught fire while he was watching television. Jack hyper-focuses. A loud beep keeps time from a nearby truck. He doesn't hear that either. There is something familiar about the drawing in front of him. At first, he can't figure out what it is. Then, he remembers. He has been forced to make a decision like this before, on one of the thousands of golf holes he has played in his life, somewhere, somewhere . . .

"It's a little bit like the tenth hole at Riviera," he says finally.

"Hmmm."

"Hmmm."

He sketches in a bunker smack in the middle of the fairway. "Length should not be the issue," he says. "The issue should be: can you challenge this bunker? So you might even make the turn point right here, right at that bunker."

He sketches a square, indicating the turn point, or where the second shot should come from. He draws in yardages. "You've got 265 right here," he says, "285 right here."

A few minutes after he began, he's finished. He is pleased by his creation. "All right," he says, sounding upbeat, "let's get the hell out of here."

When they get through every hole, Jack goes back to the hotel, a beachfront bungalow. Cope is off to the airport, taking the company Citation jet back to West Palm Beach. In the hotel bar, the Nicklaus team reconvenes. They're laughing about Cope, who escaped with compliments and not a reaming.

"I bet he's had about seven beers," one says.

Focused on the Future but Pulled into the Past

Before he can wake up and head off to do the design work he so loves, Jack's got to go be Jack for a few hours. The night is rich with nostalgia, and he works the room at the clubhouse, signing autographs, telling stories. He seems older than he did two hours ago on the eighth hole. The only time he doesn't seem half his age is when he's telling stories about his golf career. When he talks about golf course design, or his family, he comes alive. Want to see the real Jack? Ask about a grandson's middle school lacrosse game. But when he starts telling about Oakmont or St. Andrews or Pebble Beach, he seems to be reciting a well-polished script. "People say, 'Jack, do you go back and reminisce?'" he says. "I don't ever reminisce. The only time I ever do this is when I've got an interview. I'm never interested in talking about it, but I talk about it *a lot*."

When it's time to go, he works his way toward the door. The owner of the Dominican golf courses shakes his hand.

"Jack, you will never die," he says. "My father used to tell me there were three types of lives. There is the life you live. There is the life that lives on in someone's head and heart after a loved one dies. Then there are the famous people who live forever. Jack, you will live forever."

Jack smiles. Sometimes, it does seem like he has lived three lifetimes. He doesn't feel sixty-eight years old. What if he has only a decade left? Even two? That's not nearly enough. Even Air Bear cannot outrun time. Yes, forever would be nice.

"Forever, my friend," Jack says.

After the cocktail party, Jack and his team can finally eat. The restaurant they choose happens to be full of senior golfers playing in the tournament. There's Ian Woosnam. Nick Price. And, at a long table, Tom Watson, so linked with Jack's old life. Jack lingers for a moment with Watson, who sees the designers at the nearby table, the men responsible for creating the dastardly number 13 that undid him today.

"One-three," he says loudly. "Thirteen. We need to change thirteen."

Soon, the food comes. Stories are told. Plates are shared. Tequila is poured. Eventually, the restaurant empties. Watson stops by to say goodbye. In just a few days, they'll be together at the Masters in Augusta, Georgia. Tonight, they part ways. Once, they were young and brash. Now, they carry those memories around like a locket.

"See you next week," Jack says.

"See you there," Watson says. "Hope you're feeling better."

Finally, an Answer

The old stone wall captivates him. It's grown over, partly hidden, running down the left side of where he wants to put this golf hole. The sun is rising high in Anguilla, and the water is the color of his eyes, with St. Martin and St. Barthelemy just across the stretch of ocean. This is why he pulled himself out of bed yesterday morning. Because of this piece of land and its story, because it represents the hopes and dreams of an entire family, and because of the commitment he's made. He didn't do it for his paycheck. He did it because he knows what it means to trust someone else with your future. "If the wall is more than one hundred years old," he says, "it'd be ridiculous not to restore it."

Standing near him is a tall, commanding woman named Joyce Kentish. This is her family's land, sitting high above the water. As a child, she ran barefoot through these same rocks. Her grandfather settled the land, raising crops, tending goats, feeding his family. His name was George. He was born in 1866 and lived for 102 years. The grandchildren idolized him. He loved this land. For the last forty years of his life, he was blind. He couldn't see the place that made him feel at peace. But he had a friend take him on walks around the property, pointing out any changes. He stood out here, a blind man who could hear the waves crash into the rock, and could feel the salty spray on his face.

For two generations, the family resisted any attempt to develop this land. Now, they simply cannot afford to keep it. But even with all the logical reasons to move forward, it was not an easy decision. They agonized over it. They asked themselves what George would have wanted. Joyce talked to him like he was still alive, made sure she pointed out all the changes. "I tell him at night," she says.

When the family knew development was the only option, they knew they had one shot to get it right. They turned to Jack Nicklaus. This burden sits on his shoulders like a boulder. And so this wall cannot be destroyed. Something of George's spirit must remain amid the hotel and villas. A local tells him that activists have been trying to save these walls. "I love history and tradition," Jack says. "You won't get me knocking down stuff that shouldn't be knocked down. I love that stuff."

The years are slipping away. He moves a few holes, creating more oceanfront property, adding $10–20 million in potential real estate value. Jack is giddy, bouncing around, trying to make sure that Joyce and her family have someone fighting for them. Nobody understands the importance of legacy more than Jack.

It's what drives him to keep this frantic schedule. With an increase in the Nicklaus Companies' branding, and the income generated from it, Jack is actively working to make his business viable without relying on the income from the courses he designs himself. Last year, in the biggest financial move of his life, he sold a minority stake in his company for $145 million. This generated a large amount of cash for his family, but mainly the sale is to spur aggressive growth, counteracting the effect his one day being unable to work will have. "With most of his decisions today," O'Brien says, "he makes them with family in mind and how it will impact his family in the future . . . and after his passing. You can look at both the big and the small decisions — he factors the family first in almost every case."

Now he's focused on Joyce's family. The developers have a gathering scheduled, with local politicians and potential buyers, a gathering that will break up before he arrives. There are silver shovels for a groundbreaking. They have a gold one for Jack. Deep down, part of him knows that some of his clients only want his celebrity and either don't understand or don't care about the course. They want a photo op. He simply cannot do that. There is too much of Charlie Nicklaus's blood flowing in his veins. And these courses will be around after he's gone, defining his name, and his family's name. They have to be perfect.

Later, back at the airport, as he walks through the small island terminal, he thinks about Joyce and her family, and the trust they've shown him. It is a trust he treasures. He will not let them down.

"We take this very seriously," he says.

Family Values

The Anguilla golf course is laid out on a topographic map, each hole represented by a transparent plastic model built to scale. The team is gathered in the back of Air Bear, which is flying at Mach .83 toward home. The developer, IMI CEO Mike Collins, points to an open area of land. This, he tells Jack, is where Joyce and her family will be able to make the most money.

Jack looks at the map. He's barefoot. He picks up a hole in his hand, sliding it around. He moves another. What if we took two holes and ran them around that big open area, added value to that real estate? The pieces slide that way. Jack calls over people as he needs information. He looks down where the hotel is supposed to be. The hotel hasn't been very cooperative. "Do you have a deal with Fairmont?" he asks.

"We might," Collins tells the group. "At some point, Jack's got to pick up the phone and say, 'Who do you think is the damn brand here?'"

Jack looks up. "They think they're the brand?" he asks.

Did some competitive switch just get flipped? Once, golf satisfied those urges. Not as much anymore. Oh, a week ago, playing with amateurs, he grinded out a putt on 18 at Augusta to shoot his age — Barbara says he took extra time to make sure he had the line, never letting on how much it mattered to him — but mostly, he gets his kicks from business now.

"Tim!" he calls toward the front of the jet. "Tim!"

Kenny, his executive vice president, turns around.

"We're talking about getting rid of the hotel," Jack tells him.

All of this is happening instantly. Jack does not flinch. "What if I gave you a wild one and we did a Nicklaus Hotel?" he asks Collins. "If we're gonna get into the hotel business, it might as well be in a good place."

While that's being considered, he turns back to the empty space on the map. He folds his arms. They cannot move on until they've done right by their clients. "I'm concerned," Collins says. "I've been concerned since day one. It scares me to death for Joyce and those guys."

"Why don't we come up here with a par 3 course?" Jack asks. "A little par 3 course would amenitize this whole area."

Everyone loves the idea. It should add enough value to take care of Joyce's family for generations. A good day's work is almost complete, and, soon, the plane lands. When his grandson Jackie gets out of school on Tuesday, they'll leave for Augusta. The eighteen-year-old will caddie for him, both in a Masters practice round and in the annual Par 3 Tournament. Jack is excited to show him a place that's always been so special for him. He waves at the crew.

"See you Tuesday," he says.

A Gift for Jackie

He's in the right rough, and the ball is sitting down. Even though he doesn't compete in the Masters anymore, he did agree to play nine holes with his friend Gary Player. Jackie stands just beside him with the bag, and Jackie's father, Jack II, watches in the gallery. For most of the people following them, the Nicklaus-Player pairing is a walk down memory lane. They are living museum pieces.

"Save your good drive for tomorrow," a fan says to Jack.

"You won't find me here tomorrow," he says. "You'll find me fishing some place."

"Does it feel strange?"

"What?"

"Not playing."

"Not in the least. Not the way I play."

He looks at the ball in the rough. "I have no clue where this ball might go," he says. "I have absolutely no clue where I might hit it."

"Keep your head down," the fan offers.

"Thanks," Jack says. "I didn't think of that."

Standing nearby, his grandson laughs. The round goes as expected, with Jack too old to play the lengthened course. In the Par 3 Tournament, he's okay. Barbara watches, as she has done for years, urging each shot toward the hole. "Okay, Jack," she says to herself. "Let's make some noise." Barbara doesn't like going to tournaments much anymore. "It's no fun when your horse is out of the race," she explains.

They're nearing the final hole, and Jackie is nervous. It's tradition for kids and grandkids to caddie in the Par 3, and many players let their caddie take the final putt. Jack has done it the past two years — "Jack will have to play until he's one hundred so all the grandchildren can caddie," Barbara jokes — and Jackie has been apprehensive all day. There are tens of thousands of people watching in person and a million more on television. He's a senior in high school.

They are on the final tee. Jack doesn't have much of a golf game anymore. His hip is fake. He is sixty-eight years old.

His grandson stands next to him and asks for a favor.

"Hit it real close," he says.

Jack takes aim, as he has done for most of his life. When his family needs something, he wants to deliver. He swings smooth and pure, the ball traveling high into the air, across the water, every eye and television camera following it. It reaches an apex, then starts down, tracking, tracking, tracking . . .

The ball lands softly, stopping two feet from the hole.

Ho-hum, another glory dance about the Golden Bear, Fat Jack, patron saint of good golf. No, not exactly. This portrait shows an edgier, more business-oriented character than we've come to know, a man with the quiet sadnesses and demons we all share. A far more interesting Jack than we ever suspected existed.

BRYAN CURTIS

The Free Agent Adjusts His Truss

FROM PLAY MAGAZINE

"Grandpa," I asked the wrinkled, eighty-five-year-old athlete sitting before me, "will you tell me about the time you collapsed between third base and home plate?"

In the storied career of Gil Miranda, the sluggin' pride of Albuquerque, New Mexico, the Great Collapse is regularly cited as one of two signature achievements. The other is the Carding. The Carding was when Gil, then seventy, was hitting the ball with such power, such youthful vigor, that an opposing manager felt obliged to venture out of the dugout and demand to see some identification. Gil is a senior softball player. In many years of following my mother's father, I have come to believe that he is one of the greatest players in the history of the senior game. But until recently I remained relatively distant from the man, like a kid watching Mickey Mantle in slack-jawed wonder. I resolved to get to the heart of the athlete who, in the words of one teammate, "has more rings than fingers."

Gil is the kind of senior citizen who is constantly being told he looks great for his age. In his ninth decade, his bulk has transferred southward to his midsection, but no one would dare call him paunchy. He speaks in a slow, carefully modulated manner developed during his years as a teacher, occasionally tolerating interruptions from my grandmother Jo Nelle, who is a sub-five-foot ball of high energy. Not long ago, the three of us sat down to lunch in Phoenix, the site of the Senior Softball World Championships, which Gil was attending with his team, New Concepts (named after a construction company and not, as I hoped, an optimistic comment on the possibilities of seniorhood).

He took up senior softball in 1986, at age sixty-four, after a forty-year layoff from organized sports. He does not remember anyone in the family raising any objections. Over the next twenty seasons, he won eleven senior-softball world titles and has the medals, team photos, and souvenir T-shirts to prove it. "Some things I remember well," Gil likes to say. "Other things I have to reconstruct to put in their proper place." Thus reconstructed: some two dozen lesser tournament titles won in cities from Manassas, Virginia, to Richardson, Texas; berths on senior softball's "All World Team" in 2001 and 2002; a barnstorming tour of New Zealand in 1988; enshrinement in the San Diego Sports Hall of Champions; and an astounding win-loss record in his hometown league, where downtrodden opponents have regularly called for his team of seventy-year-olds to play in a more talent-appropriate fifty-five-and-up division.

Gil won his first world title with Albuquerque's Duke City Seniors in 1988. That might have been the extent of things, but for his Curt Flood–like determination to test senior softball's free-agent system. He jumped from the Duke City Seniors to a team called the Arizona 70's in 1992. Gil won a second world title playing with Arizona, hitting for the cycle in the championship game against the San Diego Silver Hawks. The manager of the Silver Hawks, Don Berg, was awestruck by the way my grandfather was gliding under fly balls in left field. "Outfield gets harder to play when you get older," Berg told me recently. "You gotta be able to run a little bit and catch it when you get there." Gil could do both, so he bolted once again, from Arizona to San Diego. He was seventy-two years old.

Several years and titles later, Gil was taking some cuts in the on-deck circle with San Diego when someone whispered "Gil!" through the chain-link fence. It was Ed Casada, the manager of the Palm Springs Nationals. Gil, by this point, was used to being a coveted senior free agent, so he pointed to Jo Nelle up in the bleachers and said, "Give her your name and number." After the game, Gil became an outfielder with Palm Springs, his fourth traveling team. He won another championship ring there and later found himself back with San Diego, where he won four more. That Gil has never lived a day in Palm Springs, San Diego, or Arizona bothers neither him nor, apparently, the authorities of senior softball.

But we were talking about the Great Collapse.

"Oh, that was in Las Vegas," Gil said. "I was playing with Denver." Denver was yet another stop on Gil's free-agent tour of the West.

Before the tournament, he wrenched his hamstring — one of the more common injuries among seventy-year-old softballers, whose muscles tend to stiffen at roughly one thousand times the rate of those of thirty-year-olds. His manager, Lou, told Gil to hang around in case he needed his bat. Gil hobbled to the plate in the last inning of the championship game with the bases empty and the score tied.

"I hit a line drive to right-center that rolled all the way to the fence," he said. "I'm limping around first base. Then I'm limping around second. Lou's the third-base coach, and I'm thinking, *Oh my God, I hope I can stop at third.*" But either Lou was suffering from temporary amnesia, or he had figured Gil, not unreasonably, for a superannuated Pete Rose. He waved Gil home.

Gil made the turn at third and then felt a fearsome pain shoot through his good leg. He belly-flopped about seven feet short of home plate.

"I called it the point of no return," Jo Nelle said. She had left the other softball wives to document her husband's trip around the bases in a remarkable series of photographs, which sadly have been lost to one closet or another. But I remember a montage of pumping arms and gritted teeth, followed by a final, heartbreaking shot of a prone figure lying in the dirt, as if my grandfather had dropped abruptly for Muslim prayers. But Gil — who was both a Marine and a high school principal and has retained the flamboyant impudence of both professions — was not waiting for the paramedics. No, he pushed himself up onto all fours and began to crawl toward the plate. He lunged forward and touched home a few seconds ahead of the relay throw.

"All the wives were hugging me," Gil said with a wink. It was hard to tell whether he regarded this or the gold trophy as the greater reward for winning the tournament.

Amid the Ace bandages, knee braces, and ever-present smell of Ben-Gay, Gil's squad arrived at the World Championships in Phoenix with a wrinkled but formidable lineup. In the outfield was Bob Kirchberger, an ex-banker who was also a star on the senior tennis circuit; Chuck Hughes and Charley Martinez, who had live bats; and seventy-year-old Eusebio Duran, whom the players referred to as "Chevo" or "Louie," and who had the rubbery batting stance of Vladimir Guerrero. Around the infield there was Daton Hill, a big man who hit for power; the gnomic shortshop Bobby Balphaser; and second baseman Charlie Romero, who maintained the eternal vigilance of someone raised in the Bronx. Ray Trujillo and Dick Brown played catcher — catcher being the senior softballer who is best able to bend down. Aside from a few nagging injuries — knee replacements, double vision — the New Concepts squad looked as well preserved as any group of seventy-year-olds had a right to. "We sure do have a nice-looking team," observed Peachie Brown, one of the softball wives. "I don't see any big ol' potbellies. And most of you have straight legs."

An exception to the latter was Mike Saul, who pitched and played first base. Mikey ran like he was wearing skis. This condition helped when he played first, however, as he could stretch out his glove hand while doing a split.

Gil's devotion to senior softball should not be thought of as a physical struggle against old age so much as a mental one. Playing right field with an enlarged prostate requires a certain singularity of purpose, a steadfastness of mind. A 2006 survey from the National Sporting Goods Association estimated that there are more than half a million senior softball players in the United States. There is no maximum age limit; Frank Murano, an eighty-six-year-old ex-firefighter from Boston, claims to be the oldest traveling senior player. About one-third of all senior tournament players live, like the New Concepts team, in the southwestern United States, and every winter, the area of Arizona where we were staying becomes flush with free-agent "snowbirds" who come south for the weekly pickup games in Scottsdale.

Senior softballers are divided into five-year age divisions — the fifties, the fifty-fives, and so forth, up until the eighties. According to Terry Hennessy, the CEO of Senior Softball USA, there was a period in the late 1980s when younger players added a few years to their ages so they could move up divisions and pummel their elders. You now need two pieces of ID to play senior softball. There

have been other reforms: the introduction of restricted-flight soft-
balls to prevent injury; liberal rules about "courtesy runners," as
pinch runners are known in senior softball parlance, to aid the
movement-impaired; and the "scoring plate," which sits a few feet
up the third-base line from the real home plate to avoid Ray Fosse–
style collisions. Even with all that, the senior softballer lives in fear
that the game has suddenly passed him by. "I have to tell the team,
'Relax, everyone here is seventy,'" says Charlie Romero.

As the New Concepts squad took their positions, Gil and I sat
down in the dugout. Though he was dressed in game gear (up to
and including knee pads), Gil wouldn't be playing in Phoenix, his
career having reached an unsatisfying impasse. No senior softballer
has ever been 100 percent. But Gil's body had undergone a thorough beating in the last decade. A partial roll call includes mild
stroke, subarachnoid hemorrhage, macular degeneration, and a
form of intestinal cancer, which resulted in the removal of his pancreas, gallbladder, and parts of his stomach in 2003 and led, as a result of the surgery, to adult-onset diabetes. "At seventy-nine, I ran
well, I felt good, I had a lot of energy," Gil said. But the injuries had
forced him to retire to the position of manager and occasional
pinch runner. Lately, even the latter was a struggle. "I picture myself going around the bases," Gil said wistfully. "Then I go out and
run and I realize it's all in my head."

A ring's a ring, though, and as New Concepts took the field
against Cape Cod, it was clear that Gil had transferred his bound-
less energy to managing. He stalked the dugout like John McGraw,
watching as his ace, Ken Wischman, delivered the first high-arcing
pitch. A senior softball game is like a baseball game played underwater. Everything moves at half-speed, but the game is marvelously
well played. Double plays are turned with regularity, and some
sixty-five-year-old power hitters can regularly clear the three-hun-
dred-foot outfield fence. Some seniors can only "hit and sit" and
are replaced by a pinch runner as soon as they reach first. Others
can hardly bend down to snag a grounder, and though that describes no one on the New Concepts squad, the outfielders began
the first inning against Cape Cod with some uncharacteristic errors and endured a thorough ribbing from teammates when they
returned to the dugout. ("No sprinklers out there? You didn't
trip?") Gil, who was unamused, kicked the chain-link fence in dis-

gust. The game went rapidly south from there, Cape Cod winning, 17–10.

We stayed in the same dugout for the second game, against a team from Syracuse, which proved to be the first test of Gil's managerial prowess. With Syracuse rallying from a five-run deficit in the seventh and final inning, Gil jogged onto the field to pull the pitcher. A mid-inning pitching change is rare in senior softball — few would even bother. But Miranda had a hunch and brought in Ken to pitch in his second outing of the day. He earned the save, and New Concepts ended its first day with a split. Several of the players invited me to meet them in the parking lot to celebrate with a cold Bud Light. It was 10:30 A.M.

Beer was passed around, shin guards removed. Senior softball has a strong undercurrent of black humor. As one player put it, "We'd play in a wheelchair if you gave us a shove." The softballer makes no secret of his advanced age, and he is constantly reviewing his most recent game for mental mistakes, lapses in ability, "senior moments." (Charlie Romero, to Mikey: "I jumped too late on that line drive." Mikey's reply: "You jumped?")

The thing the senior softballer fears most is getting burned, which occurs when you're playing the outfield and the ball gets hit over your head. This is generally humiliating at every level of softball, but in the senior game it can take several minutes to track the ball down and a half-dozen relay throws to get it back to the pitcher. I've seen guys get burned, and you could use the restroom, eat a hot dog, and drive around the block by the time the pitcher throws the next pitch.

Death is somewhat less of a concern. It's just part and parcel of getting old, and teammates see it as both a tragedy and a natural opportunity to shuffle personnel. "That's how we move players around — they die," Romero says. A well-managed team like New Concepts, which plays in the seventy-and-up division, is constantly fortifying itself with young talent: the team arrived at the World Championships in Phoenix with four spry seventy-year-olds and five youthful seventy-one-year-olds. Death occasionally occurs on the diamond: at least five players have died during Senior Softball USA tournaments in the past fifteen years. But senior softballers have a certain equanimity about death, and in at least one instance, as the deceased was loaded into an ambulance, his bereaved teammates elected to continue the game. Some years ago, one of Gil's teammates suffered what turned out to be a nonfatal heart attack at a tournament in Arizona. When Jo Nelle ran to find help, a man told her, "Calm down, lady, they die around here all the time."

As Gil nursed his beer (I noticed some of the other players had already had two or three), I could feel him struggling to maintain his composure. It was killing him not to play and, moreover, to leave his twelfth ring to elements he could not control. When we left the ballpark, he told me, "When I see a guy hit a grounder with the bases loaded, I think that's a disgrace." He quickly added, "I don't tell him that, though."

For much as senior softball consumed his life, I have no memory of playing catch with my grandfather. I do remember him rousing me early on summer mornings, zipping me into my windbreaker, and driving me to the field to serve as his one-man cheering section. He would point to a seat in the dugout and then jog to his position in the outfield. Once he overheard a teammate telling me that the guys were playing to have fun. Gil came up and offered a mild corrective: "It's fun when we win."

Success was Gil's most obvious outward feature. One of twelve children born to a family in Lincoln, New Mexico, he became a highly decorated and much-admired figure in the Albuquerque public schools, the kind of principal who could dole out punishment and be loved for it the next day. Among his four children and two grandchildren he commanded a similar veneration. He was such an impossibly heroic figure that I sometimes found it difficult to think about him on a human level. Gil seemed to tower above the rest of us like a gold figure on one of his softball trophies.

The news that he was suffering from cancer, in 2003, did little to shake him from his perch. Cancer reduced him to a puny, jaundiced form, the opposite of the lithe figure who danced to the outfield. But his self-assuredness didn't diminish, and shortly after a doctor told him he might survive surgery (if without several vital organs), I found myself standing beside him in the parking lot of an Albuquerque hospital. His first words, uttered sotto voce, were: "I guess I'm going to get to play a little more softball." He was back on the field a year later, though mostly pinch-running.

"I never dreamed he would play again," Dr. James Houle, his

physician, said recently. "He had lost so much weight, he was struggling at that point . . . If he wasn't so strong going into it, if he hadn't been so physically active — well, most mortals would not have made it through that." Immortality is a satisfying attribute for a sports hero, but I found it a strangely puzzling one for a grandfather. It seemed that softball, where he made himself vulnerable to defeat and humiliation, was the one place to see him in his natural state.

"Ballplayers hate to tell a manager when they're hurting," Gil said. The two of us were standing in the lobby of the Premier Inn, the team hotel, which had been selected because it met the most important criterion: it was cheap. "But the players tell each other when they're hurting," Gil continued, "and then the word gets back to the manager." Indeed, on Tuesday afternoon, the second day of the tournament, Charlie Romero appeared before us with a bit of grim news.

"Marvin was getting out of a van and he hurt his knee," Charlie said. Marvin Spallina was a well-built seventy-five-year-old who hit for power.

"When did this happen?" Gil asked.

"Yesterday," Charlie said. "He would prefer not to play the field, but he thinks he can pinch-hit."

Miranda said later: "I knew someone was hurt."

With or without Marvin, the tournament's second and third days saw New Concepts turn a corner. The team's play grew confident to the point of ostentatiousness. I saw Bobby Balphaser, the shortstop, turn a 6–2 double play: scooping up a grounder, tagging second, and then firing home to catch a senior trying to sneak home from third. I saw Ray Trujillo throw himself into a fence while tracking down a foul ball. I saw the Murderers' Row of Bob K., Chevo, Daton, and Charley M. sock the ball to all fields with regularity. After the creaky performance against Cape Cod, New Concepts won its next six games in a row by a combined score of 91–44, including twenty-run eruptions against teams from Texas and Sacramento. Moreover, the old men seemed to be gaining confidence, and for the first time, you heard the Albuquerqueans giddily whispering about the idea of winning the championship.

There was only one moment of discomfort. During a game

against Colorado, Gil was coaching third base and waved a runner home from second on a hit to the outfield. It was obvious a second later that this was a bad decision — the runner was out by ten feet — and Gil put his hands on his cheeks, as if to feel the burn of embarrassment. The team won anyway, and nobody breathed a word about it.

In penance, he recommitted himself to the lineup, putting in hours after the games were completed. The tournament was lining up perfectly. Cape Cod had been sent packing, a whole host of lesser teams had fallen by the wayside, and New Concepts found itself staring at a berth in the World Championship game on Thursday. Most of the team took dinner in groups around 6:00 P.M. on Wednesday night and, having little interest in carousing, went to bed early. When Jo Nelle woke up at four o'clock Thursday morning, she saw that Gil was already up and out of bed. He was sitting across the room, bathed in lamplight, fiddling with the lineup card. He was already wearing his uniform.

The groans were loud and determined. New Concepts had begun its pregame stretch, a chance to warm up muscles that had endured a week's worth — nay, seventy years' worth — of pounding. As Gil surveyed his team before the championship, he didn't like what he was seeing. Marvin still hadn't fully recovered from his encounter with the minivan. Fred Chavez and Ray Salazar were limping. Bobby, the vacuum-cleaner shortstop, was rubbing SportsCreme on his quadriceps.

"If we get real desperate for runners, I can run," Gil announced. "I can run better than the crippled guys." He was completely serious. He began loosening up next to one of the ball fields, running sprints of perhaps ten yards. Informed of this potential comeback, Jo Nelle made a face like she had bitten into a lemon. Coincidentally, the New Concepts players made miraculous recoveries and the subject was dropped.

The opponent was Syracuse, which had worked its way up from the losers' bracket to earn another shot at New Concepts. Syracuse had a manager who wore his hair in a ponytail and a ferocious lineup that included a giant, mantis-like senior in left field. They came out hot. After a pair of errors by Mikey and Kenny, the New Concepts gang found themselves in a 7–1 hole. The game re-

mained in a kind of uncomfortable stasis until the bottom of the
fourth, as if both teams were too nervous to make anything happen. "You'd think, 'They're seventy — they never get like that,'"
Charlie Romero had told me. "But they do, even at our age." The
dugout, which had been so jolly, began to fill with a frightful flop
sweat. Gil exhorted the players to play with some "huevos," and his
batters reemerged from the dugout as if they'd just come out of the
whirlpool. They rallied for five runs in the bottom of the fourth inning and another five-spot in the bottom of the fifth. Gil's auda-
cious new lineup was working. When Fred Chavez came to bat with
two outs in the bottom of the sixth, Marvin called out, "Fred, remember your prowess!" I asked him what he meant. "Fred came up
to me moanin' and groanin' about his place in the batting order,"
Marvin said. "I told him, 'Fred, there's a good reason for that. It's
your prowess.' He said, 'My what?' . . . I told him it was a compli-
ment." Fred's prowess led a two-out rally, and New Concepts added
five more insurance runs. The championship game had taken a miraculous reversal. Going into the seventh and final inning, the
good guys led, 16–9.

Nobody could quite believe what was happening. Even Gil, the
old pro, was wandering in a kind of daze, and Marvin had to remind him to sit down. Kenny was on the mound, lobbing balls into
the teeth of the Syracuse order. After three singles to lead off the
inning, the Syracuse left fielder burned Chevo in left field for a
two-run triple. The score was 16–12, with nobody out, and Gil was
up and pacing. A sacrifice fly scored another run. Now Gil was sta-
tioned at the far end of the dugout, bouncing on the balls of his
feet. But then Bob K. made a beautiful running catch in left-center,
and the next batter hit a foul ball with two strikes — which, in senior softball, counts as strike three. Game — and championship —
to New Concepts, 16–13.

What happened next is largely a blur. I remember a bunch of old
men doing joyful half-leaps. And then I remember the celebration
coming to a quick and jarring conclusion, as if the guys had realized, all at once, that no good and much harm could come from
this much exertion.

Gil shook hands with the conquered Syracusans and then took
hold of a giant trophy near home plate. Through choked-back
tears he said, "I'm so proud of you guys." The guys yelled back,

"We're proud of you, Gil!" Then he straightened up. The moment of vulnerability was over.

It was enough. Baseball people talk about a player who's "just a winner," someone who possesses that intangible quality that goes beyond home runs and RBIs. Gil, I realized, was just a winner. Not so much for his ability to collect rings but for how he had mastered the quality of winning. Gil enjoyed it because it afforded him a kind of halo of respect. It was not aloofness, it seemed, so much as his comfort zone.

I walked out to congratulate him, and he received me like he would have received any other visiting sportswriter, patting my back and letting off a satisfied laugh. Within minutes he was talking about next season, about two sixty-nine-year-olds who would be senior enough to join his team, about his desire to strap on a glove in an eighty-year-old league, provided he could find any eighty-year-olds in Albuquerque who weren't "crippled or dead." Gil Miranda wasn't immortal, of course; he was just most comfortable acting like it.

Gil Miranda is my new idol. Eighty-five is the new seventeen. May we all be swinging an aluminum bat when we're eighty-five. Bryan Curtis not only has written a good tale, he apparently also has very good genes.

AMBY BURFOOT

Running Scared

FROM RUNNER'S WORLD

EIGHTEEN MILES into the 1968 Boston Marathon, I looked up and didn't see another runner on the road ahead. Not one. I had dreamed every night for years about winning Boston. And now I was almost there. I had just turned the corner at the Newton fire station and begun the run eastward on hilly, serpentine Commonwealth Avenue. Ahead, thick crowds edged onto the road — grandparents and their children and their children's children — shading their eyes and peering at the colorful stream of runners, all 890 of us. Three motorcycle policemen led the moving spectacle, and a photo truck, and a yellow school bus containing the Boston press.

For five years, I had set myself the singular goal of winning Boston. I ran up to 175 miles a week, entered every road race I could find, broke down on occasion, as all runners do, but then resurrected myself and trained even harder. Always with Boston as the focal point. If I could hold on, my name would go into the record book with the likes of Clarence DeMar, Les Pawson, Tarzan Brown, Gerard Cote, "Old John" A. Kelley, and my coach-mentor, "Young John" J. Kelley, the 1957 winner.

Only one thing stood between me and a Boston victory — the shadowy specter that was stalking me. I couldn't hear him, only my own desperate breathing. Couldn't see him, for he was a stride back. But when I glanced down at my feet, I saw two dark shapes — my own, tall and angular. And my pursuer's — shorter, more compact, with arms that pumped more vigorously than mine.

I had come so far. I was so close. I had given so much. I was a twenty-one-year-old senior at Wesleyan University in Middletown,

Connecticut, who in four years of college had set new records
for dullness. Hit a Saturday night keg party? No way. I detested
beer and, more importantly, had to rouse myself at 6:30 for the
ritual Sunday morning twenty-miler. A weekend skiing trip? Not
a chance. Skiers twisted their knees and broke their ankles and
risked countless other injuries. Go on a simple dinner or movie
date? Not those either. I had no time for flirtations or anything that
might muck up my marathon ambitions.

As we reached the first of the three hills on Commonwealth, I
drove myself harder. Sweat flew from my forehead. My throat was
dry and scratchy, the sun having targeted us from the start, produc-
ing a perilous dehydration. Like other marathons in those days,
Boston offered no water stops. I reached the top in a near swoon,
but the extra shadow was still there. Moments later we started up
the second hill, and I dug deeper, gritting my teeth with each
stride. Nothing changed. The haunt stuck with me — silent, apparently effortless, mocking my furious exertions.

That left only the third and last hill — the storied Heartbreak
Hill. It was longer, steeper, and deadlier than the others, peaking at
the twenty-one-mile mark — beyond The Wall, beyond the marathoner's last reserves, deep in the zone of zombie running.

In my youthful racing career, I had already lost scores of races at
the end, outkicked by others with superior speed. Every time I ran
the mile, I led for three laps, then the field sprinted around me.
Same thing in the two-mile, only it was worse because I would lead
for seven laps before the floodgates opened. I found some solace in
road racing with its longer distances — ten miles, 20-K, and beyond. But I lost even those races when another runner tailed me to
the final yards before blowing past. This Boston Marathon was feeling far too familiar.

Worse still, I knew my shadowy rival's name, Bill Clark, and he
knew mine, and we both knew he would beat me. Clark, twenty-
four, was one of those distance runners I envied for their speed. He
could run a 4:06 mile — much faster than my best — and had marathon endurance as well. I was in deep trouble.

My day hadn't begun well either. After passing the "physical
exam" in the Hopkinton High School gym and picking up my race
number (17), I headed for the locker room patrolled by de facto
race director Jock Semple. I had changed there the year before,

thanks to my friendship with John J. Kelley, Semple's protégé. The year before was when Semple gained worldwide infamy for attempting to bulldoze Kathrine Switzer off the course.

That was the very same Semple I encountered as I swung open the locker-room door. With head down, he charged me: "Oh, fer Chrissakes, will you git the hell outta my locker rhume." At the last second, he looked up. "Oh, Ammmby, Ammmby. It's okay, Ammmby. C'mon in."

I was still rattled when the race began at noon. But once in motion, I calmed down, happy that we had finally begun the journey to Boston. I drifted into the front pack, the miles passing quickly, almost silkily, that's how smooth I felt. Near the ten-mile mark in Natick, I decided to make a full race assessment. I edged to the side of the road and turned for a wide-angle scan of our lead pack. It included a Finn, three Mexicans, and a half-dozen Americans. Bill Clark lolled a few yards back. I audited myself most closely of all. Breathing? Blisters? Leg pains? Overheating? The answers came back one by one and led to a rare conclusion: nothing hurt. Everything felt great. I was having a dream day — one in a million.

At fourteen miles, I mounted a little surge — the most middling of accelerations — to stretch my legs and gauge how the others would react. I shortened my stride, veered from the group, and broke into a quicker, more flowing rhythm. There was more air around me now, and it felt invigorating. When I slowed again after about two hundred yards, I expected the whole gang to circle around me.

Instead, there was only Clark. I looked back in disbelief. In shock. The others had drifted twenty yards behind. They were struggling. Just two of us remained. This was terrible, the last thing I wanted. No more comforting cocoon. Now it was a race. Man against man. A winner, a loser. With twelve daunting miles to go.

What to do? It was too soon to begin a charge for the finish, yet I didn't dare slow and let the others regain contact. For certain, I needed a plan that would save me from getting outkicked again. An insistent voice in my head said: *Maintain for now. Wait for the hills, wait for the hills, wait for the hills. Then run your guts out.* At the bottom of Heartbreak, Clark's shadow still taunted me. With every stride, my chances of winning grew slimmer.

*

In my tenth-grade biology class I was enjoying a peaceful post-lunch nap when the public-address box startled me awake. "Harrumphhhh" — the despised sound of our principal clearing his throat. "We've just received the first radio update from the Boston Marathon, and our own Mr. Kelley is running with the leaders after six miles." A sports report sure beat another lesson on cell division. And I had actually seen this Kelley in the high school hallways. He was the short one with the suit jackets that dwarfed his thin torso.

The principal returned with several more updates in the next ninety minutes. Kelley fell back, but he still finished fourth that year, 1962. Five months later, I joined the cross-country team he coached at Robert E. Fitch High School, high atop Fort Hill in Groton, Connecticut, and competed in my first distance races.

I had been a baseball fanatic, but running gave broader compass to my obsessive personality. I had a stern, Germanic mother, and from her I learned self-discipline. It required no particular effort to run thirty-five miles a week during my senior year at Fitch or to double that to seventy my first year at Wesleyan. I believed that whereas success in other sports depended on raw physicality — your height in basketball or your weight and strength in football — distance running rewarded those who trained the hardest.

On our Sunday morning runs, Kelley filled me with alluring tales of Boston's improbable history. The pull was irresistible. One April morning in 1965, my father drove me to Hopkinton to run the marathon for the first time. A light dusting of snow covered the colonial rooftops and a few hardy forsythia blossoms. On the town green, five Japanese runners warmed up in spotless white sweats. I also caught a glimpse of "Old John" Kelley in a crimson Harvard sweatshirt. I had never seen so many runners in one place — 358 that year — and I couldn't wait to join them.

I remember passing through Framingham at six miles and spotting the first of the Boston Athletic Association's bright orange checkpoint signs in the road. It said: BAA MARATHON: 19⅜ MILES TO GO. *How puzzling,* I thought, and then: *Too bad I've never run that far in my life.* This frightened me enough that I kept a conservative pace, and with every passing mile caught one or two struggling runners. At the crest of a modest slope near Boston College, I yelled out to the crowd, "How much farther to Heartbreak Hill?"

The response came quickly: "You just reached the top."

In the last five miles, I passed clumps of spent runners and continued running strongly to my twenty-fifth-place finish in 2:34:09. Two days later, I had to run the mile and two-mile in a track meet against Brown. I was outkicked in both races.

Every year after that, I tried to train longer and faster. One crisp October day in 1966, my cross-country teammate Jeff Galloway, a precocious young marathoner, proposed a stunning workout: 40 x 440 yards in 75 seconds with a 110 jog. We ran barefoot on the grassy field surrounding Wesleyan's cinder track and adjacent football field — Jeff with his muscular chest and shoulders and his light forefoot prance, me tall and skinny with my shuffling heel-strike. When we finally finished the fortieth 440, the sun had set behind the hulking Wesleyan Library, my feet were freezing, and we still needed to jog a two-mile cooldown to complete the nearly seventeen-mile workout. Of course, I had already run seven miles that morning. And would again the next morning.

The winter of my senior year, I ran a series of uninspired indoor track races, except for a two-mile in 8:45 that far outstripped my wildest expectations. In mid-March my Wesleyan track team took a spring training trip to Quantico, Virginia. With Boston just a month away, I wanted to pile on the miles. The first morning, I was up early for a seventeen-miler. That afternoon I talked my teammate Bill Rodgers (yes, *that* Bill Rodgers) into joining me for what I promised to be a relaxed twelve-mile run. And it was, until we got totally lost in the twisting trails of Prince William Forest Park. After two hours in low-eighties heat, we walked a couple of times, then started up again, and eventually emerged to some roads. The run took three hours. I wrote it down in my log as twenty-two miles. That gave me thirty-nine for the day, a good beginning.

Over the next two weeks, I averaged 25 miles a day, hitting 350 miles for the fourteen days. After a few days of recovery, I noticed that I was running fresher than ever. Even when jogging, I skimmed along at six minutes per mile. This had never happened before. It has never happened since. But in April 1968, I was in the "flow," to use a term psychologist Mihaly Csikszentmihalyi wouldn't coin until 1990. I was totally focused on the upcoming Boston Marathon and totally energized by the process.

In the late '60s, we knew nothing about visualization or positive self-talk. No one talked himself up; that would be presumptuous bragging. I did tell my brother Gary and one trusted training partner that I thought I could win. Then I swore them to secrecy.

When Clark and I reached Heartbreak Hill, I closed my eyes, groaned loudly, and ran for my life. This was it — now-or-never time. If I didn't drop him here, he would outsprint me later. But I was a good hill climber. I had won many races on hilly courses, my low shuffle chopping the hills down to size. I still had a chance.

Out of the corner of my eye, I saw a young boy, perhaps seven or eight, rushing my way with a slice of orange. I wanted it badly — any liquid, any calories, any citrus jolt. But I couldn't spare the effort to reach out for it. I had only one mission: to run to the edge. I saw the child turn away, chagrined, and retreat to his parents. I felt guilty for rebuffing him.

I was pumping, pumping, pumping to drop the shadow. Halfway up Heartbreak, no luck. I had nothing left to give. Zilch. My breathing rose to a wail. I remembered what my former coach Kelley once told me about Roger Bannister's 1954 breakthrough in the mile. Kelley believed that Bannister and others of his era were impeded by a primal fear. Many prominent doctors and academics argued that four minutes was an actual physical barrier. The human body wasn't designed to run that fast, they contended, and the man who dared a sub-four would risk death. The heart might explode, the lungs burst, or the arteries rupture.

Bannister proved the naysayers wrong, but now I wondered if it was the brevity of the mile that saved him. The marathon — that surely wasn't a distance intended for human recreation. I didn't imagine that I might die, but I figured that my body might simply stop functioning at any moment. I was imploring it to go faster. What if it had other plans?

One hundred yards to the top of Heartbreak Hill, and my vision closed to a narrow slit. There were no more sidewalks, lawns, trees, or houses. No more cheering spectators. No more blue sky overhead. No sound, no colors. Just driving arms, leaden legs, stinging salt, a thin patch of asphalt dead ahead. And two shadows. I gave a final big heave.

It didn't work. I hit the top of Heartbreak, and my tormentor was still there. I almost stopped on the spot. What was the point? I felt my body sag, deflated and depressed. I stumbled briefly, but caught myself and staggered on. We were heading downhill now, beyond the Boston College spires and toward Evergreen Cemetery on our right. I knew it was only a matter of time before Clark stormed past.

And then the shadow was gone. I blinked a couple of times and rubbed my eyes. This made no sense. I was a lousy downhill runner, Clark a fast finisher. Where was he? In 1968, I didn't know this stretch of the course was named "Cemetery Mile" because it had buried the hopes of many Boston runners. Here the stiff downhill slope forces the quadriceps muscles to contract eccentrically, opposite to the concentric work demanded by Heartbreak Hill. The abrupt change often induces muscle cramping, and that's exactly what happened to Clark. His spirit, heart, and lungs were willing — perhaps more willing than mine — but his legs were not.

Suddenly the press bus zoomed past with Jock Semple hanging from the front door. "Give it hell on the downhills, Ammmby," he bellowed at me. "Give it hell on the downhills." In the big rear window, I saw "Old John" Kelley brandishing his fists for me. Kelley had recently had hernia surgery; this was one of the few Bostons he didn't run, among his fifty-eight finishes.

I would have loved to seize the moment and press my advantage, but I had nothing. I had completely spent myself on the hills. Even as my small lead grew inch by inch, I knew my pace was slowing. The race had become a survival of the least defeated. Crossing the trolley tracks at the bottom of Cleveland Circle near twenty-three miles, where the course joins Beacon Street, I felt a stabbing pain in my left side.

Ahead, a throng of spectators gathered in the street, literally filling it. The downtown crowds were immense and police control almost nonexistent on this warm Friday afternoon in April. As I approached, the spectators would move aside at the last moment and then close behind me. Yes, I felt a little like Moses parting the Red Sea. But I was also filled with torturous doubts about the army of marathoners behind me. What if Clark regained his rhythm? What if someone had paced the race better than I had and was now gaining fast? I was fading, no doubt about it.

When you're alone at the front of the Boston Marathon, surrounded by thunderous crowds, a burning sun overhead, your body's sugar-supply depleted . . . this is not a good time for an aptitude test. I grew faint and confused. Where was I on Beacon Street? I couldn't tell; all the blocks looked the same. Why wasn't I making any progress toward the damn Fenway Park light towers? Time nearly stopped. I was going nowhere, running with an awkward tilt — bent over, trying to knead out that side stitch — at what seemed like a ten-minute pace. I had never been so parched in my life. Two hours earlier, David Costill, a PhD studying sports drinks, had weighed me in the gym at Hopkinton: 138 pounds. At the finish, I would barely top 128.

I must have looked back a hundred times in the last several miles. The first time he saw this, Clark thought, *Aha, I've got him now!* I couldn't imagine anything worse than losing the Boston Marathon at this late stage, and yet it seemed certain to happen. How could I win Boston when I was falling apart like this?

I reached Fenway and lurched into Kenmore Square, twice as crowded, twice as tumultuous as anything before. I felt so small, so vulnerable. A half-mile later, turning onto Hereford Street and seeing no one on my heels, I finally started to believe. One hundred and seventy miles to the north, my brother Gary sat on Mayflower Hill, high above Colby College in Maine, a small transistor radio jammed against his ear. "One of the runners has broken away," he heard. "It's Burfoot." He jumped to his feet and danced a little jig. At a track meet in Storrs, Connecticut, the news spread quickly, reaching Bill Rodgers. "It was hard to comprehend," he says today. "To me then, a marathon was like a race from another planet." Jeff Galloway, on a Navy ship off the coast of Vietnam, heard nothing for two weeks. But after he reached the Philippines and caught up on the news, he wrote me a letter. It said: "After I heard about your 8:45 two-mile, I knew you were going to have a great year."

I've seen video of my last hundred yards in front of the Prudential Center, where we finished in 1968. I don't look at all like a marathon champ. I look more like the tottering Scarecrow in *The Wizard of Oz* after he's lost all his stuffing. When I hit the finish line in 2:22:17, just thirty-two seconds in front of Clark, I collapsed into Jock Semple's arms. I vividly recall how weak I felt, how utterly wasted. And how warm he was, how strong and solid.

But even more I remember Jock's words. And his tone. As he held up my full body weight (what was left of it), Jock spoke with a soft lilt I had never heard from him before, not once. He wasn't roaring now. He was purring, and his mouth formed the sweetest words I have ever heard. "You did it, Ammmby," he said. "You won the Boston Marathon."

Amby Burfoot is a rarity, a world-class athlete who becomes a fine writer. Forty years after his win in the Boston Marathon (and not long after his stint as editor of Runner's World*), he can describe the race in a way nobody else can. A fascinating look into the head of a champion at work.*

THOMAS LAKE

2 on 5

FROM SPORTS ILLUSTRATED

IF YOU COULD unbreak the bones and erase the scars, recall the bullets and sever the chains, recap the bottles and catch all the smoke, if you could swim sixteen years up the river of time and find a town called Stevenson, you just might see something glorious.

Stevenson lies between two ridges in north Alabama, by the Tennessee River, a dark blue vein on the earth. There, on Valentine's Day 1992, the North Jackson Chiefs hosted the Fort Payne Wildcats in high school basketball. It was not a playoff game, not even a conference game, and neither team was especially good. But in the 117-year history of organized basketball, it was one of the few times a team with only two remaining players beat a team that still had five.

If this were a movie, the story would end at the final buzzer. The winners would always be winners, fists in the air and black jerseys glistening, and the losers would always hang their heads. This is not a movie. Morning came and they all woke up.

These officials can be blamed for this. They let this thing get out of hand completely.

That's the voice of George Guess, apothecary and Chiefs radio announcer, with 2:53 left in the fourth quarter. He's perched on a stage at the end of the court, next to a colossal painting of an American Indian with a headdress of blood-red feathers.

Until a few days before the game, North Jackson had ten players. Then the leading scorer quit because the coach wouldn't let him play every minute. Now, as the game winds down, the Chiefs' best all-around player, point guard Chris Stewart, has fouled out. Eight Chiefs standing. Already the referees have called about seventy fouls.

The Chiefs lead 58–55. Their best remaining player has the ball, facing the basket.

Robert Collier pulls up from fifteeeeen —

Robert is the largest Chief, six-foot-one, 245 pounds, the only true post player on a roster full of guards. He has been playing with four fouls since the first half. He lives in the projects. He can't afford a varsity jacket or a class ring. He owns one pair of pants, which his mother washes every night and dries on the heater because she has no clothes dryer. On warm days he wears his mother's shorts to school and hopes no one can tell.

Tonight Robert's mother is in the bleachers, as always, and his father is on Death Row.

— no good. Murphy Thompson with the rebound. We've got a whistle and a foul . . . Did they call it on Murphy Thompson? If so, he's gone.

Seven Chiefs standing. Their school is on the north side of Stevenson, a rusty old town of two thousand where goats graze in meadows above the vacant red-brick buildings of Main Street and a farmer hands out free yellow squash from the bed of his pickup truck.

Fort Payne is about six times larger than Stevenson and forty miles to the south. It has mansions on the eastern ridge and enough cotton mills to justify the self-proclaimed title Official Sock Capital of the World.

Fort Payne scores, cutting North Jackson's lead to one. Both teams turn the ball over. The Chiefs get it back on the baseline with about two minutes left.

Collier will trigger the ball inside.

His father has been on Death Row since 1978. They used to be Big Robert and Little Robert, and they rode in Big Robert's Chevy Chevelle convertible to go fishing and to football games. Then Big Robert lost his job and the money dwindled, and he was too proud to ask for help. He drove the Chevelle to Georgia and put his .32 revolver in a grocery bag and walked into a flower shop and pulled the gun and got the cash and sped off. Two deputy sheriffs caught up to him and pulled him over, but he wrestled a gun away from one of them and shot both men. One died. Big Robert drove home and gave his wife $70 from the flower shop. The police caught him the next day. Little Robert was two months from his fifth birthday.

We've got a turnover against North Jackson. Collier moved along the baseline. And you can't do that [after] a turnover, which is what it was. You can do it after a score.

Little Robert became the man of the house. When his mother got tired on the 205-mile drive to the prison in Georgia, he dropped chips of ice down her back to keep her awake. By thirteen or fourteen he was taking turns behind the wheel. He always said he would grow up and get rich so he could bust his daddy out of jail.

The Wildcats turn the ball over with about ninety seconds left. Chiefs by one. Now *they* turn it over.

So here comes Fort Payne with an opportunity to take their first lead of the game. And they do!

Fort Payne leads 59–58 with about 1:15 to go. Another whistle, like fingernails on a blackboard.

And we've got a foul called. They're gonna call it on Chad Cobb.

Somehow this is Chad's first foul. He is Robert Collier's distant cousin, a grinning coil of muscle and fist, the quickest Chief and probably the shortest. He is only five-foot-eight, but his vertical leap is so good that the coach sometimes puts him at center court for the opening tip.

Chad rides his Yamaha along the ridges above town, daring the hillbillies to chase him, and he drag-races in the streets, leaving long black rubber trails. Robert sometimes rides on the back, big man on a little bike, one arm around Chad's midsection at 100 mph, popping wheelies, jumping hills, leaning together on sharp curves, running from their enemies. Chad has Robert's trust. They never crash and never get caught.

Fort Payne makes both free throws to lead by three. After a

Chiefs turnover a Wildcat is fouled but misses the front end of a one-and-one. The Chiefs rebound with forty-five seconds left.

Still got a chance. Sixty-one to fifty-eight . . . Out to Chad Cobb. Needs to crank up for three!

Chad was a small-boned kid who took his share of whippings growing up. Lately he has been doing the whipping, especially on the white boys who hurl rocks and the n-word in his general direction.

He puts it up from three —

Chad is a streetballer: fast and reckless, prone to turnovers and wild shots, feet sometimes kicking to the side on his jumper.

— it's no good.

Two years after the game, a car will run Chad's motorcycle off the road, sending him hurtling into a fence post. His right leg will bend upward till the foot is past his shoulder, leaving the kneecap hanging by the skin and blood vessels, but he will walk again nine months later and then climb back on his bike and twist the throttle and go.

Fort Payne with twenty-eight seconds. And the ball stolen away by Travis Smith! He puts it up. It's good! One-point game.

Clinging to the lead, Fort Payne milks the clock to five seconds. Another foul, another Chief gone. Six left now. Fort Payne makes the first free throw, increasing the lead to two.

They've pretty well sealed the fate of the North Jackson Chiefs.

Fate goes by many names. Sixteen years later, on August 24, 2008, Little Robert Collier will tell a stranger that God still has a plan for him. But he won't blame God, or anyone else, for the way his life has turned out.

"We make our own choices," he'll say.

Thirty-two minutes of basketball, seventy-four fouls. That's over two fouls per minute of playing time. I think you'd have to check a long way to find very many games that would even come close to such.

George Guess is right, although a seventy-fifth foul is called as time expires. That's one foul every 25.6 seconds. The NBA record for total fouls in regulation since the twenty-four-second clock was installed, eighty-four, was set by the Indiana Pacers and the Kansas City Kings in 1977. That game lasted forty-eight minutes: one foul every 34.3 seconds.

Fort Payne is on the foul line, up by two with five seconds left. The team has made only ten of its thirty free throws. A man yells from the bleachers, long and low, to distract the shooter.

I don't know whether there's anybody made a film of this game or not, but this will certainly be one for study by the officials' association.

A film of this game. Near the end of the following decade, the people of Stevenson will still be searching. At dusk one summer day Chad's father will sit at home, thinking about it. "I'd give anything to get that tape," he'll say. "If I had the money, I'd put out a reward."

Frank Cobb lugs his camcorder to most of his son's games. But tonight, late in a mediocre season, he decides the Chiefs are a waste of tape. Later he will look back on the mistakes in his life and conclude this was the biggest.

Nevertheless, Frank and others will swear they saw camcorders in the bleachers that night, at least one and as many as three, over on the Fort Payne side. They'll conclude that whoever made those tapes must have set them on fire.

The shot is missed. Chiefs with the rebound.

Five seconds. Four. Three. Chiefs still down by two.

Travis Smith down, he pulls it up —

Travis will think back on this game sixteen years later, and it will give him chills. He grew up with Robert and Chad in Stevenson, playing backyard ball on the iron-rich clay. One day in agricultural-science class when the teacher wasn't looking, he and Chad conspired to climb through the suspended ceiling and liberate Little Debbies from the snack room.

— we've got a whistle . . . Wai-ait a minute. It's not over yet . . . No time shows on the clock . . . Travis Smith goes to the line . . . And he will get three because he was shooting from three-point range when he was fouled.

Travis bounces the Wilson Jet-Pro on the hardwood. Every day at the end of practice he shoots free throws and doesn't stop until he's made ten in a row.

He hits the first. It's a one-point game.
Travis wants to play for the Detroit Pistons, like Isiah Thomas and Joe Dumars.

Next one is up. It's good!
Instead he will pour concrete and drive a truck. He will have six children by three women.

Travis Smith. All the pressure on his shoulders. Does he make it? No. We've got overtime.
Travis fouls out fifty-nine seconds into overtime. Five Chiefs standing.
One night five years later, on January 26, 1997, he will quarrel with one of his former teammates. Travis will borrow a pistol and find the man in a drugstore parking lot and raise the gun and pull the trigger.

Robert Collier gets the ball. Robert may have to be the guard. He takes it down the floor.
Sixteen years later Robert's name will still come up in conversation at Friday's, a restaurant in Stevenson, especially at the table known as the Liars' Table, where retired men gather to tell tall tales over biscuits and gravy. The memory of this game will be one of the few things that can stop them from talking football. David Smith, the boys' old ag-science teacher, will stop by occasionally.
"You hope," Smith will say, referring to Robert and the magical game, "that will be a turning point in his life. You hope and pray." He'll think about Robert for a moment. "I don't know where Robert's at right now," he'll say.

It's a two-point game in favor of Fort Payne, 64–62. Comes in to Stafford Henry, off to Chad Cobb.
After high school Chad will attend motorcycle mechanics' school in Florida, working part-time to pay his way, just scraping by.

One night he will go to the gas station to put a gallon in the tank. The price will be ninety-two cents, and he'll scrounge up exactly ninety-two cents. He'll go inside and try to pay and the clerk will tell him he can't pay with that much small change, and Chad will see other customers staring. Finally he'll slap the pennies on the counter.

"Here it is," he'll say. "I paid for it. I'm leaving." He will drive away with tears in his eyes.

A moment later he'll stop for a homeless man with no legs. He'll let the man cross the road, wheeling his wheelchair with one hand, pulling a cart with the other. The man will look Chad in the eye and smile.

From then on, whenever he feels a twinge of self-pity, Chad will remember that smile.

We've got a whistle and a foul.

Stafford is gone with 1:41 left. Four Chiefs standing.

Two seconds later, another whistle.

And Thomas Hutchins is gone now. Hutchins is out of the game with 1:39 to go.

Thomas is best friends with Travis and Chad. They play secret games of Rook in the back of Mr. Smith's ag-science class. One day nine years later, on February 26, 2001, Thomas will drive through a stop sign and hit a man playing basketball in the street. The man will fly toward the power lines and land in a field, cracking his vertebrae and puncturing a lung.

Three Chiefs standing: Robert, Chad, and Chris Shelby, who comes from deep on the bench and fouls very hard.

And coach Jay Sanders has elected to use his only remaining timeout.

Sanders knows what it's like to be poor. His first bed was a dresser drawer, and he played in the snow wearing socks wrapped in bread bags. He lent Robert a tie to wear on game days and never asked him to give it back. He spent all season trying to persuade Robert to use the pump fake. "The kids'll go flying," he told Robert, "and you're wide open."

No one could remember Robert using it in a game.

*

This is an ugly thing, folks, for a high school basketball game, and it's all a result, in my opinion, of the officiating. . . I don't know the names of any official that's working this game and don't really care to know. But I certainly think that games of this nature should certainly be evaluated by whoever is in charge of the officials' association.

The referees' names will be forgotten. One will be rumored to live down the road in the town of Hollywood, but when reached by telephone he will swear he was not in Stevenson that night.

Both teams are given to slap-happy defense, and the storm of whistles may simply be the refs' best attempt to stop the boys from knocking each other around. They will ultimately call eighty-four personal fouls; Guess counts forty on North Jackson, forty-four on Fort Payne. The Wildcats had more players to begin with and so will have more at the end.

And we've got a foul called now on Fort Payne . . . Chad Cobb goes to the line.

The game will end and the years will pass and sometimes Chad will still hear this crowd roaring.

Chad Cobb misses the free throw, and Fort Payne claims the rebound. They're playing five against three. They'll just back it out and wind [down] the clock . . . Sixty-seven to sixty-two. All over but the crying.

Nothing in the manual could prepare a coach for this. In retrospect it will be easy to say what Fort Payne coach Phillip Collie should have done with 1:38 to play. Poured it on. Pressed his two-man advantage. Widened the lead until it was insurmountable. But Collie does what seems to make sense at the time. He bleeds the clock. Sixteen years later, in an e-mail to a reporter, he will write, "I want to ask that if in your story there is blame concerning the North Jackson game, that you put it all on me." Fine. But he is a better coach than his players think. He came to Fort Payne to be near his only relatives and his in-laws after his wife, Dixie, died in childbirth, leaving him with a newborn and a toddler to raise alone. The North Jackson game will drive him to work even harder. After the next season he will leave Fort Payne for Buckhorn High in New Market, Alabama, and two years later he will win a Class 5A state title.

Another whistle, another foul on Chris Shelby (his fourth), another missed free throw by Fort Payne.

Chiefs get the rebound. Chad Cobb, just take it on in. Pull up from three, he is fouled and will go to the line with fifty-four seconds to go. So now Chad Cobb will have the pressure on his back. And Chad Cobb drops it in.

Chad will finish mechanics' school and become service manager at a motorcycle and ATV shop across the Tennessee line. His marriage will fall apart and his wife will leave for Texas, but he'll go to court and win primary custody of his daughter, Shanele, and his son, Chad Jr. He'll coach Chad Jr. in football and teach him to fix motorcycles and tell him he can be anything he wants, even a doctor.

Chad hits. So it's sixty-seven to sixty-four.

Chad will decide he should be in the *Guinness Book of World Records* for this game. He'll want to make a movie about it. He'll say it's something not even Michael Jordan ever did. He'll remind his children about it, especially at their sporting events when he thinks they might give up. He will put them in a room with the audio recording of this game and close the door so they can't walk out.

"Oh, Daddy," they'll say. "Again?"

Chad's third free throw is no good. Rebound, Fort Payne . . . thirty-nine seconds to go. Somebody's gotta foul . . . HE WALKED WITH THE BALL! And the Chiefs get it.

A month or two after the game Guess will hand Sanders a cassette tape of his broadcast. Fourteen years later, when he is sixty-six, George Foster Guess Jr. will die of a heart attack. They will lay his bones in the clay on the side of a hill, next to his ancestors, between the river and Russell Cave. On his headstone they'll carve a five-word epitaph: THE VOICE OF THE CHIEFS.

Two years after that Sanders will have the tape transferred to compact disc. He will gather the old Chiefs at Western Sizzlin' and give them copies. Robert will not be there.

Thirty-two seconds left. Still got a chance. Three against five . . . Robert Collier in to Chad Cobb, gotta take it down the floor. Chad's gotta do his stuff tonight. Pulls up for three —

After high school Chad and Travis will run together, ride together, raise hell together. They will always be linked by this game. Travis's steal, basket, and two free throws sent the game into overtime and set the stage for Chad's singular achievement. They will vow to protect each other.

— *AND HE HITS IT AND WE'RE TIED AT SIXTY-SEVEN!*

One night five years later, on January 26, 1997, they will quarrel about whether or not Travis has been two-timing Chad's female cousin and whether or not Chad told on him. Chad will still be on crutches from the motorcycle crash. "Chad, you can't fight me," Travis will say.

"I've got other ways of handling you," Chad will say.

Travis will borrow a pistol and find Chad in the drugstore parking lot. He'll raise the gun and pull the trigger.

We've got a foul called on Chris Shelby . . . Shelby's out of the game.

Two Chiefs standing.

He's gotta miss this. The Chiefs need the rebound.

Travis will say he was only shooting at the ground. He'll swear the bullets bounced.

We don't have any time-outs. It's Robert Collier and Chad Cobb against five.

One bullet will pierce Chad's left thigh and another will smash his fibula. He'll look up and see Travis aiming the gun with his eyes closed.

He missed the free throw and —

With seventeen seconds left Fort Payne gets the rebound and scores. Another whistle.

— *there's a charging foul called against Fort Payne! No goal. And it'll be Chief basketball!*

After the gunfire Chad will drive himself to the hospital, thinking hard about permanent vengeance. From time to time after that he will drive around with his black Tec-9 semiautomatic and he will look at Travis from a distance and wonder if he can line up a shot.

Travis will plead guilty to second-degree assault and serve five months in prison. On February 26, 2001, as he plays basketball in the street, he will see a man barreling toward him on a motorcycle. It won't be Chad. It will be their former teammate Thomas Hutchins, one of Travis's best friends. Thomas will be showing off for a girl and coming too fast to stop. He'll plow into Travis, knocking him out of his shoes, cracking two vertebrae and puncturing a lung.

Seventeen seconds to go. They're gonna surround Cobb. And Chad's gotta break free.

As Fort Payne makes a substitution, Sanders calls Robert and Chad to the sideline. He tries to sound very calm. He tells Robert to throw the ball in. He tells Chad to walk along the baseline toward Robert, lulling the defenders, then do a jab step and run back toward the corner and catch Robert's bounce pass and go.

Sanders figures Cobb will run so fast that he'll overshoot the basket. He tells Robert to run hard for the left block.

So we've got three or four people around Chad Cobb. So the ball comes in to Cobb. He runs it down the right sideline. He may take it all the way in. He will. He'll put it up —

Robert is fast for a big man. He reaches the left block. Five on two, and nobody boxes him out.

— No good. Robert Collier on the follow —

Robert grabs the rebound and at last he pump-fakes. The kids go flying, and he is wide open.

After high school, Robert will bounce from one coast to the other, doing demolition work here, pouring iron there. He will come home, get married, and coach his stepson in football. His wife will die in 2007 from complications of diabetes and hypertension. Robert will be in rehab at the time, for his addiction to alcohol and cocaine.

— IT'S GOOD! ROBERT COLLIER MADE THE SHOT!

Years will go by and Robert will think of this game only when someone else brings it up. Even then it will feel hazy, dreamlike, as if maybe it never happened.

Robert won't set his father free from prison. He will follow him in. In 2005 police will say Robert stole a man's wallet and inhaler and beat him. He will plead guilty to second-degree robbery and be put on probation. In June 2008 he will break a man's jaw and steal his cell phone and cigarettes. He will be charged with third-degree assault and third-degree theft, and his probation will be revoked. Big Robert Collier will win an appeal to change his death sentence to life without parole. Little Robert will be scheduled for release in 2023.

Five seconds. [Fort Payne's] Mosteller down. He missed!
Two old hoops will hang above the jail yard, but basketballs will be scarce. Robert will fashion one from white socks and string.

The Chiefs get the ball and —
Chad will have his chance to join Robert in prison. He will not take it. He will look at the smashing of Travis by their old friend's motorcycle and see a certain cosmic symmetry. He will consider his children and his personal myth, forged in this three-minute over-time, and he will put down his gun.
On July 13, 2008, he will see Travis in the street. He'll pull over and get out and walk toward him and they will both smile and throw their arms around each other.

— the Chiefs are gonna WIIIIINNN! AND THE CHIEFS HAVE WON, SIXTY-NINE TO SIXTY-SEVEN!
At the sound of the buzzer the fans engulf Robert and Chad at midcourt, nearly suffocating them, until they hear Chad screaming from the bottom of the pile, "I can't breathe!" In the visiting locker room a few boys weep, and Coach Collie says he wishes they could all float away in a submarine.

And Chad Cobb and Robert Collier are the heroes of the night, in a historical game.
After the game, Robert thinks he and Chad will go on TV, talk on talk shows, sign autographs. He will sign one, for a woman in a doctor's office in Birmingham. That will be all.
A few years later Sanders will mail Robert's and Chad's black polyester jerseys to the Basketball Hall of Fame in Springfield, Mas-

sachusetts. They will not be displayed. In the summer of 2008 someone from the Hall will mail them back.

That same summer, on the same wooden floor at North Jackson, the latest crop of Chiefs will come in for a practice. Someone will ask them about the two-on-five game. They will say they have never heard of it.

What a game, and what a night it was —
Time is a dark blue river, and it rolls one way. Outside in the cold it rolls on.

I read this story when it appeared in the magazine. Loved it. Loved the history, the twists and the turns. This was the first story I read and said, "This is a definite choice for the book." Nothing changed my mind.

DAVID FLEMING

The Ball That Just Won't Die

FROM ESPN: THE MAGAZINE

JUST DOWN THE MOUNTAINSIDE from the ancient Sicilian town of Piazza Armerina sit the massive ruins of La Villa Romana del Casale. The crumbling walls of this 1,600-year-old estate contain the world's richest collection of Roman mosaics, including the slightly scandalous "girls in bikinis" mosaic. The famous work, which spreads across the floor, depicts ten golden-haired women in various stages of athletic competition. On its upper level, a pair of women in burgundy two-pieces works out; one hoists dumbbells, the other lifts a weighted, oblong orb. The Romans called it a *paganica*. We call it a medicine ball.

Similar references to this early piece of fitness equipment dot the ancient world. Medicine balls appear in the texts of Greek physicians and in drawings of Persian wrestlers from 1000 BC. "Someday we will discover drawings of two cavemen throwing a round rock back and forth," says Istvan Javorek, a former Romanian Olympic weightlifting coach and a member of the USA Strength and Conditioning Coaches Hall of Fame. "As long as there have been athletes, there have been medicine balls."

From the dawn of athletics to the first round of this month's NFL draft, the medicine ball has rolled through the centuries, its elemental formula unchanged and unsurpassed: sphere + gravity = fitness. The medicine ball has toned presidents, altered Olympics, and sculpted empires. It has survived wars and plagues. Thanks to a recent resurgence, it just might outlast performance-enhancing drugs *and* Jack LaLanne. And though most people, when they think of the medicine ball at all, think of it as a smelly, brown-leather boulder abandoned in a dark corner of a middle school gym — or as the thing Rocky used after beer-bonging his eggs each morning — nothing less than the course of humankind's athletic evolution can be traced by its epic, transcultural path.

Gladiators in Alexandria, Egypt, trained with medicine balls. Renaissance physician Hieronymus Mercurialis recommended them as a principal component of "medicinal gymnastics" in *De Arte Gymnastica,* a seminal work on fitness published in 1569. The U.S. Military Academy has trained soldiers for every battle since its inception with the medicine ball, and Herbert Hoover stayed in shape by tossing one around the South Lawn. Now, after a lull brought on by the clean-machine era (Universal, Nautilus), you'd be hard-pressed to find an elite athlete who hasn't gone old-school in search of more explosive muscle strength.

To help them burst off the line, Cowboys blockers regularly run through a series of overhead med-ball slams inside the racquetball courts at their training facility in Valley Ranch. Strength-and-conditioning coach Joe Juraszek knows the drill is going well, he says, when "the entire facility shakes and people in the building think the walls are about to fall down." To build hip strength, Red Sox catcher Jason Varitek has destroyed several med balls by whipping them against a cinder-block wall. Michael Jordan's dynasty in Chicago was fine-tuned by trainer and med-ball enthusiast Al Vermeil. Helio Castroneves swings an eight-pound ball in a core-strengthening drill he calls the Tornado. Lorena Ochoa recently tweaked the top of her swing using only a weighted sphere. And everywhere the German national soccer team travels, it is followed by a snaking trail of rolling luggage. Guess what's inside. "In three thousand years of athletic training, only two things haven't changed: man and the medicine ball," says Mark Verstegen, a trainer, author, and founder of Athletes' Performance (AP) Institute, a multisport training facility in Tempe, Arizona. "When you're talking about optimizing performance, from gladiators to the French Open, this simple ball might have more power to unlock an athlete's potential than any other tool ever invented."

Matt Ryan grits his teeth and stares up at a chilly, cobalt Arizona sky. As the potential number-one pick in the 2008 NFL draft, the quarterback from Boston College is about to become a household name (not to mention $30 million richer). On this particular March morning, he's at Athletes' Performance preparing for his bright future with nothing more than the scuffed six-pound orange ball he cradles in his arms. Like most elite athletes, Ryan's large-muscle groups and cardiovascular system are in top form. But with critical workouts with the Dolphins and Falcons on his schedule, he has turned to the med ball for some fine-tuning. Already this morning, Ryan, all perfect form and posture, has run through one hundred med-ball reps aimed at QB-specific strength. He's tossed the ball at a cinder-block wall from a deep-lunge position (working his back, hamstrings, and triceps); he's twisted with it held at his waist (hips and glutes); he's slammed it to the ground from overhead (calves, quads, stomach, and shoulders) and heaved it thirty feet backward over an eleven-foot wall (working nearly every muscle group).

Med balls used to come in only one style: large and leather. Now, as proof of their reborn popularity, they can be found in every imaginable size, shape, style, and color. Even Nike makes one. Old-school balls are still made with hand-stitched leather, but most now feature hard, grippable polyurethane covers. Some bounce. Paper-fiber fillings have been upgraded to silicone, rubber chips, and sand. They come in sport-specific shapes, like baseballs and footballs, with weights ranging from two pounds to two hundred. The typical ball, like the one Ryan uses, is the size of a basketball and weighs between eight and twenty pounds. It's essentially the same piece of equipment heavyweight champ Jack Johnson trained with in 1910, just a whole lot prettier.

Prompted by his trainer, Ryan squares his feet and lowers his center of gravity. He moves his hands under the ball, then uncoils his body upward. This is no traditional resistance training, which isolates small areas of the body. All the muscle fibers in Ryan's frame, from toes to fingertips, fire in rapid succession as he first balances, then propels the ball into the air. It shoots thirty-five feet skyward with the force of a small geyser, crashing into the metal roof and just missing the sprinkler pipes before landing at Ryan's feet with a thud.

Shooting baskets nearby, Jake Long, a former Michigan lineman and soon-to-be fellow first-rounder, jumps back, startled by the display of power. As he bends over, limp with exhaustion, Ryan is told that Spartan soldiers used med balls to keep in battle shape. "I always felt a little like a Spartan," he says with a wry, satisfied smile.

As Ryan finishes his workout, a TV plays highlights from the teary-eyed press conference of the retiring Brett Favre. In each of the previous three off-seasons, the Packers quarterback trained with a med ball for eight weeks at his Mississippi home under the guidance of Ken Croner, director of NFL training at Athletes' Performance. Hooked to resistance cords, Favre would simulate a seven-step drop, at the end of which he'd pick a med ball off the ground, then chest-pass it as far as he could. During these drills Favre's heart rate jumped so quickly that Croner made him wear a pulse monitor. Each morning, a hopeful Favre asked Croner what was in store. When the answer came back, "All med ball," Favre glared back as if Croner were a rookie who'd just dropped a touchdown pass. "I'd ask, 'You like the med ball, right?'" says Croner. "And he'd just give me that Favre look. He'd shake his head and stare at me in silence, like he loved it and hated it at the same time."

There is speculation inside the gym on this day that pondering another summer of that torture hastened Favre's decision to hang 'em up.

"Most pro athletes are obsessed with training and always looking for the next thing," says Saints fullback Mike Karney. "The med ball is so simple it makes people skeptical. You see commercials for all this complicated, expensive stuff, and you think, *You want me to train with a ball that's how old?*"

A staple of national fitness programs in Germany and Sweden for hundreds of years, the medicine ball's first recorded appearance stateside was in a photo of Aaron Molyneaux Hewlett, curator of the Harvard College Gymnasium from 1859 to 1871. Hewlett sits at his desk, one foot propped on a med ball. Not long after, in 1895, the term *medicine ball* appeared in an English-language dictionary. Proclaimed by fitness historians as one of the Four Horsemen of Fitness (along with dumbbells, weighted wands, and Indian clubs), the med ball's ThighMaster moment occurred in 1931, after a *New York Times Magazine* piece headlined "At the White House at 7 A.M." explored President Hoover's unique training regime.

Traveling back from South America on the battleship *Utah*, Hoover had joined soldiers on deck who were playing the keep-away game "Bull in the Ring" with a medicine ball. At fifty-three, his weight above 210 pounds, the president reported rediscovering muscles he'd long since forgotten. When the White House physician suggested regular exercise, Hooverball was invented. A version of volleyball, with three to a side and a six-pound ball between them, the game was contested every morning at seven by the "Medicine Ball Cabinet," a group that included former Amherst football star and Supreme Court justice Harlan Stone ("When he hurls them, they stay hurled," said one witness) as well as First Lady Lou Henry Hoover and her secretary, Ruth Fessler.

"There is no rank or distinction while the leather sphere is in the air," reported the *Times Magazine*. "The deportment of the contestants was not unlike that at a town-lot ball game. Players were often subjected to a treatment technically known as 'the raspberry.' All of which confirms the not so well understood fact that male members of genus *Homo* never grow up."

Hoover never managed to get the country into any kind of shape, of course, and he was voted out of office in 1932. After that, the ball slowly faded from its popular peak back into army barracks and boxing gyms. It fell further into obscurity in 1957, the year the Universal weight machine was introduced, and further still when the Nautilus system became the rage.

While hoisting weights on a bar controlled by a machine is a user-friendly and efficient way to build muscle mass and fundamental strength, it also reduces the dynamic elements of balance, explosion, and sport-specific movement that are gained from resistance training. In fact, the very idea of functional training got lost during the machine craze as performance took a back seat to looking good. With static, mass building training ascendant in the States, the Soviet Union and East Germany began to dominate Olympic-medal counts in the 1960s and 1970s. Heavy doses of illegal drugs aside, athletes in Eastern-bloc countries had developed faster contractions from dynamic methods kinesiologists call jump training or plyometrics — lighter weights and faster reps that produce more elastic, efficient, and explosive muscle contractions. Soon, as the Cold War fizzled and Eastern European athletes, coaches, and their training manuals made their way to the United States, the same phrase kept appearing: медицинский мяч, Russian for *medicine ball*.

The ease and effectiveness of the med ball give it something of a

Forrest Gump quality, allowing it to jump among centuries, continents, and ideologies, all the way from pharaohs to Favre. Three
thousand years after it was invented, the medicine ball is back.

While the ball itself is simple, the kinetic science behind it is anything but. The unpredictable path of a med ball as it flies through
the air forces the exerciser to use entire muscle groups instead of,
say, just the biceps or deltoids. After eons of evolved movement, the
body can still grow more kinetically efficient as it links dozens of its
smaller muscles to adjust to the ball's flight. Adaptation is the key
to athletic development, and no two med-ball reps are the same. "If
the game you play is chaotic, you have to train chaotic," says Titans
tight end Alge Crumpler. "How are you going to do that with a machine?"

Human power is determined by the level of contraction in the
muscles. By lengthening the muscle just before contraction (more
so than in static weightlifting), the med ball creates stored elastic
energy that dramatically increases the speed and strength of the
contraction. (The farther you stretch a rubber band, the more it
stings your little brother when it snaps back.) It's the difference between standing flat-footed as you take an arms-only chop at a golf
ball (static) and the violent entire uncoiling Tiger uses to explode
off the tee (dynamic). "That's the foundation, the operating system
that has developed all human movement," says Verstegen. "The
med ball has always been smart. It just had to wait three thousand
years for athletes to catch up."

And these days, it seems like everyone has gone ancient-school:
from synchronized swimmers to power lifters, from Mia Hamm to
Adrian Peterson, from New Zealand rugby stud Jonah Lomu to
fitness historian Dr. Ed Thomas, who's pioneered a medicine ball
exercise program for middle school kids in Iowa.

In 2006, after dedicating twelve years to free-weight training, Karney, the Saints' five-foot-eleven, 258-pound fullback, hit a
strength ceiling just as he entered the make-or-break point of his
career. A fifth-round pick in 2004 out of Arizona State, Karney had
amassed impressive "barbell" strength. But that skill was isolated
and linear, one-dimensional, while Karney's job required him to
jump sideways to chip a blitzing linebacker and twist around to
catch a flair on his downfield hip while sprinting full speed toward
the sideline in the other direction. "I wish the game was square,

slow, and straight," says Crumpler, imitating Frankenstein's walk. "I could block guys and catch passes all day. But you got all these crazy defenses and guys like Dwight Freeney twisting, jumping, bending, turning all over the place. I know a lot of very strong guys who aren't very good players, because they can't apply what they have to the football field."

That used to be Karney. But in the summer of 2006, trainers persuaded him to switch over to the med ball. At AP there is a grueling two-hundred-rep routine Crumpler nicknamed the Beast. A month into his new regime, a gung-ho Karney was using the Beast as a warm-up. Positioned in his exact blocking stance, he rapid-fired a med ball against the wall, making mirrors on the other side of the gym wobble.

At his best, Karney could bench-press two hundred-pound dumbbells twelve times. No matter how hard or how often he lifted, he couldn't improve on that. Hitting this kind of wall is often what leads athletes to think about steroids. But after a summer of med-ball training, Karney arrived at the Saints' facility feeling "freakishly strong." After the team's first training-camp practice, he walked into the weight room and grabbed a pair of 135-pound dumbbells off the rack. Teammates, still exhausted from the 105-degree heat, watched in silence as he pushed out thirty reps with ease. "What the hell did you do?" came the whispers.

Med ball, Karney told them, just med ball. (Says Javorek: "Medicine balls can develop better and more explosive muscles than drug enhancement.")

That season the Saints made it all the way to the NFC championship game, and Karney earned second-team All-Pro honors. In Tempe, they began to refer to him as Captain Med Ball. These days, whenever he speaks to high school players or youth coaches, Karney preaches the benefits of the simple sphere.

Even now, as he holds one up, Karney stares at it keenly, as if the weighty orb had mystical powers. "What can I say — I'm a true believer," he says, with a laugh. "This ball flipped my world."

No, I don't want to read a story about the medicine ball. Okay, maybe just the first paragraph. Okay, maybe the second and the third and . . . wow, that was a great story about the medicine ball. Education always should arrive so easily.

MICHAEL LEWIS

Commie Ball

FROM VANITY FAIR

BEFORE HE BECAME a casualty in the immigration wars, Gus
Dominguez was just another agent in Los Angeles. Then, on October 20, 2006, the United States government issued its first-ever in-
dictment for smuggling athletes into the country, with Dominguez
cast as the mastermind. The alleged contraband: five Cuban baseball players. Specifically, the U.S. attorney for the Southern District
of Florida claimed that Dominguez had identified four pitchers
and a shortstop in Havana and then paid $225,000 to smugglers to
sneak them by boat to Florida and drive them to California, where
he auctioned them off to Major League Baseball teams.

Intriguing as it sounded, the case didn't receive much attention,
at least not at first. Outside of professional baseball circles no one
had heard of Gus Dominguez. But inside baseball Dominguez had
made his mark as the agent who, back in the early 1990s, invented
the market for Cuban baseball players, and still sat somewhere near
the middle of it. When the sports media finally picked up on the in-
dictment, the Bush-appointed assistant secretary of homeland security for U.S. Immigration and Customs Enforcement (ICE), Julie
Myers, issued this statement: "Though this case involves a Beverly
Hills sports agent and talented baseball players, it is remarkably
similar to the human smuggling operations that ICE encounters
every day. The ringleaders put the lives of illegal immigrants at risk
and sought to profit from their labor."

But there were several aspects of the case remarkably dissimilar
to anything that had ever happened before. Up to the moment he
turned himself in to the law, Dominguez had been a model citizen.
He was forty-eight years old, with nothing worse than a parking

ticket against his name. He'd come to the United States from Cuba in 1967, at the age of eight. His parents had abandoned their property in the Cuban province of Camagüey to become janitors in Los Angeles, to give their three children a new country. The eldest, Fernando, became an editor with the *Los Angeles Times*. Gus graduated from Cal State–Northridge, married his high school sweetheart, Delia, and then opened his own graphic design firm. He'd become a sports agent practically by accident, and baseball writers who covered the Cuban beat considered him the honest end of a squirrelly trade. The players who'd hired him thought of him as a friend and family man first, a businessman second. "I signed with Gus," says Henry Blanco, the Chicago Cubs catcher, "because of what other players told me. One said, 'He might not be the best businessman, but he's the best guy. You can trust him with your money and your wife.' And you can."

Then there was the potential value of the cargo. There may be no entrapped pool of human talent left on earth with the dollar value of Cuban baseball players. "I compare Cuba to the Dominican Republic," says Phil Dale, an Australian who played in the Cincinnati Reds' organization and now scouts players in the Far East for the Atlanta Braves. "But the Cubans are better. Their island has bigger and stronger athletes." Their island also has more people — 11 million to the Dominican Republic's 9 million. There are now more than 1,700 Dominican players under contract to U.S. professional baseball teams — compared with just 40 Cubans — and close to 100 are playing in the big leagues. Back in the old days, before Cuba was closed for business, it supplied more players to the major leagues than all the other Latin American countries combined. In 1961, Cuba entered its first post-revolutionary baseball teams in international competitions and proceeded to beat the hell out of everyone, including the Dominicans. For a ten-year stretch, starting in 1987, the Cubans were 129–0 in major international competitions. "There are plenty of Cubans who are big league [caliber] players," says Chuck McMichael, who scouts the Latin professional leagues for the Atlanta Braves and helped hire Cubans to play shortstop and catcher for his team. "We just don't know who they are. But I can't recall a guy on the Cuban national team [which competes in the World Cup and the Olympics] that you wouldn't at least sign. You'd sign every guy off that team."

*

For the thirty players who traveled with the Cuban national team, quitting communism for the big leagues has been as simple as missing the bus or hopping the wall in left field. But relatively few Cuban players have left their island and almost none of the best. What has come to the United States, instead, is a rattlebag of players past their prime, players in political trouble, players injured, and players who were never very successful in Cuba. Orlando "El Duque" Hernandez escaped by boat in 1997, when he was in his early thirties, and became a star with the Yankees — but he had spent most of his prime in Cuba, and insisted that he never would have left had he not been banned from baseball by the Cuban government because his half-brother, Livan, had fled Cuba two years earlier. Gus Dominguez's former client Rey Ordoñez, who spent seven years as the starting shortstop for the New York Mets, left Cuba in 1993 only after it became clear that he was blocked by better players from starting for his Cuban team, the Havana Industriales.

The haul that landed Gus Dominguez in a U.S. federal court were cases in point. All five were in their mid- to late twenties and yet none had ever been selected for Cuba's national team. Three — Allen Guevara, Osmany Masso, and Yoankis Turino — failed to elicit even faint interest from professional scouts. The other two signed professional contracts, but in the minor leagues. Last season Osbek Castillo pitched for the Mobile Baybears, the Double A affiliate of the Arizona Diamondbacks, and Francisley Bueno for the Atlanta Braves' Double A affiliate, the Mississippi Braves. "There's at least half a billion dollars of baseball players in Cuba right now and probably a lot more," says Joe Kehoskie, an agent who has represented a number of Cuban big league players. "Of all the people to bring over, it sure as hell wouldn't have been those guys."

That was another strange aspect of the U.S. government's case: it accused Dominguez of ruthless profit seeking, but he'd lost a small fortune. It shouldn't have been that hard to make a killing in Cuban ballplayers, especially for the one man outside Cuba with perhaps the most information about them. But that just begged the question: what did Gus Dominguez think he was paying for? He admitted that he'd wired $225,000 into the account of a smuggler turned U.S. government witness named Ysbel Medina-Santos. He admitted, more damningly, that the money wasn't his: he didn't have that kind of cash. He'd borrowed it from the account of a client, Henry Blanco, the Chicago Cubs catcher. Blanco said he didn't mind. "Gus is like my brother," he told me. And in any case, Dominguez had refinanced his house and replaced the money before Blanco even knew it was gone.

But why had he done it? The more you looked at the numbers, the less sense they made. At the time, Dominguez kept no more than 5 percent of a player's signing bonus and 4 percent of his contract as long as it was above the league minimum. Simply to recoup his investment Dominguez would have needed the players to be worth something more than $5 million to big league teams. There was never much hope that these players would ever make that kind of money. The U.S. government needed the jury to believe that the American best informed about Cuban ballplayers didn't know which ones were worth stealing; that he'd refinance his house to smuggle the wrong guys; that Cuba was a mysterious black hole, about which this sort of ignorance was plausible. And it did! After listening for seven days the jury quickly reached its verdict: guilty.

Soon after he seized power, in January 1959, Fidel Castro banned professional sports from his island. The next year he tossed out the first pitch to open the Cuban amateur league and even took a few cuts with a bat. The ramrod-straight stance, plus the whiff of fourth-grade girl in the cock of his bat, should have dispelled the rumor that the Maximum Leader had once been a pro prospect, but the myth survived this brush with reality. ("Total bullshit," says Ralph Avila, who is in charge of scouting in the Dominican Republic for the Los Angeles Dodgers and played ball in Havana during what was meant to have been Fidel's prime. "Fidel never played any sport at university. He didn't have time. In Havana there was a pitcher named *Felix* Castro. Fidel used his name to say that he played baseball.")

For the next thirty years no Cuban ballplayer left. Then, on July 10, 1991, the Cuban national team, returning from a tournament, spent the night in the Miami airport hotel. A pitcher named René Arocha walked out of his room, found his way to his aunt's Miami apartment, and never returned. From that moment, until the end of the 1990s, the most common route out of Cuba for a baseball player was to make the national team and then, when the team was abroad, walk away. Sneak out of the hotel late at night and run to the nearest blood relative you had in Miami.

The funny thing was, at least in the beginning, they had no idea of their market value. René Arocha, for one, never imagined he could play in the big leagues. "I didn't leave Cuba because I wanted a baseball career," Arocha says. "I didn't think I was at the same level as the big leaguers. I thought the quality of the major leagues was light-years ahead of me." But then he got a call from a Cuban American named Gus Dominguez, who explained how thrilled he was "that someone finally told Fidel to go and shove it," and that "you are better than you know." At the time, Dominguez still worked at his graphic design firm, in Los Angeles, but happened to be in Miami on business. They arranged to meet. "If Gus hadn't called, I don't think I'd even have tried to play baseball," recalls Arocha. "He took me to a big league game. That's when it dawned on me, *Jesus, I think I can play with these guys.*"

Arocha flew with Dominguez to California, where Dominguez planned to introduce him to Jose Canseco's agent, whom Dominguez knew slightly. (Canseco, the famed Oakland Athletics slugger, came to this country from Cuba as an infant with his family.) The morning of the meeting, Canseco's agent called and canceled. Dominguez had taken the call and tried to put a happy face on things, but Arocha demanded to know exactly what this big-time American agent had said: "We have someone more important to meet with."

"Okay," Arocha recalls saying. "I'm not important to them. They're not important to me. You be my agent."

"I have no idea how to do it," said Dominguez.

"Don't worry about it," said Arocha. "We'll figure it out together. You're the only one who has helped me so far."

A year later René Arocha went 11–8 for the St. Louis Cardinals and found himself in the running for Rookie of the Year. "After a while," says Arocha, "I'd look at all the players on the field and think, *I have a friend back in Cuba who is as good or better than everyone who is here.*"

That's how Gus Dominguez had become a sports agent. He took an interest in these Cubans when no one else did, and so he became, by default, their guy. The players in Cuba learned of Arocha's success — and saw the Cuban government's decision not to punish his family — and thought, *If he can do it, I can too.* In 1993, two years after Arocha defected, the Cuban national "B" team flew to Buffalo, New York, for the World University Games. Eddie Oropesa, a twenty-one-year-old pitcher on his first trip abroad, sneaked out of the college dorm in which he was housed, but couldn't find the cousin who was supposed to be waiting. Terrified, he wound up wandering around some graveyard in the dark. He ran back to his room and stared at the ceiling. The next morning, as the team warmed up, Oropesa handed his spikes to his good friend short-stop Rey Ordoñez, then dashed for the fence behind home plate. It was at least twelve feet high, but he went up and over in his stocking feet. "I didn't know where my cousin was," Oropesa recalls. "I just started climbing the fence. I heard Rey shouting, 'Oropesa! Oropesa! Oropesa's gone crazy!' But I didn't look back. When I hit the ground I just started running." Newly liberated, he heard Gus Dominguez was the man to see. "I wanted to leave not because I thought I could play baseball," says Oropesa, "but because I didn't want my son to go through the experience that I had. And the only way for him to get out was for me to get out first." (Dominguez helped Oropesa extract his wife and son from Cuba three years later.)

Two days after, Ordoñez fled too. He followed Eddie Oropesa's tracks to Gus Dominguez and became the shortstop for the New York Mets.

A few made it to the big leagues, most did not, but they all needed a great deal of help. From the outside it all looked so easy for the likes of Arocha and Oropesa and Ordoñez. None of it was. Nothing in their experience had prepared them for American life. One of Gus Dominguez's new Cuban clients, Ariel Prieto, took his $1.2 million signing-bonus check from the Oakland A's, stuck it in his jeans, and ran them through the washing machine. Eddie Oropesa, awed by the size of American refrigerators, bet a fellow player he could stay inside one for fifteen minutes — and might have suffocated if Dominguez hadn't opened the door and found him shivering. Latin players were just then flooding into American professional baseball, but these Cubans weren't like the others: they'd been governed by fear, and when you took the fear away they were rudderless. They ate too much and listened too little, all the while longing for their loved ones back in Cuba. Dominguez took them in, even the ones who didn't stand much of a chance of making it big. He housed them with his family, sometimes for months, and helped them to cope with the shock of freedom. And they were grateful. Sprung from the fridge, Oropesa debuted for the Philadelphia Phillies on opening day 2001, against the Florida Marlins. In a tight game, with men on base, and his agent in the stands, Oropesa came in to face Marlins slugger Cliff Floyd. Floyd popped out. "And when I went to the dugout," says Oropesa, "I was crying. It was my most beautiful day playing baseball. And if Gus hadn't been here, I don't know if I would have played."

In the late 1990s and early 2000s the free market became even more elusive for the Cuban players. To flee the Cuban national team you needed to be selected for it, and after several small waves of defections, the Cuban government became shrewder in its selections. Any player deemed a flight risk was kept on the island. Families became hostages: older players with wives they loved and lots of children were preferred to younger ones without emotional attachments. A player caught talking to an American, or on the phone with a defector, might find himself suspended from baseball. The paranoia became self-fulfilling. After Orlando "El Duque" Hernandez left, the sports ministry dropped from the national team a pitcher named Adrian Hernandez, who shared not only a last name (he was no relation) but also the same quixotic high-leg-kicking wind-up, which they took as a sign that he admired the defector. His blackballing compelled Adrian Hernandez to flee Cuba in 2000 and sign a $4 million contract with the Yankees.

The road from Miami to Key West is narrow and slow and ill designed for a Cuban baseball player in a hurry to get to the big leagues. Osbek Castillo has driven it twice before. The first time was in the dawn of August 22, 2004, when he crawled out of the ocean and headed off to find a market for his services. The second was almost three years later, in April 2007, when he drove to Key West to be a witness in the trial of Gus Dominguez. His third trip was with me late this past winter, a few days before he was scheduled to report to spring training in Tucson with the Arizona Diamondbacks. Not much has changed since he first laid eyes on the place. "You never saw a single American flag in Cuba," he says, pointing out the car window. "Here they are everywhere." And they are: American flags and the signs in English that he cannot understand.

It's a gorgeous sunny day, and Osbek's clearly enjoying the trip. A small plane flies overhead. "That plane reminds me of the Coast Guard," he says, with a big yawn. "That's how they caught us the first time. They spotted us from a plane like that."

That first trip had been in July 2004. He'd let a Cuban with contacts in Miami know of his displeasure. "I had absolutely no plans to leave," he says. "But I wasn't even preselected for the national team. Then I realized they had no plans for me." A few days later he received a call from a man in the States, who said his name was Javier. Javier told him to be ready to leave at a moment's notice. A few weeks later Javier called back and said, "Today's the day." Osbek filled a small bag with family photos and drinking water. Everything else he left behind. He told no one of his plans, not even his parents, for fear that they might tell someone else and he'd be tossed in prison.

That night a stuffy, windowless van drove him from his apartment outside Havana to a beach in Matanzas, a few hours away, picking up along the way twenty-one other people who would ride out on the same boat. Among these were the four other baseball players: Francisley Bueno, Allen Guevara, Yoankis Turino, and Osmany Masso. The motorboat was just big enough to hold them, but the ballplayers were still treated as the first-class passengers. Racing from the shore in the dark, they nearly collided with what they feared was a Cuban police boat. "The driver said some people would have to jump out into the water, to slow the police boat down," says Osbek. "They would have to stop and pick up the people. They were trying to decide who would jump out, and the driver said the baseball players had to stay in the boat, because we were the most valuable. Then everyone on the boat started swearing they were baseball players, so they wouldn't have to jump out."

The police boat turned out to be a fishing boat, and so no one was forced to jump into the ocean. But four hours later, as they approached the Florida coast, they hit a reef, and one of the engines failed. They slowed to a creep. The sun rose, and they became visible. "That's when a plane came over, and they saw us," recalls Osbek. The boat was achingly close to the shore. "The water wasn't dark but light blue. And we could see the beach." Out of nowhere came a pair of U.S. Coast Guard cutters. Everyone in the boat knew that if they got to the beach they were free — they'd be granted asylum. But no one thought to swim for it, mainly because the cutters had big guns trained on them. "The Coast Guard shot bullets into the engine that turned it off."

Osbek was taken off one boat and put onto another, where, for the next six days, he was questioned by various Americans in uniforms. He begged them to take him to Guantánamo, but they handed him back to the Cuban authorities instead. "The first Cuban police guy I talked to asked, 'What are you going to do now that you can never play baseball again?'" What he was going to do was try to get out again. In Cuba, not only was he banned from baseball, but his former teammates didn't want to be seen with him or even talk to him on their cell phones. He was at risk of being jailed. He didn't know who Javier was, but prayed that he'd call again. He was the only hope of getting out of Cuba.

Getting *into* Cuba, it turns out, is also a problem, especially if you have anything to do with baseball. It may still be possible to sneak in, but you'd be insane to try. The governments of the United States and Cuba now agree on at least one thing: Americans with a commercial interest in springing Cuban ballplayers should be jailed for pursuing it. Gus Dominguez is now serving a five-year sentence in a California prison. In 1996 another American sports agent, Juan Ignacio Hernandez, was sentenced to fifteen years in a Cuban jail for traveling to Cuba and trying to persuade ballplayers to leave. "When you roll into Havana and they figure out you're from Major League Baseball," says the Braves' McMichael, "right away they shut you down. I've seen guys try it. I've seen guys try to get a radar gun in [to clock pitches]. And they get put right back on the plane going out. To know what a Cuban player is is now just this side of impossible. You can't legally lay your eyes on them." The Florida jury that convicted Dominguez was on to something: the flow of information and of baseball players out of Cuba is slower now than it has been in a long time. "What's strange about Cuba," says agent Joe Kehoskie, "is that the money given to Cuban defectors is increasing. But the number of Cuban defectors is decreasing."

You aren't even likely to be allowed to enter Cuba as an American baseball journalist — at least not without an extraordinary amount of hassling from the Cuban government, which, since Fidel took ill, has become much more vigilant in preventing foreign reporters from going where they want to go and seeing who they want to see. But there remains a path from the outside into Cuban baseball. It runs through Canada — specifically through a fifty-nine-year-old retired high school history teacher named Kit Krieger.

Krieger lives in Vancouver, where for seventeen years he taught in the public schools. In 1997, by what he describes as a series of accidents, he was elected head of British Columbia's 41,000-member teachers' union. He began a tradition of sending teachers and school supplies to Cuba twice a year. "Because of Cuba's isolation they have very few friends," says Krieger, "and my union quickly became Cuba's best friend." Much as he loved teaching, Krieger loved baseball more. He isn't an ordinary fan. He is the sort who when asked for the date Babe Ruth made his debut not only will give it to you off the top of his head, but will also list the lineups of both teams, along with their batting averages for that year. He is also the sort of fan who from a shockingly young age hounded professional baseball players for autographs. When he was thirteen he leaned over the outfield wall and asked Joe DiMaggio what it was like to be married to Marilyn Monroe. (DiMaggio ignored him.) "Mickey Mantle told me to fuck off once," he says with a hint of pride.

There were no official Friends of Cuban Baseball, and so Kit Krieger became an unofficial one. "I have the largest collection of Cuban-autograph baseballs in Canada," he says. "The second-largest is 31 million people tied with none." Once he went to Cuba with paper and pencils and schoolbooks; now he goes with bats and balls and gloves. He meets with team managers and players and league officials. He became close friends with Communist Party officials who shared his love of baseball.

It strains the resources of a retired schoolteacher living on his pension to medicate half of Cuba's old-timers and equip some large number of young Cuban baseball players, and creates domestic problems in the bargain. "My wife thinks I'm being used," he says. "And she's right. I *am* being used. But so what? These people have nothing." In 2001, to supplement his pension, he created a small company, called Cubaball, to introduce baseball fanatics to Cuba. Most of the people who go on these trips aren't anyone's idea of normal. They all know more than any human being should about Cuban baseball history, and perform, for the benefit of the locals, astonishing feats. One day, for instance, they drove three hours from Havana to a town called Cruces. Cruces is the burial place of Cuba's most legendary prerevolutionary player, Martín Dihigo. (He's the only player in the Hall of Fame in three countries: the U.S.A., Mexico, and Cuba.) They'd hoped to find Dihigo's tomb, but this proved difficult, and as they wandered around town they stumbled upon a museum of local interest. Inside they met the director, who said he had a box of memorabilia donated by Dihigo's son. The director had no idea what most of it was. "Dihigo was forgotten," said the Cuban interpreter who told me of the incident. "Dihigo's tomb was forgotten. Dihigo's son handed a box of old stuff to the museum, but they didn't know what any of it was. So, Kit fished a baseball with signatures on it out of the box and started to read the names: Carl Erskine. Rafael Noble. Silvio García. Solly Hemus. Lefty Gomez. He knew every player. He knew their batting averages. He knew their career histories. In less than five minutes he looked up and said, 'Cienfuegos, 1947–48.'" (Cienfuegos was a Cuban winter league team.)

The local museum's box of unidentifiable objects became a roomful of exhibits, with detailed labels and interesting footnotes. Silvio García, Kit explains, "was the great Cuban player removed from the list of players who might be used to break the [U.S. major league] color barrier, because of his response to the question 'How would you respond if a white player called you a nigger?'" (García said he'd beat the crap out of him.) How could Cuba simply forget him?

The Cuban government treats this baseball obsessive with something like respectful indifference. So long as he brings money to Cuba and doesn't meddle with the chief political assets, young ballplayers, it welcomes him. They allow him to excavate whatever he wants of Cuba's baseball past. Their official lack of interest in prerevolutionary professional baseball has given way to some unofficial curiosity. Kit Krieger is a bit like a guy who wanders into your house and takes a deep interest in the beige wall-to-wall carpeting that you yourself have never actually noticed and, after calling it a rare collector's item, begins a disquisition on the shade of beige, the length of the pile, and so on. By the time he's done you can barely stand to walk on the thing. Whenever Krieger visits Cuba now the sports ministry dutifully rounds up whatever old-timers are still alive and creaking for his delighted inspection — but you get the sense that this is basically the only time anyone pays them any attention. Driving past the ballpark our first morning in Havana, Kit spots a little old man standing in the street. There is no game this day, nothing happening inside the park. The poor fellow looks to be either homeless or lost. "Ernesto!" shouts Kit, leaping from the taxi. The man turns, delighted to be recognized. "His name is Ernesto Morilla," Kit explains, "and in an exhibition game in 1946 he struck out Stan Musial."

"Musial just threw the bat and said, 'Son of a bitch,'" Morilla recalls with a little grin. "'Curveball.'"

My third day in Havana there is a game, and we arrive at the ballpark just as it is meant to start. The drive has taken longer than expected, and Kit was uncharacteristically late. ("Sorry," he'd said as he trotted from the elevator. "I'm monitoring the online auction for Dale Mitchell's 1953 Cleveland Indians jersey . . . Dale Mitchell is the guy Don Larsen struck out to end the 1956 perfect game. Checked swing.") When we pull up we find that the game is delayed for lack of a policeman to open the gate. The day is hot, the gate is locked, and several hundred men are clamoring to get in. Today the Havana Metros — one of Osbek Castillo's former employers — will play the team from Villa Clara, on a baseball diamond that has been built in the middle of the grounds of the Hospital Psiquiátrico de la Habana. "We could probably think up a whole team of major leaguers who belong here," says Kit. "The All-Insane team." He begins to list the many baseball players who were certifiable. "Jimmy Piersall playing center field . . ." But before he can finish, the police appear and open the gate. A cheer goes up and the crowd rushes in.

Behind home plate are parked three Chinese-made bicycles — two of which turn out to belong to players, who had peddled to the ballpark on them. Roaming around freely are several chickens, a gaggle of mental patients, and a few doctors in hospital greens. The foul lines are not painted but laid upon the field, in strips of old rubber tires painted white. Just off the field, down the foul lines, are the long, single-story hospital buildings, presumably filled with Cuban lunatics. But the most unsettling aspect of the place, for an American baseball fan, is the concession stand.

It may be possible to create a daily economic life more confusing than Fidel Castro has concocted in Cuba, but you'd have to work at it. Start with the money. Inside of fifteen years, the U.S. dollar has gone from being illegal to legal to banned from use. René Arocha made up his mind to defect after his uncle was sentenced to two years in prison for the possession of a $5 bill. Three years later $5 bills were perfectly legal. On the street two different currencies are traded, both called pesos. One kind of peso is what the locals get paid and is worth roughly four cents, while the other is what foreigners are given when they fork over their euros at the foreign-exchange centers, and is worth roughly a dollar. All prices are in pesos, but even the locals are sometimes not sure if the peso in question is the four-cent kind or the dollar one. The rule of thumb is that when a vendible good resembles even remotely the sort of thing one might actually desire or a thing only a tourist would buy, the price tag implies expensive pesos. A copy of Che Guevara's memoir of the revolution costs twenty tourist pesos, or the monthly salary of a Cuban doctor. A cheap Cuisinart costs 54.50 tourist pesos, a boom box 329.25, and for 109 of these dear pesos, or six months' salary of a tenured professor of international economy at the University of Havana, you can dine alone on the roof of the newly renovated Hotel Saratoga, survey the ruin of Havana, and contemplate the consequences of antimaterialism.

But down on the streets you can never be sure. As this is my first Cuban baseball game, I failed to anticipate that a Cuban ballpark is, in effect, a tourist-free zone. Up in the stands are three ladies with trays of peanuts and cookies and whatnot. I grab a few sacks of peanuts and some weirdly wrapped cookies and ask them how much for the lot. "Five pesos," they say, and so I give them five of what the foreign-exchange lady at the Havana airport had given me. Wrong! I'd paid them twenty-five times the going rate for peanuts and cookies, and the ladies are so delighted and startled that they try to give me their entire store. It is sweet, really. They don't

correct me or make change, but they feel guilty about just stealing my money and so begin piling up vast quantities of what appear
to be the world's most toxic foodstuffs: Cheetos without cheese,
strangely flavorless chocolate wafers, and various other Michael
Pollan nightmares. They stop only when it becomes clear we have
reached the limit of what I can haul back to my seat.

What's even odder is what is not sold: souvenirs. It's hard to
imagine an American baseball game without jerseys and autographed balls and bobble-head dolls being hawked for outrageous
sums. There's none of that in Cuba. Walking into the main Havana
stadium one night, I come upon a crowd of several hundred people, gazing into the side of a trailer. It is dark, and the only light em-
anates from inside. It is as if the baby Jesus had been reborn, and
people had come for miles to see him. But what the people are gazing upon, taped to the wall of the trailer, are baseball caps. Six er-
satz caps bearing the logo of Havana's main team, Industriales, to
be exact. Nothing else. Just six caps. I assume the crowd is in line to
buy the caps, but at three tourist pesos a pop they are far too expensive for Cubans. The crowd gathered not to buy but to stare at the
caps. It is the first time since the revolution that the crass capitalist
act of selling souvenirs has been permitted at Cuba's most famous
baseball stadium.

On the field the finances become, if anything, more bewildering.
Officially the players aren't paid at all for playing baseball but for
some other "job" they hold. "Coach," say, or "sports counselor." For
their phony jobs they get 250 Cuban pesos a month. The 520 players in the Cuban National Series receive, in total, $60,000 a year. In
theory, the entire Cuban league could be bankrolled with roughly
one-seventh of the salary of a rookie big league benchwarmer.

Like everyone else in Cuba, baseball players earn far less than a human being can survive on. And like every other Cuban, to cover the
difference between what they need to live on and what they are
paid by their government jobs, the players turn to the black market. Playing baseball is just the loss leader that gets them into their
actual trade: retailer of stolen baseball merchandise. Before he fled
on a boat and into the arms of Gus Dominguez, for instance,
Industriales pitcher Yoankis Turino pilfered baseballs, forged the
autographs of his teammates on them, and flogged them to tourists

for $5 a pop. A player's labor may belong to the state, but his jersey, at the end of the season, is his to keep: after the two seasons he played with Industriales, Osbek Castillo sold his for $30. The jersey of a lesser player on a bad team might fetch as little as $5, but that of a big star might sell for $50. The jersey for a national team member is worth twice the jersey of a Cuban Series team, and a jersey sold outside of Cuba goes for multiples of a jersey inside Cuba. In the last World Cup, a pitcher with a 95-mph fastball, named Pedro Luis Lazo, was caught by a Cuban government official in the lobby of his Taipei hotel selling his uniform to a Taiwanese businessman for $217.

All this goes on with the more or less full knowledge of the authorities, who use that knowledge to instill fear in the players. The 2006 Cuban batting title was won by a twenty-seven-year-old named Michel Enríquez. This year he's not on any roster, and word is that he's been suspended. No one knows why — no one ever knows why. But it's a fair bet that he got caught selling something on the open market that he shouldn't have — probably his baseball talent.

At any rate, the ruling idea in Cuban baseball is that the players are not only amateurs but interchangeable. Stars are unimportant; team is everything. But there's nothing like a baseball field to remind you that all men are not created equal. A few, when they walk onto a field, might as well own it. As it happens, one of these players is here today, only he's no longer a player. He's the manager of the visiting team, Villa Clara. Like his players, he's dressed head to toe in what appear to be Halloween-orange pajamas. ("The Oranges" is Villa Clara's team name.) Although his players get little attention, half the people in the stands are pointing at him while he pretends that they aren't.

"Víctor Mesa!" says a fan near us.

"El Loco [the crazy one]!" says another, which, given that he appears to reside in Havana's psychiatric hospital, seems a bit rich.

Soon everyone is either looking at or pointing to or chatting about Víctor Mesa. Mesa is one of the few baseball people in Cuba who can be fairly described as a living legend. As a center fielder he was widely regarded as not only supremely gifted but totally nuts — the sort of player to whom no fly ball was so insignificant that he wouldn't crash into a wall to catch it. He was the only player in

Cuba who routinely stole home — and he'd yell as he was stealing it. He was one of the few Cuban players with a nickname, and by some measure the most popular player on the island. Hearts of fifty-year-old Cuban women still flutter when they describe watching Víctor Mesa play ball. It's fair to say that he never played against anyone better than he was. He was on the Cuban team that played against the United States in the Amateur World Series in 1984. Mesa was twenty-four at the time, and Barry Bonds, on the U.S. team, was twenty. The Cuban team won, and Mesa was the MVP. "He wouldn't have been just a regular in the All-Star Game," says René Arocha. "He would have been the star of the All-Star Game." "He would have been more than a star in professional baseball," says Eddie Oropesa, who, before he climbed the fence in Buffalo, surrendered to Mesa his two-hundredth home run. "He was a show. He would do things other people wouldn't even think of doing." After he'd tried — and failed — to talk Víctor Mesa into becoming an American citizen, Gus Dominguez saw one of those things at one of the international tournaments. Mesa hit leadoff and was the first batter of Cuba's first game. Before the first pitch Mesa turned and began to argue with the umpire. The first pitch he hit out of the park. After he rounded the bases and touched home plate, he turned back to the umpire to argue some more. The umpire tossed him out of the game.

A penchant for arguing with the umps isn't usually a recipe for success in a police state. But Víctor Mesa's new career as a baseball manager has made his playing career seem measured and balanced. He's been thrown out of more games than all the other Cuban managers put together. Once, he got himself thrown out of a game before it started, which is hard to do. (The umpire was warning him in advance not to make trouble or come out on the field, to which Mesa replied, "Are you fucking blind? I'm on the field right now.")

Before the game starts we find Mesa down on the field, looking troubled, though when he sees Kit Krieger he brightens and throws his arm around him. He has the animal elegance of someone who was clearly once a marvelous athlete, and one of those bodies that could have played any game well but because he had been born in Cuba was destined for baseball. (When he was nine years old two Cuban government officials spotted him playing in the streets and packed him off to a baseball academy.) With a huge grin he apologizes for his state of mind (gloomy, he swears), but it can't be helped. What troubles him is exactly what troubles U.S. big league managers: kids these days. "You have to tell them the same things over and over," he says, pointing to his team, huddled in the out- field around the team's psychiatrist. (All Cuban teams have a psy- chiatrist, but perhaps none is so usefully employed as Villa Clara's.) "I have headaches from shouting at them." In case Kit has missed his point, Mesa rubs his head and winces. It's a handsome forty- seven-year-old head, the color of café con leche, perched on a thick, strong neck.

Hard as he is on umpires, Víctor Mesa is harder on players. He has been known to rush out onto the field in the middle of innings to physically pull his players off it when they show less than perfect commitment to their jobs. The Villa Clara fans, when displeased by his relentless hard-assedness, carry a casket around with Víctor Mesa's name on the side.

A few minutes later the game begins, and it's clearly a mismatch. One big difference between Cuban and American baseball is that Cuban players must play for the province in which they were born. This creates an imbalance much like the financial imbalance in Major League Baseball. Havana has a lot more people than any other province, and so it tends to have a disproportionate share of the better players. The Metros are the Cuban baseball authorities' answer to this: a second Havana team. The first team is Indus- triales, the most famous team in Cuba. In theory, having to field two teams should force Havana to dilute its talent; in practice, be- cause the Havana officials who run the thing want to win, it concen- trates it. The Metros are used as a farm team for Industriales — a place for raw youth and decrepit old age. The minute a Metro looks promising, he becomes an Industriale. If Industriales are the New York Yankees of Cuba, the Metros are the Pittsburgh Pirates. Their seasons begin without hope and end with relief.

The Metros pitcher's first pitch hits the Villa Clara batter. The next batter whacks a grounder that bounces over the Metros sec- ond baseman's glove; the guy after him lines a shot between the right fielder's legs. Thus begins the rout. The game started at 1:15; when the 1:45 Air Canada flight to Toronto takes off from the José Martí airport, just behind the center-field wall, we're still in the top of the first inning, and the Metros are down by four runs. Alcohol is banned, but the Metros fans drink anyway — rum from unmarked bottles. This is the moment they've waited for, when the Metros have earned the insults they have come to holler at them.

"Hey, don't you have food in your town?!" (at the skinny pitcher).

"When's the last time you got laid?" (after the muffed ground ball).

The place is small enough that every remark is heard and appreciated, and pretty soon everybody is hollering and laughing. The players don't even pretend to be indifferent. Particularly ripe jabs are greeted with laughter in both dugouts. When a fight breaks out in the stands, players come out of the dugout and crane their necks to watch. When a fan takes a foul ball off his forehead, the players come out again, to gawk. Here is one effect of keeping money out of sports: it lessens the distance between the players and the fans. The players are as poor as the people who watch them, and in many cases poorer. For anything above and beyond their meager salaries they depend on the generosity of these fans. "When it rains," says Kit, "I've seen the players just come into the stands and sit with the fans until it stops."

"If Víctor Mesa had fucked your mother you might be good!" someone shouts. And even Víctor Mesa leans out and laughs.

But he quickly goes back to being serious. Even though his team is winning, he frowns, he stomps, he cheers, and he rages, and in general lets his players know that life with Víctor Mesa will be exciting, but not easy. "If I let the players do what they want," he says, "they're screwed. They will not be anyone, and they will go back to the street. And there is nothing on the street." But, for his better players, the street is not the only option. After Industriales, Mesa's Villa Clara team vies for the lead in an important stat: player defections. Live through a season with Víctor Mesa and a few days on a raft surrounded by sharks doesn't seem so terrifying. Mesa's shortstop and catcher were banned from baseball for speaking on the phone with Cuban defectors. His shortstop Yuniesky Betancourt hopped a boat to Florida one night in 2003. Established as Seattle's starting shortstop two seasons ago, Betancourt was asked if he had problems adjusting to big league managers. "We have a manager in Cuba, and that manager is worse than anything you

have in the major leagues," Betancourt replied. "His name is Víctor
Mesa."

An invisible line runs from Víctor Mesa, yelling from his dugout,
to Gus Dominguez in his cell inside a California prison. For the
one thing that the U.S. attorney general and the jailed sports agent
agree upon is that all the trouble began when Yuniesky Betancourt
fled Víctor Mesa's ball club.

After the trial, the prosecutors said privately that Gus Dominguez's
biggest mistake was to try to tell his story to the jury. On the stand
Dominguez struck his prosecutors as naive and unprepared. He
was dressed in black, for instance, which no one trying to seem innocent does. Under cross-examination he came across as pushy
and even indignant, rather than contrite. Before the trial he'd declined the government's plea deal on the grounds that he'd done
nothing wrong: the first he'd heard of the five Cuban players he
was accused of smuggling, he says, is when his former client (and
New York Yankee) Andy Morales called and told him they were in
Miami and needed his help.

To his jury, Dominguez told an outlandish story that no one
had heard before. The whole problem started, he explained, with
Yuniesky Betancourt. Like every other Cuban ballplayer, Betancourt, when he landed in Florida, needed help. He'd gotten in
touch with a friend, Atlanta Braves catcher Brayan Peña, who sent
him to Gus Dominguez. Dominguez arranged for Betancourt to
move to Mexico and train with a winter-ball team while he cut a
deal on his behalf with the Seattle Mariners — which came in at
$3.8 million guaranteed, with another million or so in incentives.
For Betancourt to join the Mariners, all they needed was the approval of the U.S. Treasury Department's Office of Foreign Assets
Control, which must sign off on any deal between Major League
Baseball teams and Cubans. As he waited for Betancourt to return
from Mexico, Dominguez told the court, he got a call from the
man who had served as a go-between for Betancourt's smugglers.
His real name was Ysbel Medina-Santos, but baseball players in
Cuba knew him as Javier.

Medina-Santos told Dominguez that Betancourt had promised
to pay his smugglers 5 percent of his first major league contract.
They heard he had a deal with the Mariners, and they wanted their

money. Now. The contract was unenforceable, but the smugglers were prepared to collect on their own. If Dominguez didn't pay them, Medina-Santos threatened, they'd break Betancourt's legs and end his career. What point would there be in that? Dominguez asked. Break his legs and you'll never get your money. Medina-Santos seemed to agree with him. But then, a few hours later, he called back and said if they didn't get their money they were coming after Dominguez and his kids. Those kids were both students at Tulane University, where they were planning careers in law enforcement. They sat in the Key West courtroom, hearing this story for the first time, from their father on the witness stand. The daughter, Desiree, says, "I thought, *What's happened to our family? We used to be so normal.*" Now she was hearing that her life had been threatened to pay for the Seattle Mariners shortstop's boat ride from Cuba. Her dad tried to explain to the jury why he'd never told his children, his wife, his business partner, or, for that matter, the FBI of this threat. He'd kept it to himself and paid the Cuban smugglers because he feared what they might do if he didn't.

It all sounded too bizarre to be true, but the only contradictory evidence was the testimony of this deeply shady character, Ysbel Medina-Santos. Medina-Santos had come from jail to the courtroom and would go right back afterward. On the stand he admitted to so many crimes the audience lost track: insurance fraud, Medicare fraud, tax evasion, theft. He'd done jail time in Florida for dealing drugs and was about to do more. Even one of the prosecutors described him privately as "a scumbag." But he was all they had. In exchange for a greatly reduced prison sentence, he swore that the $225,000 Gus Dominguez had wired into his account was for picking up from a beach in Cuba and ferrying to the Florida Keys five Cuban baseball players selected by the Los Angeles sports agent.

It was the smuggler's word against the agent's, and there was really only one person who might have broken the tie: Yuniesky Betancourt. The Dominguez side never called him as a witness, mainly because they had no idea what he might say. He'd already told three different stories, two of them to immigration agents, about how and when he'd come to the United States. He declined to return phone calls, and slammed the door in the face of the private eye they'd hired to track him down. As his former agent went to trial, Víctor Mesa's old shortstop was back in Seattle, playing in their home opener. And on top of it all, he'd unwittingly provided the U.S. government with an explanation for why Gus Dominguez needed to smuggle ballplayers in from Cuba: to make back the money he'd lost on Betancourt — for, having stiffed his smugglers, Betancourt then stiffed the agent who had fed and housed him for six months. He signed the contract with the Mariners that Dominguez had negotiated on his behalf, but paid whatever commission he paid to someone else. (A grievance regarding the allocation of the commission is ongoing.) The money Dominguez lost on Betancourt, the U.S. government argued, threw his business into disarray. He became desperate — so desperate that he ordered up five more players from Cuba.

And was now in jail for it. The U.S. attorney treated his conviction as an explanation. But it wasn't; they never even really tried to get to the bottom of what exactly happened in the black market for Cuban ballplayers. They didn't determine, for instance, who ultimately wound up pocketing Dominguez's $225,000. (They still don't know.) The original indictment accused Dominguez of actually having been in the motorboat that fetched the players from Cuba, but then it turned out he was in New Orleans at the time, dropping his kids off at college. In the end the prosecutors claimed that Dominguez had given the money to Medina-Santos, who distributed it to the people who did the dirty work.

Those people, whoever they were, may have learned a lesson from their experience with Yuniesky Betancourt: once a Cuban player was loose in the United States, he couldn't be relied on to fork over 5 percent of his big league paychecks for an illegal five-hour boat ride. A year after Betancourt crawled ashore in Florida another group of players landed. They were met by their smugglers, who then set out to auction them to agents. One agent, Joe Kehoskie, says he got a phone call from a defector's girlfriend telling him that some Cuban ballplayers had arrived and asking if he'd like to represent them. He flew down, was picked up at his hotel by the woman and driven to one of the smugglers' houses, where he found a lawyer, two smugglers, and six Cuban baseball players. One of the players Kehoskie knew: Yunel Escobar, then backup shortstop for Industriales (and now the starting shortstop for the Atlanta Braves). "The smugglers said, 'We can let you represent them if you pay us 150 grand,'" recalls Kehoskie. The players had just arrived by boat, had been collected on the U.S. shore by smugglers, and without a dime in their pockets or a word of English at their disposal were at their mercy. "The players were effectively being held hostage until someone paid to have them freed," says Kehoskie. "This wasn't a referral fee. It was ransom. A member of the Florida bar was sitting in the room, helping them to arrange their smuggling fee, so they could get out of there. It was one of those only-in-Miami moments."

Havana's Estadio Latinoamericano is a 50,000-seat stadium that seems like a slightly run-down version of a big American stadium until you realize something's missing: a parking lot. Cuban baseball is very nearly carbon-neutral. The fans arrive by bicycle or on foot or haphazardly attached to the back of whatever pickup trucks happen to be passing this way. And so it comes as a shock when out of nowhere roars a bright-orange BMW. Inside is Víctor Mesa, still in his pumpkin-orange uniform. His team just finished another whooping of the Metros, 18–4, and is filing onto its bus, probably relieved that their manager isn't coming along to tell them what they did wrong. "Come over to my house tonight and we'll drink rum," Mesa shouts, tossing out his address, and then zooms off into the night.

Mesa's house turns out to be something more than a house. It's not quite a mansion, but close. Havana is a spectacular ruin; it's as if someone had glued together the ten richest, oldest residential neighborhoods in America and passed a law forbidding anyone to touch them for fifty years. The number of Víctor Mesa's house is gone, but beside it there's a green metal gate, chained and locked, and on the other side is the bright-orange BMW. Cars are precious here — a Cuban can buy his own car only after he's convinced the authorities that he's earned the money in Cuba. They'll sit and look at how much you've made, deduct some plausible sum for living expenses, and conclude whether or not you could possibly have saved enough — which of course you couldn't have on what you've been legally paid. And so Víctor Mesa's car, like Víctor Mesa's life, is a tribute to his guile. "I don't know very many stupid Cubans," Kit

Krieger says as we bang on the front door. "Here you have to know
the system in detail or you're in trouble."

The car doesn't go with the house, because the car is in peak
condition and shines, while the house, on the outside, hasn't been
painted or improved or repaired in any way since the revolution.
But then the door swings open onto what might as well be another
world. Pink-and-white marble gleams. The tablecloths are lace. The
appliances are new, though of odd or indeterminate brand. (Could
there really be such a thing as a Frigidaire TV?) The kitchen is in-
distinguishable from a kitchen in a million-dollar American home:
there's even an island. Martini and wine glasses hang from wooden
racks. I've seen bigger houses, but foot for foot there can be no
house back in the Free World with more stuff inside it. The paint-
ings, portraits of Elvis Presley and Marilyn Monroe and John
Lennon, climb all the way up the fifteen-foot walls and nearly touch
the pristine crown molding. Two are almost too large to fit: one of
a bat and a ball, another of Mesa scaling a palm tree to catch a fly
ball.

"It looks like I was born with God," says Víctor Mesa now, reading
my mind. "I've been very lucky." He points to a big painting of himself. "That's a $25,000 painting. A gift from the artist. Even if I only
sell it for $5,000, he just gives me another for free." This is another
little wrinkle in the Cuban economy: art arbitrage. Artists can sell
what they create in Cuba abroad, and they pay little tax. In Cuba,
it's the artists who get rich.

Kit has found a book of Cuban baseball statistics in a local bookstore, and it's now open on his lap. As Víctor Mesa opens a bottle of
rum, Kit flips through it. No fifty-nine-year-old man ever looked
more like a ten-year-old boy.

"Ask me anything you want!" says Mesa.

"You earn three hundred Cuban pesos a month?" I ask. Eleven
bucks.

"Less!" he says.

"Then how the hell did you get all this stuff?"

It takes him a while to explain. At the end of his Cuban playing career, he says, he was still poor. But the Cuban government allowed
him, as it has a few other big stars, to play for a couple of years in
China. Castro rents out his baseball players after they cease to be of

use to the national team, just as he rents out his doctors and teachers to Venezuela, in exchange for cheap oil. These years abroad were given to Mesa in the spirit of a gift, but the Cuban government nevertheless kept 90 percent of his foreign earnings. The real gift was allowing him to inflict his charm and energy on rich foreigners. By the time he came home he had a harem of financial backers. "Everyone wanted to be my friend," he explains, plausibly. Among his friends is a wealthy Spaniard who still sends him big sums.

Throughout his career he'd been offered many little hints that government people officially disapproved of him: gratuitous slights in sanctioned histories of the Cuban game, forced early retirement as a player, and a long wait before he was granted his rightful place as a coach on the national team. But no one ever succeeded in shutting him up or making him any less happy to be alive. The Cuban defector and former Red Sox bullpen coach Euclides Rojas recalls that the morning after René Arocha defected, as the rest of the Cuban national team flew back to Cuba, Víctor Mesa leapt from his seat to dress down the Cuban government officials. "He shouted, 'I hope you learn from this. I hope you learn that you need to treat us better.'" When Ariel Prieto failed to make the 1992 Cuban Olympic team it was Mesa who told him that he should flee to the United States. "He came to me," recalls Prieto, "and he said, 'You better get the hell out of here. You can play in the big leagues.' Before that no one talked to me about it. Everyone was scared." When star second baseman Rey Anglada was thrown in jail for refusing to testify against teammates who'd been accused of gambling, Mesa was the only player in Cuba to publicly voice his outrage.

"You had 2,171 hits," says Kit, looking up from his stats book, as if Mesa didn't know. "And that's in a ninety-game season." There are 162 games in a major league season, so if you want to compare the career stats you need to multiply the Cuba ones by roughly 1.8.

The member of Cuba's version of the three-thousand-hit club drains a glass of rum.

"You're second all-time in Cuba in stolen bases," says Kit, "and famous for going in with your spikes up."

Mesa frowns. "There was a bad thing about the way I played," he says seriously. "I wouldn't respect my opponent."

"Three hundred fifty-one doubles," says Kit. "Two hundred and seventy-two home runs."

"Two hundred and seventy-three," says Mesa with a smile.

"I'm sorry," I say, "but you had to feel tempted to leave."

Mesa leans forward. His forearms are thick, the forearms of a construction worker. "I'll tell you something and this is true," says Víctor Mesa. "When I was a little boy in Sagua, it was just my mother and three kids. It doesn't mean I have more conscience than anyone else, but we were very poor. When I didn't have anything, I still got everything for free. I got the education for free. I got a place to live for free. I got food for free. I didn't have to pay a cent for any of it. That's what I had on my mind. There was a [major league] scout who would tell me, 'Víctor, youth is just one stage. You're not going to be young forever. If you come to the major leagues, you can make money to take care of yourself when you are no longer young.' But I couldn't: my head wouldn't let me do anything else. It wasn't political. It was my conscience. My mother, before she died, asked me not to leave Cuba. She didn't know anything about sports. She said, 'You could make lots of money, but I don't want you to leave.' So no one made me think the way I did."

He means it. Víctor Mesa may have had the best defense a Cuban ballplayer can have against his government: he actually believed in the revolution. In this one respect he perhaps was not a total freak. The great players of his generation, for whom leaving would have been as easy as walking out of a foreign hotel room, stayed in Cuba. They did what they did for love rather than money. But then, the money wasn't what it is now. And Cuba was not what it is now.

It's taken the better part of three hours, but I finally ask the question that makes Víctor Mesa uneasy: "Would you stay here if you were twenty-one right now?"

Instead of answering, he leads us to his trophy room. It's not decorated but stuffed with more awards and honors than would seem possible for one man to earn in a lifetime. There are half a dozen pictures of Víctor Mesa with Fidel Castro, and a few others of Víctor Mesa with Fidel's brother and current Cuban president, Raul Castro. Scattered among these are pictures of American ballplayers: Joe DiMaggio, Mickey Mantle. "I love American baseball," Mesa says. "It's the best baseball in the world. And, yes, I would have loved to play in the major leagues. I would have loved to be with all these big players and see just how good I was. I am going to die and I'm not going to know."

That's when I spot the picture of Mesa with his former shortstop Yuniesky Betancourt. Even now in Cuba, ballplayers who defect are officially forgotten. Their stats are stricken from the record books, and their names aren't meant to be spoken. And yet here stands Víctor Mesa with his arm draped over the shoulders of the kid who is now the Seattle Mariners' shortstop. "He was like my son," says Mesa. "My very, very difficult son."

It is past two in the morning when we finally stumble back onto the street, but Víctor Mesa is still full of energy. He follows us out and insists on giving us a lift even though we lie and swear to him that we're fine and can find our way back to the hotel. Unchaining the precious BMW, he leaps behind the wheel and drives after us and badgers us to climb in. Even sober he drives like a madman, and now that he has had more than a few glasses of rum he's more confident of his ability to do ninety on Havana's broken streets. Perhaps to slow him down Kit mentions that he plans to be in Seattle soon and hopes to look up Yuniesky Betancourt. "Would you like for me to carry a message to him?" he asks.

"Tell him I said, 'Don't smoke and don't blow it,'" says Mesa.

He's still pushing ninety, and I'm gripping various handles as tightly as I can, as if that will help. "If you crash this thing and we all die," I finally say, "how would they play it in the newspapers?"

"They'd say, 'A bunch of foreigners died with Víctor Mesa,'" he laughs, and floors the gas pedal.

One afternoon I sneak away from Kit Krieger and visit the man who runs the U.S. Special Interests Section — which is what we have there instead of an embassy. His name is Michael Parmly and he lives in a mansion outside of Havana. There I stumble into a creepy conversation with an ambassador from a European country (who asked that I not mention which one). His fellow Eastern Europeans in Cuba, he says, all share the same feeling: it feels like their own countries just before the fall of the Berlin Wall. Tense. A very anxious state police is monitoring the population with special vigilance. "They are a very efficient secret police," he says. "They learned from the Stasi."

"How do you know?" I ask.

"We know," he says.

"Yes, but how?"

"We send information back to test it," he says. "They've never failed to intercept it."

"What do they know?"

"They know everything," he says. "They know, for example, that you are an American journalist and are here right now."

Which is the creepy part.

And if true, then they also know that an American journalist using a Canadian baseball nut as his cover and looking for Cuban baseball players worth stealing has found a rare rental car in Havana and talked a bright young Cuban into driving him across the country, unsupervised, with stops at various baseball games.

On either side of the highway as you leave Havana you see to the horizon fields now fallow that under better management would be making someone rich. Much closer, right beside the highway, you see Cubans selling the items most easily pilfered from the government and resold on the black market — fruit, milk, eggs, giant cheese rounds, live turkeys — while everyone from small schoolchildren to little old ladies waits for buses that run only in theory. On the road itself you see horses, mule-drawn carts, bicycles, army jeeps, ancient tractors, sugarcane cutters, and Soviet dump trucks belching hot black smoke. What you don't see is anything resembling an automobile. The moment we leave Havana, in a 2003 Korean-made rental car, we become an object of wild curiosity. Everyone we pass stares in to see what sort of important person must be inside this exotic vehicle. "They probably think we're either artists or musicians or maybe famous baseball players," says the young Cuban guide I'd talked into coming with me.

By the time I reach the province of Camagüey — birthplace of Gus Dominguez — I've seen almost all the Cuban teams, talked to managers and players, and gotten a general sense of the caliber of play (high). But there are two things, in addition to cars, that I never saw. One is other tourists, who seem to be well imprisoned either in Havana or at beach resorts. The other is journalists. I'd been to a dozen games but had yet to encounter a single Cuban reporter. The games are on national television, they get written about in the national paper and get argued about on the streets — and yet no one interviews baseball managers or players. "The journalists don't even want to talk to us," the Camagüey manager tells me. "They think they know everything. I tell my players: Don't read or listen to them. They don't know anything."

Tonight, Camagüey will face the hated Industriales, whose fan base makes the Yankees' seem docile. My young Cuban traveling companion is a rabid Industriales fan. After I've dragged him down to the team's dugout he still can't believe he's there, standing next to his heroes. But to know who they are he needs to see their numbers. Their faces he doesn't recognize: he's never seen them before. There are no TV close-ups, and there are no newspaper profiles. They never appear on posters, because there are no posters, and they never appear in product endorsements, because there are no products, and even if there were, it would be against the law to endorse them. The Cuban baseball fan knows every name and every statistic, just like an American fan, but he can walk past his favorite player in broad daylight without a hint of recognition. And the journalists haven't the slightest interest in changing that — even though there's no law stopping them. "Sometimes we ask them to come down so that they can write something they know rather than something they think," says Industriales manager Rey Anglada. "But they usually don't come."

The upshot is that Cuban baseball games go undescribed. The papers tell you who won and who lost, who hit and who didn't. The columnists froth and fume. But you never read anything about what actually happened — which is a shame, because a great deal often does. Major disruptions don't cost anyone much, so far less effort goes into preventing them. Take the ball boy, for instance, who is always at risk of running out of baseballs. Before every Cuban game the ball boy sets himself up in a folding chair, about fifteen feet behind home plate, and puts his life on the line for his country. He wears no helmet or protective gear of any kind and is usually physically unsuited to evade fast-moving projectiles. Here in Camagüey the ball boy is a toothless old man named Miguelito, who spends much of the game dodging rockets and complaining about all the foul balls leaving the park. "How can you work in these conditions?" he grumbles loudly enough for the Communist Party officials to hear.

Then there is the Industriales equipment manager: before the game he discovers that he's got no batting helmets. The government sent them a shipment but in the wrong color — brown instead of blue. And so right up until the first pitch, the poor fellow's scouring the stands and the opposing dugout for helmets that match his team's colors. As he does he's watched, without interest, by the first secretary of the Communist Party of the municipality and at least half a dozen other local party officials.

You can tell who works for the government by who bothers to sing the national anthem. They belt it out while everyone else does the American thing of waiting around for it to end so that what they really care about can begin. You can also tell who works for the government by where they sit: the best seats, behind home plate, are reserved for them. Apart from that, as the game starts, much is familiar. The managers do dopey things to remind everyone they exist — like bat their best hitter seventh or bunt the DH in the top of the first with runners on first and second and nobody out. There are players who clearly like to get dirty and players who don't. The catchers have the same subtle ability to distance themselves from pitchers in trouble — refusing to make eye contact as they hand him a new ball after a home run. Even the body language is the same — right down to the same startling amount of unselfconscious public crotch grabbing when things go wrong.

At the start, to the delight of the Camagüey fans, nothing goes wrong. The hated elites from Havana find themselves not only without batting helmets but also without runs — down 4–0 at the end of the first. The next six innings, however, they claw their way back, and going into the eighth inning they lead 7–6. The tension builds, and when Industriales puts men on first and second, even the government officials can't stand it anymore. The head of sports administration for Camagüey rises from his seat behind home plate, skips down to the net behind the Camagüey dugout, and begins to holler at the Camagüey manager. Prudently, one of the coaches gets up to listen to what he has to say.

"Our first baseman is playing too close to the line!" he shouts.

Once he got to be president, Richard Nixon had the nerve to send plays to Washington Redskins coach George Allen, but Allen didn't pay them much attention. Here you need only to be a local party official and you get to move the first baseman off the line.

But the first baseman is still a bit player in this drama. The main character — the one you have to try *not* to watch — is the Camagüey center fielder. He moves with the assurance of a player who knows he is the best; he sets himself apart by wearing, under his jersey, the sleeves of the Cuban national team. He runs and throws like a big leaguer and in the first six innings makes several sensational catches in center field. He singles in one run, doubles in two more, and does everything with the grace and ease of a young man playing an imaginary game against imaginary opponents. His name, oddly for a Cuban, is Leslie Anderson. The game isn't an hour old before it becomes clear that, whatever happens, Leslie Anderson is likely to be in the middle of it.

At least that's how it looks to me. But it isn't just any old opinion, it's my opinion, and so naturally I look around for someone to inflict it upon. The only person at hand is the Communist Party official. After moving the first baseman off the line, he's returned to his seat behind me.

"Your center fielder can really play," I say, knowingly.

"Yes," he says, indulgently. "He used to be good."

Used to be good? Leslie Anderson has just turned twenty-six years old — an age when baseball players are still improving, sometimes dramatically. At the age of twenty-three he made the national team and played in the World Baseball Classic. (Cuba lost to Japan in the finals; the U.S.A. team, stacked with major leaguers, didn't place.) Later, when I mention Anderson's name to an agent who follows Cuban baseball, he says that "if he washed up on Miami Beach he'd be a millionaire. The only question about him is his power."

"He's off to a bad start this season," says the government official.

"The season's only been going for a week!"

"We don't like how he's started this year," he says. "I don't know what's going to happen to him."

What Anderson thinks about this is close to unknowable. If he says the wrong thing he might find himself banished from the game he was born to play. As he leaves the on-deck circle and heads to the plate, his team down by a run and two men on base, he may be thinking about nothing more than the glory of playing for Camagüey. But, for all anyone knows, he may be wondering when he's going to get the call telling him the boat from Florida is on its way.

Either way, it's the bottom of the eighth inning, and the game is on the line. The kid on the mound — a reliever named Alexei Gil, brought in an inning ago — has just hit 96 mph on the radar gun. He shouldn't have that kind of heat. He's twenty-one years old, which means he was four in 1991, when the Soviet Union pulled its subsidies. Soon thereafter, the average weight and height of Cuban children collapsed too. The Cold War ended, and East Germany ceased to send powdered milk, heavily discounted, in exchange for lemons. The shortage of calcium expressed itself in the bones of Cuban children, including those children who became pitchers. Thus you can count among the many consequences of the fall of the Berlin Wall the temporary decline of the Cuban fastball — and a temporary reprieve granted to Cuban hitters' with long, slow swings.

Leslie Anderson doesn't need it. His body is long, but his swing is short. The fans have been dancing through much of the game. Cuban baseball is one of those rare sporting events where the spectators burn more calories than the players. Now they're out of control, raving. Even the ancient ball boy has forgotten entirely what he's meant to be doing and is instead screaming instructions. "Watch the damn ball!" he shouts at Anderson from ten feet behind him. "Watch the damn ball!"

In the opposing dugout, Rey Anglada shifts forward. Every strength is a weakness and every weakness a strength: the weakness in his pitcher's ability to throw the ball 96 mph is that he's never had to learn how to throw anything else. Most hitters can't catch up to his fastball. This hitter is different. For the past ten minutes, Anglada will later tell me, he's been wondering what might happen if Alexei Gil tried to throw the ball past Leslie Anderson.

Between the release of the pitch and the crack of the bat is only a split second, but it's long enough for Anglada to think: *I was afraid of that.* The ball rockets off Anderson's bat and down the right-field line; it exits the park so quickly that Anderson doesn't have time to do anything but watch it leave. The only question is whether, after it clears the fence, it will clear the parking lot too. But there is no parking lot.

"*Ru-je le-o-na!*" the crowd chants sarcastically. ("Roar lion!")

The male lion is the Industriales' mascot. But a stadium full of rabid Havana-haters puts the feminine ending on the word to turn it into a girl, just for fun.

"Ru-je le-on-a! Ru-je leona! Ru-je leona!"

Anderson just throws his bat in the air and waves his arms like a dictator. It's good to be twenty-six and a star, even when it doesn't exactly pay.

As Anderson trots around the bases, the crowd keeps up its mocking chant, saved for just this opposing team, for just this moment. Even Miguelito neglects, for a moment, the cost of the lost ball. Fifteen minutes later the Camagüey closer secures the final out, the local Communist Party official throws his hands in the air and screams, and the stadium erupts. The evil empire has been defeated: 9–7.

Down inside the visitors' dugout Rey Anglada rises and shakes hands with his players. If a Cuban journalist were around to ask him the question, Anglada would have said that he blamed himself: he'd trusted in Alexei Gil's fastball too long. A few years ago, when his bullpen was more talented, he might have pulled Gil and brought in someone else. His tempestuous hard-throwing right-hander, Yoankis Turino, perhaps. Or his lefty Francisley Bueno. Or a pitcher with good off-speed stuff, like Osbek Castillo. Osbek didn't have Gil's raw talent, but he was wily and good under pressure. But when Rey Anglada looked to the pen he was reminded that Yoankis and Francisley and Osbek had all left, on a boat to Florida. "They aren't the ones I would have picked to try to make the major leagues," says Anglada. "They had too much in their heads. Osbek, especially. Osbek had a problem thinking about the American Dream."

Osbek Castillo is still a month away from learning that he's been released from the Arizona Diamondbacks and is no longer a professional baseball player. On the highway, as we reach deeper into the Florida Keys, we pass a boatyard, with small motorboats stacked high on racks. They're the size that might fit four bass fishermen comfortably, but on the night Castillo tried to leave Cuba the first time, it held twenty-two. Osbek points and says, "We came over in one just like that. That could have been the boat."

Three weeks after the Cuban police released him, Castillo had another call from the man in the United States calling himself Javier. Once again a windowless van picked him up, along with eighteen others, including all the same ballplayers from the first escape attempt. This time, before they left the Cuban shore, the ballplayers drank a few beers to calm their nerves. But the weather was bad and the seas rough. To keep the nose of the boat down and minimize the bouncing, the men had to move to the front, and the women and children to the back. Halfway across, the engines went out, and the boat bobbed like a cork. "The driver pulled on it for ten minutes, and it wouldn't start." All five players knew Cubans who had died crossing. The bobbing made them sick. Francisley threw up on Osbek, and Osbek threw up on Yoankis, and all three wished they hadn't downed so many beers before they left.

At length, the engines caught and they raced on to they knew not where — no one had told them where they would be getting off. But at some point the driver said they were getting close, and they must all lie flat and be silent. They did as they were told, more or less, but every now and then someone on the floor would ask urgently, "Are we here yet?"

Each time, the boat pilot replied, "Just pray to God." In Cuba, God did not exist, officially. "Everyone in the boat believed in God," says Osbek, but what he really means is that everyone was intensely superstitious. On the beach, for good luck, Francisley had rubbed himself, head to toe, with an egg in what to the other players was a familiar Santeria rite. Yoankis had brought a sack of candies and, as they crossed over, tossed them one by one into the ocean — until the engines died, whereupon he dumped the entire sack. That was what a fellow Cuban had told him: feed the ocean candy and the ocean will be good to you.

Osbek carried with him a small stone statue, along with his beads, for rubbing. He recalls the feeling of the boat slowing as he lay curled on its floor. They were meant to remain hidden, he knew, but he couldn't resist. "I stuck my head up, and I saw trees." Nearing the shore the pilot cut the engines. "You're getting off here," he said.

"Here" turned out to be some way from shore; the trees appeared distressingly small. "People started to say, 'You can't drop me off here. It's too far.'" The boat pilot refused to budge. To show them that the water wasn't very deep he told the tallest ballplayer, Allen Guevara, to jump out. Guevara, terrified, refused. So Yoankis Turino stepped up and said, "I'll go." This was his fifteenth escape attempt — when the boat pilot had seen him he said, "You again!"

But Yoankis had never gotten this close to freedom, and he feared being caught more than anything else.

He leapt. The water was only chest-deep. Instantly, the other eighteen Cubans flew over the gunwales, the women with children on their backs. No one helped each other; it was every man for himself and for his child. Frantically, Osbek caught up with Yoankis, and they began to swim in the dark ocean. "If I could have run over the water, I would have," he says. He shared the same two fears with everyone on the boat. The first was crocodiles — they'd been led to believe that the Florida coastal waters were lousy with them. "I was thinking, *If I get eaten by a crocodile, at least it's an American crocodile*," he recalls, laughing. "An American crocodile might only eat a little of you. A Cuban crocodile would eat all of you — even the shoes." The other, greater fear was being caught by Americans before they hit land and being taken back to Cuba. And the land was elusive. "At first I thought we must be on sand, but it was hard to walk," he says. "We were in mud. We couldn't walk in it. We started to crawl."

Here entered the bizarre legal distinction between a wet-foot Cuban and a dry-foot Cuban. They all knew the deal Clinton had cut with Castro back in 1995. A Cuban on a boat at sea was a wet-foot and, by U.S. immigration law, must be returned to Cuba. A Cuban in a shopping mall in downtown Miami was clearly a dry-foot and by law could remain in the United States and pursue citizenship. But what was a Cuban crawling out of the ocean and into wet mud? The answer wasn't obvious. Cubans had rafted across the Florida Strait only to be taken off a broken bridge in the Florida Keys — which failed to connect to the land on either side of it — and sent back to Cuba. Cubans have been caught knee-deep in the sea, just yards from the beach, and been driven back by police with water cannons — and then returned to Cuba. A Cuban crawling through mud so wet and deep that it was impossible even for a twenty-four-year-old, 180-pound athlete to walk on was not necessarily free. "I crawled as fast as I could," says Osbek. "I was thinking, *I've got to make it, because land is freedom.*" His Industriales teammate Yoankis arrived at a mangrove tree and climbed it. "I studied it," Yoankis says. "My feet were dry, because they were in the tree. But the tree was in water." A tree wouldn't do, they decided.

In the dark they became separated, but Osbek finally arrived on an asphalt road. He still had no idea where he was. Florida, he assumed. Wherever it was, he was beginning to see it: the sun was rising. He spotted a road sign with a tiny deer on it. He was completely alone and feeling many things. Yoankis puts it best: "A lot of things go through your head," he says, "but the one thing that hits you, once you are on dry land, is: *I'm never going back.*" He was happy but also, oddly, sad.

A voice called his name — then the names of the other ballplayers. Then he saw a man with a car, and the man saw him. He walked up. "I'm Javier," the man said.

The ballplayers were the only ones greeted in the U.S. by car and driver. All nineteen people from the boat were drawn to Javier's shouts. They crowded around and asked if they too might hitch a ride, but Javier said the car was reserved for the baseball players. All the others needed to walk down the road and turn themselves in to the first authoritative-looking person they saw. "Javier never said anything about money, but you always know in the end you have to pay," says Osbek. The going rate, he also knew, was 5 percent of whatever contract he happened to sign, once he arrived in the major leagues. Paid under the table.

Standing on Big Pine Key, the sun rising before him, Osbek Castillo knew he was now entirely dependent on this stranger who'd come to collect him. "You don't know how it works, so you just do what they tell you to do," he says. Soaked with saltwater and caked in mud, he climbed into the car, along with the other ballplayers and a teenage boy who'd been on the boat.

Three hours later they stumbled into the Miami home of Andy Morales — who rushed to embrace the boy, his son. To baseball trivia buffs Andy Morales is the third baseman who hit a three-run shot for Cuba to help beat the Orioles in Baltimore in 1999. To Yankees fans he's the Cuban defector signed in 2001 by George Steinbrenner for $4.5 million — only to be accused by the team of lying about his age and have the Yankees try to void the contract. (They wound up settling for an estimated $2 million.) To the U.S. attorney, Morales was the fellow with Ysbel Medina-Santos ("Javier") when Medina-Santos was arrested for drug trafficking in Chicago in 2005 (en route to seeing their friend and fellow Cuban Jose Contreras pitch for the White Sox). And to Gus Dominguez he was, along with Yuniesky Betancourt, one of just two former clients who wouldn't testify on his behalf.

Even now none of the ballplayers believes a sports agent had selected them for defection and arranged their transport. On the witness stand Yoankis Turino said that, as he sat in Andy Morales's living room, he heard his hosts on the phone, trying to sell them to another agent, named Bill Rigo. "I never heard the name Gus Dominguez," says Osbek Castillo. "I don't think he paid to get me out. Why would he?"

The prosecutors did their best to portray Gus Dominguez as a fancy-pants sports agent with money coming out of his ears. The charge didn't square with the rest of the case — if he was so rich, why did he need to refinance his house to pay the smuggling fee? But U.S. government prosecutors aren't in the fairness business. They repeatedly noted that Dominguez was a "Beverly Hills sports agent," even though his business was actually in Encino. They said several times he lived in a "gated community." The Dominguez home is indeed in a gated community — along with approximately a third of new homes in their county in Southern California. Twice a month Delia Dominguez must pause to allow her black metal gate to creak open before she pulls onto the freeway behind the house to make the hundred-mile drive north to her husband's prison, the Taft Community Correctional Facility, where there is no fence.

Taft prisoners are allotted three hundred minutes of phone time and twenty "points" for visitors each month. Visiting days are Friday (a cost of four points), Saturday (eight), and Sunday (six). She'd prefer to visit her husband on Fridays. But she's been forced to take on more work to pay the lawyers, whose bill is $200,000 and counting. Having spent twenty-two years as a school psychologist for children with special needs, she had to take a second job. Now it's weekends or not at all.

We arrive at a low gray building, surrounded by miles of California desert, to find snaking out the door a trail of loved ones: parents, girlfriends, mothers with children too small to fully understand where their daddy is and why. Joining this line is still something of an otherworldly experience for Delia Dominguez. From the moment the trial started, she says, "I felt that I was outside of my life, looking down on our lives. Gus loved this country and what it stood for. He loved this country. When I heard them say, 'The United States of America versus Gus Dominguez,' my heart just sank."

A few minutes after we're admitted to the cafeteria through one door, Gus Dominguez enters through another, dressed in khaki pants and a white T-shirt. In the seven months he's been in prison he's lost forty-five pounds. If he loses his appeal he'll miss his son's graduation from college, and, quite possibly, his daughter's wedding and his parents' funerals. He may even miss the next revolution in Cuba and the mass exodus of the players he knows better than anyone outside the country. He could be sitting in the middle of a billion-dollar transaction. Instead he'll be in here, teaching math and English grammar to fellow prisoners for thirty cents an hour. "They're smart people in here," he says with a smile. "We have eight lawyers, three judges, and two mayors."

His own lawyers he hasn't heard from in six months. During the trial he worried they were distracted. Now he has reason to believe it: his lawyer Ben Kuehne — who, oddly enough, also represented Al Gore in critical Palm Beach County during the 2000 election recount — has just himself been indicted by the U.S. Department of Justice in Washington, D.C., for money laundering. (Mr. Kuehne has declared his total innocence of the charges.) Still: Why couldn't he convince the jury that Gus Dominguez was the sort of man who tried to fix it himself when his children were threatened by people he'd never met, people who made their livings doing many bad things? Why hadn't they explained to the jury how little commercial sense it made to smuggle those particular players? In his office Dominguez had kept a wish list of Cuban baseball players. The ones he'd been accused of smuggling weren't even in his top fifty. (Leslie Anderson, on the other hand, still makes his eyes twinkle.) Why didn't they hammer home the point that a man trying to hide what he's doing doesn't wire the money but pays in cash? A man who sends a wire is a man who wants proof that he's paid — as Gus had, in case the smugglers tried to deny it. Why hadn't the jury learned how the baseball-player-smuggling trade actually worked — with the smugglers doing it all on their own and billing directly the players who made it to the big leagues, without anyone ever finding out? Why had it so clearly worked against him to testify on his own behalf? "I believed the jury would believe my story," he says, "and I was wrong."

And why, in the end, was this crime he says he didn't commit so awful? Even more than ordinary citizens, Cuban ballplayers are prisoners of the state. "The most prized possessions to Fidel Castro were the baseball players," says Dominguez. A democratic government should encourage, not punish, those who seek to help victims of tyranny to escape. "If this country cannot say to those people, 'Come to us — we'll give you freedom,' where else can they go?"

For the last fifteen years Dominguez has followed the Cuban national team wherever they've traveled outside Cuba. He'd sit in the same seat in the stands, behind the bullpen, and the players would holler their room numbers so he might call them to discuss their future plans. When the national team was playing in Saltillo, Mexico, in 2002, a pitcher named Maels Rodriguez knocked on his door and announced he wanted to defect. Rodriguez was then throwing 101-mph fastballs and widely regarded as one of the finest pitchers not just in Cuba but on the planet. Gus had called around and thought Maels's first contract would come in at around $40 million. On the road to the United States, however, Maels seemed tired, so they stopped at a hotel. In the middle of the night Gus awakened to find Rodriguez gone. As his agent slept, the pitcher had called his wife back in Cuba to tell her that all had gone as planned: he was on his way to the United States. But his wife had wept, and Maels changed his mind and grabbed a taxi back to his Cuban team. A year later Maels fled Cuba again, but by then his arm had been destroyed by the neglect and overuse common in a system that didn't put a price on it, and there was no longer a market for his services. "That was a $40 million mistake," says Dominguez. "It's one thing I've never understood about Cuban players. When they have a chance to defect, they don't seize it. They're torn."

Cuban lives were defined by accident, and now so was Dominguez's. It was an accident that he ever became a sports agent. It was an accident that he didn't become so rich from Cuban baseball players that the charge of smuggling lesser players would seem risible. It was an accident that led him to this prison. Of the judicial system: the trial didn't need to be in Key West; it might have been held in Miami, and in Miami, with a jury more savvy about matters Cuban, he may have won. Of characters: if the Seattle Mariners' shortstop had been a different sort of kid he'd have come forward and told the truth about his dealings with his smugglers. Of timing: Fidel might have died, Bush might have lost, Americans might have been less hysterical about immigration. "If you want to know what I really think," Dominguez says, "I think the attorney general wanted to get someone doing something with illegal immigrants who, when they got him, hit the newspapers."

It's hard for a man in a prison uniform to seem innocent, but Gus Dominguez seems innocent. Did he do what the U.S. government says he did? I doubt it. Does it matter? No. He picked the wrong time to be caught between the United States and the strangers who saw it as a place where they might create better lives. He'd been a bridge between cultures, at a time when such bridges were being blown up.

There are reasons why Michael Lewis has sold about a billion copies of Moneyball. *The reasons are all on display here: tight prose, wonderful research, great analysis. Gus Dominguez should have had Michael Lewis as his lawyer.*

L. JON WERTHEIM

Breaking the Bank

FROM SPORTS ILLUSTRATED

WITH FLASHING BLUE LIGHTS illuminating his rearview mirror, Colin Dixon pulled his car to the side of a deserted road. It was around six on the evening of February 21, 2006, and Dixon had just clocked out from his job at the Securitas cash depot in Tonbridge, England, thirty miles southeast of central London. A purposely nondescript, brown building tucked behind a car repair garage, the depot serves as a regional warehouse of sorts, where cash for the Bank of England is stored and disbursed. Dixon, fifty-two, was the manager.

Now, driving home, he figured he was getting pulled over by an unmarked police car for a routine traffic stop. A tall, athletic-looking man in a police uniform approached. Though it would turn out that the cop was no cop at all — the uniform was fake, the Kent police badge he flashed had been purchased on eBay, and the guy's face had been distorted with help from a professional makeup artist — Dixon was compliant. He got out of his Nissan sedan and was handcuffed and placed in the back of the other car.

He would later testify that the driver, a second man in uniform, turned and said menacingly, "You will have guessed we are not policemen . . . Don't do anything silly and you won't get hurt." When Dixon tried to adjust his handcuffs, he says the "officer" who'd apprehended him brandished a pistol and barked, "We're not f—ing about. This is a nine-millimeter."

Dixon was blindfolded and transferred to a van, then taken to a remote farm in western Kent. Meanwhile, two other fake cops drove to Dixon's home in the nearby town of Herne Bay, along

with accomplices in a second van. Greeted at the door by Dixon's
wife, Lynn, they explained that her husband bad been in a serious
traffic accident. They said that Lynn and the couple's young child
needed to accompany them to the hospital. Outside the home, the
Dixons were placed in the back of the second van and taken to
the farm, where the Dixons were reunited. At once relieved and
terrified, they were bound and held at gunpoint. Colin Dixon was
ordered to give the plotters information about the depot. "If you
cooperate, no one will get hurt. Otherwise," one abductor warned,
"you'll get a hole in you."

A group of at least seven men then drove to the Securitas depot,
Colin Dixon accompanying a phony police officer in a sedan and
his family bound in the back of a large, white Renault truck. By now
it was after midnight on the morning of February 22. Surveillance
video shows Dixon being buzzed into the depot with an officer beside him. Once inside, the fake cop overpowers the security guard
and buzzes in the rest of the robbers wearing ski masks and armed
with high-powered weapons, including an AK-47. Dixon told the
fourteen staffers working the graveyard shift, "They've got my family," and instructed them not to touch the alarms. He proceeded to
deactivate the security system and hand over the keys to the vault.
The Dixons and the staff were then bound and placed in metal
cages normally used for storing cash. The truck can be seen back-
ing up to a loading dock.

The robbers clearly knew their way around the depot — where
the doors were located and how they locked — and with good reason. One member of the gang, Ermir Hysenaj, twenty-eight, an Al-
banian immigrant, was the classic inside man. Months earlier, after
just a ten-minute job interview, Hysenaj had been hired for roughly
$11 an hour to work the evening shift at the depot. It was later re-
vealed that in the weeks before the robbery, he had come to work
wearing a small video camera hidden in his belt buckle.

For the next forty minutes, the gang emptied the vault of its con-
tents, wheeling metal carts filled with cash into the truck. The supply of £10 and £20 notes was so massive that by the time the truck
was filled to capacity, it accounted for only one-quarter of the
money in the vault. Still, the conspirators absconded with a haul of
£53 million, or more than $100 million.

If the caper didn't entail pyrotechnics worthy of, say, the current movie *The Bank Job*, it seemed to come off remarkably smoothly, at least from the robbers' perspective. All their discipline and meticulous preparation had paid off. There were no surprises. No one was physically injured, much less ventilated with bullets. No one had triggered the alarms. At around 3:00 A.M., Dixon's child was able to slither out of a metal cage and the police were summoned. By then the thieves were back at the farm divvying up the money — a bounty that one British prosecutor would later characterize as "dishonest gain almost beyond the dreams of avarice."

As investigators worked to crack the case, they began to suspect that the ringleader was Lee Murray, and that he and his pal Lea Rusha were the impostors who had first abducted Colin Dixon. Murray was no stranger to London law enforcement. He spent time in a juvenile detention center as an adolescent and later was tried and acquitted in a serious road-rage incident. Ironically, he'd also been questioned by police after a traffic stop in the area of the Securitas depot the summer before the robbery. But he was a prominent figure in pockets of the sports community as well, a fearsome British cage fighter who'd recently gone the distance against the great Brazilian champion Anderson Silva. Murray lost a decision and was paid the equivalent of a few thousand dollars for that fight. Now, Kent police contended, he was a fugitive in Morocco, luxuriating poolside at a villa in an upscale part of Rabat. Lightning Lee was now worth a small fortune in pounds sterling, they alleged, having just orchestrated the largest cash heist in history.

Lee Murray came into the world in 1977 with his fists balled, and he never quite seemed to unclench them. The son of a British mother and a Moroccan father — his given name is Lee Lamrani Ibrahim Murray — he grew up poor in public housing in a rough-and-tumble section near London's East End.

His salvation, such as it was, came through fighting. It wasn't so much what he did as who he was. By his own reckoning, he was a veteran of hundreds of street fights, lining up his target, transferring his weight, and then unloading punches that would seem to detonate on impact. After so many bare-knuckle brawls, he figured, not unreasonably, that he might as well get paid for his violence. He frequented boxing and kickboxing gyms, channeling some of his primal tendencies into mixed martial arts (MMA), the increasingly popular sport that combines the striking of boxing and Muay Thai with the ground game of wrestling and jujitsu. In particular Murray had designs on competing in the Octagon, the eight-sided cage used for bouts in the Ultimate Fighting Championship (UFC), the preeminent MMA league, which is headquartered in the United States.

Murray recognized that while his stand-up fighting was exceptional, he was at a loss when a bout went to the ground. That is, he needed to improve his grappling and jujitsu, disciplines predicated less on brute strength and aggression than on technique and smarts. So in the winter of 2000 he packed a duffle bag, flew to the United States, and made his way to gritty Bettendorf, Iowa. Pat Miletich, a former junior college wrestler and five-time UFC champion, had opened an MMA training gym in Bettendorf a few blocks from the banks of the Mississippi. Aspiring fighters came there from all over the world, making Miletich's gym to fighters what Florence was to Renaissance painters — though with bloodier canvasses.

To this day, Miletich's so-called Battlebox represents athletic Darwinism at its most brutal. Under the open-door policy, anyone is welcome to come and spar against a stable of regulars, many of whom have fought in the UFC. Self-styled tough guys show up every Monday. Those with the requisite skill and ruggedness stay. The other 95 percent are back on the interstate, bloodied and bruised, before sundown. Murray was one of the few who stuck it out. All bone and fast-twitch muscle, Murray was built like a sprinter. He stood six-foot-three but could cut weight and fight as light as 170 pounds. One Miletich fighter likened the kid with the Cockney accent to a British greyhound. "Lee Murray had world-class punching power," recalls Robbie Lawler, a top mixed martial arts fighter who sparred frequently with Murray. "Man, he would hit the mitts — pop-pop-POP-POP — and you would stop your workout and look over because it sounded like gunfire."

Murray crashed with other Miletich fighters before getting a room at a shop-worn motel not far from the gym. He wasn't averse to going out for a beer from time to time, but he'd come to America's heartland to train. When he wasn't in the gym, strip-mining Miletich for wrestling tips, he was lifting weights or going for runs under a big dome of Iowa sky. "Not one sign of trouble," says

Miletich. "One of his first days, I told him, 'It's up to you how far you want to go in this sport. At your height and weight and the way you hit, you could be a champion.' It was just a question of learning what to do once the fight hit the ground."

That spring, Murray entered a four-man MMA tournament in rural Wisconsin. After winning his first bout, Murray fought a burly Canadian, Joe Doerksen, now a UFC veteran. Murray showed his inexperience and got caught in a submission hold called an arm bar. He "tapped out" (surrendered) and cursed himself the entire drive back to Iowa. Having exhausted his budget, Murray returned to England. But he kept fighting and started to win. While MMA was becoming mainstream in the United States, the sport was still an underground pursuit in the United Kingdom. Still, among the niche audience Murray was regarded as perhaps England's best fighter. "He was one of those guys who rose to the occasion when he fought," says Paul Ivens, an instructor at the London Shoot-fighters Club, where Murray often trained. "You get guys who are tough on the street but they crumble in a real fight. He was one of the fortunate ones who would bask under pressure."

In July 2002 Murray attended a UFC card at Royal Albert Hall in London. The UFC was trying to spread the gospel to the other side of the pond, and in addition to the fighters on the card, most of the organization's brightest stars were on hand, including Miletich, Tito Ortiz, and Chuck Liddell. The headline bout featured a Miletich fighter, Matt Hughes, defending his welterweight title. After the card ended, the fighters repaired to a local club for an after party, a long-standing UFC tradition. At closing time the fighters and their entourages filed out. Walking down the street, Miletich felt a body on his back. It turned out to be a buddy of Tito Ortiz's. The guy was giving Miletich a playful bear hug, but suddenly Miletich felt the man getting ripped off his back. Another fighter had mistakenly believed that Miletich was being attacked. As the misunderstanding was being sorted out, Paul "the Enforcer" Allen, a longtime associate of Murray's, approached. In what he surely thought was a show of loyalty to both Miletich and Murray, Allen coldcocked Ortiz's pal.

This triggered what might rank as the Mother of All Street Fights, a scene that's become as much a part of UFC lore as any bout inside the Octagon. A who's who of the UFC and their entourages — drunk and in street clothes — began throwing haymakers indiscriminately. One posse member was knocked into the street and his arm was run over by a cab. Liddell got cracked in the back of the head and went ballistic. "I'm hitting guys with spinning backfists, just dropping guys," says Liddell. "It was a classic street fight. 'If I don't know you, I drop you.'"

In the mayhem Ortiz and Murray backed into an alley and squared off. According to multiple witnesses, Ortiz threw a left hook. He missed, and Murray then fired off a combination that decked Ortiz. The self-proclaimed Bad Boy of the UFC fell to the pavement. (Ortiz declined to comment to *SI*.) Officially, Murray was still a promising up-and-comer. But as accounts of the melee rocketed through UFC circles, the rangy British kid who poleaxed the mighty Tito Ortiz became a minor legend. "He's a scary son of a bitch," says the UFC's outspoken president, Dana White. "And I don't mean fighterwise."

As for sanctioned fights, Murray continued to win those too, mostly with devastating knockouts. In July 2003, he took on the well-regarded Brazilian fighter José "Pelé" Landi-Jons at a London event. After getting pummeled for a round, Murray regrouped and starched Pelé with a right hand. "He's probably still in the ring, probably still sleeping, catchin' flies," Murray gloated in the post-fight interview, mimicking the dazed, open-mouthed look of his opponent. "I know now that . . . [the] UFC have gotta open their eyes to me, they gotta take me. There's no ifs or buts." Sure enough, six months later Murray was summoned by the UFC to fight on a Las Vegas card. Concealing the inconvenient detail that he'd recently been questioned about his involvement in a road-rage incident that left a middle-aged motorist in a coma — he was later charged with causing "grievous bodily harm," but the jury failed to reach a verdict — Murray flew to the United States. He won the fight in the first round, trapping his opponent's head between his legs as he tried for a triangle choke, then finishing him off with an arm bar, hyperextending the man's elbow joint. He had reached the highest level, and all of his discipline and preparation had paid off: he'd won with a classic jujitsu maneuver, proving he was no one-dimensional fighter.

Murray's next bout came in the summer of 2004 in Cage Rage, a British UFC knockoff. He was pitted against Anderson Silva, the ferocious Brazilian who is currently the Zeus of MMA. Emboldened by his recent success, Murray snarled at Silva at the weigh-in. "He talked an unbelievable amount of s—," Silva remembers. "He said, 'I'm gonna do to you what I did to your friend Pelé.'" According to Silva, at one point Murray spotted a pair of his fighting shorts hanging from a chair. Murray grabbed them, ripped off a Brazilian flag patch, and tossed it at Silva. Though both fighters dispensed and withstood considerable punishment, Silva ended up winning by unanimous decision. As the two shook hands, Silva winked and pushed a gift into Murray's palm. It was the patch of the Brazilian flag. Still, Murray did himself proud, all the more so in retrospect, as Silva would go on to become one of the UFC's brightest stars.

But in September 2005, while training for an upcoming fight at Wembley Stadium, Murray attended a birthday party for a British model at Funky Buddha, a trendy club in London's Mayfair district. At around 3:15 A.M., a street brawl broke out. Murray was stabbed repeatedly in the chest, suffering a punctured lung and a severed artery. As he explained in a 2005 interview with the website MMAweekly.com, "One of my friends got involved in the fight. I tried to help him because about six or seven guys was on [him]. That's when I got stabbed. I got stabbed in the head first. I thought it was a punch. When I felt the blood coming down my face, I just wiped the blood and just continued to fight. Next, I looked down at my chest and blood was literally shooting out of my chest . . . It was literally flying out of my chest like a yard in front of me . . . I died three times. They said, 'Because you're an athlete and all the training you put your body through, that's what saved your life.'"

In the same interview, he casually noted that he had been stabbed outside the same club a week earlier. On that occasion, he'd "only" had one of his nipples sliced off. "It was just a minor stabbing, like these things happen every night of the week," says Andy Geer, a British promoter for Cage Rage. "He had stab wounds, bullet wounds. He was a proper from-the-streets kid."

Three weeks after the stabbing, though covered in zippers of scars, Murray had resumed his training in the gym. But realistically, his promising career was threatened. Particularly as mixed martial arts was becoming gentrified, what promoter would permit a man with such serious injuries to fight again? What if a scar opened dur-

ing a fight? Murray may have realized as much, and that could have
been an incentive to turn to crime.

The thieves took too much money. Had the Securitas gang made
off with, say, a few million pounds, it might have been one thing.
But the magnitude of the heist was such that overnight it became
an international cause célèbre. Even the most staid British newspapers covered the case breathlessly and exhaustively. The surveillance video from the depot was televised nationally and, inevitably,
made it online. Hundreds of British policemen were immediately
deployed to investigate. Hefty reward money provided an incentive
to anyone with any knowledge to come forward. "The gang had no
chance," says Howard Sounes, the British author of a forthcoming
book on the heist.

The suspects, though, also did plenty to hasten their demise.
Mirroring Murray's fighting career — disciplined and methodical
in MMA; arrogant and unthinking in street brawls — the same
thieves who had been smooth and poised in the actual pilferage
could scarcely have been sloppier in the aftermath. Some gang
members boasted to friends about the heist. One of the vehicles
used in the crime was set afire in the middle of a field, attracting attention. The money was poorly hidden. *Ocean's 11* quickly devolved
into a comedy of errors that recalled the Al Pacino classic *Dog Day
Afternoon*. "That's what happens," says Bruce Reynolds, the convicted mastermind of Britain's Great Train Robbery of 1963 and
now something of an armchair analyst of British crime. "All the
planning goes into the robbery and none goes into what happens
once you have the money."

Within forty-eight hours, police had made their first arrest.
Acting on a tip, they apprehended Michelle Hogg, a makeup artist
and the daughter of a policeman. Police found a quantity of latex
they alleged Hogg had used to make prosthetic disguises for the
robbers. (Under questioning, Hogg gave a statement saying she
was too scared to identify the thieves.) Later that day, police found
the van used to hold the Dixons. The next day, acting on another
tip, they located a second van used in the robbery. When they
looked inside, they found guns, ski masks, bandannas, and £1.3
million in cash. Acting on still another tip the following day, police
raided the homes of Murray's pal Lea Rusha, an aspiring mixed
martial arts fighter, and Rusha's friend Jetmir Bucpapa. In Rusha's

bedroom, police found plans of the Securitas depot, and hidden in a nearby garage was £8.6 million in cash.

All told, within ten days, five people had been charged. Millions of pounds had been recovered. And innumerable additional leads had surfaced. "A gang of misfits and bruisers pulled off the biggest robbery ever with considerable criminal aplomb," says Sounes. "But they were also stupid. This was a brilliant caper which turned into a farce."

The fate of the accused was sealed in the fall of 2006 when Hogg "went QE" (Queen's Evidence), as the Brits say, and testified against her co-conspirators in exchange for her freedom. She explained how she created the disguises so the gang members who posed as police officers couldn't be accurately identified.

On January 28, 2008, after seven months of trial during which more than two hundred witnesses were called, five men — including Rusha, Bucpapa, and Hysenaj, the insider — were found guilty for their part in the robbery and sentenced to a total of 140 years in jail. At the sentencing, authorities urged the public to resist romanticizing the caper. Fearing for their lives after giving extensive testimony, the Dixons entered the British equivalent of witness protection. So did Hogg, the makeup artist, who, according to multiple newspaper accounts, has a £7 million bounty on her head. "This crime was, at heart, a crime of violence," Nigel Pilkington of the Crown Prosecution Service told reporters. And with more than half the loot still unaccounted for, he vowed to continue to pursue the case. "This is not the end of the matter for these criminals," he said. "We intend to seize their ill-gotten gains, wherever they may be."

As the Securitas gang was being rounded up systematically, Murray apparently did not stand idly by. He left the country, leaving his wife and two children behind. Accompanied by his friend Paul Allen — he of the infamous UFC street brawl — he drove from London to Dover. There, according to Kent police, the two piloted their car onto a ferry headed for France. Murray is believed to have then traveled from France to Amsterdam to Spain, where he and Allen crossed the Strait of Gibraltar by ferry before finally finding sanctuary in Morocco.

If Morocco has historically held a certain exotic allure for Europeans, Murray is believed to have gone there for more practical reasons. Because of his lineage on his father's side, Murray is con-

sidered a Moroccan national. And Morocco has no formal extradition agreement with Great Britain.

By all accounts, Murray lived lavishly in northern Africa. He,
Allen, and two other friends from England, Gary Armitage and
Mustafa Basar, lived in a villa in Souissi, an upscale district popular with diplomats, in Morocco's capital city, Rabat. They tooled
around town in a Mercedes and spent prodigious amounts of
money on clothes, jewelry, electronic equipment, and jaunts to Casablanca.

After a few months, Murray reportedly spent close to $1 mil-
lion on a concrete manor around the corner from a cousin of
Morocco's king, Mohammed VI, outfitting it with an additional
£200,000 in upgrades that include marble floors and a fully
equipped gym. He also commissioned a giant mural above the hot
tub, depicting his victory in his one and only UFC fight. Allen
bought a property of his own nearby.

Shortly after Murray's arrival in Morocco in March '06, the Kent
police and Scotland Yard officials handling the investigation contacted Moroccan authorities and conveyed their concerns. Likely
unbeknownst to Murray, almost from the day he arrived in the
country he was under twenty-four-hour surveillance. On June 25,
2006, dozens of Moroccan police sealed off a portion of the Mega
Mall in Rabat, where Murray, Allen, Armitage, and Basar were
shopping. Because some of the suspects were experts in martial
arts (and were potentially carrying weapons), the small army of police officers was armed. After a physical struggle, the four men were
arrested. A Kent police spokeswoman asserted that Murray was arrested "for offenses linked to the £53 million Securitas raid."

When the Moroccan police went to Murray's residence, they
found cocaine and marijuana. The four men were charged with
drug possession and for violently resisting when police arrested
them at the mall, a crime a Moroccan judge termed "beating and
humiliating members of the security forces." They were found
guilty and in February 2007 received sentences ranging from four
to eight months in prison. Armitage and Basar were released soon
after for time served and returned to the United Kingdom. Allen
was extradited by the British government and is currently in a British jail, awaiting trial for his alleged role in the heist.

Murray's situation was somewhat more complicated. Because of
his Moroccan heritage, the United Kingdom's extradition request

was initially denied. "The British government has been putting a lot of pressure on Morocco," says Abdellah Benlamhidi Aissaoui, Murray's lawyer in Morocco. "But Moroccan nationals cannot be extradited [from Morocco]. That is the law, and the law should govern."

The Moroccan government discussed swapping Murray for Mohamed Karbouzi, a suspected terrorist living in London and sought for questioning in a 2003 Casablanca bombing. But the British government reportedly declined the exchange. Aissaoui says he has also heard that Britain might file a formal request to have Murray tried for the Securitas heist by Moroccan authorities in Morocco. While the extradition mess is being sorted out, Murray, at the behest of Britain, sits in a jail cell just outside Rabat, a caged cage fighter. "It's tough for him," says his lawyer. "He states that he's innocent. He has not participated in this robbery. He made money from his fights. He doesn't need to do this."

If Murray was in fact the ringleader, the Mr. Big, it wouldn't surprise Reynolds, the Great Train Robber. He compares a heist to sport. "You're challenging the authority of the state — the challenge is what it's all about," says Reynolds, now seventy-six and living outside London. "[Same as] Jesse James and Pancho Villa." What about the money? "It's a benchmark. Everyone wants to beat the record. It's like [Formula One] drivers want to beat Michael Schumacher's record."

Murray isn't granting interviews these days (his lawyer says that for Murray to speak to *SI* "is impossible right now"), much less speaking publicly about his guilt or innocence with respect to the heist. But he told a friend this story: after learning about Murray's saga — the street fights, the stabbing, the Securitas accusation — a London casino wrote him a formal letter explaining that he was no longer welcome at the establishment. That was fine by Murray. He says he wrote a quick note back: "Haven't you already heard? I hit the jackpot."

The personal stories that come out of the evolving world of mixed martial arts are going to rival boxing stories, which always have been the best sports page stories of all. Wertheim's tale of Lee Murray, bad actor in all senses of the term, sets a tough standard to beat. I would love to have seen that street fight. From afar.

ALAN PRENDERGAST

Dropped

FROM OUTSIDE

HANGING EIGHT HUNDRED FEET above Leg Lake, ten hours into
a long summer's day of climbing in Wyoming's Wind River Range,
Steve Herlihy was just starting to get comfortable. Getting into the
bubble, he called it. He was tired but focused, feeling good about
this latest adventure with his friend and mentor, Pete Absolon.

They were at the southern end of the Winds, three-quarters of
the way up an enormous cirque that flanks the lake like a half-mile-
wide backstop. Close to twelve thousand feet above sea level, the
cliff could be glimpsed from Absolon's house on the outskirts of
Lander, fifteen miles away, a stumpy tooth among more sensuously
contoured peaks. In seventeen years of climbing the area, Absolon
had never tried the cirque before; there was better rock not much
farther away. But late in July he'd gone camping at Leg Lake with
his wife, Molly, and their six-year-old daughter, Avery. He'd studied
the cirque, particularly a long shadow where the wall turned a corner as it wrapped around the lake. Two weeks later he was back
with Herlihy to try a line he'd found.

Herlihy felt honored to be included; Absolon was choosy about
the climbers he took into the Winds. Despite their age difference
— Pete was forty-seven, Steve thirty — Absolon had drawn Herlihy
into his circle as if he were a younger brother. They'd met on a National Outdoor Leadership School instructor seminar in 2001 and
had worked together on and off since. Absolon, a sturdy blond athlete with a constant smile, had recently become director of the
NOLS Rocky Mountain branch, while Herlihy had started law
school in Laramie, at the University of Wyoming.

Absolon was amped for the climb — planning meticulously, leaving Herlihy a flurry of phone messages in the final hours before their departure. They got a late start from Lander Friday afternoon and camped by the lake. On Saturday, August 11, they rose early, left Herlihy's two dogs at the cliff base, made their way across a talus field, and then climbed up three hundred feet of steep slabs to a small ledge, where the line Absolon had spotted began in earnest.

The climb was slow and tough. They found a couple of old bolts below the ledge, then nothing farther up. The route was steeper than it looked, and there was a quarry's worth of loose rock along the way. They cleared what they could, heaving the debris onto the glacier below, watching it land with hardly a sound. Herlihy started worrying about the amount of rock they were tossing and rappelled down to move his dogs back, then returned to the ledge.

Absolon led the crux pitch above the ledge, then two more pitches. Herlihy did his part, belaying and hauling and drilling in an occasional bolt. By late afternoon, they were 150 feet from what they'd agreed would be their goal for the day, a grassy ledge below the rim. Absolon set up an intricate belay; Herlihy was just below him and to the right. They lingered a few minutes, discussing how to handle the final pitch, a widening crack that curved right.

Herlihy was tired and ready to head down to camp. But Absolon wanted to nail the last pitch, and Herlihy agreed that it didn't look like much trouble, particularly with Pete in the lead. But right in the middle of their conversation, something came hurtling down from above. There was no warning, Herlihy recalls. Just a sudden *crack!* — and then a kind of white noise buzzing inside his head.

As soon as he heard the sound, Herlihy instinctively curled up next to the wall. But whatever had ripped through was already gone, leaving silence in its wake. When Herlihy looked up, he saw Pete hanging from the ropes, staring straight ahead. His eyes and mouth were open, but he was absolutely still.

Herlihy reached up. His hand went to the back of Absolon's neck and felt a warm dampness. He turned his friend around and saw the shards of his white helmet, the blood, the crushed skull.

"His face was perfect," Herlihy says, "but I just knew he was dead."

*

To the Rodolph brothers of Casper, the Leg Lake Cirque was known as the China Wall. They'd visited the rim several times before, coming up the back way, a steep but tolerable hike through neighboring Upper Silas Canyon. Aaron, twenty-eight, had backpacked in the area for a week at a time, and Luke, twenty-three, had hiked the entire canyon rim by himself.

A large party of Rodolphs had made a three-hour drive from Casper to the canyon trailhead on Thursday, the night before Absolon and Herlihy left Lander. The group included Aaron, Luke, and their older brother, Isaiah; Eli Rodolph, a cousin from South Dakota; Eric McDonald, a family friend; and wives and girlfriends — eight adults in all, plus Isaiah's four children. They set up camp at a no-name lake and spent Friday fishing and hiking. On Saturday, Luke and Aaron decided to take Eli and Eric to the China Wall.

Although the trail up the canyon ends at Island Lake, the four kept going, to the towering headwall of the cirque. They all walked to the rim, which offered a panoramic view of the basin, the surrounding peaks, and Lander in the distance. It was a favorite spot that neither Aaron nor Luke had seen for a while. Aaron had been building a landscaping business in Casper, while Luke had spent four years in the U.S. Army's 82nd Airborne Division, including two tours in Iraq, before coming home to work with his brother.

They saw no one after leaving the trail. They spent half an hour on the rim, soaking up the scenery and tossing rocks down toward Leg Lake. Later, Aaron would estimate that the group had pushed four or five small boulders over the cliff. "It was really awesome to watch the rocks fall," he recalled. "You could see every bounce, every hit, all the way to the glacier."

Around five, the Rodolph party decided to make their way to a new spot a quarter-mile away, where the rim becomes a series of jagged overhangs above the basin — a good place to watch rocks fall, they figured. Luke led the way to a fifteen-foot promontory jutting into space. He went out a few feet, peered over the right edge, picked up a bowling ball–size hunk of granite, and launched it into the void. Then he crouched down and leaned farther over the edge to watch its descent.

His new position gave him an unimpeded view of the area below. He saw, to his surprise, two men in white helmets two hundred feet beneath him. And at the same moment he registered their presence, the plummeting rock struck one of the men directly on the head.

Herlihy couldn't see where the rock had come from, and he assumed it had broken loose naturally. In the suspended silence that followed Absolon's death, he fought a surge of panic over the possibility that more was on the way. "I was a hundred percent sure the next rock to come down was going to hit me," he says. "I tried to think like Pete."

Herlihy wrestled with Absolon's body to retrieve the gear he'd need to get down. Blood spilled all over him, on the rope, and on the haul bag. He considered bringing the body along but decided the effort would slow him down and might get him killed. Even without the extra weight, it took him an hour to rappel to the ledge. Once there, he tied the ropes together and fixed them for the final rap to the base. Then he ran — and stumbled — down the scree field in his climbing shoes.

Herlihy retrieved his dogs and dunked his head in the lake, trying to wash off the blood and spitting to get rid of the pungent, metallic taste in his mouth. He looked around in the twilight, not sure what to do. He was startled to see four young men running toward him. The first one was crying.

"I'm so sorry for your loss," Aaron Rodolph said. He was panting after the long run down from the rim.

"What happened?" Herlihy asked.

A pale, lean young man, more subdued than the first, approached him. "I threw a rock," he said.

Herlihy stared at him. "Did it hit another rock or something?"

"No," Luke Rodolph said. "That was the rock."

Herlihy took a moment to digest this. It wasn't a loose rock that had killed his friend. This kid had *thrown* the rock. Herlihy didn't know what to say. What came out of his mouth next amazed the Rodolph brothers, who were half expecting him to attack them. He looked at Luke and said, "I forgive you."

Wordlessly, the four men gathered around Herlihy. Aaron put his arm around him and asked if it would be all right if they prayed. Herlihy nodded, and Aaron began murmuring softly in the dusk.

Ultimately, it would be up to Steve Herlihy to tell people what had happened to his friend, to describe how one of Lander's most respected, confident, and skilled climbers had died because a stranger threw a rock for fun. It was an awful story to tell, bound to trigger outrage and bewilderment, but Herlihy ended up recounting the details, Ishmael-like, again and again — to sheriff's deputies, to colleagues, and to Absolon's family and close acquaintances. It was important to him that people understand how alive Pete was, how suddenly he'd been snatched away.

But nearly fifteen hours would pass before he had a chance to tell anybody anything. First he had to spend a long, surreal night with Luke Rodolph. Aaron told Herlihy he had called 911 on his cell phone from the rim and that help was on the way. Right after the impromptu prayer session, the others decided to return to the family campsite, while Luke volunteered to stay behind; he and Steve would hike out in the morning.

As the sun went down, Herlihy wandered out to the lake to be alone, but dropping temperatures soon lured him to the fire Luke had built. Over the next few hours, the two men talked, shared some whiskey, and waited for dawn. Herlihy spoke about Molly and Avery and what a great husband and father Pete was. Absolon had been his boss at NOLS, he explained, generous with his advice and hard-earned experience but never taking himself too seriously. He was, in short, Herlihy's hero. Rodolph listened quietly.

"I know it probably doesn't seem like it, but I am really sorry about what happened to your friend," he said. "I want to cry, but I just can't do it. I've seen a lot of death."

In a flat voice, Rodolph described his time in Iraq — seven months in Fallujah, five in the northern Kurdish provinces. He'd lost a close friend two weeks into his first deployment, after they changed seats one morning in a Humvee. His buddy was sitting in Rodolph's place when an IED went off. Luke said he lost five friends in all. The only comfort he could find, he added, was his Christian belief that the deaths had been God's will. Everything happened for a reason.

The remark grated on Herlihy. He could see no reason why Pete was dead. But he didn't want to argue; right now he just needed to keep talking. He asked Rodolph why he hadn't run away — after all, nobody outside his family had to know he'd thrown the rock. Rodolph said he couldn't run from God. He was willing to do whatever was needed "to make things right."

"We had a long conversation about what that meant," Herlihy says. "He thought he was going to jail."

The talk, like the fire, died down after a while. At one point in the night, a helicopter circled above them, raking a searchlight across the face of the cirque. The next afternoon, a copter-borne rescue team from Grand Teton National Park arrived and got Absolon down. By that time, Herlihy and Rodolph had hiked to Herlihy's truck and driven to his home in Lander. They spoke little on the way.

Herlihy expected the whole world to be changed, but when he reached his house he realized that almost no one in town had heard about Pete's death yet; the coroner was waiting for the body to be retrieved before contacting the family. Once inside his front door, Herlihy started sobbing as he told his girlfriend, Wendy, what had happened. Then, leaving Rodolph standing alone in the front yard, he headed over to the Absolon place to do what he'd dreaded doing since he came off the wall: tell Molly that Pete was gone.

When he returned hours later, emotionally exhausted, Rodolph was still in the yard. He'd tried to clean the blood off the rope and haul bag and waited for Steve's return so they could go together to give their statements to the police.

News of Absolon's death spread across town like a stain, then all over the country. A week later, under lowering skies, more than three hundred people streamed into a meadow near Sinks Canyon — a popular sport-climbing hub near Lander — for a memorial service. They all had Pete Absolon stories to tell, gleaned from what had been a full and remarkable life.

There were rock-climbing buddies from his early days as a guide at Seneca Rocks, West Virginia; tales of Mount McKinley's West Rib and big ice in Alberta; former NOLS students and staff who'd had life-changing encounters with Pete; people who'd met him climbing, biking, or elk hunting; and local parents who simply knew him as an enthusiastic dad, deeply involved in his daughter's school activities. Nobody could figure out how he made it all look so easy.

Lander-based NOLS instructor Gary Wilmot was once saved from serious injury by Absolon, who snatched him by the boot after he stumbled and slid headfirst down an icy gully outside of Cody, headed for a cliff. But he considers such heroics the least of his friend's accomplishments. "Pete was a very good rock climber, an exceptional ice climber and mountaineer," he says. "Maybe not world-class at any of these things, but there are very few climbers who put them all together as well as Pete did. He could always keep the rope moving up, and he got his students to believe they could make certain ascents and achieve goals far beyond what they thought they could do."

Born in Minnesota, raised in Texas and Maryland, as a teenager Absolon went from Boy Scout hikes to hanging out at the Gendarme, the legendary climbing shop at Seneca Rocks. He persuaded proprietor John Markwell to hire him as a guide and began putting up bold new solo routes. "Many of Pete's routes are thinly protected and just scary," says Topper Wilson, another Gendarme alum, now living in Colorado. "But his legs never shook. When he got nervous, he'd start muttering and talk his way through."

In 1986, while soloing at Seneca Rocks, Absolon came across twenty-five-year-old Molly Armbrecht, a Yale graduate and climber who worked for the nearby Woodlands Mountain Institute. Absolon informed Armbrecht that she and a companion weren't on the route they thought they were on. Armbrecht insisted she knew what she was doing. Molly and her friend pressed on, got lost, found their way down around midnight, and slinked past the Gendarme, where Absolon sat with his pals, watching with amusement.

The wedding came two years later, on top of the highest mountain in West Virginia. The couple moved to Berkeley, then Lander, where Pete took a NOLS instructor course and began working for the school. He called the place Blander at first but soon fell in love with it. At NOLS, Absolon emerged as a quiet but vital presence whose high spirits and people skills made him a valuable field instructor and administrator. Fatherhood compelled him to give up major expeditions, but he set up a swing for Avery at the base of Killer Cave, one of his favorite routes in Sinks Canyon, and continued to seek new adventures. He was always methodical and safety-conscious — which made his sudden death an even greater shock.

The Lander community was still reeling from other fatalities, including the 2006 death of Todd Skinner, one of the area's most celebrated free climbers, who died after his harness failed in Yosemite. But Absolon's death was fundamentally different — not an equipment failure but a rock, thrown by a clueless hiker — and it sparked anger as well as grief.

"Pete was an extremely conservative and accomplished climber who was doing everything right," says Phil Powers, executive director of the American Alpine Club and a NOLS staffer in Lander for nearly twenty years. "Climbers sign up for a certain amount of risk. But Pete didn't sign up for this kind of risk."

In the days before and after the service, reminiscences about Absolon piled up in a long-running thread on SuperTopo.com, a popular climbers' website. "He had serenity in his life," wrote Pete's oldest sister, Mary, "and we are all the better for this because it is a whole lot more fun being with someone who is living out their passions!" But the tragedy also prompted a more vitriolic thread, in which people described their own near-death encounters with rock throwers. Some pointed out that climbers cast plenty of stones themselves — not just to clean a route but for the gravitational fun of it. "Everyone who's never thrown a rock off a cliff, raise your hand," wrote one poster. "Gee, there are no hands up." Climbers even have a word for the pastime: trundling.

"Pete enjoyed trundling rocks," says Wilson, "but he always looked first."

Experienced climbers know to look carefully before they roll any rock, and the type of accident that killed Absolon is exceedingly rare. Falling objects are the third-most-common cause of climbing injuries, according to data compiled by the American Alpine Club for its annual publication *Accidents in North American Mountaineering*. But Jed Williamson, the series' managing editor, says that most accidents occur as a result of naturally falling rock and that, of some 625 reported deaths and injuries involving falling objects since 1951, only a handful resulted from rocks being thrown.

The worst case on record was a 1994 trundling incident that set off a fifty-ton rockslide down the north face of 12,799-foot Granite Peak, Montana's tallest mountain. The three young climbers who did it apparently thought there wouldn't be a problem, because the north face was a difficult, less-used approach to the summit. Unfortunately, climber Tony Rich, thirty-three, happened to be in the path of their barrage and was killed. The three were charged with negligent endangerment and received a combination of fines, community service, and jail time.

A few days after Absolon's memorial service, Fremont County district attorney Ed Newell announced that he would not file charges against Rodolph. As he saw it, this case was better suited to possible civil litigation than criminal charges. Yet he was careful not to describe Absolon's death as an accident.

"It was criminally negligent or reckless to throw the rock without first checking if anyone was below," he said. But there was no evidence that Rodolph intended harm; he simply didn't know Absolon was there. In addition, Newell noted, Rodolph had taken responsibility immediately, had been cooperative with authorities, had no prior record, and was a military veteran.

The decision distressed many of Absolon's friends. Powers believes that trundling injuries are often dealt with lightly because they happen in remote areas, but in his view that's precisely what makes them so dangerous. "If the argument is that this kind of thing happens because Pete was involved in a risk-taker's sport in a less civilized place, then I push back on both fronts," he says. "Yes, the rules are different in the backcountry: one's personal responsibility is heightened, not diminished. The frivolous tossing of a rock is even more irresponsible in the wilderness because the repercussions can be so much greater."

Not long after they came to Lander, the Absolons moved into an 1,100-square-foot log home east of town. The garage is now almost as big as the house; Pete added a climbing gym, financing the effort with $250 "membership fees" wrangled from friends. Mostly, though, it was a place where he could go to work out by himself.

"There are a lot of people who are members of that gym who have never climbed in it," Molly Absolon explains. "Almost everybody got suckered into joining."

These days, the phone rings frequently in the Absolon kitchen. Since Pete's death, Molly has been inside a tight network of family and supporters. Seeing the Leg Lake Cirque from her yard every morning triggers a wave of emotions. It's where Pete died, but it also reminds her of their last family camping trip, during which Pete and Avery sang and played games and Pete made fish chowder from the brookies that were practically jumping out of the lake.

"I remember thinking how great it was that she was comfortable in the mountains, that Pete was teaching her all this cool stuff,"

Molly says, sitting at the breakfast table as she talks publicly about her husband's death for the first time. "There are a lot of us who got to places we never would have gotten because he was willing to take us."

Molly had worked at NOLS herself, and she climbed mountains and skied down couloirs next to Pete. They never had "a huge conversation" about risk, but they both scaled back considerably when Avery was born. "It's the classic dilemma," she says. "This is who this person is, this is what you love about him, that's what our relationship is about. We thought we were being safe. It never, ever occurred to us that we had to worry about this —"

She breaks off. Molly shudders when she reads accounts that refer to Pete's death as a "climbing accident." Pete and Steve could have been at equal or greater risk from a thrown rock if they were hiking at the base of the cliff, she says. Such loose terminology is part of what troubles her about how the case has been handled by the authorities. "My anger at this point," she says, "is directed as much toward Ed Newell as Luke Rodolph."

Newell's statement that he wouldn't press charges mentioned that he'd consulted with Molly before reaching his decision — giving many people the impression that the victim's family didn't want to see Rodolph prosecuted. But Molly says she never took a position on the matter, that she told Newell it was his call to make. "I was still in shock," she says. "It's not like I could have any kind of perspective on the act or whether Luke did it intentionally. Newell showed me some law books, how this could be construed as a criminal case. Then he went into his reasons for thinking it wasn't a good idea to pursue charges. He threw in Rodolph's military service. But the fact that he's an Iraq veteran shouldn't be any part of the decision as to whether or not this is a criminal act.

"I agree that Luke Rodolph did the right thing after he did the wrong thing," she says. "But I just lost my husband and the father of my child, and I'm mad and sad. I'm struggling with this feeling that Rodolph has gotten off really lightly."

Newell declines to go into detail about his meeting with Molly but says he never intended to imply that she didn't want to prosecute — or that her wishes, either way, would have dictated the outcome. "We always try to get with victims and get their input, but we never let them make the call," he says.

His decision was based on a combination of factors, he adds, including the sheer freakishness of the accident. Locals say the Leg Lake Cirque attracts maybe one climbing party a year. Upper Silas Canyon is a popular hiking area, but few hikers go as far as the rim. For Absolon, Herlihy, and the Rodolphs to be in the same location at the same time; for Luke Rodolph's throw to line up perfectly with Pete's route — it all seemed to defy astronomical odds. "You could give somebody a pile of a thousand rocks and tell them to try and hit a dummy on the cliff, and he just couldn't do it," Newell told me. "It's like getting hit by a meteor or something."

Molly has made no decision yet about whether to pursue a civil suit. There's some life insurance, but the family lived largely on Pete's salary, and the prospect of going forward without her husband at her side, having to redefine herself and figure out how to live, seems overwhelming. "Money is not necessarily a determining factor in pursuing a civil case," she says. "It's not the point for me. I'm mainly looking for some accountability."

Recently, Molly had a dream about Pete. He said he was "98 percent okay" but missed her and Avery. He also assured her that his death had been swift and painless. But the dream was scant comfort. "I feel like my rudder is gone," says Molly. "More than anything, I'm just so sad for Avery. Pete was so involved in her life, and I was so grateful for that."

She smiles grimly. "You should go look at the gym," she tells me. "It's hard for me to go in there."

Since Pete Absolon's death, Luke Rodolph has lived quietly in Casper. He works for his brother's landscaping service and spends a lot of time praying and trying to "stay focused on my walk with Christ." The news that he wouldn't be prosecuted was no cause for celebration.

"I don't know if it was a relief or not," he says, sitting at the kitchen table in Aaron's house, occasionally wiping away tears with his sleeve. "Sometimes you feel like you should have to pay for what you have done. At this point, I've accepted that this is what God wants. But I take full responsibility for what I did. Pete's death was my fault. I can't ever justify it."

Aaron nods solemnly. "I'll never throw another rock off a cliff," he says. "My dad told me, 'That was an ignorant thing to do.'

Whether everybody else does it or not, whether you looked or you didn't, it doesn't matter. Maybe our experience up there just makes us more guilty."

Through an intermediary, the Rodolph brothers had asked if they could attend the memorial service near Sinks Canyon. They were told to stay away. They haven't tried to contact Molly directly, but they did issue a public apology during an interview published in the *Casper Star-Tribune*. One comment Aaron made to the reporter — "You know in your heart there is nothing you can do" — didn't go over well in Lander, where a memorial fund has been set up for Avery. Aaron says he meant only that he couldn't bring Pete Absolon back to life.

"There's no way to repay Molly," Luke says, "but if she asked us to do something, I'd do my best. I'd like to tell her to her face how sorry I am and be able to offer something. But I don't want it to be seen as an attempt to cover up what I've done."

The Rodolph brothers have left several phone messages for Steve Herlihy, who hasn't spoken to either of them since the accident. Herlihy says he isn't ready to talk to the brothers yet. He's still haunted by his own relentless memories of Leg Lake, including the three words of absolution he offered Luke.

"I regret that, actually," Herlihy says, "but that's how I felt at that point. I feel some responsibility toward Luke. I don't think he did it on purpose . . . but I feel guilty for not hating him. I feel guilty because of Molly. I lost a guy I knew, my hero. She lost everything.

"Maybe you don't get forgiveness that easily," he adds. "Maybe I need more time. In light of everything, why couldn't he have just looked?"

This has all the drama of a well-constructed short story except it came from real life, not the imagination. The careless act, the tragic consequence, the awkward lack of resolution . . . human beings are involved here, people we really get to know.

MIKE WISE

Searching for Answers
to a Painful Question

FROM THE WASHINGTON POST

HUNTSVILLE, TEX. — Gilreatha Stoltzfus fussed with the bandanna in her hair while she zigzagged across a patch of dried grass. Fidgety, annoyed, towing her cluttered purse over her left shoulder as if it were a backpack, the hard-featured woman of forty-three stopped suddenly and slithered her fingers through the chain-link fence of the visitors' area at Huntsville Unit, a maximum-security prison featuring thirty-foot red-brick walls, where she had come to see her son.

"Fuzzy, I need the keys to the car," she muttered to her husband in a tired rasp. "I left somethin' in there."

"Fuzzy!"

The ruckus made an armed guard motion for someone to control the woman.

Sitting on a wooden picnic table in the prison yard fifteen yards away, Carlton Dotson looked up. "Is Mom coming in today?" he asked his stepfather.

"I don't think so," Elmer Stoltzfus said quietly, looking at the ground. "Mom's havin' a hard time getting herself together today. Maybe tomorrow, Carlton."

She keeps saying she will be there for her son.

Five years ago this month, Dotson shot Patrick Dennehy, his teammate on the Baylor University men's basketball team, the first known case of a player killing a teammate in the history of U.S. intercollegiate athletics. Dennehy's disappearance, Dotson's pan-

icked drive home to Maryland, his confession to police, and the
subsequent discovery of Dennehy's body near a gravel pit just three
miles from the Baylor campus in Waco, Texas, generated headlines
across the country in the summer of 2003. The sordid tale was held
up as an example of the moral free fall of big-time college sports in
the United States.

This spring, Baylor returned to the NCAA men's basketball tournament for the first time since Dennehy's murder. As the school
celebrated that milestone, Gilreatha Stoltzfus stood outside the
Huntsville prison, wrestling with the internal demons that have
confounded her life, unable to collect herself enough to walk inside to visit her son.

Heartsick that she persuaded Dotson to plead guilty to murder
three years ago — a deal that resulted in a thirty-five-year prison
sentence — Gilreatha has a near manic obsession with visiting the
site of the killing, having convinced herself that only then will she
be able to square the stories her son has told her with what really
happened.

She got her Amish-reared husband from Pennsylvania Dutch
country to sell his home and antiques, buy a sputtering RV, and
move to East Texas last year. They live in poverty on a charitable
man's front lawn in the town of Conroe, about thirty miles south
of the prison, where she works scrubbing the impenetrable ring
around the pots used to boil refried beans at a Taco Cabana fast-
food restaurant.

She clings to the notion that Dotson, who showed signs of mental instability before and after the murder, should not be among
the general prison population, and that he was done wrong by his
attorneys, Baylor University, and the college town of Waco, which
had every reason to want the scandal surrounding the killing to go
away.

"I've never been this busted in my life," said Gilreatha, whom
people call Gail. "Anyone else would have turned around and went
home. But I can't let him down again. I let him down once. I
gave birth to this boy. That's the only thing that keeps me hanging."

The mother's guilt is layered, beginning with the pregnant girl
of sixteen from the tiny Maryland Eastern Shore community of
Hurlock, who gave up her baby so that her grandmother could

raise him and the girl could work and finish high school. The same
addictions that made Gilreatha an apparition in Carlton's life —
here one day and then gone for months, sometimes years — now
gnaw at her daily.

Closure only will come in Waco. "I've been trying to put this off
for . . . years," Gilreatha said. "I couldn't do it. But now I can't go
home until I see it."

Unshackled, Carlton Dotson ambled slowly toward a group of picnic tables where inmates are allowed weekend visits with family
and friends. The long, loping strides made through the gravel belonged to a six-foot-seven former player, who in 1999 led North
Dorchester High School to the Maryland 1A state basketball championship before ending up on scholarship at a Big Twelve school in
Texas.

His basketball now is played inside "Walls Unit," the nickname
for the Huntsville prison and its ominous, towering brick walls.
Seven Texas Department of Criminal Justice prisons dot the landscape in and around this East Texas town of about thirty-five thousand, about seventy-five minutes north of Houston. No prison in
the nation has performed more executions than the one that takes
up two blocks downtown; forty prisoners were put to death at the
facility in 2000 alone.

Dotson tugged down on the waist of his white prison jumpsuit,
sat on the wooden bench, and, in his first interview since his 2005
sentencing — the most extended public comments since the killing — tried to explain why he shot his friend and teammate twice
in the head.

"Have you ever felt fear?" Dotson said. "Not the fear when someone is waiting after school for you to fight. I mean, real fear?"

Other inmates were engrossed in conversations with visitors at tables nearby, but Dotson largely ignored them as he went back to
the beginning of the story, back to when he and Dennehy first met
in August 2002. Dave Bliss, Baylor's basketball coach, brought the
two rangy, twenty-one-year-old transfers to Waco that summer to
help fix a slumping basketball program.

Dotson began the 2002–2003 season as a key player, but his playing time decreased dramatically as the season wore on. After he
tested positive for marijuana in the spring of 2003, Bliss informed

him he would not be returning to the team, in effect rescinding his scholarship.

Dotson's estranged wife at the time, Melissa Kethley, had left Waco and returned home, so he asked Dennehy whether he could stay at Dennehy's apartment until he found another school where he could play basketball.

He and Dennehy purchased two pistols and a rifle because they felt some teammates were out to get them, Dotson said. He said he also believed Dennehy was using crystal methamphetamine in addition to marijuana — a combination that can lead to aggressive and psychotic behavior. (One of Dotson's attorneys, speaking on condition of anonymity, said there was evidence to suggest both players were using meth-laced marijuana.)

It was during this time, Dotson said, that he began to distrust his teammate. Nearly a week before the murder, somewhere between five and eight days, Dotson recalled, Dennehy pointed a gun at him. He said he was unsure if his friend was joking.

As he recounted what took place, Dotson frequently lowered his voice to a whisper — often interrupting his comments by saying, "I already told you too much." He frequently looked over his shoulder, as if fearful someone would overhear the conversation, yet he spoke with an eerie certainty of his version of the events.

"The day it happened, Patrick said, 'Hey, let's go get some weed,'" Dotson said, recalling that Dennehy pulled up to their apartment in his 1996 dark blue Chevrolet Tahoe sport utility vehicle. "Suddenly he takes all these turns. I don't know where we are. Then, while he's driving with his right hand, he points a gun at me with his left hand, like this," he said, mimicking a person positioning a pistol with his left hand underneath his right arm, which held the steering wheel.

They pulled off the road and made their way toward the gravel pit to shoot at some targets. Dennehy, Dotson said, was a good five to seven feet behind him as they walked into a clearing near a creek. They were both high on marijuana.

Dennehy fired two or three shots behind him, Dotson said, then he heard his teammate reload his pistol. That's when he panicked, he said. The next shot, he believed, was meant for him.

Dotson said he turned and fired a 9mm handgun, shooting his teammate in the head at close range, from maybe two to three feet.

But Dennehy's six-foot-ten, 230-pound frame would not go down. Dotson said he was making disturbing noises.

So he fired again.

"It was like slow motion," he said. "And he still had the gun in his hand."

"It had to happen," Dotson added solemnly. "That's the only thing I could think of when you ask if I have a regret about that day. It had to happen. My only regret is getting in the car. I wished I hadn't gotten in the car that day. I wish I'd said no."

Prosecutors were determined to sink Dotson's self-defense claim with evidence that the second shot was fired from behind Dennehy's ear — proof, they contended, of premeditated intent.

"They don't want to hear what really happened," Dotson said.

Afterward, he tried to drag Dennehy by his pant legs out of the open area and toward the creek. But Dennehy's shoes came off in his hands before he pulled him into the tall grass and out of view. He said he got the car keys out of Dennehy's pocket because he knew that was the only way he could get back to Waco. That afternoon, he would set out in the car on a panicked, 1,500-mile trip back home to the Eastern Shore, tossing the murder weapon in a lake along the way.

"I could understand tampering with evidence," Dotson said. "I moved the body. I got the car cleaned. I didn't call the police right away. I didn't stay at the scene of the crime. I realized I was trying to invent an alibi. And then I just started panicking. But I didn't plan this. It had to happen.

"I just don't want to be looked at as a bad guy. That's what everybody thinks I am, but that's not who I am."

The man called "an instrument of the devil" by Dennehy's stepfather at his sentencing hearing, who showed no emotion as he accepted the plea, said he now realizes the pain he caused.

"I'm starting to understand what his family meant to him, how his family loved him and cared about him," Dotson said. "This is the first time I've really known what family means."

Dotson's mother has spent much of the past three years convinced that her son's lead attorney had no interest in proceeding to trial because of the further avalanche of negative publicity it would bring Waco and Baylor University.

In hindsight, she said, she never would have influenced Dotson to plead guilty; he must serve at least half his sentence under Texas law. "At the time I thought I was doing the right thing," Gilreatha said. "Now I realize he shouldn't be in a regular prison."

She has spent more than eighteen months trying futilely to get someone to listen to the conspiracies eating away at her gut: that one of her son's attorneys was stunned the case didn't proceed to trial; that Dotson's mental state warrants psychiatric care, not imprisonment in Huntsville; and that her son is behind bars because Baylor, the world's largest Baptist university, wanted to cover up the truth, which may have included a drug-dealing network within the basketball team. Why else, she asked, would Dotson's lead attorney have two Baylor prelaw interns taking notes during conversations between Dotson and his legal representative?

"You'll see when we get to Waco," Gilreatha said.

Before the sentencing, part of the prosecution's report to District Judge Ralph Strother included FBI documents detailing Dotson's confession, in which he said "a higher power told him to talk to the FBI" and where to find Dennehy's body. Dotson told FBI agents that he thought people were trying to kill him because "he is Jesus, the son of God."

After initially being declared incompetent to stand trial, he was deemed competent by a state hospital psychologist who found his claim of hearing voices "suspect." But the psychiatrist also concluded that Dotson must continue taking antipsychotic medication.

Dotson, now twenty-six, sought mental health care late last year and had to be transferred from Huntsville to Rusk, Texas, where he was housed at Skyview Unit, a psychiatric facility, from November 27, 2007, until February 29, 2008.

Five years after the killing, his two court-appointed defense attorneys believe he received fair representation.

"I think that Carlton was in a paranoid state," said Russ Hunt Sr., who recommended Dotson plea to the court. "He thought there was a group of people trying to kill him. And he thought Dennehy had joined those people. He figured, 'I better eliminate him.'"

Under Texas law, differing states of paranoia do not meet the threshold for insanity defenses. "Being paranoid does not make you insane for criminal purposes," Hunt said.

The recent campus shootings by deranged gunmen at Virginia Tech and Northern Illinois added urgency to Gilreatha's decision to move to Texas from Pennsylvania, she said. She saw disturbing echoes of her son and his time at Baylor in what took place at the two schools.

"I want to get a law passed, where a college has to act like a guardian when they see a problem with a student like Carlton," she said. "If they didn't call the family, then they should have notified someone and had him see a professional. How many more kids are going to die because none of the schools know how to deal with this?"

Baylor claimed Dotson had seen a therapist while enrolled, but only attended two sessions.

Gilreatha bit her lip and shook her head. "I think back to when I had Carlton. If I ever knew I would bring a child into the world that could be in prison for killing another person, I would have . . ."

As a teenager, Gilreatha Waters got out of North Dorchester High School in Hurlock every day at 3:00 P.M. and by 4:00 P.M. had started her shift at the ConAgra chicken plant, where she cut wings and thighs and made boneless breasts until midnight. She usually fell asleep in school the next day from the exhaustion of a full-time job.

She never met her father, Nathaniel Thomas Jones, seeing him for the first time in a casket when she was thirteen. He died at age forty-two from sickle cell anemia in the back seat of his Cadillac Coupe de Ville somewhere in California. She copes with the blood disorder herself.

She married her first husband, a Haitian national, who gave her three sons. But he was violently abusive, Gilreatha said. He left her with deep, crisscrossing scars on her back, still visible today, after he cut the cord from the television and whipped her because he thought she had been with another man.

Gilreatha has five children — four boys and one girl — from three different men. She had a brief marriage to another man annulled before she met Elmer, who often weeps for his wife's past as she speaks and finishes much of her life story as if he lived it with her, including the night she said she conceived Carlton in September 1981, when she was sixteen.

Carlton was born nine months after Gilreatha and three teenage friends, all between sixteen and seventeen years old, finished a night of bowling in eastern Maryland — a night that led to an unplanned pregnancy. "I don't want Carlton to think that's why I didn't raise him," she said.

She began drinking heavily as an adult, and by age twenty-four, Gilreatha said, alcohol had escalated to heroin and then cocaine. She said she broke her addictions five years ago.

"I hated the smell of hard alcohol, but it was the only thing that killed the pain so I could go through the day," she said. "I'm a stuffer. I stuff everything I'm feeling."

In Hurlock, Mildred Waters, Gilreatha's grandmother and the woman who raised Carlton, still worries for Gilreatha. One of her fears is that she has again revived hope for Carlton, hope that Gilreatha and her demons have yet to deliver.

"She got him thinkin' things are looking good and I don't know if that's a good idea," Waters said. "Gilreatha made a whole lot of promises to him that she didn't keep."

Elmer and Gilreatha met at an antiques show in Chestertown, Maryland, soon after Dotson's arrest — a white, Amish man from Pennsylvania Dutch country, who swore off his strict religious and cultural upbringing years ago, and a black woman from a country hamlet in eastern Maryland.

After some conversation, Elmer asked Gilreatha whether she would take a paid job arranging antiques at his home. "Will you meet me here next week and help me clean up my place?"

She agreed, brought her clothes, and moved in with Elmer for a week.

"That was it," he said, as an instrumental of the Carpenters' rendition of "Close to You" played in the background of the Dairy Palace in Canton, Texas.

"We need to open this thing up because it's killing her," Elmer said. "With his mental state, we don't want him out. But the goal is to get him out of a regular prison."

They long ago ran out of cash. They have no health insurance. Among the eleven medications Gilreatha said she takes are the anti-anxiety drugs and antidepressants Zoloft, Xanax, and Trazadone. They recently spent $400 on prescription drugs, which "flat busted us," Elmer said.

They gave up a home, and the antiques they sold for income in

Pennsylvania Amish country nearly a year ago, paying off the mort-
gage and debts and using the remaining cash to purchase an RV
with a broken water pump.

"I told her, 'So what if this kills us?'" Elmer said. "'Right now
we're not living anyhow.'"

Gilreatha gazed vacantly past the tall grass, the tumbleweed, and
the creek bed, beyond the Texas prairie, maybe twenty yards from
where her son took another man's life. She had finally made it back
to Waco.

She pulled an orange bandanna tightly across her hair, and her
satin gold jacket and yellow capri pants provided the only splashes
of color amid the leaden mid-March sky and the grass just emerging from its winter dormancy.

Maybe five hundred yards off the main road, where the tracks
from four-wheel-drive vehicles led the way through the thicket, she
knelt down not far from the gravel pit, clasped her hands, and
wept.

"I could understand bein' upset, bein' angry," she said. "But
there's no way in the world you shoot somebody. Make me sick the
way I feel right now. Somethin' got into Carlton's mind, somethin'
bad."

For the better part of five years, she was convinced her son was
telling her the truth about what happened that day, that Dotson
had to shoot Dennehy to prevent his own death. Conspiracies tum-
bled about in her brain and she internalized the guilt that comes
from a mother telling her son to accept a plea bargain that would
result in a thirty-five-year prison sentence.

Baylor must be behind it, she thought. "Take this school out of
here and what you got? Nothin'. A ghost town."

But the more she walked near the creek bed, to the spot where
Patrick Dennehy's body was found, the more Gilreatha had doubts.

"This isn't how Carlton told us it went down," she said to Elmer,
who nodded. "Next time I see him he better answer me some questions about what really happened that day. 'Cause none of this
looks the same from what he told us."

Carlton Dotson's mother suddenly spun around, seething. Her
son had put her through hell for more than four years, and she
came to a realization: he wasn't well in the head, and hadn't been

for a long time. Dotson's body was here that day, but his mind wasn't.

"You know what I think? I think Carlton lured him out here. I bet Carlton brought that boy out here to kill him."

The bizarre and the tragic are in an equal mix here. How do you make sense out of insanity? You want to hold Gilreatha Stoltzfus's hand, but you have no idea what to say to her.

TRACY ROSS

The Source of All Things

FROM BACKPACKER

ALL MY DAD has to do is answer the questions.

Just four simple questions. Only they aren't that easy, because questions like this never are. We're almost to the Temple, three days into the craggy maw of Idaho's Sawtooth Mountains, and he has no idea they're coming. But I have them loaded, hot and explosive, like shells in a 30-30.

It's July, and hotter than hell on the sage-covered slopes, where wildfires will char more than 130,000 acres by summer's end. But we're up high, climbing to 9,000 feet, and my dad thinks this heat feels cooler than the heat in Las Vegas, where he lives. Four days ago, he met me in Twin Falls, a town 140 miles south of here where I grew up, after driving north across Nevada, past other fires, including one on the Idaho border. The air is thin, the terrain rugged, and his body — sixty-four years old, bowlegged, and fifteen pounds overweight — seems tired and heavy to me. He struggled the last half-mile, stopping every few feet to catch his breath, adjust his pack, and tug on the big, wet circles that have formed under the armpits of his shirt, which reads TOOT MY HORN.

At sunrise this morning, we slid out of our bags, washed up, made breakfast, and caught a few fish. When we finally started hiking, we climbed out of one basin and into another, inching up switchbacks sticky with lichen and loose with scree. When we came to the edge of one overlook, we saw smoke rising on the horizon from a fire that was crowning in the trees. And when we arrived at the lake with the dozen black frogs, we called it Holy Water Lake, because it was Sunday and we did feel a bit closer to God.

I know my dad is hurting, because I'm hurting too — and not just my legs and lungs, or the blisters on the bottoms of my feet. We have barely spoken since we left the dock at Redfish Lake three days ago, left the boat and the worried Texans who looked at our forty-pound packs and said, "You're going where?" I'm sure we seemed an odd pair: an old man and his — What was she? Daughter? Lover? Friend? When we stepped off the boat, I wanted to turn back. But the Temple was out here somewhere, and, besides, I still hadn't decided if I was going to kill him outright or just walk him to death.

We continue climbing above Holy Water Lake until, a few hundred feet from a pass, we turn off the trail. In front of us is a cirque of smooth granite towers, sharp and fluted, like the turrets on the Mormon Tabernacle. The Temple shoots out of a giant boulder field. Loose rocks slide down vertical shafts and clatter to the ground. Quickly but carefully, my dad and I crab-walk across the jumbled blocks, insinuating ourselves into tight slots and willing our bodies to become lighter, so the boulders won't shift beneath us and break our legs.

When we get to the wide, flat rock that looks like an altar, we stop. He slumps over, sips water, and chokes down a few bites of food. His eyes, the color of chocolate, begin to melt, and the corners of his mouth tremble, like he's fighting off a frown.

Hunching next to him on the granite slab, I squint into his red-brown, sixteenth-Cherokee face. I dig into my pack and take out my tape recorder.

That's when the questioning begins.

If we'd thought about it, back when I was a kid and my dad first joined the family, we might have nominated him for an award. Idaho Dad of the Year. Or the Elks Club Father's Day prize. In the mid-'70s, after he married my mom and before the trouble set in, he built us an Idaho dream.

We had a RoadRunner camper, and every Friday between Memorial Day and the end of hunting season, my dad would leave his job at Van England's store in Twin Falls, change into his camping clothes, and load his new family into his bright yellow Jeep Cherokee. While we sipped root beers and adjusted our things, he'd grease the ball on the tail of the Jeep, pull up the trailer steps, and ease us back until the hitch on the RoadRunner took hold. By the time the other dads on Richmond Drive were cracking their first weekend beers, we'd be chugging across the Perrine Bridge, past the lava flats with their searing heat, and approaching the cool, clean air of the Stanley Basin, where the Sawtooth Mountains top out at 10,800 feet.

If my dad loved being outside — hunting, hiking, and fishing Idaho's pristine mountains and streams — he quickly taught me to love it too. I was four and my brother was eight the year my parents married, following a blistering whole-family courtship that included picnics at Shoshone Falls, ski trips to Soldier Mountain, and drive-in movies watched from bean bags in the back of my future dad's 1949 Willys Jeep.

My real dad, a U.S. Navy man who held a kegger outside my mom's hospital window the day I was born, died when I was seven months old after an aneurysm exploded in his brain. My brother and I were too young to feel the gut-punch of his death — the disorienting, life-sucking loss that shook my mom so violently the doctors sedated her. But when lanky, bell-bottomed Donnie Lee walked through the door of our military-pension house, it was as if we remembered to miss something we'd never known. By the time my parents were married, the family honeymoon was already in full swing.

My new dad's pride and joy — after his new family — was the RoadRunner he bought in 1976. On Thursdays, and sometimes as early as Wednesdays, he'd start loading it with supplies: bags of chips, Tang mixed with tea, and twelve-packs of mini-cereals for my brother and me. One spring, he painted a yellow swoosh on the side to match his Cherokee. It came out looking like a streak of mucous, but we all told him we liked it anyway.

During the winter, when the roads were too snowy to pull the trailer, we feasted on elk steaks and venison stew made from the bucks my dad had harvested near Rock Creek and Porcupine Springs. But come mid-June, we were in full summer-camping mode.

In the long shadows of the Sawtooths, we built castles in the freshwater sand and swam out to a giant rock a few hundred feet from shore. Sometimes, other families came with us, and all the kids would hike together, searching for bird nests along wooden walkways that stretched over primordial wetlands, or climbing on top of beaver lodges before taking off our clothes and jumping into the murky ponds. At the time, the streams pouring out of Redfish Lake teemed with sockeye salmon on their way home from the mouth of the Pacific Ocean, nine hundred miles away.

As a little girl, I stared down at their rotting bodies, the wild look in their bulging eyes, and the long, hooked jawlines dotted with razor-sharp teeth. Though I couldn't have articulated it then, I wondered what demon drove them to travel so far inland — without food or rest, for weeks — to decompose and die at Redfish Lake.

It's early June, dusk, and the whole family is naked. We've stopped off at Russian John hot spring on our way to Redfish Lake.

Our clothes — my mom's silk bra next to my size 6 flowered panties, big jeans and little jeans in a heap, a kid's down vest, and a grown man's hunting cap — are piled near the steaming pool that's just past the ranger station on Highway 75. One by one, we slip into water that smells less like sulphur and more like infused sage. My parents slide down the algae-covered rock and laugh — at the urgency, the cold air, and the slight, acceptable indiscretion we are committing, uphill and just out of range of the car beams passing below.

We soak until the last rays of sun paint the mountains pink. We all scan the hillsides for deer. Spot one, and you earn a dollar: my new dad's rule. A star — my new dad points it out — burns itself into view. "Wish on it," he says, and we all do. When we begin to prune, we get out, tug on underwear and shirts, and rush back to the Jeep, where our black lab, Jigger, awaits.

When I think back to those early moments, I see a family, newly formed and on the front end of a great adventure. I see the four of us, back on the road after soaking in the springs. We are dried off and warming up, the blast of the heater drowning out Lynyrd Skynyrd on the radio. It's dark now, and I have moved into the front seat. My dad and I are calling truckers on the CB using our handles, Pinky Tuscadero and Coyote. Outside the window, the Sawtooths rise into the night.

In my last, best memory of 1979, autumn light reflects off a golden Redfish Lake. Decaying aspen leaves smell good, in a sad, slowed-down way. Though I am only eight, these trips to the mountains have already become a foundation upon which I will build my identity. I'm telling my dad how I want to go into the Sawtooths, next summer maybe, on a real backpacking trip. He stomps out a cigarette and puts it in his pocket, then smiles tenderly. Because I don't know what's coming, I think this is how it will always be.

He takes my hand and leads me back to the trailer, where my mom and brother are fixing dinner. We crunch hard-shell tacos and guzzle cups of milk. Later, at the foldout table, we play cards — Spoons or Go Fish. My dad drinks beer and my brother begs for a sip. When I go to bed, my mom does too, on the foldout couch directly below my foldout bunk. She reads for a while, then drifts off. I listen to my dad and brother. "Pair of jacks," says my dad. And I fall asleep.

When I wake up, sandpaper is crawling on my skin. At least that's what I think it is, until I feel hot breath against my cheek. The bunk bed where I am sleeping is two feet from the camper ceiling, and it's coffin-dark. I can't sit up, so I lay perfectly still, while my eight-year-old mind tries to understand sandpaper and beer-soaked breath. At first, I think someone has broken into the trailer. I must be alone, or my mom would jump up and scream. My dad would grab his rifle and start shooting. My brother would run out of the trailer and hide in the trees.

The sandpaper keeps moving, five round pieces the size of dimes. It scrapes my stomach, sliding along the top of my pajama pants, where it hesitates, then dips down. Completely disoriented, I try to scream, but no sound comes out. Holding my breath, I force myself to buck — away from the beer and abrasion, into the tightest ball I can make. The sandpaper stops moving. The breath grunts away from my face.

I'm swimming in tar. I will suffocate. I lie awake listening to the wind beat the trailer for hours.

The next morning, my dad and I walk to Fishhook Creek. I lead, he follows. I find a log, whitewashed and slippery, and inch across it to the center. My dad scoots behind me, lights a Camel, and sits down so that the soles of his black work boots just skim the ripples, which are metallic and bright.

I feel itchy and sick to my stomach, like I've been sunburned from the inside out. My dad puffs on his cigarette, exhaling streams of smoke that hang in the frosty air.

"I know what you're thinking," he says. "I know what you think that was."

I consider asking him what he thinks I'm thinking, because what I am really wondering is how the salmon, struggling against the current below my feet, breathe in the murky eddies that disappear under the grassy bank. I am imagining, in some abstract and childish way, that I will dive in the river and let it flush me downstream. I hold my breath and let my dad continue. He puffs on his cigarette, then throws the butt into the creek.

"I mean it, Tracy," he says. "I was only tucking you in."

"What's a pretty girl like you doing hiking alone?"

The guide at the cash register asks this when I step up to pay for my maps. It's early October, 2006, and the thermometer reads 41°F. I'm standing at the counter at River One Outfitters in Stanley, Idaho, a tiny town at the base of the Sawtooths. Two months earlier, a congressman's kid had gone missing on a solo hike. A search was mounted: helicopters, volunteer ground crews, and rangers all picking and flossing the granite teeth. There'd been no sign of him until a couple of days ago, when a corpse dog got onto — and then lost — a scent. This afternoon, I will hike eight miles into the Sawtooths.

"I'm prepared and conservative," I tell the man as he rings up the maps. But it's only a brave front. Two days ago, I flew to Boise, rented a car, and started driving east. On the freeway, the early October sun seemed too bright. But as I wound through Lowman, big stands of trees diffused the light, until the air took on a golden hue that I associate only with southern Idaho.

I didn't plan to be driving down this road, concealing an open beer, listening to Zeppelin on the radio. I have a husband and two kids at home. It's coming on three decades since my dad put his hands down my pants in the family trailer at Redfish Lake. I've been to therapy — years of it — and energy workers, astrologists, and priests. I've even been back to the Sawtooths, including once with my parents and kids. I thought it would be romantic to show the boys my favorite childhood place. They were babies, and they dug in the sand near the dock. We took off their diapers and let them wade among tiny flickering minnows that flashed like silver paperclips between their chubby legs.

Yesterday, I drove out of Sun Valley and pulled off the road at Russian John hot spring. I walked to the small, steaming pool where my family used to soak, and stood there imagining us naked under the stars. I didn't get in. After an hour, I walked back to the car and drove toward Redfish Lake. I stopped at our favorite campsite near Fishhook Creek. And I found the spot where my dad and I once balanced on a log in the early autumn light.

Some people say you can heal yourself just by returning to the scene of a crime. They do that at the World Trade Center: put roses on the approximate spot a husband or sister landed after jumping out a window one hundred stories up. I sat on the bank of Fishhook Creek for maybe half a day, thinking about the sandpaper, the cigarette in the water, and the chance my dad had to fess up.

He could have done it, told the truth right then and there, and avoided this whole damned mess. But he chose to pretend I was out of my head, a little girl confused by a scary dream. I can't remember if he tried to hug me after we talked, but I know I instantly stopped trusting him.

Sometimes, I take out a picture of myself from the early days at Redfish Lake. I am pigtailed and pink-cheeked, holding a Dixie Cup with a tadpole inside. I am beaming into the camera, proud of the new life I cradle in my hands.

I became a sad kid after that picture was taken. I've been a sad kid ever since.

I pack up my things and head toward the Sawtooths, where I hope to hike some happiness back into myself.

Looking back, there were no signs or indications to tell us my dad's desire was unraveling inside him, dragging him away from my mother, toward me. For a long time after we stood on the log across Fishhook Creek, he didn't touch me. But at age twelve, as I began to climb the wave of puberty, he came back.

At first, he really was tucking me in — just *thoroughly*. But later, he let his hands wander. Sometimes, he watched me undress through the blinds he half opened after dinner, when he went outside to smoke. When I sensed him in the backyard pretending to rake the grass, I would crouch and freeze, like a deer that tries to become invisible in broad daylight. Night after night, he ranged across my body, exploring this place and that. And sometimes he sat in a corner shining his flashlight on my exposed abdomen and thighs. The effect was so bewildering, I stopped knowing what to think.

For the growing-up victims of sexual abuse, every day becomes a test of personal perception. According to Darkness to Light, an international nonprofit dedicated to child sexual abuse awareness and prevention, one in four girls and one in six boys are sexually abused in the United States annually, and only 30 percent of all cases are reported. Most girls are molested by their fathers or stepfathers, and almost always inside the family home.

Even if my dad had stopped molesting me after that first night in the trailer, I would still carry wounds. Incest victims suffer from a wide range of maladjustments, including alcoholism, drug addiction, and promiscuity. Some experts believe that a child's emotional growth is stunted at the age of the first attack, and that he or she will not begin to recover until adulthood, if ever. As adults, many survivors (or "thrivers," as they're now being called) find themselves unable to trust. They suffer from low or nonexistent self-esteem. And they almost always have deeply conflicted feelings about sex.

As my dad frequented my bedroom, a creeping disintegration set in. It attacked my self-image, then spread, diseaselike, to my sense of morality, ambition, and trust. I now think my entire family felt ill, though no one acknowledged why. We stopped camping, drew the curtains, and hardly ventured outside. Any connection I may have felt — to the mountains, my own potential, the world — began to erode.

Stacey, Tina, and I are speeding down Highway 75, passing a giant bottle of peach wine cooler between us and cranking Depeche Mode. I'm the only one old enough to drive. As we pass the turnoff for Fairfield and 70-mph wind rips through our hair, I turn to Tina and say, "Who're you gonna screw tonight?"

It's early fall. We take acid and smoke cigarettes. We lie to our parents and drive to Ketchum, across the Perrine Bridge, away from the dairy farms of Twin Falls, to a place where nobody knows us, except for the guys who've heard.

We wait outside a gas station begging people to buy us beer. In a couple of hours, we'll go to a guy's house whose name I don't know, but who we met the last time we were here. I'll stand outside on the porch, smoking a Camel Straight. Someone named Sam will walk out the door, push me against the wall, and smash his mouth against mine. By the end of the night, I will have consented to a certain kind of rape.

I started contemplating suicide on a regular basis when I was fourteen, as it dawned on me that no one was going to help — no matter what I said or did. My grandmother, a stoic with her own skeletons, refused to get involved. She listened to my reports at her kitchen table while she prepared elaborate duck or pheasant dinners for her hunting friends. But she never confronted my dad. And my mom, who'd already lost one husband, wore her denial like a heavy coat.

I can still remember the look on her face when I handed her a poem I'd written, one morning after my dad had been in my room. She read half of it — I can't remember what it said — then folded the paper over. My dad was standing close enough in the kitchen to intercept the missive, but he didn't see it. Why I didn't give her the poem in private, I don't know. But when she peered up, her eyes burned their own message back. "Please, please stop telling me this," they said. And so, one night in the middle of August 1985, I ran away.

It's late, and I'm lying stomach-up on the living room floor, with one leg sticking out of a faded yellow nightgown with Tweety Bird on the front. I'm pretending to sleep as the wind screams across the lava flats, rattling the windows of our house. And my dad, dressed in a terrycloth robe and reeking of Old Spice, hovers a couple of inches above me, so that I can feel the heat coming off his chest.

I squirm, and he backs off. I roll over; he inches on. I jerk my head and lurch my body — still pretending to sleep, but showing him that I know what he's doing and that it's making me sick. My dad and I twist around like this until he decides I'm too restless to lie on top of tonight.

He gets up and stares at me, then goes outside for a smoke. When he comes in, he turns out the lights and heads to bed. I listen. Teeth brushed. Covers back. A little moan. Asleep.

When I hear him snoring, I put on my pink-and-black Vans and slip out the front door, careful not to let the wind slam it shut. I run

to the end of our driveway and turn north, toward the Perrine
Bridge. This is the night, I think, that everyone will remember,
but no one will understand. I am running to the bridge, which
stretches across the Snake River, nearly five hundred feet in the air.
When I get there, I will walk to the very center. I will climb on top
of the railing. And I will jump.

The nights I was abused have become like dreams, some locked in
a vault and others softened around the edges so that they sometimes seem almost tender. But there are others, terrifying after-
shocks that flash out of nowhere — visceral as if they'd happened
yesterday.

Lying in my sleeping bag a half-mile below Sawtooth Lake, I
can't get the bridge, the Tweety Bird nightgown, or my desperate
fourteen-year-old face out of my head. It's 3:00 A.M., and I'm staring at the roof of my tent. A thin layer of condensation has turned
to ice, which keeps shearing off into my face.

Yesterday, I'd left the trailhead near Stanley and headed north,
out of the showering aspen leaves and past the hillsides covered in
scree. Even if I couldn't find answers at Redfish Lake, I thought, I
would still hike into my favorite mountains to clear my head. When
I got to the dead ponderosa overlooking the limestone pipes, I'd
taken a picture of myself and my pack. And when I reached the
lake surrounded by snowcapped peaks, I'd tried to pitch my tent,
but it was slushy and muddy and I started to cry.

Around 6:00 P.M., I packed up my things and turned down the
trail. *It's okay to go to pieces,* I thought, and then I started to run. I ran
until I reached the lower basin, where I found strangers camped by
a lake. Their closeness soothed me, so I laid out my gear, cooked
some oatmeal, and went to bed. An ice cloud formed around the
moon. The next twelve hours felt endless, like how I imagine solitary confinement would be.

The summer of 1985, I stood in the middle of the Perrine Bridge
and didn't jump. It might have been that the wind was howling so
hard I couldn't balance on the rail. I might have remembered the
cat my brother told me he threw over, after he dipped it in gas —
how it didn't light on fire but seemed to scream. I stood there for a
long time, and then I turned around and walked to the house of a
friend whose mother was dating a cop.

The next day, the police knocked on my parents' door and asked them for my things. When I later testified against my dad, I learned he had denied everything, then refused to take a lie detector test. At the hearing, my mother wept quietly in the second row. I was moved into a foster home and became a ward of the state. My dad, who continued proclaiming his innocence, was sentenced to a year of abstinence — from me.

Somehow, in those darkest days when I was being shuttled from home to home and finally back to my mother, my parents decided that it would be best if they got back together. I moved to Oregon to live with a relative so my dad could go home. Several months later, when the year of our separation was over, my parents came to pick me up.

They thought they could jump-start our family and forcibly undo the damage that had been done. On the eve of their arrival in Oregon, my dad granted me a sparse admission over the phone — something like, "I did it. I'm sorry." But it felt halfhearted, and I knew he was holding out. For the next year, I unleashed my hatred upon him, daring him to touch me so I could have him locked up. I mocked him for being an Idaho hick. And I meant it when I told him I'd kill him if he weren't such a worthless fuck. A year after we reunited, when I was sixteen, I used my military pension to pay for boarding school in Michigan, planning never to return.

It almost worked. In following years, I extricated myself from my family by disappearing for months at a time. I went to places that didn't have phones, like the Utah desert and Mexico. I enrolled in college several times — and dropped out when the urge to disappear became stronger than the need to fit in. But through it all, I continued to fragment.

Some people fall into the snakepit of their lives and reach their arms, like a baby, toward God. Others discover long-distance running or opium on a back street in Bali. When I realized that there was no escaping my pain, I turned my compass north and followed it until I reached a place where it was light all day.

Alaska. I went there after a friend told me that people in the forty-ninth state partied till dawn in the endless gloaming of the Arctic summer. Our plan was to hike up glaciers and hang out on the banks of rivers loaded with salmon rumored to be as big as small dogs. We might work; we might not. The town we were headed to, McCarthy, didn't have phone service and was accessible during the winter only by plane. It was a place where nobody knew you or cared if your story was true.

I took to Alaska like I'd been born there. By December 1994, my first winter, I was living in a twelve-by-sixteen-foot cabin, just off the McCarthy road in Wrangell–St. Elias National Park. The cabin was eight hours northeast of Anchorage near the Canada border, with 10 million acres of wilderness out the front door. I was twenty-four years old — a baby. Even if they'd known where to look, my parents couldn't have found me.

In the mornings, I wake up, stoke the barrel stove, and haul water from a pond after chopping a foot-thick hole in the ice. All day, I ski giant loops through stands of birch and black spruce on waxless cross-country boards. I glide along the moraine of a wide glacier that recedes at a geologic pace, skiing so hard my body sweats — even in thin layers when it's −20°F. The miles rack up: fifteen, thirty, one hundred. When I ski, some of the rage and sorrow seeps out of me.

Throughout the winter, I meet people who don't care where I've come from, how long I'm staying, or when I'll move on. My neighbors share homemade bread, store-bought cheese, and other prized possessions. We sit in wood-fired saunas drinking nearly-brewed beer, planning climbing trips, and watching the northern lights. I stare into their winter-rough faces and think I see something I can trust.

After McCarthy, I move to Fairbanks, the coldest spot on earth, to work for a sprint musher who spends $30,000 a year on seventy huskies that never win. I am in charge of something — four litters of puppies — for the first time in my life. I will make big decisions, like who will lead us out of the dog yard, who will get extra food, and who will live or die.

Solstices and equinoxes pass. By June 1996, I'm living in Talkeetna, on the southern edge of Denali National Park. I am building a cabin on two acres of land with a dog trail out back. I make friends who admire my tenacity. I start to believe they might be right. One day, a neighbor asks me to help with her dogs as she trains for the Iditarod. She too is brave and afraid; her boyfriend is dying of cancer. When I meet her at the start of another long race, she is crying, but she pushes 150 miles to the Kuskoquim River, then turns around and brings her dogs across the finish line. When I get home, I write a story about her on the back of a grocery bag, then take it to the local radio station and read it over the air. Weeks later, on the eve of the Iditarod, my story is broadcast on radio stations across the state, and months later wins an award. A light goes on in my head.

When I look back on the years I spent in Alaska, I see a more perfect version of myself emerging. I am stronger, more trusting, and kind. In 1997, I score a job as a backcountry ranger in Denali. I roam the park protecting grizzlies from people and people from bears. Against all odds, the hikers trust my advice. I'm promoted. One day, I find myself hiking with Bruce Babbitt's secretary, talking about the power of wilderness and how it changes lives — how it's saving mine. Midconversation, I flash to a moment my dad would have loved: soaking in the kettle ponds hidden in the muskeg below 20,320-foot Mount McKinley. Maybe I think of him out of gratitude, for showing me how wilderness can shape and define. Maybe it's just the hazy mellowing of distance and time. But by September, when I leave Alaska for the Lower 48, I am ready to embrace the world — and perhaps even my father.

It would be great if a few years in the wilderness could wipe away our pain. But of course it isn't that easy. For a long time, through my late twenties and into my thirties, my dad and I airbrushed the abuse out of our family photo. We got so good at pretending, we almost convinced ourselves that we had moved on.

Truth is, my dad and I got on well together — in part because he tried hard to be good and normal again. He flew to Anchorage once, when I needed a partner to drive with down the Alcan Highway, too scared of the frost heaves and endless stretches of road between gas stations to do it alone. Over the years, he has given me cash and co-signed on cars. He has picked up the phone when I called to talk about my loneliness — or the weather — at 3:00 A.M. And it is he, not my mother, who has saved all of my stories, in big, black binders at home.

We have, as they say in psychotherapy circles, reconstructed our house of relationship. In 2000, he came to see the ultrasound of my first baby. When Scout was born, and sixteen months later,

Hatcher, my dad found a new reason to live. Indeed, my sons have become the brightest spot in his diminished life, and they love him acutely. He even babysits when my husband and I go skiing at Whistler for a week.

This easing of relations was good for my dad, and easy for me. But I still didn't trust him — not completely.

"I can't do this," I tell my husband. "I can't hold up the weight." I am lying on a trail with my legs twisted in my mountain bike, and I can't force myself to get up.

It's Memorial Day, 2006. We are riding down Winiger Ridge when I miss a turn and grind into the dirt. The sun is shining on tight blue buds that will soon flower across hillsides covered in sage. The boys are at home with a babysitter. I am falling apart.

"What happened?" my husband asks. "You were flying back there. You looked good."

Most things are looking good these days. After Alaska, I moved to Winter Park, Colorado, and skied five days a week. I kept writing too, and landed a position at a big magazine. I live on two wooded acres at 8,500 feet on the outskirts of Boulder. My family hikes out the front door. On summer nights, we sit on our deck and watch satellites cross the sky, and in the winter, with snow blanketing the ground, we listen to a quiet so vast it creates its own sound.

And yet the weight had crept back, so heavy I felt it would crush me.

It started last spring, after an exhausting stretch of work-related travel. I felt wretched and broke out in cold sores. When I went for a checkup, a physician's assistant prescribed the antidepressant Lexapro, and I took it even though I wasn't depressed.

Instead of making me feel better, the pills made me groggy, irritable, and profoundly morose. After a week, I stopped sleeping almost completely and couldn't concentrate. I lay in bed staring at the ceiling. A bobcat wandered through the backyard; I didn't try to get up. I couldn't understand why I was feeling so down. I kept saying, *My life is a million times better than it should have been.* And then I thought about my dad, and my head began to hurt.

In recent years, his apologies had become more frequent, though he still talked euphemistically about "hurting me" or "making my life hard." He suffered openly when I refused to let him give me away at my wedding, and has cried man-size tears while we've sat at breakfast joints and bar stools across the West. But he never truly came clean — to me or anyone else in the family — about the extent of my abuse. No one knew the capacity for incest he still had. I couldn't be sure he didn't harbor fantasies about me. And I began to worry about what he could do to my kids.

In the haze of my antidepressant detox, I decided I had to go back to the Sawtooths. I believed I could find answers there, at the scene of the crime.

It didn't work. I lay in my sleeping bag at Sawtooth Lake. I waited for the ice cloud to burn off the moon. By the time the sun spread over the peaks, I knew I couldn't reconstruct the past by myself. I needed my dad to complete the story. And I knew we could only do it in the one place that had formed us both.

My dad was born on March 12, 1943. His mom was seventeen. One day, her husband went deer hunting in the mountains above their Colorado home. She wanted to go with him; she'd bring the baby. He said, "No, a woman's place is in the home," and she divorced him because of that.

A year later, my grandmother married Baby Donnie a new father. He worked as a wire-stringer for the phone company. The entire family — Les, Lorraine, and little Donnie Lee — traipsed up and down the Rockies eavesdropping on people's conversations zzztzing through the line. By the time my dad was six, his family had lived in seven states, moving across the country like well-dressed gypsies.

Life was good on the road. My dad slept in hotels and ate out every night. He was resourceful and obedient. He made boats that he floated down gutters along empty backroads in New Mexico, Arizona, and Idaho. And when he was five, he was sodomized.

It was an older cousin at a family gathering. My dad says the kids were just being kids. And besides, it only went on for a couple of years. He doesn't think he was mentally scarred, but admits it formed his attitude toward sex. "It showed me sex wasn't something you should be afraid of," he told me once. "It was how you showed your love."

I'm afraid. My dad and I sit at the picnic table on the far side of Redfish Lake. The boat has left, and so have the worried Texans, who didn't offer to help with our packs but waved as they motored away.

Today, we will hike through the yarrow and sage, stopping every ten minutes for my dad to catch his breath. When we get to the slippery rocks in the river, I'll take off my boots and slide fifty feet into the emerald pool. And when we pass the giant face under the Elephant's Perch, I'll realize that this is going to take more out of us than I had expected.

After the Lexapro, and the vision, and the truncated solo that ended with a sleepless night, I called my dad and asked, "Will you come to the Sawtooths with me?" I was in the loft, at home, and felt overheated, confused, and slightly brave. He said, "Yes. Of course. I think so. Let me think about it."

Now we are heading into a mountain range that looks imposing and mean. When I called my dad months ago, this trip seemed noble, necessary, and in a twisted way, fun. This will be the first and last time we go on a multi-day backpacking trip, just the two of us, in the place we love most on earth.

I'm scared because when I am with my dad I am eight years old. We will walk for days up forested valleys. We will camp in places so lovely we'll want to weep. Fish will rise to the surface of a dozen glassy lakes. And he might try to lie on top of me when I fall asleep.

"I've made some rules for myself," he announces, then rattles them off. "I won't ask questions. I won't speak out of turn. I won't be vulgar or too descriptive. I won't get pissed off at you." I stare at him. *You won't get pissed at me? What the hell is wrong with you?* Then I check off the questions I will ask him when we get to the Temple, three days from here.

When did it start?
When did it end?
How many times did you do it?
And why?

Two hours later, we are inching our way up the dusty switchbacks through spruce trees and lodgepole pine. My dad drags his legs. A week ago, at a party in Utah, he tried dangling from a rope swing that hung out of a tree. When he caught the edge of his shoe on a root, he held on and scraped himself over some rocks, rubbing the flesh off of his knees. Now the scabs are deep, dark red, and crack open when he walks.

We continue like this until we reach the sign for Alpine Lake, where we'll spend our first night. We've hiked five miles and gained just one thousand feet, but our campsite is still a mile away and another eight hundred feet higher. My dad looks weary, like he could lie down right here with his pack on and sleep until morning. I make him eat a Clif Bar and we load up, the trail becoming steeper with every step.

At the fifth switchback, my dad has fallen ten minutes behind. I consider waiting, then clip along at my own pace. I know my dad is getting older and is out of shape, and that in his condition he could be back there somewhere having a heart attack. I keep walking until I reach Alpine Lake.

That night, after dinner, I change my clothes and worm into my sleeping bag. My dad heads to the lake and casts for rainbows. I scoot my sleeping pad as far from his as possible, until I'm lying in the corner of the tent.

I know it's weird that we didn't bring two tents, but this is my dad, my *father*, who took up the job of caring for us voluntarily when he married my mom. Like most little girls, I worshiped my dad. We snuggled in my parents' double-wide Cabela's sleeping bag. He let me brush and blow-dry his hair. And I don't know how many hours I watched him load shotgun shells in the basement of our house.

I do know that any self-respecting woman would demand her own space. And yet my weakness isn't just a longing for simpler times. As I have learned about my dad's abuse, I've begun to see him in a different light. Once, after a bluegrass show when he imbibed too much, he cried in the car and told me that he would give anything if he could go back and make things right. For better or worse, I believed him. And before all that — before everything — there were the years at Redfish Lake. I hold those early memories carefully, like pressed wildflowers that, if jostled, would crumble to dust.

Still, the tent is an uncomfortable place, and so this too becomes a crime. One of backpacking's greatest virtues is that it makes instant bedfellows out of strangers and friends. When else do we lie under a star-filled sky separated by a few cubic inches of down? In the tents of my past, I have fallen in love and whispered my greatest longings and dreams. My tentmates and I have laughed until we peed our pants, knowing that in the morning, we will have created a shared history at ten thousand feet. Herein lies one of backpacking's true beauties, beyond the stunning vistas and close encounters with wildlife: it creates an intimacy that transcends normal friendship and even eludes some of the best marriages.

This is the first time my dad and I will lie shoulder-to-shoulder since I was a teenager in Twin Falls. I will wear all of my clothes and never really fall asleep.

The next morning, we pack up, eat breakfast, and head back down the switchbacks, which murder our knees. As we walk, my dad fills the silence I create. He reminisces about bird hunting with his friend Gary Mitchell and fishing for the eight-pound trout that used to feed on freshwater shrimp in Richfield Canal.

He sifts through his better memories, until we come to a big log on the side of the trail, where we break out our lunch. Then this:

"I was sixteen the first time I killed a deer," he says. A four-point buck "that would have been an eight-point by Eastern standards" walked into the crosshairs of his gun. When he pulled the trigger, he got so excited he started shaking uncontrollably. It was buck fever, and he had it bad.

"You can hardly grab your breath," he says, grinning mischievously. "Just knowing that you can actually kill something, it's the height of excitement. It makes you weak in the knees."

My dad scans the trees, inhales deeply, and smiles. I realize that I haven't seen him in this setting, surrounded by rivers and trees, in years. In 1990, my parents moved to Nevada. They sold the camper and packed my dad's shot-loading equipment in a box. One summer a few years later, he came to visit while I was living in Jackson, Wyoming. He said he'd bring his fly rod and camping stuff. When he arrived, he was underdressed in a light wind shell and braced himself against the cold. We went to the Snake River and he sat down in a heap.

"Break out your rod, Dad," I said. But he couldn't. He'd forgotten to pack it.

My dad looks up the trail. "I got away from shooting does," he says, "after I killed one with a fawn." The fawn's cries echoed through the South Hills, and he couldn't stand the sound. So he put a bullet in its head.

We chat, nibble on sausage, and dry our sweaty shirts in the breeze.

Two hours later, we take off our boots and wade into a bottom-clear lake. The silence is back, bigger than it has been all week. A giant rock leads into the water, then drops off like a cliff. The fish are rising now, and my dad follows the ripples out to the edge of the lake. Watching him, I rehearse different ways to interrogate.

So, Dad. When was the first time you . . . abused me? (Too clinical. This isn't an after-school special.)

. . . touched me? (Too real-time.)

. . . completely fucked up my bearings? Yes, that's it. That's how I'll start the conversation when we get to the Temple and he's so tired he can't defend himself. I join him by the water. He looks up and smiles. "Feels warm enough to swim."

My dad collapses the second we reach the altar. We're in the middle of the boulder field that threatened to break us in half. Sweat drenches his entire torso. His face looks punched and weak. Before we left the trail, he stopped to peer up at the stone minarets surrounding the Temple. I heard the bones cracking as he craned his neck. "Beautimus," he whispered.

I crouch down, slightly behind him, and dig in my pack. This is the moment I've been waiting for: when the truth will shine down upon us and the heavens break open under the weight of a million dirty-white doves. I take out my dictaphone, test the battery, and push record. The entire conversation will last thirteen minutes.

The Truth (A One-Act Play)

[The lights come up on a rock in the middle of a boulder field. Don, an attractive man in his mid-sixties, sits slightly in front of his daughter, Tracy. She holds a reporter's tape recorder in front of his face.]

TRACY: [Fidgeting; tugging at her shorts.] So . . . this is going to be hard.

DON: It's okay.

TRACY: [Hands spread on the rock, absorbing its heat.] All I have are four questions. And I don't want to know details. Because I know. I was there. And so what is important to me is to know your version of the truth.

DON: [Nodding, looking down.]

TRACY: Okay. When did it start?

DON: [Clearing his throat, composed.] On a camping trip up here at Redfish. I had been drinking. I lied. I was tucking you in. My hands went to a spot, which surprised me, and I kept them there. But the severity — it wasn't that often at that age. Just periodically.

TRACY: [Agitated.] But I was eight. Couldn't you see what that did to me and say, "Oh my God, oh my God, I did that. That was a mistake"?

DON: [Calmly; choosing his words.] A person who does what I did . . . you make things up. You don't think of the other person. You just need that closeness. If I had ever known how it would have affected you, I probably would have done something completely different.

TRACY: [Still agitated.] So . . . that day on the log. I wasn't upset?

DON: I don't think so. I don't remember. I was trying to cover things up. I had feelings for you. I thought of you as my fishing buddy. The only thing I could do was lie. I wasn't thinking of you.

TRACY: Just so you know . . . in case you were wondering . . . I was thinking about what would happen if I jumped in the river and died. [Starting to cry.] I was eight. That's so fucked up.

DON: [Tenderly.] No, it isn't.

TRACY: [Sadly.] Yes, it is. When you're eight years old, you're a little kid. It wasn't a physical thing?

DON: Not then, but later I was put in a position where you were going through puberty. This was your teen years, you were probably twelve or thirteen. Your mother stopped being intimate. I leaned to you for closeness.

TRACY: [Putting her hands up as if to say "stop."] Okay, okay. So Mom wasn't interested in being intimate? Why didn't you go have an affair?

DON: [Nodding.] That's what I shoulda done. By all means.

[A break. Tracy takes a drink of water, shakes her head. Stands up, sits down. Don looks across the valley. A hawk skims the trees.]

TRACY: Okay. [Sigh.] Now, how many times did it happen? In various degrees of whatever it was. Coming into my room . . . whatever that was. Till it ended.

DON: Between twenty-five and fifty times maybe. You know, I never kept track.

[A long silence.]

TRACY: [Fighting tears.] You must have felt like shit about that, right? I mean, I didn't want that, right? [Sitting down, hugging her legs to her chest.] I wasn't a willing accomplice . . . right?

DON: You weren't a willing accomplice. I didn't expect you to be willing. I really felt screwed up. Why would I jeopardize my family like that?
And I'm not using this as an excuse, but I was abused when I was real
young.

TRACY: Did you do it to Chris?

DON: No, no. It's never boys.

TRACY: [Her eyes squeeze shut, her face registering fear.] Who else
then?

DON: I haven't had those feelings for anybody, ever since.

TRACY: Since when?

DON: Since you. It ended when you left, when you ran away.

[They're both crying now. The wind has picked up.]

TRACY: So one day it was just . . . over?

DON: No, it's never over. You have those feelings, but they're just like
this tape. It replays but you learn how to stop it. You learn how.

Some people believe the truth will set you free. I think that's too
easy. When my dad made his confession at the Temple, a weight
lifted, but only long enough for me to take a deep breath.

After twenty years of second-guessing my own memory, feeling
ashamed of my sexuality, and aching for the confirmation that others have always denied, I finally had proof. But the victory wasn't
entirely sweet. My dad's confession also horrified me. I'd always
hated that he put his twisted desire before a small girl's suffering.
Now that I had learned how often it had happened — fifty nights
lost, never to be regained — a new sadness gripped me. And yet,
things had changed for the better at the Temple. By confessing, my
dad has given me something back — power, the anticipation of a
fuller future, maybe even my life. And finally, after all of these years
in the wilderness, I might find the strength to truly forgive him.

In the dry, wild heart of southern Idaho, past Russian John hot
spring and the ranger station on Highway 75, there is a small
wooden sign, barely visible from the overlook on Galena Pass.
Through a camera lens you might not even notice it, dwarfed as it
is by the Sawtooth Mountains, which spread out before you and fall
away somewhere in Utah. But if you know where to look, you'll find
the sign, and below it, a tiny spring buried in overgrown grass.
These are the headwaters of the River of No Return, a creek that

seeps out of the earth, gathers volume and speed, and becomes so fierce one hundred miles from here that it cuts a trench in the earth one thousand feet deep.

People say the river was named this because the current is so strong it's impossible to travel upstream. But when I was a little girl, I stood on the banks watching sockeye struggling toward their ancient spawning grounds at Redfish Lake. Nine hundred miles from their starting point in the Pacific, they arrived redder than overripe tomatoes, their flesh already breaking apart.

In the early 1970s, thousands of fish returned here to lay their eggs and die. Then we put in dams along the Columbia and Snake Rivers. By 1975, eight concrete barriers stood between the Pacific Ocean and Redfish Lake, and by 1995, the sockeye population had dwindled to none.

Many people took this as a sign: that the world had become too corrupt for something so pure as native salmon to exist. I might have believed that too, until last summer, when four Snake River sockeye made it home.

I was nervous on every page of this story. Nervous for Tracy Ross. Nervous about what she would learn. Nervous. I know more about her, I suspect, than I know about some friends I have known for all of my life. This walk in the woods will not leave my head for a long time.

PAUL SOLOTAROFF

Quarterbacks Built Here

FROM MEN'S JOURNAL

THE PERFECTLY THROWN FOOTBALL, moving at a high rate of speed, makes a ripping sound as it leaves the hand, something between a whoosh and a mortar launch. If you stand beneath its path you can hear its hard whistle, an oblong arrow in flight. If you're forty yards downfield, the whistle gets louder and then the ball is on you, faster and heavier than you'd have predicted, a warhead, not an arrow, dialing in. The safest way to catch it is to spread your hands wide and try to grab the sides of it going by. Should the nose of the ball hit you in the palms or chest, you stand a fine chance of a deep edema or a four-dot shiner on your sternum that stabs like a dagger when you breathe.

Despite the rain and bluster of a raw March weekend in a manicured hilltop stadium near Pasadena, California, you hear that sound a lot over the course of the two-day session of the DeBartolo Sports University's quarterback academy. Almost a hundred of the best young passers in the country have come from thirty-two states to learn at the foot of a master. His name is Steve Clarkson, and he has sent a procession of teenage phenoms to premium college programs and then to the NFL. Ben Roethlisberger, Matt Leinart, Colt Brennan, J. P. Losman, the Clausen brothers Jimmy and Casey — the list of famed alumni goes on and on, and there are more right behind them in the pipeline. Over there, running bootlegs, is the Next Tom Brady, a high school senior by the name of Matt Barkley who's bagged every award an underclassman can win and is promised to USC. Behind him is Jake Heaps, a junior from Seattle, who at fifteen already has interest from a half-dozen Pac-10 and Mountain West schools. Joe Montana sends his sons to Clarkson. Will Smith, Wayne Gretzky, and Snoop Dogg do likewise. And less famous but well-heeled parents have brought their big-armed boys to learn from the most accomplished private quarterback coach the sport has ever produced. Clarkson's fees are sky-high — $650 for these weekend camps, and $700 an hour for private sessions, with a minimum commitment of a year — but the aim of his students is higher still: to become a three-year starter at a Division I power, get drafted into the league as a franchise-in-waiting, and spend a year or two toting a clipboard before gaining admission to the most exclusive sodality in professional athletics — the NFL Starting Quarterbacks Club. Current membership: thirty-two and holding firm.

At Clarkson's camp there's no time for standard drills or leisurely one-hand touch, as groups of ten shuttle from strength-and-speed sessions to intense film study with ex-NFL coaches, then take the field again for inch-by-inch breakdowns of their throwing mechanics. Clarkson, as brawny as a drill instructor and every bit as deft with an insult, spares no one, not even Barkley, the Gatorade player of the year, hailing bad passes with deadpan barbs like "You just sent your receiver to intensive care. Are *you* going to call his parents or should I?"

On a field with dozens of six-foot-two high school sophomores who've already made their name on scouting sites and YouTube dossiers, it isn't easy picking out an unmapped star, a kid not on the radar by fourteen. But by and by, your eye locks onto a boy whose feet are as much the story as his arm. Though absurdly tall for his age, he glides on tiptoe through his five-step drops, bouncing to unload another head-high spiral, football as ballet in two-inch cleats. A good deal of passing happens below the waist, and Clarkson spends years teaching blue-chip talents how to open up their hips and transfer weight. Max Wittek learned it cold in a couple of months and is so far along the learning curve that Clarkson can't help but gawk. "Rarely does anyone get it that quick," he says, watching Max work through his progressions. "What he's picked up in a year is off the charts — but don't even *think* of saying I said that."

When his father brought him to Clarkson in the spring of '07, Max was so raw that Clarkson almost sent him home, half-convinced he wasn't worth the bother. Six months later Clarkson sat his parents down and told them their son's talent was sufficiently robust that he'd be best served by moving from Norwalk, Connecticut, to a passer-friendly high school in California. At great personal cost, the parents, who were never married and are no longer together, agreed. Max's mom followed her son out to a suburb of Los Angeles, and the father visits from his home near San Francisco. This fall Max, a shy fifteen-year-old kid who has never been on a date unchaperoned, will attend Mater Dei, the Santa Ana prep school that has turned out two Heisman winners. At Mater Dei, he'll back up Barkley in his swan-song season, then compete for the starting slot in '09.

But that's not the kicker in this passion play about talent and its all-points pursuit. No, the kicker is what Max's and other families have staked for a preposterously small shot at pro stardom: thousands of dollars, forfeited vacations, marital breakups, and, in the case of at least one prominent *twelve-year-old* at this camp, an aggressive doping program.

Playing quarterback is the hardest position in sports not because you're running for your life half the time, but because that's the very *least* of your concerns. The job requires the thought speed of a NASCAR driver, the coolness under fire of a tank commander, the grace below the neck of a ballroom dancer, and the recall of a Vegas mentalist. You have five hundred plays you must remember and master and, as the need arises, opt out of at the line; three or four receivers running precisely timed routes that they too can alter as the coverage dictates; and seven or eight defenders in the tackle box, any and all of whom may be rushing full tilt and are themselves adept at concealing the schemes they're in. It takes apprentice QBs years just to learn protections, years more to recognize defensive patterns, and years again to trust their split-second reads and make the right decision by the count of four, when all hell breaks loose in the pocket. Film study is crucial, and the Peyton Mannings of the world do more of it than the entire staff of *Cahiers du Cinéma:* four to six hours daily during the season. It is only an adjunct, though, to the thing itself — the six-day-a-week grind of practices, forty-eight to fifty weeks a year.

"The first thing I tell a kid when he comes to me is you better be able to deal with boredom," says Clarkson. "Playing the game's the most fun you'll ever have, but the stuff leading up to it is dull, dull, dull, and if you don't have a burning desire to work, then do your folks a favor and take up golf."

When a kid is brought to Clarkson for evaluation, he typically spends a weekend assessing him, though he often knows by the start of day two whether the boy's cut out for this. "If he went back to his hotel after the Saturday session and spent hours in the mirror doing what I showed him, then he's got the makeup to play QB," he says. If not, Clarkson has neither the time nor the patience to baby the kid along. He's a phenomenally busy man, running his local camps, training an extensive and far-flung list of private clients, and rolling out a national version of all this with his new business partner, Edward DeBartolo Jr. Starting next year he and the former owner of the San Francisco Forty-Niners will stage huge minicamps for passers and wideouts at locations around the country, bringing their veteran team of coaches and coordinators to work with kids hand to hand. From there they will spread the gospel overseas, teaching kids in China and England to throw a hot spiral on the run.

It's the basis of what Clarkson now calls his life mission: to plant and nurse the grass roots of quarterbacking so that great ones emerge more than once or twice a decade almost by accident. "Aside from a handful of guys in the league, this is a real downtime now for passers," says Clarkson. "What we need is more kids coached right from the get-go, so that the quantity and quality goes up at all levels and we see six or seven good ones every draft."

It is a wildly ambitious life for a guy who was bounced out of football after the briefest cup of coffee in the NFL and who, twenty years ago, was the district manager at a Black Angus restaurant in L.A. Sitting on one of a pair of matching leather couches in his massive corner office in Pasadena, Clarkson, at forty-six, looks more like a linebacker now than the fleet QB who came out of college ready to detonate the league in '83. That, you may remember, was the annus mirabilis class, a quarterback draft so awash in passers that Dan Marino went *last* of the six selected in round one. Clarkson had twice outplayed John Elway in head-to-head duels when Elway was the consensus all-American at Stanford and Clarkson was breaking records for Elway's father Jack at rival San Jose State. But Elway went first in that mighty draft, and Clarkson —

well, Clarkson was never chosen, though in those days the draft went *twelve* rounds, not seven, and sixteen quarterbacks, all of them white, were selected. Denver scooped him up as a street free agent for the whopping sum of $9,000, then turned around and swung the huge trade for Elway, paying a king's ransom for his rights. Clarkson, a proud man who wept in his kitchen the night of that draft, went up to play in Canada for a couple of years after the Broncos cut him, then came home to Los Angeles and declared himself done with the game. "I was raised in a racially mixed part of L.A. and couldn't accept that the game would be that racist. But at the Broncos' camp, they straight set me up to fail, sending plays in to get my head knocked off. I chose to keep my mouth shut so they couldn't call me a rebel, but it really turned me off to the sport I loved."

A big-boned kid with a howitzer arm, he'd fallen hard for football as an eight-year-old at his first Rams game with his father. "We were sitting in the cheap seats with all the hippies around us smoking grass, and I'm watching Roman Gabriel, the first glamour-boy passer, throw bomb after bomb to Lance Rentzel and Jack Snow, and thinking, *That's* what I want to grow up doing. I want the ball in my hands on every play, and I want to *look good* throwing it."

Clarkson helped lead L.A.'s Wilson High to three straight city titles, two as a stylin' QB. (He played in a tailored uni and self-customized cleats, painting the school mascot on the heels.) But he never really took the game seriously until college, when Jack Elway put his own job on the line by starting a black QB. "The hate mail he got, the death threats and back stabs — man, that grew me up fast," says Clarkson. "I went to him one day and asked for film of the great quarterbacks, starting with his son, of course. To this day I've never seen a better technician. John Elway's reads and footwork? *Perfect.*"

Clarkson graduated as an academic all-American and a wised-up student of the game. That's why his treatment by the league cut deep: he wanted to demonstrate that blacks could *think* the position, not just wing it by scrambling. But if he was done with football, football wasn't done with him, luring him back with the cheapest of ruses: an ad in the local pennysaver. A man in the area was looking for a coach to tutor his high school son; Clarkson's great-aunt spotted the ad and gave the guy Steve's number. Clarkson agreed to meet the boy and watch him play. Unmoved by what he saw, he begged off politely and got back into his car. But before he hit the gas, he took a last look and saw the kid nail a string of backflips. "He was a great athlete but couldn't play a lick," says Clarkson. "I thought, if I can turn *that* kid into a quarterback — well, if nothing else, it'd make a great story."

That kid, Perry Klein, was a gangly sophomore who had inherited his gymnast father's genes. "I'd never even taken a snap from center, and went to a school with a lousy coach and very few pass plays," says Klein, now thirty-seven and a computer parts supplier after a two-year stint in the NFL. "But Steve created a whole new offense for me and said, 'You're going to set records for passing.'" Six months later, Klein was chosen all-county, having rewritten the record book at Carson High, and Clarkson was getting mentions in the local papers as the Midas who'd spun copper into gold. A handful of parents called about their kids. Clarkson took a breath and a searching look in the mirror and quit his job at Black Angus. It was touch and go for money the first ten years, but he kept churning out precocious QBs who could run the spread offense in their sleep. Then a profile ran in an L.A. newspaper, and the next day sixty teens and their dads besieged the little park where he taught. Just trying to eke out a living, Clarkson had tapped a well of parents who'd pay any sum to make their sons stars.

In short order, his small shop became a monolith. The Air 7 Quarterback University hired veteran coaches with college and pro credentials and added classrooms for chalk talk and crews to film the kids. Suddenly Clarkson became one-stop shopping for college coaches who ran a pro-style offense; they called to get his take on high school sophs they couldn't, by rule, scout in person. Word got out to the parents of these stars that Clarkson had the ear of a Norm Chow or Rick Neuheisel, and *those* kids, the Barkleys and Clausens, were lining up to be his private clients. "What you see in Steve's kids — and I've gotten four of my quarterbacks from him — is they're miles ahead of the others, technique-wise," says Chow, the offensive coordinator at UCLA and formerly a coach at USC and BYU, who has turned out six of the top twelve rated college passers ever, including Steve Young. "Just super-solid above and below the waist."

Getting the best kids was to be expected: there's only one starter

at a QB launchpad like USC, and hundreds of gifted teens all gunning for the job when the current Heisman winner moves along.
What Clarkson *didn't* count on was the other class of kids now
stepping off planes in droves: the rawboned but ambitious eleven-
year-olds. They were boys barely out of car booster seats but by far
the best passers in their Pop Warner leagues and possessed of a
blind passion to get better. As bad as they craved it, though, some
of their parents craved it worse. They yanked their sixth-graders
out of class to fly to Clarkson, hired trainers back home for additional speed-and-strength drills, and supervised film study — such
that football was a full-time, after-school job for kids who hadn't yet
hit puberty. One mother I met persuaded a doctor to prescribe
growth hormone and steroids for her son, even though he was absurdly big for a twelve-year-old and could throw a fifty-yarder by
flicking his wrist. Posted on their fridge was a jointly signed contract, stating how much money the child would earn for every pass
completed and touchdown thrown. In his primitive scrawl, the boy
had added a rider providing a $100 bonus for a Pop Warner title.

  "I try to weed out folks who want it more than their kid, but every
now and then one gets through," says Clarkson, who discovered
the woman was doping her own son when a shipment of growth
hormone, addressed to her, wound up at his Pasadena office. He
confronted the mother and dropped her son from the program,
though it should count for no surprise that the boy, now thirteen, is
still being aggressively recruited by premium high schools.

The Fairfield Country Day School in southwest Connecticut is
about the last place you'd look if you were trying to find a franchise
passer-in-training. Its honeycombed campus of Georgian manses
and terraced purlieu of ancient oaks is peopled by just a couple of
hundred boys in blazers and Lands' End khakis, dropped off each
morning by enameled mothers in German SUVs. Max Wittek has
sixteen kids in his class, and few, it's safe to say, have designs on the
NFL, unless they're hoping to one day *buy* a team. Even in uniform
Max looks alien here, a ruddy giant who dwarfs his peers, Gulliver
among these rep-tied Lilliputians. When he transferred in from
public school to start eighth grade, he was jeeringly called "New
Kid" by his classmates and frozen out of cliques in the lunchroom.
Then the New Kid started running the option as a bulling QB and

mowing down the side as a starting pitcher, and suddenly his classmates were bumping fists with Max and inviting him to parties. By
then, though, he wasn't able to hang, having thrown himself head-
long at something else.

In the spring of eighth grade, Max had gone to one of Clarkson's
camps and found his place fast among the gangly kids who could
throw a ball high and far. He flocked to three or four camps that
summer and joined Clarkson's exclusive circle of young-gun private clients. Accompanied by his father or mother, the then-thir-
teen-year-old flew cross-country twice a month, spending hours in
the film room with Clarkson and others and going out for two-a-
days at Maranatha High with purebreds like Matt Barkley and Joe
Montana's boys. He was awfully raw yet, tripping over his own feet
and driving Clarkson crazy by holding the ball low. But by that fall,
he overheard a private chat Clarkson had with his father, Kurt
Wittek. "Steve was saying I had arm strength like Matt, and slightly
better footwork at this stage," says Max. "I was like, *what?* Matt
Barkley's the *man.* How am I even in that conversation?"

Freshly showered, he is minutes removed from an obscene demonstration of power, striking out sixteen helpless hitters in a home
win over Iona Grammar, a game in which he also bashed a moon
shot over the chain-link fence in dead center. Afterward the kids
from Iona swarmed him, giving awed fives to the boy who'd
smoked them with a fastball in the low-to-middle eighties. Max,
though, was underwhelmed. He'd struck out *seventeen* his last start
here, and besides, you know, this was just baseball. If he cared
about the game — and he assuredly doesn't — he could be a high
first-rounder three summers from now in baseball's amateur draft.
But all he has thought about since the age of four, when he
watched his first Bills game with his father, is leading an offense to
the line of scrimmage with the game clock winding down and the
ball in his hands for a last drive. Max is gifted at math but has no
plan B. He is following this out as far as his arm will take him.

I stop by his house in Norwalk to join him for breaking down
some film that Clarkson has sent him. It's the right-brain work
of playing quarterback, learning every Z-shift and odd-man front
till they're stamped in the corpus callosum, and to hammer home
the point, Clarkson enclosed a blue binder with hours' worth
of quizzes and notes. But it's a splendid May Saturday, and Max

wants to show off his arm. On a wide, quiet block of pillbox Capes, he fires blue-streak slants and skinny posts to his wincing friend Wilson. It can be hazardous to your health to play catch with Max; his father, a real estate developer and onetime high school line-backer, tore tendons in his finger twice running patterns for him and knows better than to try it again. "He was throwing half-speed, and my pinkie *still* doesn't work," says Kurt over the phone from Northern California, where he, with a variety of partners, among them Joe Montana, constructs commercial buildings and hous-ing tracts. "He always had an arm, but since he got with Steve, his ball's gotten so much heavier. I'm officially retired as his receiver."

Deep in a rhythm now, Max suffers my questions about what he's learned at camp. "Well, it started with footwork; I'd spend week-ends with Steve where I never even picked up a ball. That first step from center, going straight back, not sideways — that was, like, a month by itself." He demonstrates the switch-foot, five-step drop, with its artfully explosive first two steps, and the hairpin dynamics of the throwing motion: the off-arm yanking through and down for torque; the hand with the ball turning over on release to plant the right thumb in the left pants pocket, a forkball delivery in baseball. "It was so hard to do that, the opposite of how I threw, but that's how you get it to spiral. Distance too: I could air it forty yards max. Now, I throw it sixty with no flutter."

Sixty, no flutter: it's one way to gauge the lengths Max has come since signing on with Clarkson. A year ago he was the left-out child playing football at a tiny middle school. Now he finds himself a prince-in-waiting, the heir apparent at Mater Dei High School, which has nine state titles to its credit. It's a little like being plucked out of the Babe Ruth League to do setup relief for the Yankees. But when asked if he's daunted by the leap, Max frowns and studies his feet. He can handle himself fine on the field, he says; as for off-the-field pressure, he'll do the best he can. "Besides," he adds, hanging his first big smile, "they have girls on campus there."

Still, the question bears re-asking, because he's just so young for this sort of life decision. At fifteen, Max is prone to two-word answers and is in every sense of the word a virgin. Aside from his weekends and vacations with Kurt, Max had rarely been away from his mom till he started working out with Clarkson. "He'll call from California saying he misses me, and that goes double for me," says his mother, Karen Kurensky, who works as a mas-

sage therapist. She never fought the move to California — "I'm
about his best interests" — but the decision has cost her dearly. In
2004 she married a man who owned a thriving business in town.
Last fall they split when she announced she would follow Max to
California. She's also leaving behind her parents and three sisters,
to whom she is tightly bound, and starting over in a place she has
never been to and where she knows no one except her son.

So it goes now for passers of promise, following their talent to
prime-time venues for better coaching and exposure. "Two percent of high school athletes get college scholarships," says Angelo
Gasca, the football coach at California's Venice High, who works
with Clarkson and helped grow J. P. Losman into a promising NFL
quarterback. "Talent is great, but there are thousands of kids with
the tools to play the position. What separates the ones who get to
the next level is they grab on every chance to get better."

Actually, what separates most of those who make it is the money
to see their dream through. "This isn't for the poor," said a dad at
the March camp, having brought his young passer and two of the
boy's receivers thousands of miles west that weekend. "Kids from
the inner city, I don't see how they compete," admitted Kurt Wittek
over dinner in Norwalk during a business trip back east. "No position coach, no film room, no pro-style playbook — it's not a level
field for them."

Indeed, you can't drop by one of Clarkson's camps without feeling pressed to do the math. Of the 135 attendees at the quarterback camp in March, no more than twenty were kids of color, and
the majority of those were wide receivers. It's much the same story
at the top of the line. By last count blacks made up 67 percent of
the players on active rosters in the NFL, but of the thirty-two regulars at quarterback last year, only three were black. Yes, there are
dozens of other camps for passers with NFL dreams, but none are
as costly or prestigious as the one being run by a black ex-pro
whose color may have cost him a shot at breakthrough stardom.
Clarkson treads *very* lightly, however, saying the issue is about want-
to, not whiteness. "I've worked with kids from single-parent families, but they didn't hold their end up," he says. "They'd stop coming out here or ignored what I told them. In other words, didn't
value the chance. I can make you good, but I can't make you care,
and a kid has to want this more than anything else or it's never going to work for him, skills or not."

He's every bit as careful on the subject of age, and how much is too much at twelve. "Some kids are just naturally old for their years and can handle all the things I throw at them," he says. Or *others* throw at them. The summer of 2007, while still in his thirteenth year, Max Wittek was cruised at one of Clarkson's camps by a big-name coach from the ACC. No formal offer was given, though the intent was clear. "He said, 'We'd love for you to come to our school,'" says Max, who was stunned and flattered. The NCAA prohibits colleges from recruiting middle school kids, and any contact made before their junior year in high school must be initiated by the boys or their families.

"Big-time coaches don't care about rules. If they want a kid, they'll go through a third party," says Tom Lemming, of CBS College Sports, who hosts a show called *Generation Next.* "They'll call up Clarkson and say, 'We like your guy; have him call us and we'll get it done.'" Every couple of years, he adds, schools move the process up, getting kids to commit now as high school sophomores or, in the case of major talents, as *freshmen.* "In twenty years," Lemming snickers, "they'll be offering it to newborns whose moms played some field hockey in high school. It'll be like, 'Hey, here's your blankie and your letter of intent; just make your little X there on the line.'"

The job of quarterback, like that of film star or lead guitarist, is by now so accoutred in myth and hope as to be as much a thing of fantasy as ambition. Y. A. Tittle, gored but gallant after being leveled in his own end zone; Tom Brady, wearing confetti and a dazzled grin, aloft on the Super Bowl dais — their faces are engraved in our limbic system, and no one knows that better than Clarkson. He loves to stage events at which the great ones gather, trailing clouds of glory as they go.

Memorial Day weekend he threw a gala in the Santa Barbara hills for his first annual Super 7 QB Retreat. In the courtyard of Fess Parker's Doubletree Resort the stretch limos and roadsters were wedged in tight, heralding the arrival of the gods. Off the lobby Joe Montana hugged Jerry Rice; ten feet away Wayne Gretzky shook hands with coaches. The rotundas and breezeways were clogged with college passers — Jimmy Clausen of Notre Dame and Jake Locker of Washington, among a half-dozen others — as well as the very best high school talent in the country. Meanwhile, Clarkson's current clients, who paid $3,000 apiece for a weekend of drills and dinner, buzzed like the preteen kids they mostly were at each new entrance and sighting.

The next day was a circus of sound trucks and boom mikes, as media outlets ringed the turf at the Santa Barbara City College Stadium. Much of the press pack had made the trip for their first action glimpse of Terrelle Pryor, the most talked-about signing in Ohio State history. Pryor is six-feet-six and has salad-bowl shoulders and the subzero swagger of his soon-to-be neighbor LeBron James. From the moment he shed his wind suit and took the field, all eyes and long-angle lenses were on him, the *click-buzz-whir* of the star machine. Under the north goalposts Clarkson led a group of future first-round draft picks, including Pryor and fellow entering freshmen such as E. J. Manuel of Florida State and Matt Scott of Arizona. Then Snoop Dogg rolled up, fastidiously late, in a black-on-black van with brutal rims. Out spilled his horde with their own camera crew — the one from his E! show *Father Hood.* Last down the steps was the family prince, Snoop's gifted but indolent son Corde, who, as usual, had forgotten his cleats.

A half-hour later, ignored by satellite trucks, a group of very tall high school freshmen drilled at the stadium's southern end. Among them were Trevor Gretzky, as lean as his father but, at fifteen, two inches taller, a two-sport star with a cannon arm and a future in baseball or football; Jerry Neuheisel, the surf-do'ed, handsomely gifted son of UCLA's head coach Rick; and Snoop's boy, who, in borrowed spikes, showed off the footwork that gets Clarkson excited. With these progeny of the famous was one Max Wittek, the taciturn child of no one bold-faced, yet the star, nonetheless, of this rotation. As he worked all morning on ball fakes and checkdowns and hit his slot receiver on the run, he drew approving nods from the retired QBs that Clarkson had brought in to lend a hand. Perry Klein, the ex-backup for the Atlanta Falcons, said Max's "mechanics were better than most of the seniors."

Klein nodded upfield, where Pryor was shocking everyone with his raw, almost clownish, play. Time after time he fired, wrong-footed, above and behind his target. "Five different throws from five different arm slots," tutted Clarkson. "Bend your knees so and load the hip, then point your big toe at the receiver." On several occasions he stopped a drill cold to take Pryor back to step one, making him work without a ball, at one point even showing him how to grip it. The rest of the Super 7 campers watched in consternation. "Front shoulder down!" Clarkson then yelled at Josh Freeman, who last year broke five records at Kansas State in his first full season as a starter. "You'd have cost yourself millions in draft position if you'd done that at the NFL combine!"

But Clarkson, who seldom smiles and seems to have been born wearing his game face, also has a streak of showbiz in him, and later that day he donned a body mike to host a QB challenge. Playing to a sizable crowd of parents and siblings and college students who'd strolled over from class, he put his Super 7 through a state-fair gauntlet of speed and arm-strength tests. They ran obstacle courses to fire footballs at bull's-eyes over 2-D-cutout blitzers and hurled bombs at targets strapped to moving golf carts forty and fifty yards downfield. As the E! cameras rolled, Snoop's boisterous posse heckled every underthrown ball. Max, seated in front of them but oblivious to their chatter, watched the contest raptly. Occasionally he whispered to the kid beside him, sixteen-year-old Nick Montana. Afterward I asked him what they'd talked about. "Just taking notes," he muttered, frowning. "Tomorrow they're making us do this."

It won't be airing on basic cable, but Max Wittek went out that next morning and dominated the QB challenge, easily besting Gretzky and his age-group peers in distance and accuracy. No one much noticed — his name wasn't called when the winners were announced — but Max seemed not to care. He was still on the field as the cam crews packed and the celebrities and spectators left; even Clarkson departed in his dazzling M6 with the plates that read DRM8KER. All but alone under a fickle sun, Max threw half-speed spirals to his father, a young man working at the thing he loves on a cool spring afternoon. Kurt Wittek, catching his passes, gave soft grunts.

Is it me or is there something wrong here? I suppose kids move from their hometowns to study at the Juilliard School of Music to learn how to become masters of the violin, and I'm sure this school makes a lot of sense if you have quarterback talent, but . . . really. Do you have to spend a fortune to learn how to play a sport? Paul Solotaroff shows us how far we've come from picking sides at the playground. Truly interesting.

STEPHEN RODRICK

Spartan Warriors in the YouTube Age, or, The Legend of Legend, Spider, and Science

FROM NEW YORK MAGAZINE

IT'S A SUMMER FRIDAY NIGHT in Union Square. A short-haired preacher shouts about the perils of using the Lord's name in vain. A high-on-something teenager listens for a moment, then flips off the evangelist with both middle fingers. The kids standing around them laugh, but only for a second. There's a commotion by the subway kiosk at the southeastern corner of the park. It appears to be a fight. Two young men are locked together, their arms on each other's shoulders, muscles and tendons bulging. The man on the left is a twentyish white guy, about six-foot-two and maybe 220 pounds, with bushy brown hair. He wears camouflage shorts and a T-shirt that reads I'M THE GUY YOU SHOULDN'T GO HOME WITH BUT WILL, SO WHY NOT JUST GO HOME WITH ME NOW? He could be a surf punk, except that he's too big for that. The other man — a slightly darker-skinned guy, maybe a little younger — is massive too, but he's got a smooth, red-cheeked face and a layer of baby fat that make him look vulnerable, if not a little scared.

The two men wrestle some more, then separate and start throwing punches. Surfer Guy throws a hard right that lands on the other man's kidney with a sickening *thwack*. A crowd has gathered, but no one tries to stop the fighting. Instead, people snap pictures with camera phones. The older man hoists the younger one over his shoulder. There's a millisecond's midair pause, then — *thump!* — both men crash to the concrete. The crowd lets out a cartoonish "Ooh!"

A friend of the younger man starts screaming. "Louyi, roll over him! Roll over him, and put your fingers in his eyes."

Louyi does as he is told. He wriggles off the ground, grabs hold of the other man's T-shirt, and spins on top. Surfer Guy gasps for air and whimpers.

"Finish him," someone shouts.

Several hundred people are now watching; they've formed a circle. Across Fourteenth Street, shoppers fill the windows of the Whole Foods and Filene's Basement stores, turning them into luxury boxes. Louyi doesn't stick his fingers in the other man's eyes. He merely presses his fists into them until Surfer Guy surrenders.

Louyi stands up, flashes a Li'l Jack Horner smile, and pumps his fist.

The crowd is silent, slack-jawed. Midtown office drones, girls carrying Forever 21 bags, German tourists — no one knows quite what to say.

Now a black man with short dreads walks toward the fighters. His chest is bursting out of a tight white tank top, and a dog collar hangs around his neck. He squints at the onlookers with a wild stare. Everyone gives him a wide berth. But then he breaks into a childish grin. He's just fucking with people.

"That's Legend," a bystander whispers to a man standing next to him.

Legend gives Louyi a benedictory soul shake. Louyi beams.

Then Legend turns toward the crowd and seeks out another black guy who was filming the first fight. He's wearing long jean shorts and a baseball cap with spikes on it.

"Science, you ready?"

Legend and Science go at it themselves for fifteen minutes, exchanging a series of kicks and punches and an assortment of other cinematic martial arts moves. When they're done, they bow and embrace.

The crowd claps. Legend speaks. "We're the Union Square Spartans," he says. "Who wants to fight next?"

Ever since Chuck Palahniuk published *Fight Club* in 1996, rumors have circulated about illegal underground fights held in the basements and boiler rooms of New York and elsewhere, modeled after those in the book and, several years later, the Brad Pitt film of the same name. The most quoted line from the movie was "The first rule of fight club is, you don't talk about fight club." That's not the Spartans. They fight in public, outdoors, at one of the city's busiest crossroads. They want to be seen. Where Palahniuk's characters were mostly middle-class white guys, the Spartans are mostly black city kids, some of them homeless. They put their fights on YouTube. They know many among their growing body of fans take voyeuristic pleasure in watching them fight, and they're somehow looking to make money off the whole business, but they are warriors without a business plan.

Legend is leaning against the brass railing that surrounds the George Washington statue. The neon glow from the Coffee Shop lights up the night behind him. It's been an hour since he and Science fought. He's shirtless and drenched in sweat. He has his arm around a pixieish white girl whom he calls Strawberry, except when he calls her Snowflake.

Buzzing around Legend is a tiny tough-talking kid throwing kicks in the air. He looks twelve, but he's really sixteen. Everyone calls him Chucky. The high-on-something preacher-hater reappears. He introduces himself as Shadow. He's a Spartan too. The rest of the happy few go by names like C.J., Two-King, and Joker.

Still, this is clearly Legend's show. He's attended by two faithful aides-de-camp: Science and a shy, gangly kid named Spider. A cheap cigar is hollowed out and filled with pot. I ask Legend about the Spartans. "There's always been a caste system," he says. "There's always been the clerics, there's always been the scholars, and there's always been the warriors." Legend talks in flowery, cryptic terms. "Just because you say the color gray doesn't exist doesn't mean it doesn't exist," he says. "The same thing with the warriors. We're the warriors of now." The Spartans are run by the Triangle. "The Triangle is our leadership council," Legend says. "Me, Spider, and Science are the Triangle."

A few days later, I find Legend, Spider, and Science ducking out of the rain in what they call their Bat Cave, a small overhang adjacent to the Virgin Megastore across from Union Square. Legend grabs my arm. "C'mon, we're going on a mission." I trail the Triangle and Strawberry into the rain. The mission turns out to be just a quest for slightly better shelter, which we find on a Fifteenth Street construction site across from the Park Bar. A joint is passed around, and the three men talk about how they met.

Legend says he grew up in Bedford-Stuyvesant, near the Gates housing projects. "They called it the 'Death Gates' because someone was getting murdered there every week," he says. Legend's father was a Navy SEAL. "When I was three or four, he started tossing a heavy bag at me, and I had to dodge it. It was all soft, but it would knock me on my ass, so I had to learn how to move." Legend claims his father taught him martial arts moves and secret holds he'd learned in the Navy. As he got older, he says, his father would be gone for long stretches at a time. "You know, on secret missions or supervising projects."

Legend is clever and could be inventing his myth as he goes along. Still, some of his story is demonstrably true. He says he joined the Crips at twelve. "My whole neighborhood is Bloods, but I always do the opposite." He shows me several scars on his arm, then places my hand on a small indentation on his forehead. "I went over to a friend's house in Bed-Stuy one day to smoke weed and play video games," he says. "I just opened the door, and two guys started beating me with a baseball bat with a nail on it. My friend just watched." He says the attack was random.

Legend's mother eventually gave up on raising him, he says. He was farmed out to group homes in the Bronx, where he attended Adlai E. Stevenson High School. "Nobody bothered me at Stevo, because I'd already grown into the face I have," he says. Although Legend looks black, he insists he's more than half Native American. "By the time I was seventeen, I realized I had the Native American stone face. It can be really intimidating." He spent most of his high school years cutting class and gangbanging, but talks dreamily about how much he loved learning about war and history, particularly warriors like Geronimo.

While he was working as a bouncer around town, he started visiting underground fight clubs, mostly in Chinatown. Legend says he would find himself in a basement surrounded by screaming drunks. Another fighter would enter the circle, and they would battle with no rules until one of them was unconscious. Legend says he'd leave the room with concussions, broken ribs, and maybe a couple of hundred dollars. "Those places, they only stop the fight if the crowd stops cheering or begins leaving," he says. "They don't really care if you live or die."

Legend, who is twenty-three now, says he has an apartment in Sheepshead Bay, but he spends most of his time in Union Square and often sleeps there. He drinks some, but his self-medication of choice is pot. "Weed is what keeps me right," he says. "The only time I get nervous and agitated is when I can't get any weed."

In fact, Legend has a volatile personality. At any given moment, he can toggle between wise and childlike, open and guarded, loving and menacing. Most of Legend's friends are girls, he says. "Guys are weird. I don't get along with them. They seem threatened by me. I'll be like, 'Hey, I'm just chilling, doing my thing, you just do your thing.' But they always seem to want to put out your light just because your light is stronger."

While Legend is talking, Science is drawing medieval fighters in a sketchbook. He says he grew up on the Lower East Side and has twin sisters who just graduated from college. "My dad was just a sperm donor, I didn't get along with my mom, and I was out of the house when I was twelve," he says.

Science lived with family and friends through his teens, but he's been mostly homeless for the past decade. "I've always been a *ronin*," he says, referring to the Japanese term for a rootless warrior.

Like Legend, Science once fought in underground fight club bouts to make some cash. But he's less of a tough than Legend. "It was down in Chinatown in a garage. We were surrounded by cars with their lights on, and I was really nervous. Then the fighter gets in the middle with me and it's a woman. And I was like, *Should I punch back?* By the time I did, another guy jumped in the ring and I got the shit beat out of me."

Spider, who's twenty-three, is painfully thin, and still has a trace of adolescent acne. He is the quietest member of the Triangle. He was born in Panama and moved to New York when he was six. He first lived in Flatbush and then Crown Heights. Like Legend and Science, he never really knew his father.

Spider went to Louis D. Brandeis High School on the Upper West Side but got kicked out in the tenth grade after getting into a fight with another student. Spider left home at sixteen and spent the next two years living in Union Square during the day and on the Q train at night.

In 2002, Spider headed to the Port Authority and settled in Norfolk, Virginia, before coming home. Now he's the only one of the three to have a job, working at a nearby Papaya King. "I'm the most cautious of the three of us," Spider tells me.

It's raining harder now. Spider shivers. Strawberry and Legend do a little stoned dance to stay warm. Science tucks his sketchpad under his sweatshirt to keep it dry. I suggest we get a pizza at a place on Sixth Avenue. "No, a cheese will cost you like sixteen there," says Spider. "There's a place on St. Mark's where you get one for eight."

As we walk down Broadway, Legend shares what he sees as the Spartans' purpose. "I want it to be competitive, but like a family," he says, holding Strawberry's hand. "It makes you tough, but it shows you love. I didn't have that as a kid."

The Spartans' creation myth begins at the Pyramid Club, on the Lower East Side. Science worked for the Club, but different floors would be rented out to independent promoters who provided their own security. One night in the winter of 2005, Science was summoned to handle a situation where a group of drunken men were harassing a woman. By the time he arrived, another bouncer was already on the scene.

"This guy went to the pressure point under the armpit on the first guy," says Science with awe. "Then he hit his palm under the windpipe of another guy. I was like, *This guy has moves.*" Science and Legend escorted the offending patrons out of the club. "Once we got outside, we started talking about how we had both done martial arts as kids. Then we started sparring out in front of the club right then."

Science invited Legend to hang out with him in Union Square. The timing was excellent. Legend had been living with a girl in Brooklyn, but it had ended badly, with Legend's girlfriend chucking a jar of applesauce at him, slicing open his arm. He had nowhere else to go.

At first Science and Legend had a different idea about how to make money off their fighting skills. They would spend hours talking about how cool it would be to choreograph fight scenes for the movies, then they'd work out sequences and perform them for their Union Square friends. Legend and Science taught some of their friends their moves. Spider was one of them, and the three men became close. Science nicknamed the trio the Triangle after something he read in a book about ancient warriors. "All warriors are equal," says Science. "But there's a triangle of warriors that leads the phalanx into battle. That's us."

Legend says he's been known by that name since he can remember. Science's real middle name is "Scientific" because his mom hoped he would become a scientist. Spider got his nickname because he loves Spider-Man comics. I ask Legend if he and the others will tell me their real names. No, Legend says. "When a warrior is born, he has a milk name, you know, from when all you drank was milk. But when he grows up, he gets a warrior name that is more who he is. This is who I am."

"Words are power," adds Science. "If I know your first and last name, I know who you are. I have access. I have more control over you." He motions at Spider and Legend. "They know my government name if it's an emergency. But I trust them. We've jumped out of windows. We've fought together. They've earned it."

The Spartans' fights started out informally. "We'd just spar with each other without any rules," says Science. But over time, the Triangle started pairing up friends of similar ability, and rules were drawn up. The fights would follow the basic guidelines of mixed martial arts fighting, the hybrid combination of boxing, wrestling, and martial arts moves that's become popular in recent years on cable TV. The fights would consist of three rounds of approximately five minutes each. (Fighters could surrender earlier by tapping the concrete.) There would be two critical deviations from mixed martial arts rules: no blows to the head were allowed, and fights would be about improving one's skills, not about hurting or humiliating one's opponent. The first rule was practical, the second philosophical.

"We figured out, if you were not punching to the head, it was legal to do this publicly and say we were just training," says Science. "And we wanted this to be like a family. You get humiliated by the world every day. That's not what we're about."

In the spring of 2007, the movie *300* opened at the Union Square Regal Cinema. The film retells the legend of the three hundred Spartans who died fighting the Persian horde at Thermopylae. Spider, Science, and Legend watched it repeatedly, transfixed. "I came up with the name the Union Square Spartans," says Science. "The Spartans are the fighters, but Union Square is all of Sparta. It was like we already had the idea in our heads, and the movie came out, and we were like, 'Aha.'"

Not long after the movie premiered, the Triangle watched as medieval combatants wielding spears and shields invaded Union Square. Turns out they were members of the Darkon Wargaming Club, a role-playing society that reenacts fantasy battle scenes. "They put a lifeguard chair up, and I ran up there," says Science. "I shouted, 'Spartans, what is your occupation?' And everyone shouted back, 'War!' They let us fight them with their plastic swords, and of course we won. That made us think we could build a world too."

The Astor Place cube is just ahead. Legend, Science, and Spider run through traffic and start pushing on it. Legend and Science begin chanting, "Union Square Spartans! Union Square Spartans! Union Square Spartans!" At the moment, they look less like warriors than a pack of bratty junior high kids. Then Legend shares a fantasy he has for the Spartans: "I'd love it to be the Union Square Spartans take on the Ukraine," says Legend, his dark brown eyes lighting up. "The Union Square Spartans take on Cuba." He seems to believe that there would somehow be money involved. "Everyone in the club would make the same amount," he says. "I wouldn't get an extra penny just because I'm the leader."

We arrive at 2 Bros Pizza on St. Mark's Place a few minutes later. Two large pies are devoured in minutes. It's not clear when the Triangle's last real meal was. Legend shakes hands with the manager.

"Soon, we're going to be famous," proclaims Legend. "You can put a sign up saying PIZZA CHOICE OF THE UNION SQUARE SPARTANS."

The man smiles and makes another pizza.

Although the Triangle members were enjoying their newfound camaraderie and purpose, they were still flat broke. One day in April, Science showed up with a video camera; he had the idea of filming some of the group's fights. Maybe, he reasoned, if people saw them, they would come down to Union Square and the Triangle could charge them ten bucks a lesson.

Legend and Spider thought this was an excellent idea. In April, Science created the Union Square Spartans MySpace page. He then placed some of the fights he filmed on YouTube. Alas, the Triangle's original goal of attracting fighters willing to pay for lessons was a failure; Science says no one has paid.

But there was a publicity boomlet. The blog And I Am Not Lying wrote about the fights in May, other blogs followed, and crowds began to show up at Spartan fights. The Triangle enjoyed the spotlight in a charmingly time-delayed way. A printout of the And I Am Not Lying item arrived like a nineteenth-century transatlantic letter, three weeks after the fact. Legend carried it around for a while like a holy relic. There was one line he loved to quote: he kept asking the other Spartans, "Am I really 'petite and diamond hard'?"

By June, up to three hundred people were watching Spartan fights on a Friday night. Baristas at a nearby Starbucks, who had banned them for rowdiness, now welcomed them to use their bathroom. There was even a rumor that ESPN had contacted the Spartans about filming their bouts and airing them as the ultimate-fighting equivalent of Harlem's Rucker League.

Still, Spider insists the group doesn't fight for the attention. "We fight in public because we have nowhere else to fight," he says. "And we fight because you get that rush of *Oh, shit, did you just see that move?* That's the same rush, whether there's three or three hundred people watching." Besides, he says, "if the economy keeps going bad, we could be in a civil war in two years. We're gonna need to know how to defend ourselves."

It's a hot weeknight. Legend and Science lead a wiry nineteen-year-old called Munkey and a newcomer called Mexican into the ring. Munkey expertly uses his lower center of gravity to his advantage, and within a minute, his opponent topples. Legend is impressed: "Munkey, way to use the leverage."

Then two cops shoulder their way through the crowd. The police have more or less ignored the Spartans for more than a year now, but the crowds the group has started attracting seem to have engendered a change in policy. One of the cops has a crew cut, and he approaches Legend and Science. "We're getting calls saying there's fights going on in Union Square. You can't do this here."

Science tries to reason with him. "We've been doing this for a year. It's just sparring. There are no blows to the face. Everybody does tai chi here. It's the same thing."

"Look, we can argue all night," says the cop. "Next time we come back, we're arresting people."

Science tells him that they've applied for a permit. The cop laughs. "You think you're going to get a permit for fighting in Union Square? That's never gonna happen." The cop stares down Science and laughs again. "You know, if you were doing this as a fundraiser for the troops, you could probably get a permit."

The cop and his partner walk away. The crowd disperses. The Spartans regroup under the George Washington statue. Everyone looks depressed. Legend glares into the distance.

After a minute or so, a Spartan named Flow speaks up. He's a medium-built, studious-looking black guy, in his mid-twenties, with a Star of David necklace around his neck.

"I told you putting this on YouTube was a mistake," Flow says. "We're moving too fast. This wasn't supposed to be about us getting famous."

In the brief history of the Spartans, there has been relatively little dissension. But now, Legend, Science, and Spider surround Flow. Legend speaks first.

"You don't know what the fuck you're talking about." He looks at his two lieutenants for confirmation. "What do I keep saying? It doesn't matter what the pawns do. We know the king."

Flow looks confused. "What the fuck does that mean?"

"We know a guy who knows Ray Kelly," Legend says. "We'll be fine. We just ignore the pawns."

"I thought we were going to have a roundtable meeting about this," Flow says. "What happened to that?"

"This isn't a democracy," says Legend. "You're not part of the Triangle. I tell everyone, 'Do the things you love, and we'll all get rich.' We're splitting everything with equal shares. I am not getting one dime more than anyone else. So why don't you just shut up and let us handle it?"

"This isn't what I wanted out of this," says Flow.

Legend balls his fists. He has to be held back by Spider and Science. "Where do you think I grew up? It was Brooklyn, and it wasn't Flatbush, I'll tell you. It was Bed-Stuy." Legend points at the indentation on his forehead. "Look, put your hand here," he says to Flow. He tells him the story about the baseball bat. "No fucking reason," he says. "That's what life is about."

Flow shifts his feet. Legend gets back in his face. "You're either with us or I'll cut you off. I'll cut off your legs and leave you in the woods."

Flow drifts off. Then Legend repeats the same line to no one in particular: "I am an antisocial sociopath who hates base behavior. I am an antisocial sociopath who hates base behavior."

At the moment, you believe him.

A few days later, I come back to Union Square at dusk. Legend is standing in the same place where he and Flow had been arguing. But tonight, Legend is feeding a bottle to a cooing baby boy in Oshkosh B'Gosh overalls. The baby's name is Xavier Jr.; he's the son of two Union Square regulars. Strawberry handed him to Legend a few minutes before, but now he doesn't know where the parents went.

"Let me show you something," says Legend. "Babies are so cool." He takes the bottle away for a second and touches Xavier's dimpled chin. Xavier's mouth magically pops open. "When they feel pressure there, they think it's the bottle or the nipple," Legend says as he reinserts the bottle.

We watch the baby feed for a moment. "This makes me think of my twins, Romeo and Caesar." This catches me by surprise; Legend hadn't mentioned he had children before.

"They're six. They live in Sheepshead Bay, but I don't see them that much. Soon, I can start training them, if their mom lets me."

He tells me the Spartans are in a state of flux. The NYPD precinct captain came out this week and reiterated that any more sparring would result in arrests. "We'll move to Tompkins Square or somewhere else," insists Legend. "Or get a permit." But Union Square will always be base camp, he maintains. "We're always going to be here. We're always going to be the Union Square Spartans."

I ask him about the supposed interest of ESPN in making some sort of deal with the Spartans. Legend ducks the question, but I find out later from Science that that was just a freelance promoter/huckster passing through the square and talking big. They never heard from him again Still, Legend insists, other things are happening. He says a Staten Island fight club called the Greens saw video of the Spartans and have invited them out to Staten Island for a battle. "I watched some of those dudes fight," Legend says.

"They suck. We can take them all. This is just the start. This time next year, we're going to have two gyms. One for training, one for us just to hang out."

It's not at all clear where they'd get the money, but that's only one of the Spartans' problems. In a few weeks, Legend will get picked up by the police for passing out on a Union Square bench and be hauled down to Centre Street on vagrancy charges. In the course of trying to find him again, I will find out that his real name is Glen Williams.

Tonight, Legend laughs when Xavier spits up on him and then hands the baby off to Strawberry. He looks out at Union Square. It's the same scene as most nights. A man walks around with a sign that reads FREE HUGS, a New Orleans Dixieland band plays out of tune, and cabbies ride their horns. Legend gives a little wince.

"I love it here, but, man, if we could get out, that would be great too."

Misplaced dreams are better than no dreams at all. There is a documentary feel to this story, everything shot in black and white with a shaky camera. These kids break your heart. Stephen Rodrick serves us a memorable slice of New York street life.

PATRICK HRUBY

Men Who Love Goons

FROM ESPN.COM

"F— ME." Cochrane is perplexed. That the Syracuse Crunch and Albany River Rats can play nearly two periods of minor league hockey without somebody punching someone else in the face strikes him as absurd. Seriously, that's Jon "Nasty" Mirasty down there, circling the ice like a suicide gunboat. And what about Trevor Gillies? Dude has a longer fight card than Evander Holyfield. Why won't they just go?

Cochrane shakes his head, lips pursed in budding disgust. Mind-blowing, he says. A ripple in the fabric of the universe. Yet here from his perch in the dull-blue concourse seats of the Onondaga County War Memorial Arena, Cochrane has a theory, a way to make sense of the appalling nonviolence taking place below:

It's all my fault.

That's right. Me. Forget that I've never even laced up a pair of skates. Never mind that my firsthand hockey fighting experience begins and ends with using the video game version of Bob Probert to make people's heads bleed on Sega Genesis. Somehow, I'm to blame. Who knows? Maybe Cochrane is right. Maybe I'm screwing the deck, and maybe I just can't see it.

"So disappointing," he says, surveying the ice. "C'mon, Jon! Run somebody!"

Cochrane crosses his arms, his thin blond hair topping narrow, aquamarine eyes. He is thirty-eight, a landscaper turned day trader from Mahwah, New Jersey, a man who thinks nothing of driving seven hours through a snowstorm to videotape a training camp fracas between two semipro goons he has seen only on YouTube. "You gotta pay your dues," he explains, and before I can ask the obvious follow-up question — ¿*como?* — he launches into an unprompted soliloquy on the nature of his hobby:

> Dropping the gloves is the ultimate commitment.
> Two men going to war is a unique, intimate situation.
> If you're a cook, you get greasy; if you're a landscaper, you get dirty; if you're a fighter, you're going to get banged up.

Which, when taken as a whole, makes him sound like a Saturday-morning sensei on *Kung Fu Theater.* Not to mention a bit nuts.

It's a frigid March evening in upstate New York. Like everyone else in the building, Cochrane is here to watch hockey; like almost everyone else — the guy with the Mohawk and the girls in the MIRASTY 41 T-shirts and the kid with the sign reading THE CLIMATE IN OUR ARENA IS ALWAYS NASTY — he's also here to see a fistfight.

As am I. For months, I've been immersing myself in the world of hard-core hockey fight fans, the Cult of the Goon. (Quick taxonomy: A hockey fan watches a fight and cheers, and maybe gets another beer. A hockey *fight fan* watches fifty fights in a row on DVD, then goes online to argue about them.) I've traveled from New York to Saskatchewan, watched dozens of knockouts on tape (yes: actual Paleolithic VHS tape; more on that later), had one enforcer show me his sparring routine and another give a hands-on, on-ice demonstration of just how badly he would break my face (conclusion: Jacko glue-on nose territory). I've even signed up for a goon fantasy league. Problem is, my fantasy team sucks, I still don't understand what goon lovers see in a bloody mouthful of missing teeth, and, worst of all, *I haven't even seen a hockey brawl in person.*

As such, I'm feeling Cochrane's pain.

"If Gillies doesn't go," he tells me, "I'm going to rip the hell out of him on the message boards."

Right. The message boards. Specifically, those on Fried Chicken's Hockey Fight Site, the oldest of its kind on the Internet. A place to bemoan the ongoing sissification of the NHL, judge hockey scraps like Olympic boxing matches, track down 1993–1994 Tacoma Rockets fight tapes, and debate the maddening question: who was a badder, er, badass, Probert or Behn Wilson? A virtual church for the faithful. It's where I first met Cochrane — which, by the way, isn't even his real name. His given name is Steve. Cochrane is his online handle, chosen to honor Glen Cochrane, a former Philadelphia Flyers enforcer best known for (take your pick): (a) terrorizing the New York Rangers; (b) fighting with reckless, g'head-and-punch-my-nose abandon; (c) sporting a memorable mustache and a chin to shame the Geico cavemen.

The upshot? After spending some time with Steve, I've decided "Cochrane" is probably more appropriate. (Actually, using board names seems more appropriate for every fight fan I've met online.)

"This really pisses me off," Cochrane says, still fuming. "This was about as guaranteed a fight night as you could get."

Cochrane has a point. Look around: The arena's outer walls bear inscriptions such as ALGIERS and CORAL SEA. A banner hanging below the press box reads WELCOME TO THE HOUSE OF PAIN. Syracuse has won eleven of its previous thirteen contests on the strength of what owner Howard Dolgon calls "old-school hockey," and what the ancient Romans might call *Visigothic*. The Crunch like to fight. A lot. And no one likes glove-dropping more than Mirasty, whose rock 'em, sock 'em bouts have made him a YouTube legend, the Tila Tequila of the goon-loving set. Blessed with a cinder-block head, sporting a goofy, charming Mohawk, Mirasty has been taunting the River Rats since pregame warm-ups, all but begging for a tussle.

"No balls, eh, Gillies? May as well retire, old-timer! You're done!"

"Rechlicz! You f—ing get beat like that last time, you f—ing fight again! That's what you're here for! Don't be a p— like Gillies!"

No one takes the bait. Not Gillies, a former NHLer who missed twenty games of the current AHL season after breaking his hand against Mirasty's skull. Not Joel Rechlicz, an up-and-coming enforcer Mirasty pummeled the last time they tangled. In fact, Rechlicz won't even look at Mirasty, and when he finally sneaks a peek through the Plexiglas separating the Syracuse and Albany benches, the result is swift and strange: River Rats coach Tom Rowe grabs Rechlicz's helmet with both hands, then points his head toward the ice.

"Look at that," Cochrane mutters. "I knew it."

The whole scene is wrong. Gillies owes Mirasty a fight. Rechlicz owes Mirasty a fight. That's the code, the unwritten order that has governed hockey fighting since just about forever. They know. Everyone knows.

There should be blood. Only there isn't. So Cochrane smells a rat. Namely, me. His theory goes like this: Another fight fan, Peatycap, knew I would be in Syracuse to see Mirasty fight. Peatycap got excited and posted a note on the message boards. Cochrane told him to take it down. Too late. Somebody associated with Albany saw the note and told Rowe, who in turn has ordered his players not to fight . . . *out of sheer spite.*

Cochrane nods. He's convinced. I'm confused. Two hours ago, I didn't know who Rowe was. Now, apparently, we have some sort of Death Row–Bad Boy records feud going. When I bring this up — specifically, when I mention how ridiculous this sounds — Cochrane looks at me with pity, as if I just asked him for subway fare.

"It's not your fault," he insists. "Peatycap doesn't realize the power the boards have. You wouldn't believe how many coaches and players read them."

To recap: I'm here to see a hockey fight to better grasp what people like Cochrane see in hockey fights, only no one will fight because I'm watching, and I have no idea why this is the case. Nevertheless, I'm supposed to write a story that explains the whole thing or, barring that, at least help you win your goon fantasy league.

F— *me.*

A Full-Time Obsession

"You should have seen my old house. It was NASA." Nicky V. grins at the memory. Four televisions. A $4,000 satellite dish on the roof. Four Sony SLV-1000 videocassette editors, each of them worth a grand. *Twenty-eight* cassette copying machines. A bushel of remotes and one very important piece of plywood he installed in the middle of the basement to keep them from interfering with each other. Everything devoted to Nicky V.'s part-time hobby — or more accurately, his full-time obsession: recording and collecting hockey fights.

Like, all of them.

"I was a nut for quality," he says. "A control freak. Teams used to beam their stuff to twenty-four satellites in the sky. I'd capture games right off those satellites."

Nicky V. pulls a VHS tape off a nearby shelf. (Correction, he says, "a $6 Super VHS tape." There's a difference.) The label reads "NHL PRE-REG 1993–94, VIII." "This is my master," he says. "Big-dish quality. No degradation due to copying. Prior to DVD, as good as this gets."

Nicky V. pops the tape into a black VCR, one of the Sony SLV-1000s, tucked below a DVD player and above a big-screen television. Pixels flicker to life. "Now, nobody cares. But ten years ago, if I had told a hockey-fight collector, 'You can have my master for a season,' they would have flown out here to get it."

Before YouTube, before the message boards and the Internet and all things digital and easy, there were guys like Nicky V. The pioneers. The old-school fight fans who devoted countless hours to recording and trading and compiling footage, going from icebox-sized VCRs in the 1970s to standing on the roof in the middle of 1990s ice storms, aiming dishes by hand. The guys who racked up $300 phone bills calling to Canada at twenty-five cents a minute, who scoured old *Hockey News* box scores for penalties, who developed sore thumbs from hitting RWD and FFWD over and over again. The guys — and let's be honest, they're all guys — who spent three months waiting for fight tapes from Philly, then tore open the UPS packages like snakebite victims fumbling for antivenom.

"We were like drug addicts," Nicky V. says. "With games that weren't televised, local news stations used to put up feeds. I'd record six hours of news on a Montreal channel, just to see if there were fights, spend the next day fast-forwarding through. It was a full-time job."

Nicky V. rests his feet on a brown plastic cooler, a remote control in one hand, a Philadelphia Flyers coffee mug in the other. (He drinks two pots of Starbucks a day.) We're sitting in the storage room of his home-remodeling construction company in Stamford, Connecticut, which doubles as his office. Plastic trash bins are stacked by the half-dozen against the wall. A metal shelf teems with tubs of Sheetrock joint compound. Nicky V. just turned forty, is married, and has a two-year-old son whose pictures surround a Flyers clock that hangs above his desk. He doesn't collect and trade fight footage like he used to. But he remains one of the most knowledgeable fans in the hobby, a walking database of who punched whom in the jaw, and why.

On the screen is a brawl. A bench-clearer, the kind hockey doesn't make anymore. Rangers versus Flyers, late 1970s. Frank Beaton and Mel Bridgman go toe-to-toe. "Great stuff," Nicky V. says. "If these guys took their pants off, their balls would fall to the floor." The camera cuts to center ice. Some two dozen gloves and half as many sticks are scattered like dead cockroaches. The officials separate the teams. Nick Fotiu jumps out of the penalty box to fight Jim Cunningham *for the second time.* The Flyers gang up on Fotiu. A new scrum erupts. Ron Duguay is bleeding. "This," says a broadcaster, "is the kind of thing that sets a team back fifty years!"

"As a fan, this is almost like reliving my youth," Nicky V. says. "Watching the same fights I watched as a kid. They pan the crowd, you see the hairstyles, the big plaid shirts. I just like this era."

He scans his shelf. "Have you ever seen the fight in the stands with the Rangers and Bruins? I gotta whip that out for you!"

Nicky V. taped his first fight in 1984, but he didn't get serious until after college. His early tapes were terrible — twenty seconds of players skating around, fights joined halfway through. But they quickly improved. Nicky V. bought blank Super VHS tapes by the carton and mailed them to his contacts in other cities, fight fans and team video guys, anyone who could supply footage. He developed protégés in New York and Arizona, teaching them to do the same. He wouldn't just find one contact for footage in St. Louis — he'd find three, "so no one could f— up a fight." He scribbled fight logs on index cards, cataloged his growing collection on a computer, produced tapes on request for NHL players.

At his peak, Nicky V. had a system. Come home from work. Shower. Eat. Call his contacts. Pop in tapes at 7:00 P.M. Change the tapes at nine. Get back on the phone, figure out the late games. Make a pot of coffee. Repeat the next night.

On Saturdays, he might go to a bar — a nearby bar, so he could come home, make the nine o'clock switch, and head back out. "I was really thin until the 1990s," he says. "I put on weight from sitting around making tapes. You get corns on your feet. I would stand up and my back would hurt."

That was then. Nicky V. now rents out his former mission-control house. He married eight years ago, and his wife told him he could keep taping, with one condition: no more late-night phone calls. Next came his son. So Nicky V. cut back. Adjusted. Learned to live with YouTube's low-res footage. These days, he wakes up at 4:30 A.M., gets to the office by five, spends an hour on the Fried Chicken boards before starting his workday. He still loves the stories, the arguments, the sense of community. One guy on there just got engaged. Nicky V. might know him better than his fiancée does. And why not? They've been talking hockey fights, and life, for almost twenty years.

Nicky V. decorates his trucks with Flyers logos. Driving to those New York construction sites, he'll catch hell from Rangers fans. Yet with two words — "Dale Rolfe," the former Blueshirts defenseman who was infamously beaten up in a Flyers-Rangers playoff game while his frightened teammates did nothing — he can even the score. There's an understanding among fans, a bond.

Every fight fan has a Holy Grail. For Nicky V., it's footage of Bob Gassoff. Gassoff is a legend, maybe the toughest brawler ever. He played four seasons in St. Louis and was killed in a 1977 motorcycle accident. Just four of his fights are on tape. Nicky V. has them all. But once, supposedly, Gassoff took on Flyers tough guys Paul Holmgren (the Flyers' current GM) and Bridgman in the same game, and beat both of them into submission. Nicky V. likens it to Buster Douglas shocking Mike Tyson.

"The fight I wish I had," he says with a sigh. "Gassoff's a folklore hero. We all believe it."

Nicky V. takes me to his office. He goes online, hunts for some old scanned magazine photos of Gassoff fighting Holmgren. The images are in faded black and white. None shows an actual punch being thrown. There is just Gassoff's left fist, cocked up by his ear, hanging over a prone Holmgren like Damocles' sword.

"People that are new to the hobby, they can't get into it the way I did," Nicky V. says. "Don't get me wrong, YouTube is phenomenal. You get to see all the fights. But it takes away the imagination."

He laughs. "I have to admit, though, if there wasn't the Internet, I'd still be taping fights."

"We Have Sad Rivalries Now"

Bob Probert is punching someone in the face. Again. Could be Craig Berube. Or maybe Dave Brown.

Honestly, it's hard to keep track.

I'm stuck in an airport terminal, watching a Probert fight DVD on my laptop. Fight fans consider him the greatest ever: best record, most feared, knockout power, took punches, never ducked a scrap. Decent player too. I figure I can learn something. Twenty minutes in, I'm pumped. Probert battling Dave Richter and Rick Tocchet back-to-back is *way* more exciting than the neutral-zone trap. I even have a new name for my struggling fantasy squad: Probert Throws Best. Yet after another dozen fights, my adrenaline fades. The beatdowns seem robotic. I feel numb. Wham, bam . . . is this it?

When I mention my malaise to Posux, a Fried Chicken regular and West Coast editor of a popular men's magazine, he asks me whether I follow hockey. Not really. That's the problem, he says. You have to know the teams, the rivalries, the personalities, the story lines. It's like a soap opera. In the context of hockey, fights are the straw stirring the drink. In the context of no context — a fight tape — they're human cockfights on ice.

I decide to go to a game.

Peatycap offers to come along. He gave me the Probert disc. He's twenty-eight, works for the federal government, and has a master's degree in organizational psychology. He also owns a golden retriever. So I feel safe. We pick a March game between the Caps and Penguins. While NBC focuses on Sidney Crosby and Alex Ovechkin, we're anticipating a rematch between Georges Laraque and Donald Brashear. The two have tangled twice this season. A third bout could decide the NHL's heavyweight championship, at least on the boards:

> I'm predicting they fight midway/late in the second, or early in the third.
>
> Laraque is going to have to do something pretty significant while Brashear is on the ice for this fight to happen.
>
> If the Caps or Pens go down by two goals, it should happen. Knowing Brash, he probably figures twice in a season is enough. Winning this game is way more important than his personal fighting rivalry . . . It is important to us, though. LOL.

Game day. The Verizon Center scoreboard displays a text message from a fan reading "We want a goalie fight." Peatycap is worried. Yesterday, Brashear dropped Boston's Shane Hnidy with a glove-on sucker punch, a blow that made the opening montage on *SportsCenter.* The Caps enforcer could be suspended; even if he plays, the club might keep him on a short leash.

I check the official game notes. Brashear is in the lineup. Excellent. We make our way to the lower bowl and take our seats behind the goal. On the other side of the glass, the teams are warming up. Brashear is six-foot-two, 235 pounds; Laraque, six-three, 243. In skates and pads, they look even bigger, as if they could park small cars just by picking them up.

"Brashear-Laraque, round three!" says a guy in a Crosby jersey, turning to face us. "Man, I hope we see it."

Crosby Guy has beer breath. Overpowering beer breath. Then again, it is nearly half past noon.

"We'll see them hug each other for three seconds," says Hannibal, Peatycap's older brother. "Then they'll both fall down."

"Both those guys, they could land one punch and it's done," says Crosby Guy, shaking his head.

"If you really want to get into this, you should go see the Quebec league," Peatycap tells me. "They take off helmets, skate around, come to center ice, shadowbox a bit. Then they fight. They're showmen!"

Where Peatycap is bullish, Hannibal is dismissive. Ready for a letdown. Styles make fights, he says, and the problem with Brashear and Laraque is that they're boring. Dominant, yes, but dull. Both follow the same formula: Lock up opponents with overwhelming strength, land a few hard punches for effect, end brawl. Do just enough to win without getting hurt, just enough to continue in a line of work in which one lucky punch can leave you unemployed and drinking your meals with a straw. (Laraque is an eleven-year vet; Brashear is in his sixteenth season. Neither number is an accident.) Fight fans call this "seatbelting," and they find it maddening. They aren't moved by play-it-safe technical prowess. They want Julio Cesar Chavez, bloodied but unbowed, taking fifty punches to deliver fifty-one. They want total abandon, toe-to-toe wars, pulp-faced passion.

"I think Brash fights more on business than emotion," Hannibal says. "That's not what I want to see. What leads to a powder-keg situation? History. Genuine dislike."

"That's what builds a rivalry," Peatycap says.

"We have sad rivalries now," Hannibal says.

"It is sad," Peatycap says. "Atlanta had a no-fight rule, didn't even dress [its] tough guy the game after all those fights with the Caps." (In November 2006, the Caps and Thrashers engaged in a series of late-game brawls that produced 176 penalty minutes, three suspensions, and $40,000 worth of fines. A December rematch, however, produced zero fights.) "It's the infamous phone call from the NHL," Peatycap continues. "They say, 'If this happens, we're watching and you will be punished.'"

"I would have been embarrassed to be an Atlanta fan," Hannibal says. "Their team was soft."

"Even if your team loses, if they fight, at least you go away knowing that they cared," Peatycap says. "That they have heart."

Peatycap tells a story. When he was eleven, his parents took him and Hannibal to their first hockey game, a Washington–New Jersey contest at the now-demolished Capital Centre in suburban Maryland. Fans were screaming at Devils goalie Chris Terreri: "Hey, Terreri, you suck!" The boys turned to their mother: "Can we yell too?" Late in the third period, they were about to leave when a fight broke out. Peatycap and Hannibal ran down to the glass, transfixed. So did their mom.

"My mom is a eucharistic minister, and she was banging on the glass," Peatycap says, laughing. "At least, that's how our dad tells the story."

Back to this game: Three ponytailed girls, none older than twelve, sit behind the net. No one curses out Penguins goalie Marc-Andre Fleury. The NHL is changing, chasing corporate dollars, competing against the NBA and Netflix and the Nintendo Wii, positioning itself as family entertainment. A sports product suitable for the Hannah Montana set (not to mention sanctimonious sports columnists who liken the league to glorified roller derby). This means more emphasis on goals, less emphasis on blood. Since the hockey-fighting apex of the 1970s — *Slap Shot* in theaters, Philadelphia's Stanley Cup–winning Broad Street Bullies in penalty boxes — rules changes and stiffer penalties have slowly squeezed fisticuffs out of the sport. The NHL's last bench-clearing brawl was in 1987. According to unofficial statistics at the website dropyourgloves.com, fights per game are down from an average of

1.29 per game in 1987–88 to 0.40 last season. Teams that used to dress two or more enforcers — like Detroit with Probert and Joey Kocur, the much-hyped, much-feared "Bruise Brothers" — now dress none.

The league knows violence still sells tickets — a study published in the *American Journal of Economics and Sociology* found a correlation between brawling and attendance, and the website hockeyfights.com draws 8 million page views per month during hockey season — but it also knows too much violence gives the sport a black eye.

"It's a balancing act," Caps owner Ted Leonsis says. "The day after that Atlanta game, I probably got four hundred e-mails. Half of them went like this: 'How dare you, I took my son or daughter to the game and have never been more embarrassed. I will never go to a game again. Fighting should be outlawed, and Donald Brashear should be suspended for life.'

"Meanwhile, the next e-mail would say, 'That was the greatest game I've ever been to in my life. I love seeing the team stand up for each other.'"

Leonsis laughs. As a hockey fan, he respects and appreciates fighting; as an owner, he says his franchise wouldn't build a marketing campaign around it. "Now, one complaint is too many. But let's not forget that Atlanta did TV commercials promoting the rematch."

If the NHL is like a presidential candidate in a general election — moving to the center, trying to be everything to everyone — then fight fans are like the hard-core wing of the party. They're the true believers, the no-compromise ideologues. They liked the league the way it was, and as glove-dropping becomes less common, they feel betrayed. Sold out. On the message boards, they direct most of their ire at commissioner Gary Bettman, who is alternately seen as: (a) a clueless basketball guy, thanks to his previous stint as an NBA senior vice president; (b) a soulless corporate vampire, concerned only with enriching owners, no matter the larger cost; (c) responsible for every problem in the game, and probably global warming too.

"I have no idea what that man thinks," says Peatycap, who once created a website (hockeyfansunite.com) to voice his displeasure with Bettman. "He's a poor ambassador for hockey."

Peatycap might be right. But he's missing the larger point. In blaming Bettman, fight fans are punching a brick wall. Fifteen years ago, NHL video games let you cross-check Wayne Gretzky — the very face of hockey — after the whistle, dumping him in a pool of pixelated blood. Today, a game with the same feature probably would prompt a congressional hearing. Culture evolves. Hockey arenas are no longer dumpy old frozen barns. They're value-added sports theme parks, housing teams originally named for Emilio Estevez star vehicles. Time moves on.

Back at the Verizon Center, time is running out. Laraque and Brashear have yet to tangle, and with the game tied 2–2 in the third period, a fight seems unlikely. Neither squad can afford the resulting penalty time — five minutes for throwing punches, two additional minutes for the player who instigated the fracas. Not when a single power play could prove decisive.

A break in play. The scoreboard flickers. A video montage. On comes Al Pacino, delivering his "Inches" locker-room speech from *Any Given Sunday*. Peatycap sighs. That the arena ops crew is using a football movie is bad enough. That the speech is intercut with ten seconds of Brashear fight footage is downright cruel.

"If we were just here to watch fights, I'd have to root for Pittsburgh to start racking up goals," Hannibal laments. "I don't think fight fans go to games anymore. They'd be wasting their money."

With 27.9 seconds left, the Penguins score a go-ahead goal, then add an empty-netter. Game over. Fans stream to the exits. The heavyweight championship will have to wait.

"This sucks," Hannibal says.

Respect the Code

Derek Boogaard works the angles, cutting off the ring, moving his younger brother Aaron into the corner. Ceiling fans twirl under dull fluorescent lights, casting faint, flickering shadows against the flat-gray walls of the Lonsdale Boxing Club in Regina, Saskatchewan.

Thump-thump! Derek throws a jab, then another, his left arm extending into space like a curtain rod. Short of breath, he pulls back, flashing his neon-blue mouthpiece. He dips his left hand. Aaron jabs back. *Thump!*

"Ow!" yells Derek, popping out the mouthpiece. "You punched my collarbone!"

"Break!" yells boxing coach Frank Fiacco, clicking a stopwatch. "Keep that left hand up! Don't slide!"

Derek leans against the ropes, shoulders sagging, his long-sleeved shirt drenched with sweat. Fiacco grabs a bottle, squirts water into Aaron's mouth. He turns to Derek. "You're getting lazy," Fiacco says, holding a hand over his chin to demonstrate. "The left hand should be *here*. You threw a couple of jabs, but you didn't follow with the right.

"If you don't do it on a moving body, you're not going to do it on the ice."

Derek nods. He's gassed. It's an early evening in August, and the Minnesota Wild enforcer has already spent his afternoon at a rink, skating himself into shape for the upcoming NHL season. He's here with Aaron, a minor league winger, to become a better brawler. A scary proposition, given that many fight fans consider the six-foot-seven, 270-pound "Boogeyman" to be the league's most destructive puncher.

"You should watch when he trains with the heavy bag," says Curtis Kemp, a local policeman watching from outside the ring. "The whole place shakes."

Derek has been training with Fiacco for three years. He wasn't supposed to spar tonight. He was supposed to teach at the Derek and Aaron Boogaard Hockey Fighting Camp, open to kids twelve to eighteen, a two-hour clinic so popular the previous edition drew twenty-plus participants and a write-up in a Minneapolis newspaper. The article was picked up nationally, controversy ensued, and tonight's event was scrapped.

Josh Kemp came anyway. A fifteen-year-old with close-cropped blond hair and a broad, lanky frame, Josh is Curtis's son, captain of his youth hockey team. Last season, he played in a provincial all-star tournament. He also led his league in penalty minutes and has been working with Fiacco since he was ten.

"Josh has a great shot, and he's a good defenseman," Curtis says. "But he's not going to be Wayne Gretzky. He brings another element."

"Other kids are pretty much sitting there flailing their arms around," Josh says. "I actually know what to do."

"He has learned to hit hard," Curtis says. "One hit and it's over."

"I love doing it," Josh says.

"Last year, we're in a tournament in Prince Albert, a real dirty game, and Josh knocks out one kid, then another," Curtis says. "The coach sends out a third guy. Josh knocks him out too."

"That was fun," Josh says with a laugh, looking slightly embarrassed. "I didn't even know what had happened until my team told me after."

"Josh is going to the Kelowna Rockets' WHL camp next week, his first real taste of what junior hockey can be," Curtis says. "I can say unequivocally that he wouldn't be going if we hadn't come here."

"I just like fighting," Josh says.

"Not one time did he get in trouble for it," Curtis says. "He filled a role with the team."

He filled a role with the team. Baseball has designated hitters. Hockey has designated punchers. Why? The answer lies in what author Ross Bernstein calls "the code," the unwritten rules of hockey brawling that govern everything from who fights whom to Laraque's famously wishing fellow tough guy Raitis Ivanans, "Good luck, man," before pummeling him. It's no coincidence Boogaard and Josh Kemp have fathers who are cops, and no accident the puckheads use the term "enforcer" instead of "goon."

Goons enforce the code. Fight fans admire them for it. "They're kind of like antiheroes," Posux says. "Like Dirty Harry. When you need to take the law into your own hands, they do it. They walk into town and take names."

At a basic level, the code owes something to both beanball wars and the Book of Exodus. An eye for an eye. You plunk one of ours, we plunk one of yours. Justice via swift, painful retaliation. Hockey is a fast, full-contact, no-stoppage sport played by large men with sharp blades and curved sticks. Referees can't police everything. Enter the goon. Anyone who roughed up Gretzky in his Edmonton Oilers heyday, for example, knew he'd have to pay a price — a punch in the face from bodyguards Marty McSorley or Dave Semenko. As such, maybe he would think twice. Or maybe he wouldn't bother in the first place. Could Gretzky have fought for himself? Sure. But he wouldn't have been very valuable sitting in the penalty box, bruised and bleeding from the nose, any more than Semenko would have been useful drawing face-offs. Fill a role. Tough guys act as score-settlers, proxy gladiators, nuclear deterrents.

"With a guy like Donald Brashear," Leonsis says, "it's mutually assured destruction."

Fights themselves follow a set of guidelines as complex as an arms control treaty. The overriding principle is fairness. But the gray areas are extensive. Cheap shot? Clean punch? Uncalled for? Had it coming? On the message boards, every brawl is fodder for ethical debate. "That's the drama," Posux says. "Part of the fun."

In general, fighters don't beat up nonfighters. But sometimes they do. Big guys aren't supposed to fight small guys, unless the smalls ask for it. Anyone is free to turn down a fight, especially if he's injured or liable to hurt his team via penalty minutes. Turn down the wrong fight at the wrong time, however, and you're considered a "spot-picker." Which is two shades over from "coward." Never challenge someone at the end of his shift — he might be tired — but always try to pull an opponent's sweater over his face, because he can't hit what he can't see. Punching someone while he's on the ice is bad, and punching someone in the back of the head is worse, yet hitting someone directly in the kisser until his bones are the consistency of applesauce is good. Very good. Oh, and don't dip your helmet forward in a scrap, because even though your dance partner is trying to pound you, you don't want him to cut up his knuckles, otherwise he won't be able to do his job. *Good luck, man!*

Back in Regina, Derek Boogaard has just finished sparring. One year earlier, he fractured then–Anaheim enforcer Todd Fedoruk's cheek and orbital bones with a series of hard punches. Fedoruk ended up getting four titanium plates inserted in his face. Even some fight fans wondered whether the brutal brawl was good for their hobby.

Boogaard leans forward in his chair, which beneath his hulking frame resembles baby furniture. He's friendly and relaxed, maybe a bit sleepy. He asks whether I follow football. "Look at quarterbacks," he says, shaking his head. "They get smoked. And if it's not the guy hitting them, it's their head bouncing off the grass."

"In a hockey fight, you know that things are coming in front of you. I couldn't imagine grabbing a guy and just launching into him. I would find that hard to do, to blindside a guy."

Er, right. So the code, all these little rules, they're designed to protect fighters, even though they're, you know, fighting? Got it. And when the other guy takes his helmet off — which happens a lot in the minors — that's to protect . . . *your* fists?

Boogaard smiles. He shows me his hands. They look like mangled tree branches: scarred knuckles, knobby joints, a reddish purple lump atop his right middle finger that wouldn't be out of place on the surface of Mars.

"You punch someone in the skull, and it's like, 'F—!'" he says. "It still hurts."

It's all very honorable. And all very confusing.

Knuckles Like the Protruding Edge of a Kitchen Countertop

Jon Mirasty has the round, friendly face of a mischievous cherub. He stands five-ten, weighs 220 pounds. On the ice, however, he seems bigger and taller, definitely more menacing, less cherub than pissed-off grizzly bear.

Of course, this is probably because his fist is pressed against my chin.

I'm back in Syracuse. The Crunch's morning skate is over, and Mirasty is showing me the ins and outs of a hockey fight, up close and personal. I'm wearing jeans and a team jersey, and thankfully, we're play-acting — otherwise, I'd be on my back and unconscious, or possibly reading through insurance premiums. Mirasty squares up, engages, throws a baby jab. Yipes. His knuckles feel like cold granite, the protruding edge of a kitchen countertop; his death grip on my collar brings to mind Mola Ram from *Indiana Jones and the Temple of Doom.*

"You see a little blood," Mirasty says, "and you keep punching."

Hockey fighting is a dance. With, as mentioned, ample hemoglobin. Throw in some C-list celebrities, and it would make a pretty decent prime-time show. (*Glove-Dropping with the Stars* — who wouldn't want to see Mark Cuban get decked?) The first step is the grab. Right-handed puncher? Snatch a fistful of the other guy's jersey with your left hand — around the neck if you want to open up, around his right shoulder if you want to keep him from throwing. This gives you leverage, sets up your overhand right, even lets you throw small, irritating jabs with your left fist. A good grab is akin to a good punt return — it makes all the violence to come a whole lot easier.

Be warned: your opponent also is trying to grab you.

Next comes punching. You want to punch first. You want to punch hard. (Mirasty trains with thirty-pound dumbbells: hold one in each hand, cock fist above shoulder, punch for thirty seconds, switch hands, repeat.) Remember to duck your chin into your shoulder pads too, because you're getting punched at the same time. Worn out? Time to "seatbelt" — grab both of the other guy's shoulders and squeeze your arms like a vise. (When Mirasty does this, the sensation is downright claustrophobic. Oh, and look out for kidney punches. That's the counter.)

Feeling bold? Try switching hands. Mirasty does this when taller opponents hold him at arm's length, and also for the hell of it. Just to put on a show. It's something of a signature move. Works like this: My left hand is grabbing Mirasty's right shoulder. His left is grabbing my right. We're trading right-handed punches. My reach is longer. My punches are connecting. He has me just where he wants me. "You might be winning at this point," he says, grinning. "But watch."

Mirasty's right hand shoots under my left arm, grabs just under my neck. At the same time, his skates and shoulders reverse, while his left hand cocks back. He's coiled, ready to punch, weight and momentum behind his fist; I'm off-balance, arms neutralized, somehow pulling Mirasty *toward* my wide-open, soon-to-be-rearranged face. This happens in an instant and makes me happy I never learned to skate.

Later, as we're sitting on the team bench, two teenage boys take to the ice. They might be in high school, though neither looks old enough to get a driver's license. The boys circle each other, shadowboxing, then grab each other's shirts. I hear them grunting, and I think they're horsing around, until one slips and falls on his back with a loud *thwack!*

"Welcome to the Syracuse Crunch," Mirasty says, "where even the water boys fight."

He's joking. Sort of. The Crunch are bound for the AHL playoffs, largely thanks to playing "heavy" — hitting hard, talking trash, turning games into pain-endurance tests. Intimidating opponents, daring them to fight back. The ice becomes a schoolyard. Mirasty is the toughest kid in class. In a recent game against Grand Rapids, teammates tell me, Crunch captain Zenon Konopka issued an in-game challenge to the Griffins' bench.

Let's have a fight. One of yours against one of ours. Fair and square. Show us what you're made of.

The Griffins declined. And the Crunch muscled their way to a 5–2 victory.

"We win games before we even play," Konopka says. "People just want to get out of here with their bodies intact. With Jon, we feel physically invincible on ice. You see him fight, and it's kind of a warm feeling inside."

He pauses and notices my face is all scrunched up. "That's weird to say," he admits. "But it's true. When the team was bringing Jon in, they asked me what I thought. I said, 'Get a guy who likes fighting.' Ninety percent of fighters don't. Six percent do. Four percent love it. Jon loves it."

He didn't always. Here's the thing about enforcers: none of them grows up dreaming about becoming the next Probert. They want to be Mario Lemieux. But somewhere along the line, they realize that's as likely as the NHL's expanding to Mars. To stay in the sport, they have to adjust. Do whatever it takes. Like taking punches.

Mirasty is no different. He grew up on a farm, loved horses, was a peewee goal scorer. At age fifteen, he was invited to a junior camp, where the reigning tough guy challenged him to a fight. "He was twenty," Mirasty recalls. "I beat him. The coach didn't want me to go home."

He had a gift. Didn't know where it came from. Maybe it was residual anger after his parents divorced. Maybe it was the kids on the Flying Dust First Nation Indian reservation mocking his mixed-race heritage — Cathy has Irish ancestors, Gary is a Cree Indian — calling him "white boy" as he skated along the ice. Maybe it was just his cinder-block skull, a blessing from the goon gods. "I've never played with a guy who can take a punch like him and not swell up," Konopka says. "You see him in the penalty box and he's fine. It's unbelievable."

Mirasty fought his way from Prince Albert and Moose Jaw in Saskatchewan, from Bakersfield, California, to Danbury, Connecticut. He spent three seasons in Quebec's Ligue Nord Americaine de Hockey, the most brutal, fight-happy league in the sport. He made good money, had a son, met his fiancée, had a tooth removed from his left hand and a steel plate inserted in his right. (The tooth severed the tendon above his middle finger; the plate sets off airport security metal detector wands.) He became a fight fan cult hero, his fearless style winning converts, YouTube clips of his bouts drawing 80,000-plus views. Yet by last summer, he was ready to retire, go home to Meadow Lake, Saskatchewan, and spend time with Tristan, his son, now six years old. Camp and fish and hunt. Coach youth hockey. Maybe compete in mixed martial arts (MMA). He didn't see a place for himself in the changing NHL. "Being a tough guy, I felt this is pretty much as far as I can go," he recalls.

Enter Eric Beman. Eric is Mirasty's agent and a good friend. More importantly, he's a fan. A hard-core fight fan. Saw his first hockey brawl in 1978. Been hooked ever since. As a teenager, Beman made contacts with NHL teams, met enforcers at their hotels, amazed them with his knowledge of their *junior* careers. Later, he'd travel up and down the East Coast and into Canada to watch and film fights. He knows Nicky V. He knows the guys who came before Nicky V.

"Say you and your girlfriend are going to Hawaii on vacation," he says. "Where am I going? I'm driving nine hours to Quebec City to film training camp, film fifteen fights. That's like a dream vacation for me. Nowhere else I would rather be."

Beman makes his living as a personal trainer, owns a chain of fitness stores in New Jersey. But he never lost the fight bug and, about ten years ago, decided to become an agent. For tough guys. Exclusively. He wasn't motivated by money — you'd be better off digging for oil in Central Park — but rather by a desire to preserve his hobby. He met Mirasty four years ago, helped talk the Crunch into signing him, and has spent two years filming Mirasty on and off the ice with $10,000 worth of video equipment he bought himself. He'd like to make a documentary, something along the lines of the well-received MMA film *The Smashing Machine*. He'd really like to see Jon get invited to an NHL training camp, then fight his way onto a roster — if only to show that tough hockey isn't dead.

I ask Beman whether he plays hockey. Nope, he says. Roller and street. But never on ice. Never had the opportunity.

"I'm just a guy who will do anything for hockey fights," he says. "As sick as that sounds."

Ugly and Strange and Beautiful

"F—ing Gillies, man." Cochrane remains perplexed.

The third period of the Crunch–River Rats game is about to begin, and still no face-punching. Never mind that Konopka has pretty much called out Albany's entire team — his mouth could fuel an electric wind farm — or that parts of *Slap Shot* were filmed in this very building. Mirasty's gloves are safely wrapped around his hands. The crowd is restless.

"Definitely orchestrated," Cochrane says, staring a hole through the back of the River Rats' bench.

I reconsider Cochrane's theory: Albany's coach won't let Gillies fight Mirasty because I'm here to see it. The more I turn it over, the more it seems preposterous. Wait. Not preposterous. Small-minded. Don't blame me. Blame change. Blame a culture that likes its violence restricted to MMA and *Grand Theft Auto*. Guaranteed fight? Maybe those days are over. Maybe there's no such thing, not anymore, not when a much-replayed brawl involving the son of former NHL goalie Patrick Roy prompts howling, widespread outrage. Maybe Cochrane and all the other fight fans, the apostles of aggression, will just have to get used to a world in which goons are museum pieces, in which Mirasty retreats to rural Canada to fish with his son.

Cochrane looks at me like *I'm* the crazy one.

"Fighting is something that is necessary in the game," he says. "You can try to discourage it, but you can only accomplish that for a certain period of time. It's like stripping an animal out of an ecosystem. It will be back. We will repeat the tough hockey cycle again. The clothes are back, the hair is back. Enforcers will once again be a hot commodity. As they once were."

He gets a faraway look. "There aren't any boards for the pretty drop pass or the breakaway goal. Rome doesn't change. Rome loves the gladiators."

Are we Rome? I should have read the book. Needing a change of scenery, I leave my seat, turn a corner, head down into a stadium tunnel. I'm below the bleachers, making my way to the other side of the arena when I hear the crowd. *Oooooh!* Something's up. I scramble to a section behind the glass, almost directly opposite of where Cochrane is sitting. A fan fills me in: "Frischmon nailed Borer and now they're gonna go!"

Right. Syracuse's Trevor Frischmon checked Albany's Casey Borer right out of the game, wrecked Borer's knee. Someone on the River Rats has to retaliate. That's the code. Mirasty and Gillies line up together on the outside of a face-off.

"Are we going or what?" Mirasty asks.

"Yeah, yeah," Gillies says. "Okay."

Off come the gloves, followed by the helmets. Mirasty and Gillies skate past center ice, circling each other, hands bobbing up and down. Gillies grabs Mirasty, lands three overhand lefts. He leans back, out of Mirasty's reach, keeps his right arm locked. Mirasty ducks his head, takes some shots to the back of his skull, moves in closer. The two trade punches, abandoning defense, Mirasty with his right hand, Gillies with his left: *one, two, six, eight* . . . I lose count. It's thrilling and horrifying all at once. I think about Dimitri, a fight fan I met online, who runs the goon fantasy league site and grew up in Russia playing pond hockey. Dimitri saw his first fight during a USSR-Canada Summit Series; at that very moment, he remembers, the sport was no longer just a chess match. It was a war. Ugly and strange and beautiful. And he couldn't turn away.

Three seats to my right is an elderly woman. Her face is wet with tears. She has never seen a hockey fight before.

She is Mirasty's grandmother.

Two seats over is a blonde with a ponytail, wearing a Mirasty jersey and Ugg boots. She's standing on her chair, screaming and whistling and waving her index finger in the air.

She is Mirasty's mom.

In the seat next to mine is a young guy holding a digital camera, angling to tape the brawl. "Kill 'em," he screams. "Kill 'em, Jon!"

He is Mirasty's cousin. He's in the Navy. Later this year, he'll ship out to Iraq.

A minute passes. The punching slows. Gillies grabs Mirasty's shoulders, attempting to seatbelt. "Good fight," he says. The refer-

ees approach. Mirasty waves them off. "Hey, get out of here!" He
then does something I've never seen on a fight tape.

He smiles.

I see it. Gillies sees it. Everyone sees it. Mirasty is enjoying this.
He wants more. I glance across the ice at Cochrane. He's standing,
arms crossed, nodding his head. He looks . . . content. Almost se-
rene. And now I understand. All this time, I thought fight fans just
wanted to see someone punch someone else in the face. Bloodlust
and raging id. And that's part of it. But not all of it. And it's not
what really moves true believers in the Cult of the Goon. What
moves them is the willingness to *get* punched in the face, and then
get punched again. To suffer for your teammates, for the sport, for
everyone who cares about it, all so someone else doesn't have to.
You don't have to win. You just have to show up.

Show up and give.

"Kill 'em, Jon!"

Gillies jabs Mirasty in the jaw. The punching begins anew, amid
the crowd's adoring roar, fists landing like lead. Every blow an act
of love.

*The hockey goon always has been one of my all-time favorite sports charac-
ters. The word "goon" alone makes me smile. Apparently, though, it makes
some guys smile a lot more than I do . . . wow. Patrick Hruby should take
this story to some college and get a grant to do a sociological study.*

MICHAEL J. MOONEY

Royal Flushed

FROM MIAMI NEW TIMES

AT A POKER TABLE, perhaps nothing is more disturbing than a well-tanned man. This is a man of luxury. He has the time in his schedule to lie beneath the sun so that it may color him. Or worse, he has the time and money to lie in a tanning booth. He never wants for food or shelter. He doesn't have to wake up to an alarm clock or show up late to meetings, unshaven and smelling of last night's intoxicated adventures.

Nor does he care about a stack of chips worth a few hundred dollars. And this fact makes him dangerous in a poker game filled with men who really can't afford to go home light five big bills.

That was the trouble with Norman, the bronzed gent in his thirties with sparkling teeth, coifed hair, and a Ralph Lauren pullover, as he sat at a no-limit table in the back of the card room at Isle of Capri Casino and Racing at Pompano Park on a Sunday evening in July. Anytime that anyone else at the table bet, Norman raised an ungodly amount, calling out the bet in what seemed like an intentionally ambiguous foreign accent. A few other players knew he played here almost every day, and more than once that evening, a brave soul had doubted Norman and called his huge bets only to see the tan one turn over an unbeatable hand. He sent player after player away from the table looking down into an empty wallet.

When he dragged a tall stack of red chips from his sizable pile and planted them deliberately in the middle of the table in front of me, I quickly shucked the pair of kings in my hand. Like everyone else, I didn't think he had a better hand every time, but I could never be so sure that I'd stake every dime I'd brought to the table.

Norman had more than $600 in chips in front of him when Harold Persaud arrived at the other end of the table. The fifty-three-year-old Caribbean man, who always seems to be in a good mood, is a familiar face around here. This night, he had his long, braided ponytail under a red ball cap and wore a gold earring shaped like a musical note.

Persaud makes his living at these tables. He pulled a crisp $100 bill from a roll in his pocket, greeted the dealer in his island brogue, and sat down. Norman immediately recognized Persaud. "This guy will give me action," Norman said to me under his breath. He sneered as he thought of separating this smiling man from his money.

Over the next half-hour, Persaud was calm, even jovial at times. He casually tossed his chips into the middle; twice he engaged in conversation with someone at another table and didn't miss a beat in the game, throwing his chips in for a call without even turning around.

Soon enough, the two men got into a hand together. Persaud bet. Norman raised; his bright tan was essentially winking at Persaud, begging for a call. Persaud obliged. When the first round of community cards came out, Persaud bet again, pushing the pot over $50.

Persaud knew Norman too, and he'd watched him play. Though this was a lower-stakes $1/$2 table, the two had played at the $5/$10 tables, where the pots often go over $1,000. So when Norman raised again — this time $50 — Persaud sat back and thought. He looked at the bet. Then he counted the money in the pot. He looked at the cards on the table. If Norman had a deuce or a three or another pair in his hand, Persaud knew his pair of fours wouldn't hold up.

He folded, pushing his cards to the dealer — sending all the money he'd put in the pot to this tanned nemesis. Norman, looking smug, turned over a king and an eight. He had nothing. Persaud nodded. A scruffy-looking retiree called to Persaud: "He got you to drop too, huh? I knew he didn't have it."

Persaud calmly leaned forward. "Listen," he told the old man, "you play by your rules and I'll play by my rules." His voice was as soft as the green felt on the table. "We'll see who comes out better."

He was confident that if he stuck to his system, he'd prevail.

A self-described "pro," Persaud plays cards to supplement his income as a cruise-ship musician. As Harold Caribbean, he has recorded eight albums over the past twenty years, but now he's what you might call an amateur professional poker player. He is one of dozens of men — and a few women — who go to the legal poker rooms across South Florida every day, hoping to grind out the money to pay the bills. They go to places such as Pompano Park, Mardi Gras, and Miccosukee Resort & Gaming, to card rooms full of businessmen who cut out of the office early, young men wearing hooded sweatshirts and listening to iPods, foul-smelling degenerate addicts, and more retirees than a Sunday buffet.

These amateur pros feast on the tourists with bloated pockets and yentas who can't quite see all the cards — and guys like Norman, who have the money and know-how but not the drive or desperation.

They show up from open to close as if the poker room were an office. They take their meals at their desk — the poker tables. Their friends are their coworkers: the other regulars, dealers, and floor supervisors. And the massage girls — the attractive young women who, for $10, will rub your back and laugh at your stupid jokes as you play.

The goal is somewhere between carving out a semblance of a normal existence while playing a game for a living and making it big as a poker icon like Daniel Negreanu, Phil Hellmuth, Chris Ferguson, or the ultimate amateur-made-good, Chris Moneymaker.

Battle between the patient Persaud and the tanned Norman continued for hours. The other players at the table could only watch as the two went back and forth, each trying to study and trap the other.

By 11:00 P.M., Persaud was collecting the last of Norman's chips.

After seeing his fortune melt away, Norman stood up quietly, with the empty gaze of a punch-drunk boxer. He went home, possibly to tan.

To his heckler, Persaud was curt. "You think I'm going to risk all that on a little pair of fours?" he asked, referring to the hand he had lost earlier. "He can have all the small pots he wants. I'll get him in the big ones. And look" — he pointed to the $600 of chips in front of him — "here's all his money." He grinned. "This is what I do."

*

The days of poker as the sport of bearded degenerates with tall hats and nicknames that involved geography are gone. Delaware Donnie has been replaced by Donald Johnson, an accounts manager from Dover who likes getting together with buddies and sometimes, while on vacation, plays at a casino.

Everyone in the industry can chalk up at least some part of America's poker fever to the work of Chris Moneymaker. And seriously, who could ask for a better name? The Tennessee accountant who began playing dollar games online and ended up winning the World Series of Poker main event in 2003 was a story too good to resist. This was the first live tournament he'd ever played. His small frame, soft build, and Southern drawl told millions of Americans they too could bluff out a Vegas pro and win a few million dollars.

Then came the constant replays of that event. And the rise of online poker. And the barrage of poker commercials and poker books. Poker movies. Scripted poker TV shows. Poker cruises. Poker video games.

Poker players became celebrities, drinking champagne with movie stars, appearing on television, and receiving large winner's checks. And then thousands of poker enthusiasts across the nation debated "going pro" — as if they were Heisman Trophy candidates forced to choose between friends on the team and the money in the NFL. Except, of course, with poker, turning pro doesn't mean you're signing a contract with a franchise. A thin sliver of players in Las Vegas and Los Angeles receives sponsorships from poker websites, but the only real requirement to turn pro is the willingness to gamble — and lose — large sums of money.

An industry centered on corporate-owned casinos such as Isle of Capri Casinos and Hard Rock International benefits from these individuals spending more time at the casino, where they eat, drink, get rubs, and tip, tip, tip.

Card Player magazine's twentieth-anniversary issue, which is handed out free at several local card rooms, featured a column about "understanding what to expect before turning pro." Among the tips: "If needed, take a leave of absence from work. It helps to play every day (or whatever schedule you expect to work as a professional). If you decided to move to Las Vegas or California, go there for a few months to try it out."

Casinos found a way to make big bucks dealing poker. Though

players are competing against one another and not against the house, as in blackjack and roulette, the casino still takes a cut of every pot. That portion, called a "rake," is normally 10 percent, with a cap at $5 every hand. A rake also means that even if two players tie in a hand, they both lose money.

Harold Persaud learned the game when he was a lounge performer ten years ago in Las Vegas. But only in the past year and a half has he decided he could play full-time. He goes to Pompano or the Hard Rock most weekdays and at least one weekend day — to cash in on the weekend tourists looking to get a few hours away from the family. He told me he averages $1,000 a week from cash games, tournament wins, and the lessons he offers in his Boca Raton home. He also told me that he's never read a poker book but that as long as he brings positive energy and sticks with his rules, he likes his chances against anyone in the world.

Brian G. was ahead of the poker boom. Now thirty-three years old, the Brooklyn native first played for cash at age fourteen. He told me he doesn't like to call himself a pro, but he spends eighty hours a week playing in live cash games, playing online (as "BrooklynBman"), dealing in high-dollar home games, or dealing at the Palm Beach Kennel Club in West Palm Beach, where he lives. His arms are tattooed, his head shaved, his face thoughtful.

I sat down next to him at a table in the Seminole Casino Coconut Creek, where he plays about twenty-five hours a week. It was past 1:00 A.M. Right now, four Broward poker rooms are open around the clock: Coconut Creek and the other two Seminole casinos, plus Mardi Gras Racetrack and Casino in Hallandale Beach. A poker room in the middle of the night is a symphony of coughing, clacking chips, and loud sports television played over a sea of sunken eyes and crooked backs. Behind all the interaction is the mutual understanding that nobody in the room will be doing anything productive for society the next morning.

While we played, Brian took several smoke breaks, and each time he returned, he made his way around the room to see how his friends were doing. His mother taught him to play Uno and Yahtzee as a kid, he says. Then gin rummy. Then a handful of poker games he can list off in his Brooklynese: "Omaha, acey-deucy, follow the queen." His father trained — and bet on — racehorses. By age eighteen, he had a fake ID so he could play poker and blackjack in Atlantic City. By twenty-three, he had spent every dime of his bar mitzvah money and pawned every bit of jewelry he owned just to keep gambling.

One night he broke into his roommate's safe to get the $1,500 inside. When he came back from the three-day binge — where he lost it all — his stuff was gone and his key didn't work.

He says he's finished with betting on sports and playing black-jack. But not poker. Here he has some control of the outcome. And there isn't much in the world that feels like a good run of cards. He has seen people turn $100 into $20,000 in hours. Brian says he doesn't keep very good records, but he places his annual poker in-come at $50,000 to $70,000 before taxes.

Recently, he's played more live games and less online. He doesn't trust the offshore gambling companies that run now-illegal sites such as Pokerstars.com and FullTilt.com. For years, players have worried about the validity of online games that benefit from two players both getting top-quality hands at the same time, so they both end up betting a lot, raising the rake.

"I'm a dealer; I see thousands of hands every day," Brian says. "You just don't see four-of-a-kinds and straight flushes like you do online. It's gotta be fixed."

While we spoke, a bearded old man at the table was telling us how close he was to the bad beat earlier that day. Most casinos dis-play an ever-growing "bad beat jackpot" to be split among everyone at the table after the most improbable poker defeats. Which hands qualify as the bad beat vary from place to place, but generally, if someone loses with a full house of aces over kings or better, the hand is jackpot-worthy. Each casino also has a complex set of fine-print rules and technicalities for the bad beat, so no player is sure what qualifies at any given time.

"I was an ace away," the old man said. "I've been at the table when we hit once. We couldn't believe it. We split more than $100,000. Dealer, let's get a bad beat."

The dealer had just told the table about her new baby grandson. She had pictures. When any of the men around the table folded his cards to her, she'd say, as if talking to the toddler, "Bye bye now!"

Brian got into a hand with an older Asian man. He was disap-pointed that the guy had stayed in — and won — with a jack and a seven, which is, by any standard, a subpar starting hand in Texas hold 'em.

"What kind of asshole calls two raises with jack-seven?" he grunted to the other end of the table, showing that he had a pair of aces.

"The winner, that's who," the Asian man replied, stacking Brian's chips.

Brian unfolded another $100 bill and slid it to the dealer. "Jack-asses who stay with jack-seven . . ." He trailed off.

When I asked him about the hand an hour later, he was still bitter. "You should call your story 'Fishes of the Sea,'" he said. "Donkeys like that, they don't know the right way to play. I guess in the long run, you want guys like that, but then sometimes they get lucky and get you." He pursed his lips. "That's poker."

The expression "That's poker" has come to symbolize the ultimate noble defeat at the whim of the poker gods. Playing poker is one of those rare opportunities in life when you can do everything right (go all-in with a pair of aces in your hand, for example) and still lose all of your money (to some horrible, lucky schmuck with a two and a seven). No matter the pronouncements in movies like *Rounders* about poker being a game of skill; it is popular, in part, because a donkey (a popular nickname for a bad player who gets lucky and wins) can beat a pro on any hand, given the order of the cards.

For the majority of players, the compulsive nature of the game keeps them coming back to places like Pompano Park, where the new poker room, with its wood paneling and high-tech tables that allow for faster play (and more rakes), is the center of a $140 million renovation project that includes a steak house, a New York–style deli, and a top-shelf bar.

In the early afternoon, players begin to arrive, a ceaseless stream of poker zombies traversing the vast, sweltering casino parking lots, called to the cool air inside. Once in the door, they grip their wallets inside their pockets and march past the slots and over to the escalator going to the second floor. From the first floor, they can already hear stacks of chips shuffling and clacking together in a rhythmic, soothing cadence. The sound alone sets the neurochemical receptors in motion, a Pavlovian response in anticipation of the gamble.

The regulars, however, require more stimulation. Sitting in these cold, anonymous rooms for hours on end, they need something to root for. So after a pizza or a smoke break or a series of unlucky hands, a player might pat the table gently and call for the elusive bad beat. Most players have actually never seen one. It's the dream — the prayer — that gets the weary through a disappointing stretch.

On a recent Wednesday back in Pompano, Persaud had suffered a string of bad beats at the higher-stakes $5/$10 table, though none qualified as so bad it was good. After losing $500 ("That's the most I'll buy in to a table for," he told me. "If it's not your night, it's just not your night."), he saw me at a $1/$2 table.

Across the table, a man sat next to his wife. He wore a poker T-shirt, an open button-down shirt with cards on it over the T-shirt, a poker-themed hat, and poker sunglasses. His gold wedding band had aces carved into it. As they played, the man criticized his wife's play.

"No way you should have called that," he said.

"I'm sorry," she said. "I don't know what I was thinking."

Persaud sat next to me, across from Mr. Poker.

"How's it going, Harold?" the dealer asked.

"Not so good," Persaud replied. "Not so good."

Most dealers also play, though they can't play where they deal. But on their days off, they go to other card rooms — and tip the dealers especially well — so many of them seem like a happy little community. Except when they're losing.

A woman with a round belly walked by. "Hi, Gina," the dealers called out as she passed. Gina, the wife of one of the dealers, made eye contact with a dealer friend of her husband's and sat at the table. She was eight months pregnant.

"I'm just trying to get it out of my system," she joked to another dealer who'd come by to rub her belly and pay his respects.

"You mean the poker or the baby?" he replied.

"If I hit the bad beat, it'll be both," she said.

"Awww, we'll have a great little poker player, won't we?" he said as he rubbed her stomach a few seconds more.

Playing at a table nearby was Trevor Nesbit, a Jamaican-born man in his twenties with an underbite. He told me he plays to pay the bills, painting a picture of himself as the stoic grinder who can gut out the emotional roller coaster that poker provides. His family owns a coin-operated laundromat where he sometimes works when he isn't playing cards. He doesn't go to the laundromat much.

Trevor, or T as he's known in most card rooms, told me I should write about him. "I'm the best player in Florida," he said with an accent. "You follow me around and write about me and get me a sponsor." He said he could take anyone in the world one on one, that he can play all day, every day, and that he never makes a bad move. "Just when you think you might have me, I got you," he said, closing his hand quickly. "I was born with a straight flush in my hand."

He left Pompano around 10:00 P.M. He said he was off to Coconut Creek, where day and night cease to exist. He vowed that he wouldn't leave that casino until he had $2,000, enough to pay his bills for two months. "Come watch me get rich the easy way," he said as he left.

Back at my table, Persaud's bad luck continued. He went through half of his $100 buy-in in just a few hands, losing once to Mr. Poker's wife. His sorrow was interrupted by the shrieks of a woman a few tables away. A swarm of players from other tables stood up and walked over to see about the commotion. The woman was throwing white chips — each worth a dollar — into the air, laughing. "We got it!" she announced in a shrill voice.

Indeed, the cards were still on the table as the dealer waited for a floor supervisor. The woman had four queens ("quad queens," in pokerspeak) and had just lost the hand to another player who showed four kings. As the woman danced around, though, Scott, the dealer, sat calmly and quietly. Something was wrong.

When the floor supervisor arrived, he confirmed that the hand did not, in fact, qualify as a bad beat. "The eight didn't play," he told the gathering crowd. In Texas hold 'em, to have a bad beat, both players in the hand have to use their initial pocket cards when making their final, five-card poker hand. Since there were three queens face up along with two kings and she had a queen and an eight in her hand, the eight was not part of her final five-card hand. (She had four queens and a king; her opponent had four kings and a queen.)

The woman collapsed into her chair, despondent.

The crowd dispersed. As close to the bad beat as most will ever get.

For some people, life as an amateur pro player is like one big bad beat without the six-figure payoff. In theory, all luck evens out and the players with more skill profit in the long run. But the numbers game is hard. The poker commercials that promise "yesterday's average Joe might be tomorrow's millionaire" don't explain how difficult it is to beat the rake. For a player to be successful, he not only has to skim excess money from the whales rolling up with fat stacks of cash, but also pull in enough to cover the $5-a-pot cut that goes to the house, the dollar or two tip to the dealer for each win, and the cost of food, which can range from disgusting fries to a gourmet spread at your table, such as is available at Isle of Capri.

Catherine, a Pompano dealer, estimates that about one in twenty players in her card room tell themselves they're playing poker for a living. "Kids see this on TV and it doesn't look like gambling," she said. Poker fans are inundated with commercials that promote a luxury lifestyle and programming built around the suspense of turning over cards with millions at stake. "Parents are telling their kids to go play poker over at a friend's house to keep them off the streets. What's really happening is an entire generation of boys is going broke very young."

She also thinks television teaches people to play the wrong way. ESPN takes four full days of poker and boils it down to forty-five minutes of action, so viewers don't see that most of the time, professional poker is a tedious, unending sequence of receiving cards, deciding they're not good enough, and folding. "I love the game as much as anyone," Catherine said. "It's fun. It's the reason there are hundreds of people here tonight. But some of these kids bring in all their money, trying to build up a bankroll. And who takes care of them when they have $40,000 worth of credit card debt?"

When I last saw him in Pompano, T told me he wouldn't leave Coconut Creek until he had enough to cover his expenses for two months. And sure enough, more than twenty-four hours later, T was at a $5/$10 table in the small, crowded card room on the second floor of the Seminole casino. He was wearing the same Aston Villa soccer jersey I'd last seen him in. Every ESPN channel played from one of the plasma screens on each wall. Some showed high-lights from the Home Run Derby. Others showed poker.

I was at a table with Brian. He was telling me about the hand in which he lost $40,000. "By the way, does *New Times* cover your buy-in?" he asked.

"We'll see what the editors think of the story," I said, noting my longtime desire to list "gambling losses" on an expense report.

"Losses are a part of this game, like everything else," he said, taking on a slightly wistful tone as he ruminated on the game he has built his life around. "If you love poker, you have to love losing. You have to love winning. You have to love donkeys. People bitch after a bad hand, but you can't complain when you agree to sit down and play with those other people at the table. And deep down, people know that. If poker players didn't love losing, they'd choose to get up and walk away."

When I looked up from our conversation, T, who'd accumulated a hill of expensive chips when last I looked, was gone. Someone else was in his seat, surely still feeling the body heat he'd generated sitting there for more than a day.

It was nearly 4:00 A.M. when I headed out to the west parking lot. I spotted a white truck off by itself near the edge of the lot. It looked just like the one I'd seen T driving when he left Pompano a few nights earlier.

As I got closer, there was a glimmer in the window. Moisture, it seemed, had built up along the inside of the windshield and was re-flecting the tall, yellow lights of the parking lot.

I was next to the driver's-side window on the GMC pickup before I could see inside. There, resting against the door handle, were two large, black Nike sneakers. They connected to jeans that bent around the steering wheel. Beyond that was an Aston Villa jersey twisted around the thin Jamaican man sleeping with his hands next to his cheek. In the quiet of the night, under the glow of the casino lights, he looked like a child taking a post-lunch nap at day care.

Now, at any given time outside a twenty-four-hour casino, you might find a handful of people sleeping in their cars. Generally, they're too drunk to drive or so desperate to get back to the slots that they can't bear to drive away. Once in a while, a security guard told me, you'll find couples having sex right there in the open.

I walked around to the passenger side, where T's head was resting gently. As I looked down at his sleeping face, I thought about this life as a wannabe poker pro. Like so many Americans, part of me is envious that some people get to play a game for a living. They feel the everyday buzz of hitting an open-ended straight draw or bluffing an opponent off a big pot. But there aren't too many jobs where an employee can walk into the office, do everything exactly as the manuals recommend, and still walk away a few thousand dollars poorer. And as an adult, there aren't many respectable occupations that lead to spending the night in a truck parked at the edge of a casino parking lot.

As these thoughts bounced around in my head, I saw movement. T's eyes opened. He looked up at me. I looked back, notebook in hand.

It was weird.

He opened the passenger door and swung his legs around, still groggy. "What are you doing, man?" he asked.

"How often do you sleep out here?" I asked, still jotting down notes about his scuffed Nikes.

"Man, don't go telling people I sleep in my car," he said.

"It's part of the price you pay as a local pro, right?"

"C'mon, man. Don't tell people I sleep in my car. How are people gonna respect me if they think I sleep in my car?"

A week or so after finding him in his truck, I saw T back at Pompano. He was at the $2/$5 table, popular among serious players because you don't have as many idiots as the cheaper table or as many ridiculous gamblers as the highest-stakes tables.

Two seats to his right was another regular, a man the dealers call Wild Bill. T and Bill got into a hand together. T bet big. Bill raised him. T pushed all of his chips into the center and stood up, daring the older man to call. Bill lifted his cards to get a better look. He sized up T's stack and then his own. He tossed his cards into the muck. T turned over his cards, revealing a complete bluff. He scooped the chips into his chest with both arms, grinning brightly.

The thing about poker is, no matter how bad the beat, a few seconds later, you get another hand. A new chance to get rich. A new chance to go broke. And it takes only one win to forget about all the losing.

Still beaming, T tossed the dealer a $5 chip as a tip. Then he turned to the woman sitting next to him. "This guy over here," he said, pointing at Bill, who was within earshot, "this guy is a chump."

Is this a sport? Must be. I see it on ESPN and actually watch when there is nothing else on television. I always wondered how many folks had been burned up, burned out, simply burned before the lucky few win "the bracelet." Michael J. Mooney has the graphic answers. The flop has a deeper poker meaning than three cards laid across green felt. Or so it seems.

JOHN SPONG

Untitled Mike Flynt Project

FROM TEXAS MONTHLY

THE MOVIE WOULD HAVE TO OPEN with a shot of Jackson Field, in Alpine, home of the Sul Ross State University Lobos. Built in 1929 and having seen little touch-up since, the rock-walled stadium would give an instant feel for what it means to play small-college football in a West Texas ranching town. Narrow stacks of metal bleachers face off on either side of the gridiron, but there's no horseshoe seating behind the goalposts, just practice fields, a few rooftops, then long stretches of scrubby desert floor. An ancient press box sits atop the home-side stands, its Plexiglas windows bowed and yellowed, with busy train tracks running just twenty yards behind it. In the film's opening moments, an old freight train could roll by the field, hinting at a resilient power ignoring the passage of time. If the scene were filmed after a rare rainy period, as Alpine experienced in 2007, the hills around the stadium would be unbelievably green, implying a sense of renewal and rebirth. If by the time of filming the regular drought had returned, the verdant effect could be created in the editing room. Reality can never be allowed to interfere with the telling of a good story.

Set the scene at a practice. Since Mike Flynt didn't see action at linebacker until the season's final game, make it the Friday workout before that last contest, a home game against Mississippi College. Script it as much like that real November afternoon as possible: The players stroll onto the field in bunches, dressed in red shorts and jerseys, no pads, most carrying their beat-up gray helmets with the bar-SR-bar logo. Flynt stands out, but not because he's forty years older than his teammates. At five-nine he's a little short, but his barrel chest, reputedly still capable of bench-pressing four hundred pounds, dwarfs everyone else's, and his sleeves are bunched above better-defined biceps. His helmet never comes off, a nod to the old-school virtue of always being ready to go into the game.

Shots of other players reveal a ragtag bunch that couldn't have played anywhere else, the Bad News Bears of Division III football. They're all shapes and sizes, the tall and the short, the ripped and the rippled. Their mood is loose, and the trash talk is constant. Though their playoff dreams dissolved with a week-eight homecoming loss, they still hope for a victory on Saturday to cement a winning 6–4 record, an impressive feat for a team that played six games on the road. Finishing with a win would mean even more to the team's seniors, most of whom — except Flynt, of course — have recently endured winless seasons at Sul Ross.

The comic relief comes from head coach Steve Wright. As the players assemble, he lounges on a sofa on the sideline. One of his players points out that at least he's not chipping golf balls or lying at midfield talking on his cell phone, as he often is. After some brief words of inspiration, Wright sends the team off by position for drills, but the camera stays with him as he heads for a goalpost to visit with alumni and journalists. In his Smoky Mountain drawl — his "y'alls" sounding like "y'owls" — he tells them how unusual their presence is at a frontier program like Sul Ross. Traditionally, reporters and alums have been scarce even at Lobos games, forget Lobos practices.

Mike Flynt has changed all that, Wright tells the reporters. Big media outlets from all over the country have looked in on Alpine this season — CBS, NBC, ABC, Fox News, ESPN, the *Los Angeles Times*, *Sports Illustrated*. There have been movie and book offers by the dozens, blog posts and radio interviews in the hundreds. Flynt has even been writing a weekly column for the Associated Press. It's been a strange autumn.

The camera finds Flynt. He's jogging across the field with the linebackers, and by his gait you can tell he's still a player — up on his toes, with his elbows in and his fists high and together like a boxer's. Instead of pumping his arms, he swings them slightly side to side, as if he's conserving his energy in case the chance comes to cream someone. He stops with his group to practice intercepting passes, and his voice can be heard over everyone else's. "Attaboy, Milo!" "Good hands, Nate!" "That's it, Kyle!" And then, when he takes his turn, his teammates give back. "Nice job, Mike!"

But some moment in this scene will have to explain why Flynt's here. Maybe now he turns to a teammate and repeats the line he's told reporters and players all year, that he has come back to right an old wrong, to make up for having been booted from Sul Ross for fighting during two-a-days in 1971. Have him add his invariable reality check, that though his aging body has kept him from contributing on the field the way he'd hoped, being teammate to these young men has been reward enough. But one thing will need to be made absolutely clear, maybe by having Flynt squint his green eyes at a tailback goofing near midfield, juking in and out of stationary teammates: Flynt has returned to Sul Ross to play linebacker, and tomorrow's game will be his final opportunity to make one last big play, to deliver one last good hit.

The scene should probably end there, though if the movie were to depict the whole of that day, it would have to keep rolling through a curious moment after practice. As the players retired to the field house, two of the team leaders, seniors Austin Davidson, the school's all-time leading passer, and his best friend, Zach Gideon, a giant defensive tackle with a Mohawk and perfect nickname, Giddy, lingered on the field for a field goal–kicking contest. They made a ridiculous sight, the pretty-boy blond quarterback versus the hulking lineman, who finally won the battle with a straight-on toe kick from twenty-five yards.

Afterward, they talked about their years at Sul Ross, the fun they'd had playing despite all the losses, their readiness to get their degrees and get on with their lives, and Flynt.

"Mike's a great guy," began Giddy, "and if this brings attention to the program, that'll be great. But we've got nine seniors on this team, and he's the only one that anyone notices."

"Nothing's about us or anything we've done," said Davidson.

Giddy paused, then added, "Mike's first day on scout defense was at the second-to-last practice. He's not contributing to the team. He's only worried about getting a movie deal."

That's probably not a scene that would make it into the film. It's a little too sour — and too self-conscious — for a feel-good sports flick. It's also not a sentiment expressed by any of the other players

I spoke with in the three months I followed the Lobos last season. Every one of them talked about the inspiration of seeing someone Flynt's age survive two-a-days without ever once complaining. These late gripes sounded like the envy you might expect from kids ending their playing days in a newcomer's shadow. There'd be no place for something like that in a movie about Mike Flynt.

The legend of Mike Flynt begins in Odessa, where his family moved from Mississippi when he was three years old. His father was a World War II vet who'd fought at the Battle of the Bulge, one of the few soldiers in his company to make it out of the Ardennes. Toughness mattered to J. V. Flynt, and he instilled it in his only son, a small kid, by teaching him early to never shy from physical confrontation. From the time Mike could hold up a pair of boxing gloves, his dad would get on his knees in their living room and they'd spar. Mike came to live by the lesson of those encounters: "There is no sin in getting whipped. The sin is in not fighting."

The football field was the first place where he would distinguish himself, though it took a little time. As an eleventh-grader, he played sparingly on defense for the Odessa Permian JV team. But the next year, 1965, Coach Gene Mayfield took over the varsity squad and opened up the depth chart; every player would have to earn his starting spot. Flynt, already a dedicated weight lifter, busted his ass to impress the new coach. He went with the varsity players on unsupervised training trips to run in the nearby sand hills. He made first-team offensive back, one more scrappy oil patch kid on a legendary squad that would go undefeated and win the school's first state championship. It was the birth of the Mojo dynasty. Mike made all-district.

After graduation, he passed on chances to play at the University of Arkansas and Sul Ross to follow a girl. He ended up at Ranger Junior College, eighty-five miles east of Fort Worth. When neither the girl nor Ranger football nor a subsequent semester at Fayetteville worked out, Flynt wound up back home in late 1967. His football career apparently over, he began to make a name for himself as a bar fighter.

"It wasn't something I broadcast," he told me. "But people coming into Odessa knew me one of two ways. Either 'Flynt played football here,' or 'There's that ass-kicker.' And then it's a fastest-gun-in-

the-West-type thing. Somebody wants to be talked about more fa-
vorably than you."

The fights weren't limited to punching and kicking. "It was
chairs, pool cues, gouging . . . all of those. It was winning." Before
too long, word made it to Alpine that Flynt, that old Permian standout, was living in Odessa and not playing football. The Sul Ross
coaches gave him a scholarship to come play for the Lobos.

In those days Sul Ross competed in the National Association
of Intercollegiate Athletics' Lone Star Conference, a powerhouse
akin to baseball's Negro Leagues. Since the Southwest Conference
was still effectively segregated, the best black athletes in Texas
played in the Lone Star. It was no minor league. From 1967 until
1973, the Lone Star's two dominant teams, Texas A&I and East
Texas State, had twenty players drafted by the NFL and the AFL.
And beginning in 1969, Flynt's first season at Sul Ross, a Lone Star
school would win the NAIA football championship every year until
1979. But Sul Ross wasn't one of them. It was the conference step-
child. Where every other school had a natural geographical area
for recruiting, the Lobos were out in six-man country, where the
few local recruits didn't rate with the other schools' and imports
typically came because they couldn't start anywhere else. Sul Ross
made its way by being a little bit tougher, hitting a little harder.
Flynt fit right in.

A natural leader, he'd take guys into the weight room and organ-
ize informal track meets on Jackson Field, just like he had at Permian. He was a second-string defensive back when the 1969 season
opened, but by the fifth game he was starting at outside linebacker,
and he proved to be a terror in the Lobos mold. Before an East
Texas State game, Coach Richard Harvey had instructed the defense to neutralize the opposing quarterback, a brilliant passer
named Dietz who was considered a showboat for wearing white
shoes. At the end of a long scramble with Flynt in pursuit, Dietz
turned and smiled as he stepped out-of-bounds. Flynt laid him out
anyway, explaining to Coach Harvey later, "If I'm going to run that
far, I'm going to hit somebody." Sul Ross finished a disappointing
4–5–1, but the season did feature the single greatest moment in
Lobos gridiron history, a bloody 13–12 homecoming victory over
A&I. It would be the Javelinas' only loss on their way to the national
championship.

The Lobos started the 1970 season on fire, winning their first four games. An early highlight was a win against Tarleton State, in which Flynt recovered four fumbles and picked off a pass, earning conference Defensive Player of the Week honors. The next week they beat seventh-ranked Sam Houston State, in Huntsville, a game made famous after the Lobos' bus broke down ten miles outside town. The players had to hitchhike to the stadium, trickling onto the field in groups of three and four until just before the coin toss. They went on to win 50–18, then the next week beat fourth-ranked Howard Payne, 31–21. The Alpine City Council declared 1970 "the Year of the Lobos."

But the season turned south the following week, when A&I avenged the '69 upset with a 27–0 thumping. The Lobos then dropped two of their next three, to McMurry and East Texas, before closing the season with two wins for a 7–3 record and a tie for third place. Flynt made honorable mention all-conference, won team awards as most conscientious player and a defensive standout, and was named a team captain.

By then he was known all over campus. A good-looking kid with a great shock of brown hair, he was considered not a kicker but a cat daddy for his snappy dress. But he had also cultivated his fighter's reputation in Alpine. If the phone in the athletic dorm, Fletcher Hall, rang on a Sunday morning, the players assumed the caller was the sheriff and that he was probably looking for Flynt. In early 1971, there was a famous fight in the all-night truck stop café just outside town, followed by a trial that was well attended by Lobos and locals. Flynt and his roommate, Randy Wilson, were fined $100, and the team was banned from the café.

Flynt didn't participate in spring football workouts but was back with the team for two-a-days in August. And like a lot of Lobos, he was hoping to turn the previous year's success into a conference championship. But then came the fight that got him kicked out of Sul Ross. Last year's newspaper stories called it "one fight too many." Flynt calls it the great travesty of his life.

His comeback was born over beers at a Lobos reunion in San Antonio last summer. When a former teammate said that Flynt's dismissal had killed bright hopes for the '71 season, Flynt said he had never forgiven himself for letting the team down. Randy Wilson, still Flynt's best friend, suggested he do something about it, and within days Flynt had phoned a former coach to inquire about eligibility. He discovered, to his surprise, that according to Division III rules, he could still play, but there would be administrative hurdles to doing it anywhere but Sul Ross. That was irrelevant to Flynt. "There was no consideration of doing this somewhere else."

We were talking in the student center cafeteria on campus, where we visited periodically through the season. Still dressed like a cool kid in tight T-shirts, loose jeans, and cross trainers, he was impossibly solidly built, his head shaved clean and colored deep red from the Indian summer sun. The media spotlight had restored him to "big man on campus" status, and students walking by interrupted to wish him luck. They'd read the stories and knew him as that old guy on the football team. Used to be a troublemaker. Went on to be a strength coach at Nebraska, Oregon, and Texas A&M. Dabbled successfully in oil wells and gold mines. Had spent his recent years in Tennessee, selling a fitness device he'd invented called Powerbase.

He was soft-spoken, nothing like the mean-ass of legend. "I've had people tell me I'm the most changed person they've ever known," he said the first time we talked. "I always hope that's because they can see God and Christ in me, not through me preaching but through things that I do. And things that I don't."

When he decided to return, there were only a few weeks remaining before practice started. "I drove to Alpine," Flynt said, "met with Coach Wright, and went out and ran with the freshmen. He watched me and saw that I could run with them. He said he was expecting chaos but that I blended."

Flynt and his wife, Eileen, quickly sold their home outside Nashville and moved to Alpine, where he reenrolled at Sul Ross, signing up for "History of American Sports," "Health in Public Schools," and "Seminar in Management." He changed up his training regimen to get into football shape. He ran sprints twice daily. He concentrated on explosive lifting in the weight room, medium weight with intense reps. After sweating through two-a-days in the blistering August heat, he made the team.

Where to play him was a problem. He had strength, size, and speed, but his lateral movement was lacking. Coach Wright said that in a ten-yard square, Flynt would be fine, but with more room to cover, he'd be a liability. Wright listed him at linebacker, but far down on the depth chart.

Then there was the matter of injuries. In the first weeks of practice Flynt suffered a stinger, tore an arch, discovered two bulging vertebrae, and pulled a calf and abdominal muscle. He learned quickly that his body didn't recover like a young man's. He spent much of his time at practice alone, high-stepping on the sidelines to keep his muscles warm in case a coach put him into a scrimmage.

But there were things he could do that the young bucks couldn't. At a weight-lifting session, the coaches called two offensive linemen and Flynt to the middle of the room for a contest. They'd each lie on the floor and bench-press a forty-five-pound disk as many times as they could. The last one to stop would win. With the whole team circled around them, Flynt looked up and saw only one face, a player he'd met during two-a-days, with whom he'd discussed the power of Christ. "It was like God saying, 'Okay, Mike, you can do this.'" Flynt asked the kid to say a prayer for him, then shut his eyes and started lifting. "I was thinking the whole time, this is such a blessing. I opened my eyes, and the guy on one side had stopped and the guy on the other was slowing down. I knew I had it won."

The feeling was sweet, but it didn't get Flynt any closer to the field. As a coach said later, bench-pressing talent only matters when you're on your back, which is not where you want to be in a game. Flynt didn't even travel to the first two games, a gutsy rally to win against Texas Lutheran, in Seguin, and a blowout over Southwest Assemblies of God, in Waxahachie. He suited up but didn't play in the third game, a 55–14 loss to fourth-ranked Mary Hardin-Baylor that could have been a lot worse. (The Crusaders returned the opening kickoff for a touchdown and led 21–0 after barely three minutes of play.) Between the runaway loss, the national news crews, and the MHB band chanting, "We want Mike!" the game turned into a circus. Lobos alums in attendance were livid at Coach Wright for not playing Flynt in a game that had gotten far out of hand.

None of them knew that his injuries had already caused him to reimagine his dream. After standing on the sidelines during another lopsided loss, to East Texas Baptist at home, Flynt explained, "Initially I had visions of being a starter. But I'm not good enough.

I see myself now in a support role, playing on special teams, giving guys a break when it's hot, being their friend and teammate and keeping them motivated and focused on what we need to do to win."

As he talked about the off-the-field aspect of his quest, he began to sound less like an old warrior and more like a modern business-man. "I never thought about the number of people that would be so interested and captivated by what I am doing," he said. "And in-spired. Gosh, I've gotten so many encouraging e-mails and phone calls about how I'm changing lives. But at the same time, I'm inun-dated. Book deals. Movie producers chomping at the bit. Some came in and met with the school president, Coach Wright, and me. They said there was going to be a writers' strike and we needed to get this done. I told them, 'I can't sign anything right now. I'm not going to jeopardize my eligibility.'"

He stressed that there would be no deals until the season was over. He was distinctly aware that what Hollywood wanted were de-tails about his past, specifically about the fight that had gotten him kicked out of school. But he intended to keep that card close to his chest. "I was told that when the AP story ran, my life became public domain," he told me, referring to the first in-depth article written about him during the historic season. "That if somebody wanted to make a movie or a book out of my life, they could, without my co-operation. From a business standpoint, if *Texas Monthly* delves into my past, what's to prevent you from selling that to someone who wants to do a movie?

"The story for me is about now. It's Sul Ross and my teammates and Coach Wright and the sacrifices he makes to do what he does. That's what has value to me."

Steve Wright looks exactly like a fifty-one-year-old football coach running a modestly successful program in a small town. His bowl-cut blond hair spills in a mess out over a white visor bearing the school's logo. His lean, sturdy bowlegs hold up a potbelly clad in a wardrobe of only school colors. He projects a slightly beleaguered but ever-upbeat quality, though you won't get much sense of this by looking into his eyes. They're hidden behind heavy lids and wire-rimmed glasses, and when he's talking about serious matters re-quiring serious contemplation, they're usually closed.

His statements are also tough to decipher. He talks like Sparky

Anderson auditioning for the starring role in a Casey Stengel bio-pic. His rambling addresses open with "Folks . . ." whether he's talk-ing to fifty people or one. He'll tell you that football is not just about "wons and losses" and insist that the Lobos' winning season in 2006 "was not an abolition."

So you figure him out not by listening but by watching. His mouth puckers round when he senses that you're missing his point. It purses flat as he sees you starting to understand. And when he realizes he's taught you something, it blooms into a gap-toothed, coach-that-ate-the-canary grin, his teeth covered with to-bacco flakes, like he's just napped for an hour with a pinch of snuff in his mouth. Typically the lesson is that what matters most is not what happens on the field but what you take with you when you leave it.

Like when he talks about losing his first twenty-six games as head coach of Sul Ross, beginning on opening day 2002. "You have to trick your human computer, your brain," he said, sitting in his of-fice on the Monday morning after the week-four loss, to East Texas Baptist. "The first game Austin Davidson played, we lost 79–14, at Richard Simmons," he said, referring to the school that everyone else calls Hardin-Simmons University. "That's a pretty good whip-ping. To get in the bus and try to get to practice and play the next game, yeah, there was a lot of soul-searching. But the trick in the belief was 'We can get this done.'"

He fiddled with a paper clip while he spoke, eventually making perfect sense. "The low point was at the end of the second season. The next-to-last game. We were getting beat pretty handily, getting ready to go 0–9, which is actually 0–19. There's about twenty peo-ple in the stands at the end of the game, and one of our kids makes a play by crawling. He gets blocked out of the play, gets his butt kicked, and then, as the other guy is running down the hash mark, our kid crawls and makes a shoestring tackle. And folks, there's no-body there to see it, because we weren't successful in people's mind.

"I remember watching film that night, then going home and say-ing, 'That's a shame.' So I went to the kid's dorm, found him, brought him to my office, and made him watch it. And I told him, 'This is one of the greatest plays I've ever seen, and you need to know someone appreciates it.'"

Coach Wright's office befits the brain trust of an underfunded program. The cinder-block walls are painted white. A space heater stands unplugged in the corner. A laptop sits on his cluttered desk. There's a whiteboard with stick figures positioned in the Lobos' 3–4 defense, a game ball commemorating his 1989 junior college national championship at Navarro College, and a D3Football.com Regional Coach of the Year plaque honoring the Lobos' 5–4 finish in 2006. His most precious keepsakes are an Olan Mills portrait of his two daughters, Stephanie and Synthia, and a painting of a red-brick dormitory at Carson-Newman College, in Tennessee, where his grandfather was the school president for twenty years and his dad played football. In the painting, the ghosts of legendary Carson-Newman gridders are depicted running through the clouds above the dorm. "I've been offered five thousand dollars for that painting," Wright told me. "I said, 'Uh-uh, baby, no way.'"

Try to find his salary inside a $247,000-a-year program and you'll see the sacrifice he made by keeping the painting. Only two of his seven assistants are full-time, and they all pull double or triple duty to augment their paychecks. The defensive secondary coach is the head of the school's equine science department. One of the line coaches is a graduate assistant who leaves practice early on Wednesdays to play a weekly gig with his country band. The defensive coordinator washes uniforms after games.

His players are issued one helmet, one pair of shoes, and one set of pads for the season. Socks, jocks, and underwear are the kids' responsibility. Much of that goes with being a small Division III program, where scholarships are prohibited. As Wright frequently points out, his Lobos are actually paying to play, and getting them to do it in Alpine is no easy task. "Folks, we're two and a half hours from the nearest Super Wal-Mart," Wright said. "So a lot of these guys recruit us. They call, and we'll tell 'em, 'Send us your film. Let's see if you can play college football.'" He winds up with kids who learned about Sul Ross because an older brother played there or because one of their buddies is going there. "Hell, we're all misfits here," Wright explained, "even the coaches."

None of the Lobos have dreams of playing on Sunday, so Wright emphasizes enjoying what football they have left. He keeps practices unbelievably relaxed. He doesn't have a playbook, calling his improvisational offensive scheme "basketball on grass." The result is a program based on the only cliché he'll use. It may be the only one he can afford or, as he might joke, the only one he can remember: "These kids play because they love this game."

He paused to look out his office door at a group of players waiting to turn in proof-of-attendance slips. "This may be the only place where this Mike Flynt deal could have happened," Wright said. "A guy walked in, and yeah, he's fifty-nine, and after listening to him, I felt, 'If I do this, I'm stepping on loose branches, because it's so unique.' But to me, out here, it's not unique. If he could physically do this, why not give him a chance?

"Mike's got his rationale. He's trying to right a wrong. Well, there's a hidden thread to why I let him do it. My oldest daughter, Stephanie, has an undiagnosed autoimmune neuromuscular disease. That's what they call it when they don't know what it is. And having her be handicapped, at times, I've had firsthand experience with the limitations we put on folks, for a disability or gender or age."

He lifted his visor and scratched his head, then shut his eyes. "But you know, my younger daughter, Synthia, was also affected. When the doctors came in to see Stephanie, they didn't address Synthia. I'm not sure that wasn't good practice for this Mike Flynt deal."

His lips puckered. "There's no doubt we have a story here that can benefit people. There's no telling the synergistic multiplication effect that this exposure can have. But this is not a publicity stunt. Mike will not bump in front of those other kids for publicity. I will manage this through the program first and then each individual athlete, whether it's Mike or Fernie Acosta or Milo Garza or one of those freshmen who hasn't seen the field yet."

He seemed to be saying that Flynt was just one of eighty players, no more or less important than any other. When I asked if that was what he meant, Coach Wright leaned back in his chair and grinned.

As the season progressed, alums eager to see Flynt play felt their frustration with Coach Wright fester, then mushroom. Each week the coach passed on uniquely fitting occasions to return Flynt to the field. The East Texas Baptist game had been the home opener, a chance for a triumphant return to Jackson Field, yet Flynt spent the afternoon rooting on the sidelines. The next week's game,

against Howard Payne University, in Brownwood, was attended by
Flynt's three kids, his year-old grandson, and his eighty-two-year-
old mother, a manager at the local Wal-Mart. Again, no Flynt.
Though the contest was a double-overtime barn burner — won by
the Lobos, 34–31, when Giddy blocked a field goal that would have
sent the game to a third OT — the alums who rushed the field after the win weren't looking to celebrate. One former teammate of
Flynt's found Wright in the end zone and took him apart, pointing
a finger and saying, "Nobody cares about you. These people are
here to see Mike. You're squandering an opportunity to make history!"

Over the next two weeks — the Lobos' bye week came next —
Wright received scores of ass-chewings in thousand-word e-mails
and half-hour voice messages. On an Internet message board set
up by an alumni group called the Sul Ross Baby Boomers, com-
menters likened him to a jackass and demanded he be fired. Randy
Wilson posted a message urging the Boomers to complain to the
school, providing e-mail addresses for the athletic director and
president. The two officials declined to tell Wright what to do, but
they frequently inquired as to just what he *was* doing.

Flynt, however, had become even more aware of his physical limitations and had asked Coach Wright to let him take it easy in practice. He explained in his weekly AP column, "Coach wants me to do
what I can in practice at what I feel like is an acceptable risk to my
body. He doesn't want me going 100 mph in practice then not being able to play Saturday. I really appreciate that."

The strategy worked. In a week-six rematch with Texas Lutheran,
after Davidson threw a long touchdown pass on the opening drive,
Flynt sprinted onto the field with the extra-point team. In the
stands, there was bedlam. Hugs and kisses rained on the Flynt family, and a Boomer giving play-by-play on his cell phone screamed
himself hoarse trying to be heard over the crowd. But there was no
time for wonderment down on the field. Flynt lined up at left end.
With the snap and the kick, the kid across from him didn't make
much of a move, and Flynt just gave him a little touch. What the
moment lacked in excitement it made up for in history. Three
months shy of his sixtieth birthday, Mike Flynt was back in the
game.

And he wasn't finished. The game proved to be another shoot-

out, with either the score tied or the lead changing hands fully thirteen times. As the scoring mounted, the extra points and field
goals carried greater import, and eventually Flynt's man was challenging him. Flynt answered every time, standing him up when
he came out of his stance, then patting him on the butt when the
play was over. When Lobos kicker Mike Van Wagner's field goal
clinched a win in the third overtime, 45–42, Flynt was on the field.
He wrote for AP the next week that he'd felt like a kid again, then
closed by explaining how much these young men meant to him.
"Come to think of it," he wrote, "that's another part of the script
that's been better than I could've written it."

When the homecoming game with Hardin-Simmons came two
weeks later, Flynt had two games under his belt. The team was riding a three-game winning streak and eyeing the playoffs, and the
unprecedented attention to Sul Ross guaranteed a monster turn-
out. Flynt's old teammates arranged a reunion of the '69 and '70
squads, and some forty of them made the trip. They were introduced on the field before the game, where Flynt joined them to receive a gubernatorial proclamation. Then he returned to the field
house to get ready to play, and his contemporaries found places in
the stands.

They saw the Cowboys take an early 7–0 lead but quickly noted
— between comments on how much better the grass looked now
and how much bigger the players were — the fight in the '07
Lobos. The defense stiffened, and Sul Ross scored a touchdown at
the end of the first quarter. Flynt's old teammates were so busy
pointing at him when he lined up for the extra point that most
didn't notice that the kick missed wide right.

The lead seesawed back and forth, and Sul Ross was up 19–18
early in the second half when Flynt got the chance everyone was
looking for. It was storybook perfect. The Lobos lined up for a field
goal attempt directly in front of the alums, with Flynt on the end
nearest the home bleachers. Once again he hit his man, but this
time the kick was blocked, and the ball bounced toward the near
sideline. A Cowboys defensive back scooped it up and looked
downfield. Flynt was the only player between him and the end
zone. Flynt squared off and the old guys rose to their feet, remembering the way he used to take off players' heads. But the
kid, rather than run at him, headed for the pack at the center of

the field. Flynt watched him go, then trotted gingerly behind. He would say later that he could feel his groin muscle with every step, that he knew if he had to perform, it would have ended his season. But he said he'd been ready for whatever he had to do.

Four minutes later Hardin-Simmons scored another touchdown and a lead it never relinquished. The Cowboys won 46–36, and the Lobos' playoff hopes were done.

Spirits had picked up by the time the former players gathered at the Alpine Country Club for a barbecue dinner. Flynt had made them cool again, and they seemed to have drifted back in time to when they owned the school. Though nonplaying alums were presumably welcome, none came by. The only partygoers who hadn't played football were the wives, Coach Wright, a couple reporters, and a Hollywood producer named Mark Ciardi, the money behind movies like *The Rookie* and *Invincible*.

War stories floated on a stream of free beer, some more believable than others. The men talked about driving opponents into the concrete wall just beyond the sideline and a New Mexican hotel they couldn't enter before a game because a traveling whorehouse was using the rooms. When Coach Wright arrived, the players' wives introduced themselves and said they'd never heard his name without the prefix "that SOB." Everyone marveled at Flynt, how he had remade himself and pulled off his comeback. Throughout the night the running gag for everyone was "Who's gonna play me in the movie?"

The Thursday morning before the last game, Flynt and I met again in the student center. Until that point we'd not talked about the fight that ended his first tenure as a Lobo. But when we sat down, I gave him a document he'd requested, a short letter stating that *Texas Monthly* wouldn't sell his story to Hollywood without his participation and approval. He read it, then started to explain the pivotal event in his legend and life.

It began in the summer of 1971, with Flynt's telling Coach Harvey that he thought the Lobos had a chance to win conference that year. But he insisted that to make that happen, Harvey would have to enforce curfew. The coach asked him, a returning team captain, to mete out punishments when teammates came in late. That's what led to the momentous fight.

"We had an athlete here named Jacob Henry, a world-class runner," Flynt recalled. "His older brother had spent four or five years in jail and then walked onto the team. The coaches didn't know much about him, but they felt that if he had Jacob's genes, they'd give him a shot.

"So I was checking rooms at curfew, and Henry's brother and his roommate weren't in. Forty-five minutes later they still weren't. But Fletcher Hall was horseshoe-shaped, and looking over the balcony, I saw them in the courtyard, on the steps smoking cigarettes. I could see the cigarettes.

"I walked down there and said, 'You guys know what time it is?' I could smell alcohol on them and felt it was pretty brazen to be smoking. The coaches definitely didn't want us doing that. I said, 'Tomorrow morning at six A.M. we got some cars that need washing.' The Henry guy had a few things to say, and now I could see it coming. I knew this guy's history. I figured, *Well, he doesn't mind fighting, so that's what's going to happen.* When he thumped his cigarette and came off the step, I hit him. Broke his nose. He went down and out."

Flynt said the roommate began hollering, waking up the dorm, including Coach Flop Parsons, who lived there with his wife. Guessing Henry had a concussion, Parsons called an ambulance. Then things got crazy.

"Everybody's awake and screaming now, and the ambulance comes and loads the kid up. Then on the way to the hospital, he gets out of the ambulance. And he tells the driver, 'I've got a gun, and I'm fixing to kill Mike Flynt!' and heads back for the dorm. So the driver calls the police, who send squad cars and call the coaches and the university president, Dr. McNeil. And then they locked down the dorm, sent us all to our rooms. Well, we've got practice the next morning, so I just went to bed.

"The next morning, Coach Parsons came in around seven o'clock and said Coach Harvey wanted to see me down in the dressing room. When Coach Harvey let me in, he said McNeil had called and told him it was either him or me. The graduate assistants were in my room packing my luggage. They loaded me up and took me to Odessa.

"That fast . . ." He trailed off. "It all was over."

Flynt nutshelled the rest of his life. He married Eileen in 1972, then finished college at UT-Arlington. In 1976 he talked his way into a strength coaching job at Nebraska with Boyd Eppley, a legend in his own right who all but invented modern football strength training. (Notably, Flynt got in a shoving match with Nebraska's all-American center in the weight room his first day on the job.) In 1978 he went to Oregon and became the first strength coach in the Pac-10. The next year he took the same job at Texas A&M.

He left in 1981 and started working with children. He created a children's workout video that he sold at home-school conferences and eventually invented his Powerbase equipment, which he now sells to individuals and school districts. And somewhere in there he got right with God. "It was just depression over things that weren't going the way I thought they should. I was drinking too much, really at rock bottom." One night he went on a walk with Eileen. She quoted scripture to him. "All of a sudden, it just sort of settled in on me."

It was a remarkable story, of a life begun in prideful mistakes and redeemed in peaceful humility. Flynt spoke eloquently and at length about how humble he felt. It was no wonder that for more than twenty-five years some of his old friends had been expecting a big-screen depiction of his legendary life.

But legends are tricky. At their essence they're stories crafted of memories that, with the passage of time, can come to look more like the legend than the events they recall. There's not always room in the legend for being merely human, for the moments in a real life that point away from the pedestal.

Flynt didn't talk much about the eighties. But buried in the mountain of media coverage of his historic 2007 season was an October blog post written by a Baptist minister who'd taught Sunday school to the Flynts after they moved to Tennessee, in 1985. He thrilled at the comeback, described praying with Eileen, and called Flynt a friend. He also recalled Flynt's frequently approaching him with investment opportunities. "I never bought the stock he offered for Gold Mining in Arizona," he wrote, "or the stock he offered about raising the *Titanic*. A little off-the-wall for someone like me." When I asked Flynt about that in a December phone call, he said he'd once done consulting work for a man who was doing contract work for RMS Titanic, the Florida company that began retrieving artifacts from the shipwreck in 1987. But Flynt insisted he would not have offered stock because he had never held a license to sell securities.

The gold mine reference was more complicated. It was related to a series of investments Flynt had entered into in 1981 with a child-hood friend from Odessa. The deals were ultimately determined to be a pyramid scheme that bilked hundreds of people out of tens of millions of dollars. Flynt had been close enough to the pyramid's top to have been indicted, along with his friend, on four counts of felony fraud in 1985. The friend was convicted, but the charges against Flynt were dropped three years later, according to court filings, after he paid restitution to an investor who'd gotten in through him. When I asked Flynt about the scam, he said he'd been a victim too. He called the experience a painful nightmare. Presumably, that was the rock bottom to which he'd referred.

As for the fabled "one fight too many," the hinge on which the Flynt legend swings, I talked to thirteen of his 1971 teammates about the infamous fight. Some had witnessed it in the courtyard, some had been inside the dorm and come out for the ensuing melee, and others had merely heard the next morning's reports. Their memories had diverged over thirty-seven years, and they told conflicting stories. Some cited the curfew violation, but others re-membered the fight's taking place in the early evening while the sun was still out, and most said that the real crime was that Jacob Henry's brother, whose name was George, had shirked his fresh-man duties. The team had a tradition of initiating newcomers, who had to shave their heads and wear beanies until the Lobos' first win. They were frequently made to wash upperclassmen's cars. "Even in the rain," a friend of Flynt's joked.

Every player I talked to said that when Flynt made his demand of George, the freshman mouthed off and Flynt coldcocked him. But what Flynt left out of his version was that George was black. Though no former player, black or white, suggested or implied that race had anything to do with the punch, they all said that the commotion that followed, which was described as either a face-off or a gang fight, was divided along racial lines. They said no ambu-lance had come for George — most said they didn't think Alpine even had an ambulance in 1971 — and that he had never threat-ened to kill Flynt. Coach Harvey told me that the police had not been called, nor had President McNeil called him. Harvey's con-cern had been that the fight would split the team, that bad feelings would resurface throughout the season. He said that was why he had made the hard decision to kick Flynt off the team.

But the bigger problem with Flynt's story had to do with George

Henry, whom I reached on the phone in December. He had recently retired and was moving to Kentucky from Denton with Jacob, who was actually his *older* brother. It turned out that George had been a true freshman in 1971 and that he had never, as Flynt stated, been in prison. He was nineteen years old and, at barely 150 pounds, the smallest player on the team. He also said he didn't smoke back then.

"It was getting on to dusk," George recalled, "and Flynt told me, 'You're going to wash my car tomorrow.' I said, 'Wash it yourself.' He got pissed and threw the first punch. I don't know why he's saying this stuff now. I've always said I hated to see him kicked off the team. He was a good football player. We could have used him that year."

After talking to George, I called Flynt to reconcile the stories. He quickly grew angry. "Look, I didn't even have a car," he said. "Apparently it's pretty foggy to a lot of people if you're getting this many stories."

He tried to make his version fit with the others. He said that he had not actually seen the ambulance himself but had heard about it from Coach Parsons. He said that perhaps Coach Parsons, who's now dead, had told him about the ambulance and the gun to get him to stay in his room. And he said that Coach Harvey had definitely mentioned McNeil, maybe to pass the buck. As for George, he said, "It was my understanding that he'd been in jail. I didn't create that. As far as I'm concerned, the fight took place for whatever reason it took place, and it was the straw that broke the camel's back. Whether I hit him with a left hook or an uppercut, all that's immaterial.

"If you can't get comfortable with the facts, just don't write the story."

With 3:39 left to play in the season finale, against Mississippi College, Flynt finally saw game time at linebacker. The Choctaws were up 56–35, and Davidson, trying to engineer another miracle, had just been intercepted at Mississippi's 14-yard line. Even in a season in which anything seemed possible, this unmistakably ended any chance of a Lobos victory. But it did nothing to the excitement level in the Jackson Field bleachers. Flynt's five games spent blocking on kicks had been inspiring but uneventful. Here was his chance to complete his dream.

After watching a four-yard pass, Coach Wright called a time-out to send Flynt in. The crowd reaction was exactly as expected. The Baby Boomers, who were as hungry as Flynt, started chanting, "Push 'em back, push 'em back, way back!" Camera crews and photographers jockeyed with Lobos players for angles, and reporters scurried to find the Flynt family. As before, Flynt had no time for kudos or reflection. He later told the AP, "I was totally focused on my responsibilities."

The first play was a run to his side. Flynt hooked up with a 270-pound offensive guard who was pulling on the play and watched the Choctaws tailback dart inside, gaining three yards. The next play was a handoff that went the other way. Flynt started in pursuit, then tripped and fell on teammate Chris Vela. The two watched the end of the play from their bellies.

On third down, Mississippi ran up the middle. Flynt was blocked out of the play but, refusing to quit, followed the ball carrier and jumped on the pile of tacklers six yards down the field. There was less than a minute to play as an official signaled first down. One more snap and the quarterback took a knee. Thirty-nine years after it began, Mike Flynt's Sul Ross football career was over.

If the postgame scene on the field could have been viewed from above, the crowd would have looked like ants running for a dropped piece of candy. Everyone wanted a picture taken with Flynt, the players, their parents and girlfriends, the opposing coaches, and the referees. Reporters lingered on the periphery, trying to be respectful before moving in.

There was one person in the crowd who did not hustle to Flynt. Near the visitors' benches, Coach Wright was lying on his side, picking at the grass. I walked over and sat down next to him.

"You know," he said, "it's so impressive to have bounced back after the way the first half ended. What were we down there, forty-two to fifteen? And for us to start the fourth quarter down only thirteen? Folks, if we convert that fourth down, we're one play away — or one holding call or one interference call — from winning that ball game."

He sat up, put his hands on his knees, and looked at the scoreboard. Then he watched the crowd.

"Isn't this team fun?" he said. "God, if the injuries hadn't hit us this year. I tell you, they've got something that in thirty years . . ." He grabbed another piece of grass and flashed a washed-out grin, looking significantly more worn than he had at the start of the year. A football season will do that to you.

He was already thinking about next year. He said Flynt had promised to be the liaison to the Boomers, to help realize his comeback's institutional benefits by organizing fundraisers and game-day reunions. Then he talked about players he hoped would return. "Jamal Groover should eventually be able to replace T. J. Barber. And Carlo Dominguez will be a hell of a lot of fun to watch, wherever we play him." He showed no indication that in a month's time he'd resign.

I left him to find Flynt. As he finished talking to an El Paso news crew, I jumped in and asked what he felt he'd accomplished. "Personally, I came back and helped a group of young men I didn't know, and that's what I set out to do — to right what I felt was a wrong. I'd like to think these young men are better off for having known me. I know I'm better off for having known them." Humble to the end, he gave no sign of the big developments coming his way. In mid-December, shortly after Coach Wright's resignation, Flynt would sign with the sports marketing firm started by NBA superstar LeBron James. The agency would negotiate his movie and book deals, as well as arrange endorsements and speaking engagements. There would eventually be talk of a Mike Flynt–model Nike shoe. As a second news crew fired up its camera and nudged me away, Flynt fell into the crowd for more hugs and handshakes.

Somewhere in there, Flynt would later tell me, he had a short conversation with one of his teammates. He said he thought it was Kyle Braddick, an eighteen-year-old linebacker who saw most of his action on kick returns. Braddick played recklessly and left nearly every game banged and bruised. But he kept coming back, and Flynt was part of his inspiration.

"Kyle said, 'Mike, I wanted to see you intercept a pass and run it back for a touchdown.' And I said, 'I know, Kyle. Maybe we can do that in the movie.'"

I love the enterprise involved in this story. Mike Flynt sort of dissolves in front of our eyes as writer John Spong digs deeper and deeper. This is good journalism of the first order.

IAN THOMSEN

Russian Revolution

FROM SPORTS ILLUSTRATED

THE WORLD'S MOST ELEGANT CHEERLEADERS take the court like a troupe of ballerinas, dressed simply in lilac tops and low-rise black pants for their role as arm candy to the star of this brief show. The iconic main attraction is decked out in the telltale white body suit and has the familiar upswept hair. During his brief time on earth, the original Elvis Presley typified the Western entertainment that was banned by the Soviet Union as "tumors on the social organism." But in this incarnation he is belting out bastardized Russian-and-English lyrics to the tune of "Blue Suede Shoes" as the twirling ladies encircle him. "Come on, SESS-ka!" sings Elvis, leaning into the crook of his glittering elbow.

SESS-ka refers to CSKA, or Central Sports Army Club, the home team for this February basketball game in Moscow. The celebrated organization dates to the Soviet days of Stalin and Khrushchev and Brezhnev, who ruled the army generals and also, by chain of command, the gold medalists competing for CSKA. The Red Army athletes were the most intimidating of competitors: fundamentally disciplined basketball stars, ice hockey players, and figure skaters who tormented the United States in the Olympic Games every fourth winter and summer.

Then in 1989 the Berlin Wall fell, and soon the Soviet system collapsed. But the teams of CSKA Moscow have continued to thrive, though they bear little more than symbolic allegiance to the military. Instead, they answer to a former disc jockey.

It's true: CSKA is run by a deejay named Sergey Kushchenko, a genial, outgoing forty-six-year-old who was spinning LPs of the Beatles and bootlegging cassettes of the Rolling Stones even as Soviet coach Alexander Gomelsky and five CSKA players were leading the Soviet Union to an 82–76 win over the United States at the 1988 Olympics in Seoul. That Sergey the deejay happened also to fall in love with basketball has resulted in his spectacularly unpredictable rise to president of CSKA. Sitting courtside in a dark suit and tie — uncomfortable attire during his deejay days — he watches the team that he has reinvented to become the best in the world outside the NBA.

Two decades ago Soviet stars such as Arvydas Sabonis and Sarunas Marciulionis earned disposable income by selling athletic gear and black-market caviar out of their hotel rooms during international road trips. Now, the high-end clubs of the Russian Superleague have more money to spend than most of their European rivals. Russia's vast natural resources and the ambitions of President Vladimir Putin (who will move to the prime minister's office on May 7) have recast basketball as a metric of the nation's new identity — even if that identity is often cast by foreigners. The coach of what is still commonly referred to as the Red Army team is Ettore Messina, an Italian. He yells at his three American players, two Greeks, a Slovenian, a Lithuanian, a Belgian, an Australian, and a half-dozen Russians in English — *English!* — proof that the new Russia is competing for talent on a global scale.

Sergey the deejay is driving this revolutionary trend in Russian basketball. He is striving to create an open-market environment for the American-born sport within an old-world government of Russian secrecy (in which investigative journalists are routinely found murdered) and strong-arm politics (as manipulated by Putin, who prolonged his influence by handpicking his presidential successor in a March election that was free of viable opposition candidates). The NBA has recognized the ambitions of Kushchenko, and over the last three years he has patiently negotiated a unique relationship between his progressive club and the NBA. Commissioner David Stern usually prefers to marry himself to international federations or leagues, but so important is CSKA to all of basketball in Russia, and so visionary is Kushchenko, that in February the NBA was ready to sign a deal with CSKA that would open the Russian frontier to opportunities benefiting both sides.

On this afternoon the Superleague meeting between CSKA and

visiting Khimki is tight into the fourth quarter as CSKA's cheer-leaders return yet again to the court. Their elegance is part of Sergey the deejay's larger vision for basketball in the CSKA Universal Sports Hall, a steeply tiered arena of 5,500 seats built for the 1980 Moscow Olympics. As the young women sweep gracefully onto the floor, they are met by dozens of colored lights spinning and strobing from the ceiling, another of Kushchenko's innovations. "Like disco," he explains.

An and-one drive by the visitors cuts CSKA's lead to 65–64 with twenty-five seconds remaining. Trajan Langdon, the former All-American guard at Duke who is one of CSKA's go-to scorers, responds with a free throw. Another drive by Khimki fails and CSKA seizes a 68–64 victory, one of twenty-three it will earn (against just one loss) domestically this season to claim first place in the Superleague.

Basketball is important to Russia because, in the beginning, it was important to the United States. The Soviets embraced basketball after World War II for no other reason than to try to prove they could beat the United States at its own game, to demonstrate that their collective approach could overcome superior talent. They started by dominating the sport in the old world, dividing the first six European Champions Cups among ASK Riga, the army team of Latvia (winner of the first three titles, all coached by the legendary Gomelsky); Dinamo Tbilisi, the police-sponsored team from the Soviet republic of Georgia; and, of course, CSKA Moscow.

Today there are at least 1,500 Americans playing basketball professionally around the world, but this trend began in Europe when they were imported like mercenaries to repel the Soviets. In 1962 Real Madrid became the first Western European club to break into the finals of the Champions Cup (known today as the Euroleague) after its Hall of Fame coach, Pedro Ferràndiz, had traveled to Philadelphia to recruit six-foot-eight power forward Wayne Hightower, an African American who had left Kansas a year before he was eligible for the NBA draft. Europe had never seen an athlete like Hightower, and though he would return home to spend eleven years in the NBA and ABA, his one season in Europe created demand for more Americans to stand up to the Soviets.

The Soviet Union ratcheted up the standards of international competition by turning games into metaphorical life-and-death struggles with the free world. The common denominator for many of the nation's significant basketball victories was Gomelsky, who began an eleven-year term as CSKA's coach in 1969 and later served as the team's president while guiding the Soviet national team on and off over three decades. "He was a wily little guy, politically shrewd, considered one of the one hundred most powerful men in Russia, disliked by many, connected with higher-ups in the Politburo," says Dan Peterson, the expatriate American who coached in Italy during the Gomelsky era. "A ruthless winner, a brilliant guy."

Gomelsky's most important — and final — triumph was the 82–76 semifinal win over coach John Thompson's collegians in the '88 Games, which prompted USA Basketball to assemble the original Dream Team four years later. That last Soviet team, like the Soviet Union itself, was on the verge of splintering amid ethnic quarrels and demands for freedom, but Gomelsky achieved temporary unification in his locker room, according to Peterson, by persuading Mikhail Gorbachev to allow the players to sign with clubs outside the country provided they won the gold medal.

After the 1991 dissolution of the Soviet Union, most of its famed basketball generation scattered throughout Europe and the NBA, for in the first tortured decade of independence there was little money for Russian hoops. The proud clubs of the former empire were unable to pay their bills — CSKA included, though that did not stop the team from winning nine straight Superleague titles. Gomelsky's search for his eventual replacement as team president, someone capable of responding to the problems and opportunities of the new millennium, led him to the isolated Russian city of Perm, a former Soviet weapons-manufacturing base eight hundred miles east of Moscow that was closed to foreigners until 1989. Perm was home to a small start-up club known as Ural Great, which had dethroned CSKA to win the 2001 Russian championship and which was owned and operated by none other than Sergey Kushchenko. "I visited Perm in 2001," recalls Roy Kirkdorffer, an American financial adviser based in the south of France who represents European basketball players. "And I had breakfast with Gomelsky, who said of Kushchenko, 'He's our bright young hope.'"

*

Three things that illustrate the paradox of Russian basketball:

1. *It is not run as a business.* While the NBA exists to make money, there is no tradition for profitability throughout European basketball. The major clubs are funded by private financiers or parent sports clubs and exist simply to win games for their city, region, and country — red ink be damned.

2. *Kushchenko wants to run it as a business.* Kushchenko, who took over CSKA's basketball team in 2002, talks of creating a market for basketball, of eventually developing sources of revenue that will equal or exceed his club's budget of more than $40 million, which makes it among the richest in Europe. (The average NBA team's budget is more than $100 million.) Over the last three years he has made several trips to the United States with his CSKA employees, and together they have studied everything from the marketing to the merchandising to the administration of the NBA website in hopes of acquiring the perspectives of an organization that is built for profit. As foreign as this may be to his Russian colleagues, Kushchenko sees no other future for basketball in his country.

3. *There is no compelling need to run it as a business.* CSKA is funded by a billionaire oligarch, Mikhail Prokhorov, forty-two, who made his initial fortune in the 1980s by selling stone-washed jeans in the Soviet Union. When the state-owned industries were privatized in the '90s by Boris Yeltsin, Prokhorov leveraged his chairmanship of a bank to acquire Norilsk Nickel, the world's leading producer of nickel and palladium. He has since relinquished his stake in Norilsk, though he retains control of sister company Polyus Gold, the largest gold producer in Russia.

Despite standing six-foot-nine and having played basketball in grade school, Prokhorov has shown minimal interest in the team. It appears to Western observers that he is involved with CSKA because Putin has instructed billionaire oligarchs to invest heavily in basketball and other sports to raise Russia's profile around the world. As it is, Prokhorov, the twenty-fourth richest person in the world according to *Forbes* (net worth: $19.5 billion), rarely attends hoops games, and he tends to be impressed neither by the spectacle nor by the American need to profit from the sport. During the NBA Europe Live exhibitions in Moscow in 2006, where the carnival of NBA sideshows was on display during time-outs, he turned to a few international guests and said, "This is all bulls—."

Prokhorov's passive interest has not prevented the team he bank-rolls from becoming the most talented outside the NBA. CSKA has reached the Euroleague Final Four a record six consecutive times, and next week in Madrid the Russian power is favored to win the ti-tle for the second time in three seasons.

The leading scorer throughout the season (at just 13.4 points per game, befitting the club's balance) is six-foot-eleven center Da-vid Andersen, a twenty-seven-year-old Australian who plays on a Danish passport and is considering a move to the NBA next season. (The Atlanta Hawks drafted him in the second round in 2002.)

The point guard is a surprisingly talented player from Bucknell named J. R. Holden, thirty-one. In his six years with CSKA he has become, according to coach Messina, the best point guard in Eu-rope. The six-foot-one Holden's skills are so highly valued by the Russians that he was naturalized in 2003 — despite not having met residency requirements — so he could play for the national team. (A former national team general manager, Kushchenko helped persuade the government to grant Holden an exemption.) Last September, Holden hit a contested jump shot with 2.1 seconds left to give Russia a shocking 60–59 victory over Spain in the European championships, a victory that promised to maintain political inter-est and money in Russian basketball for years to come.

The CSKA roster is overloaded with renowned Europeans such as Theodoros Papaloukas, thirty, recently named one of the thirty-five greatest players in the fifty-year history of the Euroleague; his fellow Greek guard Nikos Zisis, twenty-four; and Lithuanian for-ward Ramunas Siskauskas, twenty-nine, who chose to leave Euro-league champion Panathinaikos to move to Moscow this season. The six-foot-eight forward Marcus Goree, who grew up playing with Denver Nuggets forward Kenyon Martin in Dallas, is a thirty-year-old who, according to Messina, "could be the European Ben Wallace." Messina himself was named one of the top ten coaches in Euroleague history, and he views his team leaders as Holden and Langdon, who last season was the only American to make first-team all-Euroleague.

The man who put CSKA together, the open and sincere Kushchenko, is in every way the opposite of the stern, cold authoritarian whom one would expect to be presiding over the Red Army club. It helps that he doesn't particularly need basketball. He and some friends from Perm also cashed in on the privatization boom of the 1990s, and their ownership of Kam Kabel — a manufacturer of electronic cables with five thousand employees — has made a millionaire of him. Today he lives with his wife, Svetlana, and their three children in a gated community outside Moscow, in a modern, four-story house with heated floors, a skylit penthouse, and fixtures designed by Italian architects.

In 2006 Kushchenko was rewarded with a promotion to the presidency of all of CSKA and its forty-one sports, which is a far more political position than simply managing the daily affairs of the basketball club. At All-Star weekend in New Orleans, he was welcomed by the NBA to finalize their long-sought partnership. The agreement appeared to be in place: CSKA would put up close to $10 million to serve as host of NBA events in Moscow, including the charitable youth event Basketball Without Borders and preseason exhibitions involving NBA teams. NBA and CSKA officials would work side by side in Moscow, enabling the Americans to grow their league in Russia while providing CSKA with expertise in transforming basketball into a market-based business. CSKA games would be broadcast in the United States on NBA TV. Left unsaid was the eventual possibility that CSKA might become an NBA franchise during the league's planned expansion to Europe over the decades ahead.

The meetings in New Orleans were expected to be a formality — sign the papers, shake hands, bring in Stern for group photographs — but Kushchenko unexpectedly revealed that he was unable to agree to the terms. He also was unable to explain why. He grabbed the arm of NBA deputy commissioner Adam Silver and whispered, "Don't worry. We'll get that done."

The NBA isn't giving up on Kushchenko. "Russia remains an important market for the NBA," says Silver. "We are encouraged by the discussions we've had with Sergey and his colleagues. We remain hopeful that we're going to work out a long-term deal with him."

But something had changed, in spite of all of Kushchenko's successes in moving basketball forward in Russia. Was he unable to persuade the politicians to run the sport as a business? Were they, in spite of their reliance on foreign basketball talent, unwilling to form a partnership with the Americans? The story of Sergey the deejay, though it is not yet finished, is that Russia, for all of the promise of its new frontier, is still mired in its old ways.

If Nikita Khrushchev were alive today, maybe he would say, "We will bury you . . . with three-pointers." This is a terrific look at capitalism and basketball in the most unlikely place. I am a sucker for anything about basketball that is removed from the overpowering NBA presence. Although the Russians seem to be copying the NBA, step by step.

LISA TADDEO

LeBron James's Magnum-Sized, Ultrashiny, Nike-Powered Lawn Mower to the Next Century

FROM ESQUIRE

RISING FROM HIS THRONE like an urban fairy tale, the great black king stands in his glass house. Looming erect, at six feet eight inches and 250 pounds, he is a pythonic force of length and clout, and all he has to do is crane his neck just so to ever so politely, gingerly, and revolutionarily break the glass ceiling.

The king is wearing sneakers, not the roughed-up kind but the endorsement kind. You can see them, big and exclamatory, through the cameras in the Cube, where he's having his video portrait taken. Twenty-four lenses shooting in adulation from every angle. It's a tiny space, and he fills it. His sneakers take up space too. They're the dark-red Air Force Ones. Shiny like status. When he misses a shot, he stamps one, a monster foot. The bright-white laces fly, the swoosh goes *slap*.

He roars. Really, he fucking *roars* when he misses. Outside the Cube, uptight people titter nervously; they drop their mouths and look up from their bottles of unfortified water.

Was that even human? they ask one another's unfamous faces.

He's a king because they are not. You take away the basketball, and that's still the point. A king can only exist if there are subjects to kneel before him.

He is encased in glass, a great fly caught in commercial amber.

Inside he's doing exactly what he wants, playing NBA 2K8 on Xbox
360 — *the hottest console!* — with a neat pile of Vitamin Water — *that
quenching endorsement!* — in the corner. Jay-Z is thumping from the
speakers like a promise. Outside are the reporters, the gawkers, the
handlers, the stylists, watching the way unimportant people do.
Waiting, charting, and hovering, like insipid gray suits selling Red
Bull at a rave, and club-loud LeBron James is on the inside playing
a video game.

This is the story of America Tomorrow. The future of this country. The supersized, jumbo-jawed metaphor for the watchers and
the watched is right here in a glass cube, endorsing himself, becoming the future so adroitly that nobody cares that the rest of us
are still standing dumbstruck in the present.

To watch LeBron James play is to know that you are not a superstar.

Watching him coming down the court, not terribly fast but not
slow for his size either, he is this game's animal, a beast made of pistons, a dark gazelle. Built in a rubber-smelling, pimple-walled orange lab by men with basketball faces. Evolved from a different species.

Picture it. Michael Jordan (his hero) and Penny Hardaway (his
full-court predecessor) made love and sprouted this beatific em-
bryo, then gave it to Kobe, who tucked it in his Armani pocket, nes-
tled and incubated it, and when it hatched, the progeny was longer
and stronger, and it had more tattoos than its parents, a bigger
smile. Love me, market me. You will do both. Love and marketing
will, through me, become inextricable.

But the truth is more like this: at twenty-three, LeBron James is
only a living thing with a ball in his hands. There is an affection between the two. Love you can't grasp. It's not a middle-class marriage; it's Romeo and Juliet high on Spanish fly and Carmelo Anthony buckling like a horny cheerleader before it. Other players
fold to it, like, "Here, you better take it, here, here, *hereherehere*,"
and they pass it off to him — a hot potato that cools to his touch,
that wants him to handle her.

LeBron plays without a discernible disposition. When a team-
mate goes to help him up when he's down, it's a dead man's stare.
An ESPN blogger dubbed it the LeBron James "Don't Help Me Up,
I Don't Even Want to Look at You Because You Suck So Much, I
Can't Believe We're on the Same Team" face.

But he's not an asshole. It's rawer, purer, and a lot less believable than that. He says, "It's just having this instinct. I see the plays over and over in my head. Even when I'm dreaming, I dream about basketball. So when I'm playing, I see the play before it ever even happens. I dream about it, and then I make it a reality."

His voice is hormone deep. Gone-through-five-changes deep. It is bearded but young.

Game 5, round 2 of the Eastern Conference Finals. Cavaliers at Boston. It smells like basketball, the sweat and the shine of the floor. At one point, Boston fans start to rally hard, and LeBron scowls at the crowd, like, *Yeah, go on and rally, motherfuckers. There are five of them. There is only one of me.*

Boston takes it, 96–89. LeBron scores thirty-five of those eighty-nine.

At the press conference afterward, diamonds glinting — earrings, ring, cuff links. A six-foot-eight badass blinged *up*. He is asked how bad the Cavs need to win *now*. He says: "LeBron James's team is never desperate." Numbly, directly. Look at my diamonds.

On his leg there's a tattoo that says WITNESS. At a game once, slight, myopic billionaire Warren Buffett sat and watched and wore a T-shirt that said the same. They met a few years ago, ate cheeseburgers together. Buffett's a big fan; he believes LeBron will sit at the billionaires' table, with his lobster bib and his golden chalice.

But *witness?*

"That," says LeBron, "is for everyone that watches me play. They *witness* something special. You're all a witness."

In his glass house, he is this brilliant museum specimen. Observe him, this great black fly mouthing the words to a rap song and toggling a controller with the zombie gaze of a child. Look at him, but don't touch. Look, you are here *to* look, but do not disturb.

One guy tries. "LeBron? Um . . ." The name LeBron on his tongue is an apology. "Um, can you . . ."

LeBron says one more minute. He's been playing for forty. He wants to finish his game.

"You need him out? I'll get him out." This comes from a dude a little older than LeBron, dressed a little more like a man.

He knocks on the door of the Cube. "Yo, 'Bron, let's go. Time to go."

Just like that, LeBron is out.

This is Maverick Carter. He's LeBron's best friend; they grew up together in the Akron projects. He's also LeBron's other half, older brother — the business partner who counts the money.

Sometimes he is Momma Bear. They are eating salads. LeBron finds a piece of bacon in his salad and is inspecting it, wondering if it's bacon. It's okay if it is bacon, he likes bacon, but he's not sure if it is. Maverick sticks his palm out, "Let me see it." Turns it over with his fingers. It's ascertained that it is, indeed, bacon, and he tells LeBron so, and now LeBron wants it back. Maverick shakes his head, smiles. He is shrewd, caring. He is both at once. Business and not-business, the fusion of the two. How this empire is evolving, as organically as talent and yet also as plastic as Taiwan.

There's a child hovering near the Cube. Maverick asks, "Who's your favorite ballplayer?"

Kid says, "Um . . . do they have to be players who are playing now?"

"Not at all."

"Um . . . Michael Jordan. Julius Erving. Um . . ."

The kid's dad teases, "You better say LeBron!"

Maverick says, "Nah, that's cool," and he's smiling, he's genuine with children, or at least wolfishly good at pretending, but you can see his brain working: how can we make sure this kid, and billions like him — black ones, white ones, Chinese ones — say LeBron James first? And LeBron James only.

In 2005 LeBron fired his superagent, Aaron Goodwin. Aaron Goodwin who represents Kevin Durant and Delonte West. Aaron Goodwin who began courting LeBron when he was a moist high schooler back in 2003. Aaron Goodwin who got him the famous $90 million deal with Nike.

In his place, LeBron hired Maverick and started his own agent and sports-marketing company LRMR: the L stands for LeBron, R for Richard Paul, M for Maverick Carter, and R for Randy Mims — all of them childhood friends. This is well publicized, the usual shit said about it: Entourage *but black* — *and basketball. Dumb move. Wait, does it even matter when LeBron James is the product? Nike would do business with a roundtable of squirrels to get LeBron to lace up their shoes.*

Except Maverick isn't a squirrel. He is twenty-six and well connected. He's got a sleepy voice and a charming sharpness to his face, plus the "I am your friend, I am not your friend" back-and-forth business in his eyes that the hottest bitch in high school harnessed like a Bubblicious smack.

He is the CEO of LRMR. Also, he is the gatekeeper. You want LeBron, you don't just go to Maverick. You have to go *through* Maverick. He didn't finish his sports management degree at Western Michigan University. Instead, Maverick went to the Harvard of sports management, Nike, and apprenticed for a year and a half under basketball senior director Lynn Merritt, who was the first convert to the Religion of LeBron. Merritt called Maverick a sponge. He listened to everything. He asked questions — he asked, Who is the best at this? At that? — and then he drew from them the answers.

But imagine the beginning, imagine the NBA hearing its newest, biggest star fired his agent and put his best friends in charge. A couple of kids in a designer tree house, watching as they burn down their parents' estate. Now imagine the smoke clearing, when LeBron and Maverick began inking more and more deals, and it became clear to Goodwin that not only did the king have a new kingmaker, but that suckling kingmaker was actually building the empire he'd always dreamed of.

At a lunch following his charity bike-a-thon in Akron, there is all manner of fried chicken being passed around. Boneless, barbecue, buffalo. Orange, red, and steaming. LeBron sits in the way corner in the way back of a pub with his inner circle, Maverick and Mims, and LeBron's Olympic teammate Dwyane Wade. Lunch is laughing, loud. They talk about their BlackBerrys, how to get the calendar to display like this or like that. Kid businessmen with Monopoly cash.

"I thought," says LeBron, fingering a pineapple slice, "if I stopped playing basketball right now, what would my friends have to look back on? They wouldn't have *anything* to look back on. For me to grow as a businessman, and for me to become a man, I decided I've got to start working with guys I can trust — my friends. Now I don't need to be there for them to get into places, high-prestige places, or to have a business meeting with somebody. LeBron doesn't have to be there."

He's the guy who started seeing the hot chick, in part to land his friends dates with her rosy clique. Everybody gets laid.

Under the table, LeBron's big-sneakered foot is underneath Maverick's. Their legs are touching, their expensive sneakers are canoodling. It is the ease of their friendship, of their closeness, that they don't even notice.

You can see they've talked this over. LeBron and Maverick. They've sat around on gaming chairs, around an Xbox campfire, and they've said, "I've got it, I've got it, we don't do sponsorships, we do *partnerships*." And maybe Maverick sponged it half off of someone in a Nike boardroom and half off of Jay-Z, but it doesn't matter. Because the reason this business model will work is, here are the most popular kids in school, and now in life, and they are the ones commandeering the bake sale. Nobody wants to be in a partnership with a loser. You want someone who is airborne, someone who can control climate, the guy who can get the girl and win the game and who looks good with his shirt off.

"What are we doing differently?" says Maverick, and you can tell he loves this question, and loves his answer more: "One thing we do differently, we like to *control* — well, *control* is a bad word — we like to be *involved* in every aspect of the brand we're partnered with: who they're advertising with, what the advertiser looks like — if it's a commercial, then who's the director? We really strive on the management side once a deal is done, so it becomes a *partnership*, not just a deal where they pay LeBron, he shows up."

And about the partners, they all need to be authentic. Capitalize it. AUTHENTIC. It is a word Maverick and LeBron found in a glen one day, a tethered unicorn they unfettered and dusted off and made their into-the-sunset horse.

So let's say some local car dealer, not even from Akron but from, say, Tallahassee, offered you guys $40 million a year, would you say no?

Maverick says, "Absolutely. If it's not AUTHENTIC to LeBron, then definitely not. We don't do sponsorships. See, sponsorship is" — he points to the State Farm logo on one of the bike-a-thon banners — "State Farm pays, then they get to put their names on it. *Partnership* is: State Farm pays to put their name on it, but they also bring something to the table. Instead of just money."

It's charming to be in control.

"The biggest deal we've said no to," Maverick says, scratching his chin and considering the options, "was $2.5 million a year. Now that's per year. Four years. *Per year.* It wasn't necessarily that the brand wasn't right. It just wasn't the right time for LeBron to do it."

It's charming to say fuck you to $10 million.

"It's mostly my responsibility," Maverick continues. "LeBron focuses on being the best basketball player in the world. I do most of the negotiations. He's gonna help, but it's not like he's involved in negotiation. That's why it's important to establish the team. He does come in on top-line meetings. But he's not going back and forth on e-mails. He's involved from a top-line perspective."

LRMR owned about 10 percent of big bicycle manufacturer Cannondale with private equity firm Pegasus. Sold it a few months ago. "LeBron and I came up with the idea," Maverick says. "We discussed it with a member of our team who handles the investments, and we said we were interested in the business of bikes. Twelve months later we sold it with Pegasus and made three or four times as much."

There is the Play-Doh sniff of little boys playing at grown-up games — Chutes and Ladders with solid-gold game pieces. They have the best of everything. LeBron chose Maverick, and Maverick in turn chose a Valhalla.

But there is also something else: LRMR isn't just looking for equity from the business of LeBron; they are looking for equity from other ballers. They are expanding into a full-blown marketing agency. So far, they've signed Mike Flynt, Ted Ginn Jr., and most notably, new Memphis Grizzly O. J. Mayo. The latter chose to enter the NBA draft over finishing college and was considered one of the best high school players in the country. Sounds familiar.

An athlete representing another athlete. This is a revolution in itself, according to Kenneth Shropshire, a professor of sports business at the University of Pennsylvania. He's never heard of anything like it. And he imagines that's the way it will go. Not just athletes representing themselves, but things happening sooner, faster, fiercer.

"The next step would be for an athlete to come out of high school with their own company," says Shropshire. "You see LeBron, and an even younger kid thinks, 'Hey, this is something we can do!'"

The LeBron Effect is that you can no longer come into the game

at twenty-five and expect to get better endorsements than the guy
who came in at sixteen, who has employed an agent since he was
twelve. You will have lost the race before you even got your number.
It's like the younger sisters of prom queens wearing progressively
shorter skirts. Show it sooner and let them taste it closer, and suddenly it's *Screw your older sister. She's class of 2008. Not just old hat, but
fucking porkpie.*

In a regular old banquet room, in a regular old Hilton in a suburb
of Akron, you'll find the Fellowship of the Ring, the hidden room
in the back where Frodo stole off to blow lines with Gandalf.

Here, powerful people from powerful companies have gathered
like gabardine moths to the halogen glow of LeBron James. There
is Nike and Lynn Merritt, the unofficial head coach of the LeBron
brand, the cool teacher for the in-crowd. There is Coca-Cola.
There is State Farm, Upper Deck, MSN, Cub Cadet, the Akron-
based lawn-mower company with the motor of gold. There is
WePlay, sometimes called the Facebook of youth sports. If you believe the hype, it will be big, huge maybe, and LeBron (along with
Derek Jeter and Peyton Manning) already owns a share.

Pockets of power are convened around tables with Evian and
cheap candies, and front and center is the inner circle again:
LeBron James, in a red-and-white-striped rugby and jeans, flanked
by Maverick and loyal Randy Mims. (Richard Paul is gone, looking
after Mayo, presumably helping him ink his four-year deal with
Nike.) Maverick gets up, stands before the room in a navy knit
school tie, jeans, and a Louis Vuitton belt. It's the outfit for the Best
Friend/CEO, the head of the New Business Phenomenon.

During his PowerPoint presentation, Maverick summarizes the
LeBron Past to reinforce that everybody in this room should be
proud to be partners in the LeBron Present. The awards flit by:
*Two-time NBA All-Star MVP, four-time NBA All-Star, three-time All-NBA,
ten-time Eastern Conference Player of the Week. November 2007 Teen Choice
Award nominee for Male Athlete. Ranked sixteenth on* Forbes*'s 100 Most
Powerful Celebrities. Ranked second on the* Wall Street Journal*'s World's
Greatest Athletes. Nominated for three ESPYs in 2007. Hosted the same
ESPYs with "his good friend Jimmy Kimmel, LeBron was the second athlete
to ever host them." Hosted the thirty-third season premiere of* SNL. *Cover of
December 2007* Fortune . . .

Maverick pauses. "A few years ago, I wouldn't even know what

Fortune was; all of a sudden, my twenty-two-year-old best friend is one of the twenty-five most powerful people in business."

Cover of April 2008 Vogue . . .

Another pause: "Now, I've had many conversations with many of you in this room about the *Vogue* cover . . ."

The King Kong comparison, the disparagement of the African male. This is LeBron fucking James. He blogged about how he felt, says Maverick, he didn't really see a resemblance, he got over it.

Next, because the past is as old as Michael Jordan, Maverick outlines the LeBron Future.

To fully inhabit the future, LRMR is occupying every media medium and fanning out its breadth like a many-necked cobra. In each medium, they are partnering with someone who is tried-and-true. They are developing a sitcom with ABC based on LeBron; they are in talks with H. G. "Buzz" Bissinger about writing a book. (Maverick says, "You know him, he did *Friday Night Lights*.") They are releasing a documentary called *More Than a Game*. Maverick's very excited about this one. He says, "It's true, it's real life, it's three hundred hours of footage — the director was *embedded* in LeBron's high school world. If you got the best writer in Hollywood, you couldn't write a better script."

Maverick says, "This is a *franchise* we're building here."

No shit?

And the *partners* — they love it. This is why they came to Akron. This is why they kneel. "We all need to play our cards right, but yes, he will be bigger than anything," says Upper Deck vice president Adam Sullins. "Michael got his own brand within Nike, which was huge. But if you just look at the way the media world is progressing, the reach that the Internet provides alone is so much bigger than anything that has ever existed in the past. If you have a guy who's as comfortable in front of the camera as LeBron, combined with the global reach of media today, yeah, you're gonna see somewhat of a perfect storm, something that's never been seen before and will be unparalleled."

When LeBron will smile, each pretty white tooth will endorse a different soft drink. Twenty-five thousand for a canine, and up to fifty for a central incisor.

The world's first billionaire athlete. The road to world domination officially begins this year, after the Olympics, with China. "Because of sheer population alone," says Sullins, "if you're popular in

China, you could be unpopular everywhere else, and you're still gonna be huge."

LeBron is learning Mandarin.

The partners have found their horse. Here in this room, they are betting wild trifectas with seersucker money. With his wide lap, LeBron James straddles all the odds:

He is self-aware and self-ecstatic, in the quietest of ways. "I grew up in Akron, and there was no LeBron James to look up to," says LeBron James.

He's kind of funny, for an athlete. "You grow up in Chicago, you got Walter Payton, Michael Jordan. You grow up in Akron, you got Goodyear!"

He thinks beyond himself, even in the third person. "Me and Mav were talking the other day: We were saying, on June 17, during the NBA Finals, we hope the Lakers win, because Kobe sells shoes, and that helps basketball. That helps LeBron. That helps LRMR."

He is unpretentious. "I was on the cover of *Sports Illustrated* when I was in the eleventh grade, and I just thought I was doing another cover of another sports magazine. I didn't know how big it was at the time. I didn't know till I was like twenty-one years old how big *Sports Illustrated* was, and then I was like, 'Wow! I was pretty big in high school!'"

He self-actualizes. "Then I've got a lion tattoo, which symbolizes me. I mean, I've always loved lions. I don't know. I love lions. They the best."

BUT.

There's this: Ask him what his favorite drink is, what he likes to order when he's out, and you mean cocktail, but right off, LeBron says Vitamin Water. Fast, like this: *Vitamiwater,* like he's spitting out a *Jeopardy!* question before anyone else in the room. It's rumored he peels the labels off bottles of water he's drinking if they're *not* Vitamin Water. He's a raging endorser; thanks to Maverick, he is always on. He knows how to be bipartisan, modeled after Jordan.

But he doesn't have the Jordan glimmer yet. LeBron hasn't proven it yet. Because he's not Jordan. Yet.

You hear this from the fans, the guys who love this game enough to recite its truths like drama majors geeking out on Shakespeare.

Go to the famous West Fourth Street court — the Cage — in New York City and ask around. These men, their kids, they love

LeBron, they wear his sneakers. But Jordan is still better. Jordan's toilet flushes with legacy. He is a proven commodity, as worshiped as the sun, the same bright need in every country.

On a hot summer Sunday down at the Cage, an eleven-year-old named Clifton is watching a game with his uncle. Clifton says, "I love LeBron, but I'd rather meet Jordan." Why? "Jordan's more famous." His uncle Wayne pipes up: "This kid probably never even seen Jordan play. I'm forty-seven, I've seen everybody play since I was his age, and I've never seen anybody play like Jordan. Man, MJ took it to another level."

Then you've got this baller, Victor "Gotti" Cherry, thirty-three, with a sly tuna-belly smile, sitting on a folding chair with his bare feet on the hot top. He's a former Harlem gang leader, but now he's straight, a poet. He says we love LeBron — where "we" means the basketball people who matter in New York. He also says something else. And this is where Maverick should cover his eyes.

"Look at Ray Allen, Paul Pierce, KG — these guys sacrificed their careers for the championship. LeBron has to want it that bad. LeBron came in as a brand, getting $90 million from Nike. *Shit.* There's almost not much room to go after that. Kobe looks up at the rafters, he sees championship banners. That's inspiration. LeBron looks up and sees nothing. That's why the campaign for him to move to New York is so important. We have a history here," says Gotti. "We love LeBron here. But he needs to just do it, know what I mean?"

What he means is, enough of the talk. Like any talent, like any promise, it is only as good as its execution. We've got to sit and wait. *Witness.*

LeBron's great bed is quilted in the authenticity of Nike and Coca-Cola, in the swooshes and the snaking scripts of eminence, and that's all good, but he needs to work on the LeBron brand itself — the emotion, the game, and the game face. He has to be the indisputable best, on the court and off.

LeBron's good friend Jay-Z part-owns the Nets, which are moving to his native Brooklyn in 2010, the same year LeBron will be free of his Cleveland contract. A move from Cleveland won't guarantee a championship, or five. But merely *existing* in the biggest media spotlight in the world will help the brand, will get LeBron nearer to owning the court of consumer veneration.

At an All-Star Weekend banquet that Jay-Z hosted with LeBron, one attendee recalls, "Jay-Z talked of a tomorrow when these two monuments to music and basketball will transform the rules of engagement for the iconic performer. He talked of making history."

Indeed, if these two perfect storms collide, it will be as meteoric as Hannah Montana French-kissing an American Girl doll at the Teen Choice Awards.

LeBron playing for the Nets "would be a dream for me," says Jay-Z. "But he's my friend first. I want the best for him wherever he is. He's my friend before he's a commodity."

It will help Jay-Z, just like Kobe winning helps sell sneakers, which helps LeBron. Brotherhood, lookin' out. Friendship and family, remixed with money and talent and fame and street cred, partnering the best of one world with the best of another.

"My logo," LeBron says, "is expanded now. An LB with a two-three and a crown underneath it." He points to it on his shoes. "You can see it right here too." He moves the massive, winking bling he wears around his neck aside to expose the LeBron logo on his T-shirt. The necklace, a gift from Jay-Z, is a cluster of diamonds the size of a child's hand in the shape of Jay-Z's own logo, for his Roc-A-Fella Records.

Logo on top of logo, coiled snakes, sweethearts cheek to superstar cheek.

Now all he must do is win. And when he does, the logos will ignite — an incandescent fire show scored with hip-hop and popping with exploding orange rubber — and melt into each other. The two brands will beat as one. Bigger than Jordan, dunking higher than the sun. This is LeBron's silent vow, and Jay-Z's (and the world's) fervent expectation.

The last hour of the summit is called "LeBron Unplugged." The room becomes an orgiastic auction block. Everyone's bidding for nearness.

Someone asks LeBron what was his business "wow" moment.

His smile fills with a thousand teeth. "When I realized I could walk into a room with people who know the business like they know they own kids and my opinion mattered to them. *Wow.* It's *wow* to have my opinion mean something, with how old I am — I mean, sorry, how young I am!"

The room laughs, like a starlet has just correctly guessed what continent she is on. "I mean, me and Mav, we just came from ABC, Fox, where else? Oh yeah, Calvin Klein's house."

Someone asks, "Are your colleagues asking you for business advice?"

LeBron answers coolly: "I think my colleagues are afraid. Afraid to sit down and do something like this with their friends, like I have done. A lot of guys are afraid to do anything more than just play basketball."

Maverick doesn't necessarily interrupt LeBron, but he slides his voice in, a dominant trombone: "You know, people tell us, 'You're really smart,' but no, we just have really smart people around us." He begins to talk about magazine covers and coverage, momentously pans the room for Keith Estabrook, LeBron's publicist. "Keith, wherever he is. Keith? I meant to tell Keith, I was looking at *USA Today*, and you know how they do that Top One Hundred CEO list? Well, I got to thinking, Why wouldn't Tiger be on that list, you know? Why not Jordan? Why not LeBron? He runs a company too, just as big . . . We do all the marketing for ourselves too." Maverick trails off into something else, then sees Keith. "Keith, I want us to call up *USA Today*," he says, prideful and smiling.

At the close of the summit, LeBron initiates a team huddle, because, see, this is not only more than *sponsorship*, this is even more than *partnership* — this is a *promise*. Family.

A moment of incredible surreality, this huddle. Adam Sullins of Upper Deck went to Yale; he is the sort of smart that never falters. Lynn Merritt's got the tested significance of aspirin. Here are these men, the top executives at the best companies in the world — hey, really, close your eyes and imagine it — here are these gentlemen folding willingly into a *team huddle*.

LeBron says, "Okay, on three, *Family*. ONE, TWO, THREE — FAMILY! And on six, *Gold medal*. FOUR, FIVE, SIX — GOLD MEDAL! WOO — HOO." Clap, clap, hug.

The suits wear tender Republican smiles, and LeBron's arms are long enough to huddle them all.

On LeBron's back the biggest tattoo says, CHOSEN ONE. It's the one that hurt the most.

"God has given me this opportunity," says stone-faced LeBron. "And I can take advantage of it or I can shit it away." Makes you think this God who chose him is up there, a NASCAR-suited deity sucking down LeBron-flavored Vitamin Water, looking out for the next young thing while idly dropping gray hairs onto Ryan Seacrest's head. *Plunk.*

The future, as ever, will be feverish. More money, more clothes, more cars, more sex, more *things,* and quicker, wanting to have things before you have even thought to want them. And youth, for the sex of it, for the cash of the bloom on its rose. For the ideas of the young, and for using the young to announce those ideas in the writing across the asses of their Abercrombie shorts. For all of this, LeBron will be the megastar ambassador of his generation.

His entourage thinks he is already bigger than most. Bigger than Pitt, bigger than Cruise, bigger than Clooney. But for right now they own more Google hits. This will taper off. More than ever, the future is about whom you are told to love. Who is in more places, whose face glints on more key chains and is emblazoned on more mouse pads.

"In ten years," says the commodity, "it should be flowing to a point where I don't even need to wake up."

But he will *want* to wake up. If LeBron James plays to his promise, the future will be his miniskirted bitch. He will be a carnival ride, an amusement park, a brand of magnum condoms. He will be shaving cream and chewing gum. Paper plates, tablecloths, table runners. He will be his own flag in the colors of Brooklyn. His mouth will be the angry grille of a lawn mower, his eyes will be the digitized binoculars into the first basketball game ever played on the moon. And the colony up there, the young-kid rulers with *Sports Illustrated* streaming across the miniscreens of their e-Readers, they won't know who the fuck George Clooney is, or what it even means to be an actor, when everything is reality television. Clooney will be an eBay autograph. At best.

吻我的真 屁股眼 操你妈的

That's Mandarin for "Kiss my authentic, futuristic, billionaire ass, motherfucker."

The megastar lives differently from you and me, a situation we love to explore as much as we can. LeBron seems to live on a level beyond the megastar. He is learning Mandarin for the marketing in China! Oh, my.

Where There's Smoke . . .

FROM ROLLING STONE

TONY STEWART IS PISSED. It's a crisp night at the Phoenix International Raceway, and Stewart's number 20 Home Depot Toyota — "Rides like a soapy dishrag!" Stewart complained to me the night before — just finished a distant fourteenth. Even worse, Jimmie Johnson won the race. Jimmie fucking Johnson: the glad-handing, charity-golf-event-hosting, Eddie Haskell–acting, California-born suck-up.

"I like Jimmie," Stewart says later. "Good guy. He stays in resorts and stuff like that on race weekend. Wish I could afford that kind of lifestyle." Stewart earned an estimated $19 million last year.

Now, furious at the loss, he exits his car and strides angrily across the pit lane and through the garages. His Home Depot fire suit is half undone, the sleeves tied beneath his stately gut. His face is sweaty and smudged, his wet eyes wide and bloodshot from exertion and the heat and fumes of the cockpit. As he seethes, a cloud of greasy black smoke from Johnson's celebratory rubber burn wafts over the Phoenix infield. Mike Arning, Stewart's PR rep, fixer, and constant aide-de-camp, walks briskly beside his client, hoping to get Stewart out of town without a TV camera catching him saying something he'll regret. Arning is not always successful.

"Tony will at times do or say things that make our skin crawl," says Jim Hunter, a NASCAR vice president who has been with the sport for forty years. "He's been an asshole at times."

Stewart barges into the mobile office at the back of the Home Depot hauler where Greg Zipadelli, the only NASCAR crew chief he's ever had, is waiting to debrief him. Stewart slams a door. He throws shit against the wall. He curses. He swigs a Coke Zero.

A short while later, still agitated, Stewart boards his seven-seat Citation Bravo jet at the Phoenix airport. He sets down a kitty caddy containing Wylie and Wyatt, his mewling Tonkinese cats. Stewart used to travel with a monkey named Mojo, but when Mojo grew into adolescence — "We realized he was exactly the wrong breed to have as a pet" — Stewart donated him to the Louisville Zoo in Kentucky.

As we take off over the Phoenix Speedway, Stewart opens a box containing piping-hot Papa John's pizza and takes a slice.

"Good race, Tony," I say, trying to ease the tension.

He takes a bite and chews.

"Oh, you think so?" he asks. "Because I think it *sucked*."

This is Tony Stewart's thirteenth year in NASCAR, and at thirty-seven he remains the most magnetic driver in the sport, even if he isn't always the most successful. At a time when the $3.5 billion industry of NASCAR has corporatized and spawned a generation of technically gifted, clean-cut racers like Johnson and Jeff Gordon, Stewart — or "Smoke," as he's called in the backrooms — is a throwback to racing's older era of bootleggers and brawlers. With his prodigious stomach, permanent stubble, and more than occasional public outbursts, Stewart reminds the faithful of scruffier icons like Bobby Allison, Junior Johnson, Dale Earnhardt Sr., and Stewart's idol, A. J. Foyt. Over the years, he has thrown his gloves at Kenny Irwin, had a shoving match with Robby Gordon, been accused of assaulting a fan in Bristol, Tennessee (but not indicted), knocked the headphones off a track official at a midget race, kicked a reporter's tape recorder (and apologetically replaced it), punched a photographer (and later befriended him), and told off NASCAR officials after they forced him to wear a helmet restraint.

"Tony represents what made this sport," says Hunter. "Drivers never held back in the old days. They said whatever came to mind. You never knew what Junior Johnson was going to say, but if he says it, you know he believes it. Tony's like that. I don't want our guys to be vanilla. We need different flavors."

Not everyone enjoys Stewart's act, however. Racing blogs burble with invective — "a big orange truckload of crybaby," "fat, arrogant punk-ass," "the biggest douche bag in sports." Before each race, when drivers ride around the track on the backs of pickup trucks and wave at the crowds, none are greeted with so thick a barrage of hate as Stewart. Partly because he can be a jerk. But also because he wins. A lot. Stewart is one of only three full-time drivers in NASCAR today with multiple championships. But 2008 has been a tough season — a "nightmare," he calls it — riddled with crashes, mechanical failures, and bad-luck endings. He's not even the top racer on his team this season — he's been surpassed by Kyle Busch, who is currently enjoying a Tiger Woods–like run of dominance in NASCAR.

Recently, Stewart dropped a bombshell when he announced he was leaving his employer, the deep-pocketed Joe Gibbs Racing, to start his own team in 2009. Haas CNC Racing, a much smaller outfit that has never won a race and whose principal owner, Gene Haas, is serving two years in prison for tax fraud, offered Stewart a free 50 percent stake in its $41 million organization. After weeks of hand-wringing, Stewart accepted.

The new team is called Stewart-Haas Racing, and it's the biggest move of Stewart's career. But it's risky. Stewart will no longer have the well-regarded Zipadelli in his ear or the Home Depot logo decorating everything in his sightline. And the recent history of owner-driver experiments is dodgy at best. Michael Waltrip, the two-time Daytona 500 winner, debuted his eponymous racing team full-time in 2007, but its three drivers are still winless, and they struggle every week to break the top twenty.

Stewart is undaunted. "Running a Cup team is a big step for me," he says. "But not too big. I mean, I worked my way up the ladder. Plus I already own a couple of race teams. I got an edge."

Of course, the switch raises a delicious question. In the past, when Stewart had one of his famous meltdowns, there was always a staffer or executive happy to humor him, absorb the anger, and pick up the pieces for one of the sport's great racers. But now that Stewart is the boss, who will he bitch to?

Flying home on the plane from Phoenix, Stewart finishes a couple of slices of pizza, opens his laptop, and plays computer mahjong as Led Zeppelin blasts through his headphones. Despite having raced hundreds of hard miles, he doesn't sleep on the plane. By the time we land in Indiana, he's relaxed and has become affable and chatty.

A beat-up Hummer H2 — one of Stewart's fifty-plus car collection — is parked beside the tarmac at the Columbus Municipal Airport. Its windshield is cracked, and fast-food wrappers litter the floor. Stewart doesn't wear a seat belt as he drives slowly from the outskirts of town to his sleepy suburban neighborhood and pulls into the driveway of his house — the same modest, low-slung, three-bedroom home he grew up in.

Stewart turns off the big V-8 and sits for a moment in the early-morning stillness. He exhales heavily.

"Getting home at dawn's pretty depressing," he says. "But it's good to be here, ain't it?"

Inside, a pile of mail awaits. He lets the cats out and opens the fridge, which is empty, save for a six-pack of Schlitz and some canned tangerine wedges marinated in rum. Mementos line the living-room walls: racing trophies, a football autographed by Indianapolis Colts coach Tony Dungy, helmets signed by NASCAR buddies like Ryan Newman (who is joining him as a driver at Stewart-Haas Racing) and Kyle Busch, who has scrawled in silver marker, "Tony, I'm coming for you!"

In the bedroom upstairs, Stewart shows off die-cast models of the dirt-track stock cars he grew up racing. There are framed photos of Stewart with his parents, his friend Kid Rock, Dale Earnhardt Sr., and Stewart's blond ex-girlfriend, Tara Roquemore, a small-town Home Depot employee from Georgia before she met Stewart at a sponsor event.

The house has the unlived-in feel of an extended-stay hotel, mostly because, like his father, Nelson, a former medical-supply salesman, Stewart spends much of the year on the road. Aside from some dirt-track racing newsweeklies and copies of *Healthy Pet,* there's no reading material. "You want to hide something from me?" he says. "Put it in a book."

Stewart was born on May 20, 1971, in Columbus, a small blue-collar suburb south of Indianapolis. When he was five years old, his father bought him an old go-cart. "I tore around in my backyard with that, and when I turned eight, I was old enough to drive racing carts," Stewart says. Of his first five races that year, he won one of them, placed in two, and wrecked in another.

"I tore a ligament up in my knee," Stewart says. "I was racing again the next week. Young and dumb."

Stewart's parents divorced when he was in high school, and his father left for Indianapolis. Tony stayed with his mother and younger sister. He tried to lead a normal life — he played city-league baseball, hung out with friends — but he was already running in the go-cart nationals. He barely graduated high school in 1989 and stepped up to racing a three-quarter midget, a sort of oversize, overpowered go-cart. He took a $5-an-hour job at a Columbus machine shop and raced at night.

"My parents mortgaged their house so that I could go go-cart racing," he says. "You get a *trophy* at the end of the night if you win. I look back on it and I'm like, 'They were stupid.'"

Stewart started winning races and made a name for himself as a gutsy, chance-taking competitor. Soon enough, local team owners started calling and asking him to drive their cars.

"One day in February of '91, I ran second in a race in Arizona, and my portion of the prize money was $3,500," Stewart says. "Well, I was making $5 an hour at the machine shop, and I thought, *How many hours do I have to work to make what I make in one day driving a race car? Shit, I can do this.*"

Stewart went from three-quarter midgets to midgets, and then to sprint cars. In 1995, he won the USAC triple-crown championship, which is the top honor in sprint-car racing, and made the giant leap to IndyCar racing. On May 26, 1996, he started his first Indy 500 on the pole, a dream come true for a boy who grew up spinning around tracks just south of Indianapolis. The next year he won the IRL championship, and offers flooded in from the more lucrative world of NASCAR. Rick Hendrick, whose stable now holds Jeff Gordon, Jimmie Johnson, and Dale Earnhardt Jr., had wanted him, but Stewart was charmed by Gibbs Racing, which is owned by the legendary Washington Redskins coach.

"We never rushed it," Stewart says. "We climbed a ladder, one rung at a time, nothing too soon."

Stewart got the nickname Smoke when he switched from dirt tracks to pavement and would race so aggressively his tires would smoke in the turns. While Stewart enjoyed the notoriety his technique brought, it wasn't necessarily smart. One of the keys to winning

NASCAR races is managing your tires between pit stops. If you don't conserve your treads, you lose grip of the track when you need it most: trying to pass late in a race.

But that's the way Stewart does it. Most NASCAR drivers blend into the pack, riding patiently in the slipstream of other cars and biding their time until a fevered sprint to the finish in the last few laps. Stewart has no patience. He works a car hard — he "gets up on the wheel" — and prefers running at the front of the pack, like a thoroughbred racehorse. But this electrifying style has increased risk — Stewart, his engine, and his tires take more punishment. Still, his fans appreciate the showmanship, as do some of his competitors. Veteran driver Mark Martin has called him "the greatest racecar driver I've watched in this era."

Stewart's number 20 Home Depot car is a hand-built technological wonder. It's a small-block V-8 unembellished with computers, turbos, or any telemetry beyond what you'd find on, say, a 1984 Chevy Celebrity. But like the deceptive country-boy image that NASCAR likes to sell, the simplicity hides a beast inside. The car generates 850 horsepower and winds up to 10,500 rpms. A single number 20 car can cost up to $500,000 to build; Stewart will cycle through as many as twenty in one year.

To see a NASCAR race in action is to understand the sensory violence of the sport. When the pack of forty-three cars roars by at full blast, the noise doesn't pass through your ears but through your rib cage. At a track, the 150,000-plus spectators sit with headphones that shield them from the thunderous din and let them dial in their favorite pit crews and drivers to listen to their communications. Often, what they hear is a driver diagnosing his car and informing his crew what it needs to adjust at the next pit stop. If the car is "loose," the rear wheels are kicking out too much as he turns; a "tight" car doesn't turn enough in the corners. Either condition makes the driver vulnerable to wrecking or losing track position to a better-riding car. Once a car is dialed in — just loose enough to carry speed out of the corners — then it's up to the driver to get around the track as fast as he possibly can, and in one piece.

Many racers consider the toughest moment of a race weekend to be the qualifying laps. The driver has just two laps to get a time that will put him at the front of the field on race day, so the car is rigged for pure speed, and a lot of bad wrecks happen. Stewart has been in some glorious wrecks in his career. He's suffered concussions, dislocated shoulders, torn ligaments, but he's never been seriously injured. In the spring race in Las Vegas, Stewart blew a right front tire going into Turn 3. He rocketed up the banking like a jet launching off a carrier and smashed the wall hard. It was over in an instant.

"I know I'm going to hit the wall," Stewart says. "I can see it coming. But I can't do a damn thing about it except say, 'Here it comes.'"

"This is the only time I get butterflies," Stewart says. He's dressed in his fire suit and is pacing restlessly in the narrow passageway in the Home Depot hauler at the Texas Motor Speedway. Guys from the pit crew pass him, and every so often he checks other drivers' times as they appear on a flatscreen. Jason Shapiro, the car chief, wanders in.

"Hey, Smoke," the chief says. Stewart reaches over and slaps him in the balls with his hand. It's a friendly little game they play.

"Payback's a bitch," Shapiro says, and exits the hauler.

Stewart looks at the screen, and another car's time pops up.

"There's the dickhead," he says to no one in particular.

Onscreen, Kurt Busch just ran his qualifying lap in his number 2 Miller Lite Dodge. At the start of the season, Busch (the older brother of Kyle) got into a skirmish with Stewart during practice before the Daytona 500. Afterward, Busch and Stewart were called to the NASCAR official's hauler to iron things out, and while both decline to discuss what happened, rumor has it Stewart decked Busch with a punch to the face.

"You know those kids in high school that talk all the time and won't shut up?" Stewart says. "And every once in a while someone gives them a good wailing? That's Kurt."

Fighting, of course, is part of the Stewart charm. His first ontrack altercation in the Cup series took place in his rookie year at Martinsville Speedway in Virginia. Racing against a field that included Dale Earnhardt Sr., Stewart mixed it up with Kenny Irwin.

"We were rivals from open-wheel racing," Stewart says. "We knew if we were at the same racetrack, we'd have to beat each other to win, and we just got in a shoving match in racecars. Every time one of us would hit the other, it was harder than the one before. Eventually Kenny crashed me bad enough to where I couldn't get it to move."

When that happened, Stewart's number 20 car came to a smoldering stop across the center of the corner. He got out and stood angrily on the track waiting for Irwin's car to pass under caution. The crowd erupted: the balls on this rookie!

"I reached in his car and tried to grab hold of him," says Stewart. "Wasn't a very smart thing to do. The funny thing is, Dale Earnhardt was in front of Kenny's car, and Earnhardt slows down to a crawl to give me time to get to Kenny. So the old man was working with me there." Irwin was killed the next year during a practice run in New Hampshire.

Over the next eight years, Stewart would accrue a racing rap sheet longer than that of any active driver. He once chased Matt Kenseth into the infield at Daytona, and he tried to climb into Brian Vickers's car, à la Irwin, after tangling with him on the track. The list of fellow drivers he's had on-track altercations with includes Jeff Gordon, Clint Bowyer, David Gilliland, Ryan Newman, and Rusty Wallace, who said he wanted to "wring Stewart's neck."

"Sometimes I just want to shake some damn sense into him," says Carl Edwards, who after getting wrecked by one of Stewart's on-track tantrums wondered to a TV reporter how "that much of a jerk" could have gotten this far in life. "But Tony's a good guy. I would say that if he got in shape he'd win even more races, but I don't think Tony needs to do that to win."

"I like to think I do things the right way," Stewart says. "It's about respect. You get into a wreck with somebody you might hold a grudge for three or four weeks, but it goes away. There's a lot of water under the bridge."

The only thing Stewart enjoys more than a racecar and a fight, it seems, is women. Over the course of a race weekend, he's approached by dozens of them, each more long-legged, doe-eyed, and blond than the last. Inside the NASCAR bubble, these gals are called "pit lizards," and they prowl the inner sanctum at tracks throughout the year.

"My parents are afraid my dick's gonna rot off," Stewart says.

Roquemore, the Home Depot girl, was a fixture for a season, until Stewart realized she wasn't the one. "Oh, we had to fire her," he says.

At a late-night fuel stop during the flight to the Phoenix race, he meets two girls, who look to be in their early twenties, working the front desk at the airport lounge in Salina, Kansas.

"Take us with you, Tony?" one of them says as he grabs a chocolate chip cookie from a tray on the counter.

"Depends," he says, taking a bite. "You gals eighteen yet?"

"Why you want to know that?" one girl asks.

"Well, we ain't just flying up there, darling," he says, winking at me. "We'll be taking pictures and hanging out and all sorts of stuff."

"*Aww,* Tony," singsong the girls.

Talladega Superspeedway. The Wimbledon of American motor sports. Set plum in the center of the lower heartland, near Atlanta. Twice a year, the reddest necks in the South travel from the swamps, bayous, and cypress groves of Alabama, south Georgia, Mississippi, and Louisiana and congregate like ill-behaved pilgrims to worship in Talladega's temple of steel, gas, beer, and high speed.

They arrive weeks before the race and build shantytowns of dually pickup trucks, beat-up Winnebagos, tarps, tents, and gleaming motor coaches affixed with satellite dishes and Weber grills. It's a full-scale bacchanal that one number 20 crew member described as "a little heartland, a little misbehaving, and a little Book of Revelations."

The night before the Talladega race, Stewart is driving through the traffic outside the superspeedway behind the wheel of a beige Camry, in search of the exit. Jody Doles, a former Alabama sheriff, is racing one of Stewart's dirt-track cars at a nearby backwater track. Stewart hired Doles, whom he calls "Redneck Jody," as his property manager in Indiana after an injury forced Doles into retirement, and built him and his wife a house. Doles is a real Southern boy and the center of Stewart's circle of protective confidants. Smoke ribs him mercilessly.

As he makes his way to the dirt track, Stewart's eyes flicker with annoyance in the rearview mirror at the car behind us.

"What in the hell does this guy have his brights on for?" he says to Tom Wetherald, another Columbus confidant sitting in the passenger seat.

Suddenly, Stewart brakes in the middle of the road, gets out of the Camry, and walks to the car behind us. Traffic honks. The driver rolls down his window, ready for a fight.

"Is there a reason you have your high beams on?" Stewart asks, in his best sheriff's voice.

The passengers are briefly stunned. Finally: "Tony! Tony!" they say, recovering. "Hey, man, sorry. Tony, can I get an autograph?"

"Just turn off your high beams," he says, and walks back to his car.

Later, we watch the dirt-track race from a rickety wooden official's tower, where fading autographed posters of Stewart line the walls. We eat corn dogs while Doles gets his ass kicked down below, and afterward we meet him at the car and drive back to the motorcoach lot.

"I'm done with racing," Doles says.

"You fuckin' quitter," Stewart says. "If I'd-a quit, you think I would have had the twenty-eight-year career I had? *Sheeee-it.* I've had enough of you tonight."

"Aw, hell, Tony. Y'all gonna call me later and say, 'Bring me some pussy.'"

"If there's one thing I don't lack, it's pussy. Between me and Tom here, there's two things we definitely don't lack, and that's pussy and money." Stewart is standing in his relaxed pose, with his thumbs hooked into his jeans. Carnival sounds and car horns float into the lot from the other side of the vast Talladega infield. "Pussy, money, and racecars. That's pretty much all I care about." Then he winks at me.

Stewart gets wrecked at the Talladega Sprint Cup race. Twice. The crew repairs the damage the first time, and Smoke claws his way back into contention. With fourteen laps to go, Junior gets into him as they race four across, and he gets caught in a melee that takes out six cars. Into the wall he goes, tearing up the front right side. The number 20 car's day is over. Bad luck. Again. "This season's like a bad dream," he says. Zipadelli kicks the wrecked car. Zippy, Shapiro, and the rest of the Home Depot team are staying with Joe Gibbs next year.

Back at the motor coach, Doles and Wetherald are sitting on the couch. Stewart strips to his tighty-whiteys and reclines on the floor. Someone hands him a plate of microwaved Chef Boyardee ravioli, and Stewart eats and watches the race on the widescreen.

"Shit, you can't blame Junior, even if it's his fault," Stewart says to the room, referring to Earnhardt's sacred status with the fans. Doles agrees. "And I think that Denny Hamlin set the goddang record for unnecessary lane changes," says Stewart. "Why can't he just ride?"

"That's what I was saying," says Redneck Jody.

"Well, he's on his own at Richmond. And I mean it."

Stewart finishes the ravioli and tosses the plate in the trash can. "This tastes like shit," he says. He fishes a box of doughnuts out of the cabinet.

The pack wrecks again, and Kyle Busch wins under caution. Pundits are now comparing Busch to Old Man Earnhardt, and I'm reminded of the signed helmet back in Stewart's house: "Tony, I'm coming for you!"

Stewart doesn't have anything left to prove in NASCAR. He can race for another ten years if he wants to, but the competition is coming of age — Busch, Hamlin, Vickers, Edwards, David Ragan, a pimply eighteen-year-old named Joey Logano who'll most likely be taking over Stewart's seat in the number 20 car. Stewart has to build a whole new team and also assemble a pit crew that understands that sometimes he loves winning so much it hurts. It ain't gonna be easy.

"You want a doughnut, Jody?" Stewart asks, chewing.

"No, thanks."

"Well, then," Tony Stewart says. "Do you want a kick in the ass?"

The do-anything, say-anything approach of Tony Stewart comes from the roots of NASCAR, not from the burnished, corporate product of today. Good for him. Good for Mike Guy, letting us ride with him. Deep into the corners.

DAVID MCGLYNN

Rough Water

FROM MERIDIAN

IF I LEAN AGAINST THE RAILING and squint, I can almost make it out. The orange buoy anchored a hundred yards off the end of the pier, a wanderer in the galaxy of wind and sea. My father and I stand together at the lookout point above La Jolla Cove. The bougainvillea is in bloom, though it is the end of summer, and the small violet flowers go all the way to the edge of the cliff. The rocky cove below is curled tight as a lower-case *c*. The hotels and condominiums on the hillside shadow the rocks and water, pushing the harbor seals toward the inland point of the cove where there is sunlight. My father sips coffee through the lid of a travel mug. It leaves a pencil-thin line of brown on the fringe of his white mustache. He sets the cup in the bougainvillea so he can scan the horizon with his binoculars, the heavy black Bushnells my mother gave him for Christmas when I was eight or nine. They're one of the few things he took with him, and seeing them returns me to the strange fact that we once lived together. He passes me the binoculars and I look north across the mile and a half of open water. The buoy bobs in the smoky haze, a twenty-foot tower of red-and-yellow balloons tethered to its northern pole turned horizontal in the breeze. The slightest shift of my wrist, a wiggle of my elbow, and it disappears. The binoculars fill with ocean. It looks like a long way to swim, and it is. And it's only halfway.

Each September, when I can scrape together the cash, I come to this tiny California beach to swim one of the oldest and most famous ocean races in America: the La Jolla Rough Water. There's a short, 250-yard race for children, the traditional one-mile, and the

3.1-mile (5-kilometer) "Gatorman." The Gatorman is my race. It runs from La Jolla Cove to the tip of Scripps Pier and back, a roundtrip distance three-quarters of a mile farther than the swimming leg of an Ironman triathlon. The cove sits at the far northwestern tip of a peninsula appended to the California mainland like an enormous ship docked against the coast. In the middle of the peninsula is Mission Bay and tucked below the crook of the southern point is the North Island Naval Air Station, where two of the Navy's largest aircraft carriers, the *Nimitz* and the *Ronald Reagan*, actually sit docked against the coast. Across the bay is San Diego.

If the peninsula is a ship, then entering the ocean at La Jolla Cove is like jumping off the prow. The course points due north while land retreats to the southeast, dipping into the crescent of the La Jolla Underwater Park before meeting the mainland. By the time the beach appears off your shoulder during the race, it is nearly a mile away. A number of swimmers enlist the company of a paddle boarder to mitigate the danger and the distance, and several more boarders paddle unaccompanied to corral the field. They ride kneeling, eyes shaded by wide-brimmed lifeguard hats as they scoop their cupped hands through the water. Yet the paddle boarders are not lifeguards, only guides. There are only about twelve of them for a field of five hundred. A true emergency, a swimmer on the verge of drowning, will summon the San Diego Lifeguards in their yellow speedboat. Short of that, short of your imminent demise, you're on your own.

Which is, of course, the fun of it, and the reason I come back each year. The allure of the swim is that it traverses a path not everyone can follow. Most of those who can follow it dare not try. Challenging the ocean is a way of feeling significant in a Kantian sense: Man confronts Nature; Nature dwarfs Man; Man is awed by his smallness in the universe, and in his solitude feels unique. It's hard not to feel this way. And ocean swimming is different from other long-distance competitions. There is no bottom to stand on, no sideline to sit on, no shady spot or port-a-potty in which to rest. No first-aid tent. No police officer holding traffic. No line of spectators ringing cowbells. No volunteers offering cups of water and orange wedges. No one to shout your name. Stop running during a marathon, or stop cycling during a tour, and only time leaves you behind. The earth will wait beneath you. Stop swimming during an ocean race and the world leaves you behind. Life leaves you behind.

The Rough Water was first held in 1916, the year San Diego hosted the World's Fair. Two world wars, the influenza epidemic, and numerous shark sightings interrupted competitions during the first half of the century, but in ninety-one years the swim has gone off seventy-seven times. In 1916, there were only seven swimmers. Today more than two thousand will race. In 1916, the course started at the pier and finished at the cove; the last finisher ran onto the shore one hour and fifty-four minutes after he went in. Today the course is twice as long and must be completed in an hour forty-five. After that, time is no longer kept. If you finish in an hour forty-five and one second, you don't officially finish. It's as though the day never happened.

Competitors in the 1930s and '40s complained that the pier-to-cove course was too long and grueling and crossed too much unprotected water, so in 1947 the old course was abandoned in favor of a shorter, one-mile route that runs in a triangle inside the safety of the cove. The Gatorman was added in 1993 as a pseudo-revival of the original 1916 course. The one-mile triangle is compact enough that a keen eye can follow a single swimmer from start to finish. It has remained unchanged for sixty years, and at the bottom of the entry sheet are the names of men and women in their seventies and eighties who have swum it every year since the first. It is also the race my father swims. This day of swimming — as well as our breakfast before dawn and the drive from his house in Laguna Beach along the coast through Camp Pendleton while the sun chalks the sky behind the Santa Margarita Mountains — is something we do together. Most years it is just the two of us, but this year my sister Devin is here to race too, and my wife Katherine and sons Galen and Hayden have come along to watch. We're a family of swimmers.

I grew up in what might be called "swim county" — the vast expanses of suburban subdivisions northwest of Houston, Texas. Land here is more plentiful than oil; cul-de-sacs of semicustom single-family tract homes radiate out from the city like a compass rose gone supernova. Geographically, Houston is the largest city in the country. The Consolidated Metropolitan Statistical Area, encompassing the city and the surrounding counties, is as large as Israel. The Metro bus system alone famously covers an area larger than the state of Rhode Island.

Every subdivision has a pool and many have more than one. They're built to attract buyers, but they're also necessities. Temperatures in the summer months camp out above one hundred degrees with 99 percent humidity, the sky like a wet towel draped overhead. When I worked as a lifeguard I learned to recognize the crowd of regular mothers who came to the pool every day. They arrived right at 10:00 A.M. when I unlocked the gate, carrying sacks of magazines and Igloo coolers full of drinks and sandwiches, their children already whitewashed with Coppertone. They thumbed their magazines with their feet in the water, once an hour slid in up to their necks to cool off, and then called their children back to the chairs for lunch and another coat of sunscreen. Many stayed into the evenings when their husbands met them there after work. The men changed into trunks and swam awhile and the family went home together after seven when the mosquitoes started to bite. Without a pool to go to many people in Houston would spend the summer sprawled out beside the air-conditioning vent.

It is a quintessentially suburban assumption, a truth universally acknowledged, that physical ability and enjoyment should be channeled into athletics, just as intellectual aptitudes should be put toward "marketable careers." In the same way that a child with a gift for mathematics is encouraged to consider majoring in engineering ("where the money is") and the voracious reader of history a career in law ("what else can you do with history, teach?"), swift runners are pushed toward organized sports in which runners excel, preferably one with the potential for a college scholarship. Football for boys, and if not football then basketball or soccer; track if you're not good with a ball. If a girl likes to cartwheel across the lawn and can land a round-off, Bella Karolyi is training the next Mary Lou Retton sixty miles north of town. To be a child without a sport is to be without childhood. People moved to neighborhoods like mine specifically so that their children could play sports. I knew families who sold one house and moved to another simply to feed into the high schools with the better teams.

When summer hits and it grows too hot for baseball or softball, swimming is the only game in town. The Northwest Aquatic League, which organizes the summer youth swimming teams *only* on Houston's northwest side — not the south side, not the east side — has grown into a Goliath of a little league. With 18 divisions, approximately 102 teams, and over 11,000 swimmers, it is the second-largest swimming organization in the country. Only USA Swimming, the national body, is larger. To put it another way, there are more swimmers in northwest Houston between May and July than in all the colleges in America.

It was not just my environment, however, that made me a swimmer. My father boasted a handful of records from his youth and a scholarship offer to swim in college. My first desire to swim was therefore a desire to imitate, fueled by the hope that by inheriting half his chromosomes and his last name, I had also inherited his talent. And I was quickly showing my lack of talent in other sports. I was tall but doughy and bowlegged; a tennis ball could pass between my knees when my ankles were pressed together. My mother used to call me "The Tank" because I ran so upright and ramrod stiff and because my first soccer coach made me a fullback and told me to "just get in the way of the ball." (I didn't have the mettle to actually tend the goal.) I played an entire season of basketball without scoring a single bucket. The first pitch at my first baseball practice — the first ball to leave the pitcher's hand — landed squarely in my groin, and after that I feared the batter's box. I can't bear to remember the spring I signed up for a jazz dance class at the studio where my sister took ballet. I was seven the first year I swam on the neighborhood team. Devin joined two years later, when she was just five. By the time I was nine, I'd quit all other pursuits to focus on swimming year-round. Never once did I consider the possibility that I could have chosen another path, and before long I had put in too much time for any other path to tempt me.

Meets were held on Saturdays throughout June and July. Away meets were often more than an hour away, which had us on the road by six. Our team camped together beneath the trees, if there were trees, or under a shantytown of blue tarps held aloft by nylon cords and aluminum poles. The sunlight through the plastic magnified the steamy heat. My mother would flap open an old bedspread and anchor it with a cooler stuffed with pimento cheese and tomato sandwiches, sliced apples marinated in cinnamon and lemon juice, homemade trail mix with Cheerios and pretzel sticks and raisins and M&Ms, dried apricots and almonds, Wheat Thins and saltines, Diet Coke and regular Coke, jugs of water and jugs of Gatorade, and my favorite, floating at the bottom like the prize in a box of Cracker Jacks, the frozen miniature Snickers. She buried them deep in the ice to be saved for after the meet. No one can pack a cooler like my mother. Each time I have set out from her house on a long drive she has packed me a cooler so tight and jam-packed that it required two hands to lift. Each time I have been thankful for it.

My father volunteered as a stroke-and-turn judge and spent the day pacing the deck in short white shorts. He was lean and liked to show off his legs. My mother wore her turquoise team T-shirt with the sleeves rolled up and a matching terry-cloth visor. She helped herd the heats from the ready benches to the starting blocks and made sure my sister didn't wander too far off. Once an hour I swam a twenty-second race and by the end of the day I'd read two books, listened to four tapes on my Walkman, played six hours of cards, and spent maybe thirty total minutes in the water: twenty minutes warming up, five minutes racing, five minutes free swimming once the meet was finished. We left sticky with sweat and sunscreen, and in the car on the way home I fished out the last Coke floating in the melted ice at the bottom of the cooler, but before I could finish it I fell asleep against the window.

We check in for the race. A line of folding tables has been set up at the edge of the park overlooking the cove, the aisles arranged by event and alphabet. Behind the tables is an archway of red-and-yellow balloons in the same helical twist as those tied to the buoys. The woman at the table uses her painted fingernail to isolate my name on a list and a ballpoint pen to cross it off. In exchange for my signature waiving my right to sue if something goes wrong I am handed a plastic sack containing a yellow swim cap, a Velcro ankle strap fitted with a digital timing chip, a Powerbar, a packet of Powerbar Gel, and a sample bottle of Bullfrog Sunscreen. A man in a khaki outback hat, one side snapped above his ear, waves me over. He marks my number on my biceps and shoulders with indelible ink.

In the ocean, however, nothing is indelible. After a coat of sunscreen and a short warm-up swim, I come out of the water with my numbers faded and smudged. Katherine darkens my numbers with a marker she keeps in the diaper bag. She writes slowly and presses hard, making sure that this time the numbers won't rub off. Hayden naps in his infant carrier in the shadow of the bougainvillea bush where we've encircled our bags, his fat face squished against the shoulder belt. Three-year-old Galen dances on the grass in my cap and goggles, the rubber cap scrunching up his face like a baseball glove, a little like Sloth from *The Goonies*. He runs between the chairs to the railing at the edge of the cliff where below a group of children play in the shore break. The children chase each wave as it recedes and then scurry up the beach to dodge the next crash. The last boy lingers, taunting, his wet T-shirted back to the ocean. The next wave jacks over the top of his head, driving him into the sand and rolling his legs over his head. He comes up with his hair in his face, his knees and belly covered in sand, hollering and laughing. Galen watches him, his eyes mirrored by the goggles, the goggles fixed on the water. I know this look. He's looking past the boy, past the group of children, his eyes set on the sea. He wants to go in. He wants to swim.

Though I have spent most of my life in pools, I've always been drawn to open water. In Texas I used to dive for golf balls in the water hazards on the course near our neighborhood, the water oily black and stagnant and potentially full of cottonmouths from the adjacent bayou. The threat of snakes and getting caught by the course marshal made the hunt feel clandestine and perilous. During summers in California, I liked to slip out of the house with my mask and snorkel after my father and stepmother had gone to bed. The beach was less than a mile away, down a long flight of stairs; I could get there without passing beneath a single streetlamp. Entering the ocean in the dark, the rolling waves undetectable until I was riding one up, I felt like I was entering a world unhinged from the laws of physics, without a floor or ceiling or sides. Every hike I took during the years I lived in Utah led to water, or what should have been water, that amoebic depression in the map beckoning me to come toward it. To this day, whenever I come to a body of water, in the car or looking down from the window of an airplane, I cannot help but ponder swimming across it. I try to estimate the time it would take to make it across and then turn around and make it back. It's the explorer's impulse: the urge to see how far out we can go and still make it back. How far a ship can sail, how high a climber can climb, the distance an untethered astronaut can float away from the Space Shuttle. The medium of travel may vary, but the need to go out and return remains constant. To make it there only is to strand yourself beyond the borders of sustainable living, beyond people, beyond shelter and comfort. To make it there and back is to bring the remote inside your radius of wandering, to make it a part of your home.

My numbers freshly blackened, I stroll around the park where the other teams have set up camp. I tell Katherine I need to use the restroom, but I really just want to size up the competition, the men and women in their thirties and forties and fifties, their skin gone a little leathery, their hair grayed and frizzled by overexposure to chlorine and sunlight. Ostensibly they're here to see if they still have the onions for a tough swim, but coming to La Jolla is also an act of nostalgia for their competitive days. Some teams come with T-shirts and warm-ups and banners hanging from the crossbars of the canopies. The swimmers — now parents and grandparents, now tax accountants and web designers and pharmaceutical representatives — sit in that old swimmers' pose: the soles of their feet pressed together, crotches open, pressing their thighs to the ground to stretch the quads, headphones stretched over their caps. I can see them nodding and listening, but also not-listening, thinking instead about the race or remembering a race from long ago.

One of my best races could hardly be called a race at all. I was a senior in high school, gunning to qualify for the USA Junior Nationals. In addition to the excitement of swimming at a national meet, the qualifying times were often the benchmarks for college scholarships. If you made the meet a letter would show up in the mail and a college coach would call your house. People took notice. The previous summer I had missed the cut by less than a second in the mile, and just the day before, at my high school regional meet, I had come within three-tenths of a second in the 500-yard freestyle. The qualification time was 4:39.69; I swam a 4:39.95. The next day, Sunday, I drove with my mother to the far side of Houston where a time trial was being held — an informal, unadvertised

event thrown together at the last minute. I learned about it by rumor. The only races swum were those the swimmers requested
to swim. Most were short, flapping sprints in which swimmers at-
tempted to shave off a few one-hundredths of a second. I didn't
have the courage to face the mile, and since I'd struck out in the
500 the day before, I decided to swim the 1,000-yard freestyle. Forty
lengths of the pool. It was a race I'd swum fast enough to believe
that given the right confluence of circumstances — cold water, an
aggressive heat, an energetic meet — I could make the cut. I had
fifteen seconds to drop to qualify. There was no concession stand,
no heat sheet. The overhead lights were left off. The sun came
through the skylights in the rafters and a line of translucent windows behind the blocks. Two officials and a time-keeper verified
the results. If you were lucky, there would be other swimmers in
your same event. Swimming beside one other person was far better
than going it alone. I was not so lucky.

By the time I stood up on the blocks, I was not only the only
one in the race, I was practically the only one in the natatorium.
The other swimmers had either made their times or had missed
them, and either way there was no point in sticking around. (Most
missed, given the utter lack of atmosphere. This was a place where
"next year" was said a lot.) I stood behind the block yawning, listening to the water trickle into the gutters, and watching the pool return to that static standstill where each molecule of water balances
against another, where the surface appears to swell above the cop-
ing. The starter spoke through the PA even though it was just the
two of us. He said, "Take your marks," in the plural, and I bent and
gripped the block. The horn sounded and I dove in. I was angry
and disheartened at having missed the cut the day before and I had
little belief that I could go any faster today. I had spent too much
time dreaming about qualifying, and now having twice failed, I had
run out of energy to dream. So I didn't dream and I didn't think. I
swam. I sang George Harrison's "Give Me Love," I'd heard it in
the car on the way down, and I listened to the water flood my ears,
and I felt my triceps stretch when I rolled. I felt the walls on my
toes, and the seams between my fingers trap and move the water. I
followed the black-tiled line along the bottom and I breathed in
and out.

About six hundred yards in, my coach started to pace. He walked back and forth at the end of the pool, just a few steps when I swam by him, and then he went farther, and soon he was traveling the entire length of the deck. He waved his clipboard and whistled. I stayed steady on, not in a hurry, not about to get my hopes up. In my mind, I had already missed the time. Then a boy from a rival high school, whom I hardly knew, unfolded his legs and climbed down from the bleachers and started to cheer. He squatted low to the water and pointed his finger toward the end of the pool, as if to say, *That's where you're going, now hurry up.* I thought, *If he's cheering, maybe I'm close.*

Sometimes a moment comes along when the world slows down, and though everything else moves around us at the same frenetic speed, we're afforded the opportunity to reflect in real-time rather than in retrospect. It is as though we slip into a worm-hole in the fabric of time and space, travel into the past and then back again to the present in the same instant. That morning, swimming, I remembered a day in late September the year before, the last day my swim team had use of an outdoor pool. The pool was Olympic length, fifty meters, located on the edge of a property owned by a steel plant. All summer long my teammates and I swam under an open sky and raced our cars along the plant's service road, past the welding shop where sparks rained out morning and night. After this day we would spend the rest of the season in a dank and moldy indoor pool at the junior high across the highway.

The triangular backstroke flags were strung across the lanes and the adjacent diving well. My teammates liked to run down the long cement deck, jump out over the diving well, and try to grab hold of the line. Many of them could jump far enough to make it. I could not, though I tried every day. I tried that day, and missed. Since I would not have another shot until May, I decided to try again. I squared up and ran, my feet wet against the pavement, and just as my foot hit the water's edge, one of my teammates called out, "Jump!" I bent my knees and pushed off hard and got my hand around the flag line. I pulled the whole thing into the water. The embankment and meadow around the pool were brown and the sky was clear and smelled of decaying leaves. Autumn was coming and I wondered if there was a metaphor in what I had just done, a fortune folded inside a cookie: my greatest effort would come when I was down to my last opportunity.

Now it was March and I was down to my last opportunity, think-ing about that day and hearing the word "Jump!" as my eyes fol-lowed the finger of the boy pointing me onward. What I under-stood — not later, but right then, in the water — was how little this swim added up to in the world. How few people were here to see it, and how few would register its ever having occurred. I had spent more than a year training for this one swim, and when it was fin-ished the world would be no different than before it began. If no one else cared, then the swim was mine alone. It mattered because it was the task before me *now*, the thing I wanted *now*. Whatever happened was up to me and no one else. Swimming, I had long un-derstood, is a constant choice between the now and the later: ex-haustion now for the sake of fitness later, all those Friday nights spent in the pool in pursuit of an end that seemed always one step farther on. I was out of laters, this was the end, and I made my choice. I tucked my chin and cleared my nose and emptied my tanks. I cashed in the energy I kept reserved for the final dash to the wall as well as the energy I set aside for climbing out of the pool and unfolding my towel and tying my shoes. I've never sprinted harder in my life, not before and not since. I hit the wall and emp-tied my stomach into the gutter. I knew by instinct, by the spasm of my tendons and the ache in my bones, before I ever turned toward the clock or heard my coach scream, that I had made it.

Over the years there have been a number of swimmers I expected to beat and accepted nothing less from myself than beating them. Boys from rival teams, or even from my own team, who seemed to show up at the meets with the sole intention of challenging me. Be-hind the blocks we would joke and laugh, talk about the other meets we'd signed up for, and make fun of our coaches. (I had three: one who drove the pink Cadillac his wife had earned as a saleswoman for Mary Kay cosmetics, another with one leg longer than the other, and a third who carried a book in his briefcase ti-tled *No Cherry Cheerleader.*) But all friendliness stopped when the starter blew the whistle. Lying in bed at night, or reading, or sitting in class, I fantasized about their gasping, asthmatic failures, their bewildered faces when they saw how far ahead I had finished, their lip-quivering, teary humiliations buried inside their towels. It was not enough to win. I wanted to eviscerate. I wanted to disembowel.

My hatred was so fierce, their names so anathema that many years later I can still recite them: Jeremy Woodley, David Donat, John Klein, Josh Kimmel, Ramon Kik, Matthew Pierce, Jamie Rausch, Jon Armstrong, David Durden, Rich Sarkisian. Several of these boys swam on scholarship in college, one won a silver medal in the Olympics, one dated Chelsea Clinton while her father was president, and one is dead. The last two, Durden and Rich, I hated the most. I hated them with a rabidity unbecoming of a sportsman.

They were my college roommates and for four years we did everything together. We spent twenty hours a week in the water, four more in the weight room, and when we weren't swimming we were eating, or showering in the big stalls in the basement of the athletic complex, or studying, or watching TV, or sleeping — all together. Durden and I shared a bunk bed for two years, Durden and Rich shared it our third year, and our fourth year, Rich and I sawed the bunk apart and set the halves against the opposite walls of our bedroom. Durden and I had been recruited together from Houston; since we were both named David and both from Texas, we were known as "the two Daves" or else "Big Dave" and "Little Dave." Durden wasn't little, but he was the thinner of the two of us, so I got to be Big Dave. He didn't comb his hair for an entire year, and in the chlorine and constant California sunlight it turned transparent, waxy as straw, and stood up from his head like an urchin. At the end of the year he shaved his head bald with a Lady Bic razor. We all did. Lady Bics were softer on our scalps. Rich was half Armenian and grew a beard so long and nappy that he carried his breakfast crumbs around in it all day, his face a nest of maple bars and Frosted Flakes. He could do an impression of Gilbert Gottfried so dead-on that Jay Leno wouldn't know the difference.

We knew one another's ins and outs, every little secret, and we knew one another's bodies the way only swimmers do. When our championship meets came we shaved the hair from our chests and arms and legs, and then helped one another shave our heads and backs. I have never in my life worn a jock strap, and am repulsed by the idea of ever putting one on, but I have shaved more backs than I can count, including the backs of women and the backs of strangers. Durden and Rich majored in engineering and math, so my classes in the Humanities Building provided my one brief escape from them. In the courtyard immediately before and after class, I was free to remake myself, to live for a time in a crowd where I could talk about philosophy and poetry and edge furtively away from my life as a swimmer. I wanted desperately to be someone else. Sometimes Durden or Rich would wander through and catch me, their puzzled eyes meeting mine across the courtyard, yanking me right out of the conversation, their smiles exposing me as a fraud. They had my number, and there was no place I could go to escape it.

We sang on the bus to our meets, and wrestled on the carpet of our apartment, and rode our bicycles to workout at 5:45 in the morning, when the entire campus was still hazed with a glowing, amber drowsiness. It felt that every big thought and thunderous sentence ever produced there belonged to us. Jacques Derrida slept in an apartment just up the hill, and though I hadn't yet read a word he'd written, I knew he was important. His thoughts felt like mine too. But beneath all this wonder lurked our unspoken, constant state of competition. We'd come to college to compete. Our abilities to compete paid our tuition and our books. Competition therefore possessed not just our time in the pool, but also the very courses we studied, the very words we read.

We challenged each other at the things expected of boys on the cusp of manhood: who had the higher grades or the better-looking girlfriend, or a girlfriend at all, who could do the most pull-ups or bench the most weight. And each day an inordinate number of smaller, stranger contests passed between us. Who could shower the longest in ice-cold water. Who could withdraw cash the fastest from an ATM machine. Who could ride a bicycle down the longest flight of stairs. Durden and I both wore contact lenses, and each morning before heading to the pool we stood in the bathroom racing to see who could get his lenses in first. He and I overlapped in two events, Rich and I overlapped in every event but one, which meant that each time I stepped up to the blocks I stepped up beside at least one person who shared my bathroom, whose snores and sneezes echoed against the wall of my bedroom, who pilfered my dresser when he ran out of clean clothes.

That brief time in the water — that harsh assembly of seconds, and tenths of seconds, and hundredths of seconds — between the starter's horn and the last lunge toward the wall felt like the fulcrum of my existence. For four years, it was the fulcrum of my existence. Had we not been swimmers we would not have been friends. We wouldn't have known one another at all. Competition was the rule of our friendship and we knew it going in. We were tired all the time, we wanted nothing more than to skip workout to sleep, and yet, as though driven by a compulsion that would one day land us in prison, we went, every morning from six until eight, every afternoon from three until five. Following the advice of a sports psychologist, we all wrote down our goal times on index cards that we kept taped to the wall beside our beds. I fell asleep touching my times while on the bottom bunk Durden fell asleep touching his. A win in the pool eclipsed everything, and no other victory could surmount a loss. And so often I lost, so often I was the one to finish gasping and asthmatic, so often I was the one to lift my head from the water to see Durden or Rich — or God save me, both of them — sitting with their goggles on their foreheads and their arms draped over the lane ropes. So many times I buried my hatred inside my heart as I climbed out of the water and slapped their backs and said "good swim" and followed them home for dinner.

I cannot imagine a life without competition, without the endless need to measure myself against the wits and talents of others. How strange it is to make a friend into an enemy, the focal point of all your angst and anxiety and malice, only to realize that you are the same thing to him, the bearer of faults you didn't intend and wrongs you didn't know you committed. Though competition can inspire excellence and move us beyond our limits, it is also the engine of narcissism. Again and again it brings us to the mirror to evaluate the states of ourselves, to hunt out our every imperfection lest they be hunted out and exploited by others. Every day presents the possibility of greatness, and in every day lurks the possibility of shame, the unavoidable worry that the competition is simply better. You glimpse it, shrug it off, and still it remains. You tell yourself your losses are the result of forces beyond your control. You talk yourself into the lie that you're better off because you're kinder, or smarter, or happier, a winner at some other contest, until kindness and intelligence and happiness all come to feel like consolation prizes. In a final, desperate attempt to save yourself, you say you don't care, maybe even quit, and still there it is, after you like a shadow on a hot sidewalk: failure.

*

The last time we swam together was the morning of my wedding. Rich was married by then and Durden was about to become engaged. It was early May and raining, cold enough that in the Wasatch foothills above the pool the rain fell as snow. The pool overlooked downtown Salt Lake City where my relatives were eating brunch. They were my best men so I got to dictate where we went and what we did. I wanted to swim. They both huffed and shivered and finally Durden said, "Come on, McGlynn, let's go eat." But I wouldn't, not until I had trounced them both. My father was there too, happy for a break from his ex-in-laws and because going in the water on the mornings of big events has become a tradition. My sister knew better and stayed away.

Competition has had a different effect on Devin and me. It's made us distant and polite; when we talk we don't talk about swimming. If one of us swam well we relied on our mother to pass along the news. When she was looking at colleges, my school and USC both showed interest, but she chose a university in the East where I had never set foot and therefore left no footsteps. It shouldn't have been this way. The years we spent together on airplanes flying between our mother in Texas and our father in California, and all the things we witnessed together, should have created between us a stronger bond. Like me, she went through some tough periods with swimming, when the weight of expectation grows so great it buckles the pleasure of the thing itself, when your enthusiasm pools into a sour puddle and you'd rather scrub toilets than face the water. We could have helped each other then, but neither of us could admit that we needed the other's help, so neither of us gave it.

Most years we visit our parents at different times; it's rare for us to be in the same place. Now, watching Devin line up with the other women for the one-mile and descend the sandy cement stairs to the floor of the cove, I have to remind myself to keep my old impulses in check. We're here for fun; she's my sister. She finds a place in the middle of the pack and stands touching the seams of her cap, checking to make sure she's got all her hair tucked up inside it. With the binoculars I scan the other women around her, trying to guess who will go out fast and who will round the last buoy and come home strong. Devin's fit enough that she has a shot of doing well, and I realize I'd like to see that happen. She lets out a long breath and jounces her shoulders. My father points his camera while Galen and I clap and yell. Everyone around us does the same, so I look like everyone else, my cheers ordinary, even routine, though of course they're not. They're not.

One of the reasons I am drawn to this race is the absence of rivals. Though 499 other swimmers go into the water with me, and the top three finishers receive cash prizes, the swim is ultimately solitary. The last real glimpse of the competition is on the beach before the gun goes off. Then it's all arms and elbows and nylon as we high-step into the surf and punch through the shore break and skim over the shallow rocks and sea grass and make for open water. It's a melee, a salmon run: lift your head to take a look around and you'll get an elbow in the eye; keep your head too low and the swimmer behind you will try to climb over your back. It's not personal. Everyone wants a clean line and no one wants to pull up to let someone else go by.

After a hundred yards, we clear the shallow water and fall into line. I spot a swimmer to my right and resolve to stick with him, or with her. (Despite the chauvinism of the name "Gatorman," nearly as many women as men swim the race.) If we stay together we'll have a better chance of holding the pack, and the pack is our best chance for staying on course. The line on the map between the cove and the turnaround demarcates not only the route but also the distance; the course is 3.1 miles only if you swim in a straight line, and in open water there is no such thing as a straight line.

As soon as my jitters settle down and I find my stroke, we hit the part of the course I like the least — the kelp bed. A flotilla of stalks and leaves so slimy and heavy that they cling to my skin like wads of wet toilet paper. Away from the shade of the coast, the kelp grows thick and close together; trying to swim through it is like trying to ride a bicycle through a rain forest. Depending on the year, the bed ranges from one hundred to several hundred yards wide, and equally as far across. It's too far to go around, so the only way past it is through it. It's a slow, frustrating crossing, each stroke a reach into a dark primordial soup that retards my glide and requires me to frog-kick to push my hips back to the surface. If the stalks get above my shoulders they'll drag me under.

When the kelp ends and the water opens, the sea floor falls away.

The view through my goggles goes from blue-green to pitch black. The Scripps Institute of Oceanography perches on the cliff above this coastline because of the two submarine canyons that bisect the continental shelf just off La Jolla, offering the rare opportunity to study deep-sea marine conditions without losing sight of land. The canyons form a V between the cove and the northern point of the coast. La Jolla Canyon runs south into the Underwater Park while Scripps Canyon goes north toward the pier. Both canyons are shifty and unsteady, constantly filling with and emptying out of sediment, and where the race crosses them, more than nine hundred feet deep. Between me and the bottom of this ocean is enough water to swallow the Chrysler Building in New York, or the TransAmerica Tower in San Francisco, or the Space Needle in Seattle. I could swim over their radio antennae and blinking red warning lights and never know they were there.

The depths of these canyons have allowed for the occasional rogue wave, generated by submarine seismic activity, to rise out of the deeps and wash out the shore. Migrating gray whales in the fall and spring swim so close to land that a mask and snorkel and a bucketful of courage are all you need to look one in the eye. Leopard sharks are common in the Underwater Park, but now and then a larger species, a Mako or a Blue, will swim right into the surf. The pack offers only the illusion of protection, and I have lost long minutes imagining a shark circling toward the sunlight with its tail curled toward its snout, mistaking me and my hop-along stroke for a wounded seal. How easy it would be for it to sink its jaws into my calf and pull me under. Who would notice? Every swimmer looks the same. We all wear the same yellow cap. If I disappeared, another body would take my place. Only hours later when I did not return to shore would my family start to worry, and by then I would be long gone. So long, chum.

By the time I've reached the buoy, the thought of a shark taking me out of the swim doesn't sound like the worst idea. The worst idea is swimming all the way back. I lift my head to spot the pier, Navy-gray and as big as a warship, not the kind of pier from which to drop a fishing line. The surf slaps against the pylons, I suck in air and put my face back in the water and move for the buoy. The field bottlenecks at the float, jockeying for the inside line as though gaining it makes a difference, and rounding it we steer for the two paddle boarders sitting saddle-style, resting their weight on their arms. Turning in front of them we turn toward home. It's important to get pointed in the right direction. Out here the variation between south and south-by-southwest makes an ocean of difference. A single degree off course and who knows where I'll end up. And as soon as the buoy is behind me the field of swimmers disperses like a meadow of geese alarmed out of their thrushes. One minute I've got a swimmer to my right and another to my left, and the next there's no one on either side. I look up and see no one. I'm all alone.

I'm not sure why, exactly, this happens — if the pack can stick together heading north, then why not heading south? — but every La Jolla swimmer I've ever met says it has happened to them. Perhaps it has something to do with the fact that the route to shore is a little farther out to sea than the route to the buoy, and that when I breathe to my right side, I don't see land, just the ocean's windblown undulations stretching from here to Japan. The sun takes up the whole sky, so bright and hot it burns my eyes through my goggles. Fatigue radiates from the back of my neck to the tops of my thighs. My ears begin to chafe from rubbing against my shoulders and my shoulders begin to chafe from rubbing against my chin. My stomach caves in while my balls crawl into my lower intestines. With each breath I whimper, just a little, just to make sure I'm moving air through my lungs. I am no longer afraid. I am in pain.

Most races I spend my time trying to control and ignore pain, but with a mile and a half behind me and a mile and a half left to go, I have come to the point where pain is all there is. I've lost my usual bag of tricks for enduring long swims, the games I play to distract myself from myself — old songs I can sing verse for verse, anagrams and crossword puzzle clues, lengthy addition problems. I cannot sing, and I cannot speak. I can only hurt. I feel myself enter into pain as though passing through a doorway from the bright of day into a windowless room, at first overwhelmed by its absolute grasp and then adjusting to it in small degrees, locating the walls and floor, the dimensions of the space I'm in. My emotions flood out as though leaking through my nose. At first I'm angry with the paddle boarder for leaving my shoulder, then I'm elated to be on my own, then I'm dejected and lonely and begin to cry, my goggles fogging at the edges as I promise to be a better husband and father, to worry less about money and to linger longer at the park with my sons. Then all emotions are finished, passed through, I'm on the other side of them, and all that remains are the raw dimensions of my anatomy. My heart beats in my chin and fingertips, in the backs of my knees, and deeper, in the bubble of my stomach, my pancreas, the tiny organs tucked in the folds of my intestines that before now I could not name. I feel them all. Then even my body disappears inside the pain, and I follow it to the very edge of being — the white flash of the sky and the black abyss below like the first sparks of the universe flicking on and then off again, hinged together at the point where my head turns on my neck. I take in air and lose it in the water. I take a stroke and then I take another. I am here and nowhere else.

The numbers on my father's arms make him look younger despite his white hair and mustache. I come alongside him as he stands in line to go down to race. He wears a Speedo one day a year, today. I ask him what time he has in mind. "I don't really care," he says. "I just want to have a nice swim." His back and neck are red with sun. He knows all about the start, the flying elbows, and wants no part of it. He's used to swimming in the ocean alone, in the late afternoon, in the crescent-shaped cove not far from his house. He's made friends with the men around him, all of them graying and paunchy, all of them over fifty. They'll be the last group to go into the water. He is far enough removed from his days as a competitor that he no longer remembers his best times. Even if he did remember, they would no longer matter. My best times too are obsolete: what was fast when I was seventeen is considered mediocre now. It pleases me to think that my time here today, like all my times, like time itself, will pass into nothing. I take a picture of him and then hand the camera to a stranger. I take off my T-shirt so my numbers show beside his. We lean into each other. His skin feels like a towel left draped over a chair at the beach. We haven't seen each other since last year's Rough Water. For most of my life we've lived in different states. "Father and son?" the stranger asks. We nod. He snaps the picture. "The family that swims together," he says, and passes the camera back to me.

After forty years of wandering in the desert, Joshua led the Israelites across the Jordan River into the Promised Land. The river marked the line between exile and home. So it was to the river that John the Baptist went to baptize, and to the river that Jesus went to be baptized. They stood together in the water. Baptism is an act of exile and return, a metaphorical journey just beyond the borders of your people, the same hands that push you out pulling you back in. The water is not accidental. We are meant to live near water, not in it; in baptism we drown and return again to life. When I wash up on the shore at the end of the race, and dash the last fifty feet for the finish line, I can't help feeling a little redeemed. I've left the world and made it back. I've made room for my heart to grow. I move across the sand with the other swimmers who have endured this too. A volunteer kneels on the sand, stripping off our timing chips as we walk away from the finish line. Another hands out cups of Powerade, the color and temperature of dog urine, and Powerbars that have been in the sun all day, like flattened Tootsie Rolls with a little Gravy Train mixed in. I chow it down hungrily. Before attempting to climb the stairs we sit for a while in the sand, our chests pink, our feet in the tide as we look out over the white-capped waves, the paddle boarders, the swimmers still crawling in. We want them to see us when they run up the beach. The tide washes over our ankles and retracts, calling us back out.

All my stories lead to water. In my earliest memory I see myself padding toward the business end of a three-meter diving board, water wings on my arms, my father treading below as he calls to me to jump. It was at a pool that, years later, he told me he was leaving my mother. It was at a pool in Houston where my team gathered the morning after one of our teammates had been shot and killed. It was at a pool in Salt Lake City that I watched a man die. I tried to save him and could not. It was at the same pool that I met my wife. Our first touch was not skin but water, I squirted her with a rubber duck, and on our first date we went swimming in the Great Salt Lake. Her legs bobbed against mine as we floated in the briny water, a conduit for my courage, allowing me to touch her calf, her thigh, to reach around her back. The water wasn't simply backdrop; it was an x in the equation. On dry land the outcome would have been different.

Sometimes I think about the friends I've lost when I swim, the two that died. I'll look to the lane beside mine and see them there, our strokes in cadence, or else either one of them coming on hard. I pick it up to stay ahead, unable to resist the urge to compete, even with my ghosts. And since, despite all the differences between pools, a length is still a length and water is always wet, I often find myself reliving old races, remembering old workouts, laughing at the old jokes — alone in the water and yet surrounded by time. It's water's z-axis that does this, allows me to think of more than one thing at once, to simultaneously remember and imagine. The present gets squeezed between the past and the dream of the future. That belly-first plunge through the summer sky, Galen's arms reaching as he steps from the side of the pool, Hayden's eyes candied and white the first time he bursts through the surface, my hands moving him.

It is after 1:00 P.M. when the Gatorman is called to line. I stand in the shade of a eucalyptus tree and wait for the stairs to clear. The last one-milers are still coming up. My father is dried and in his shorts, and stands against the railing overlooking the cove. Katherine holds Hayden beside him while Galen stands with his back against my sister. I follow the procession to the stairs. We walk silently, solemnly, uncertain of whether we walk toward greatness or danger. On the beach I edge my way to the front left, just inside the reef that juts out from the hook of the cove. The rocks push the swell to the south, revealing the line between the rocky shallows and clear water. I'll need to move to the right once I'm in the water, but I'd rather go in first and scramble than get caught in the scrum. The water is sixty-seven degrees, the top inch warmed by the wind and sun, that smoky Southern California haze. I look for the buoy, but I can't see it. The pier and the beach and the brown hills all float away in the distance, pushed back by the sea.

The paddlers gather up their boards and head for sea, the crowd around the railing cheering. They wave, and one by one slap their big boards on the water and flop down and head out. It's a long way even for them. Bodies press in tight. I can feel the anxiety in the swimmers that surround me, adrenal glands wide open and throttling. Some bounce and jump, some suck in deep breaths of air as though hoping to squirrel away extra. They exhale long, hot gusts against my neck and back. I splash in the shore break to rob the ocean of its initial paralyzing shock. Others do this too. Together we sit in the water and pee, our last chance for a while.

I look up once more at the railing, at my father and sister, my wife and children. Everyone up there shares my last name. The sun shines on Galen's red hair and glares in Katherine's sunglasses. My father waves and I wave back. *I see you, you see me.*

One last wave and then it's time to concentrate. I scoop a handful of water into my mouth, swish and spit. I scoop it under my arms and chest and then I lower my goggles. I shake my arms. A man squeezes in beside me and goes through this same series of actions, the swish and spit, the splash, the lowered goggles. He's bronzed, hairless, not an ounce of fat anywhere. When he's finished he turns and eyes me up and down. He doesn't know me and can't possibly be intimidated by my wooly stomach, but I recognize him. He's an Olympian, a former American record holder. He swims open-water races all the time, and today he's looking good for the cash. He'll beat me by a margin of seven to ten minutes, depending, and I know it, but standing with my shoulder against his I can't help allowing myself the momentary delusion that when the gun goes off I'll beat him to the water, and in the water I'll beat him to the buoy, and who knows, maybe this is my day, maybe this will be the swim that has flowed dormant through my veins ever since a starter's gun first sent me into the water twenty-five years ago. How many times have I seen those races happen, nobodies becoming somebodies in just one swim? Maybe today it will be me.

He nods and I nod back. "Good luck," I say.

All delusions dissipate when I turn back to the sea. I take a deep breath and hold it and let it leak out slowly through my nose. I touch my forehead and chest, my right shoulder and my left, drawing on my skin the mark of the pain that the next hour will force me to appreciate. I pray to make it back. I lean forward and let my fingers dangle in the water. Beneath the surface the sea grass sways, the sand sparkles like gold in a miner's pan, and an orange garibaldi drifts lazily in the tide's back and forth. A wave sweeps in and engulfs my hand. I am ocean, I am salt and water. My heart is bursting. The harbor seals are barking, great deep woofs from the rocks. From the beach the woofs sound like cheers, calling out to me as I begin to run — as the Pacific takes hold of my ankles, my knees, my thighs, as I pull my hands together and throw them forward and dive — *Go! Go! Go!*

This reminded me of a John McPhee story. Not much happens and maybe the subject isn't really interesting, but the writing alone is a wonder. David McGlynn puts us in the pool, puts us in the starting blocks, puts us in his family. We're on a trip to someone else's life and nothing else matters. That is good writing.

TODD DREW

Memories Are Forever

FROM ALEX BELTH'S BRONX BANTER

THE MEMORIES WILL NOT STOP. Sometimes they come in the middle of the night and you have to walk. So you head down five flights to Walton Avenue. You pass the spot on East 157th Street where a bat boy once found Satchel Paige asleep in his car after driving all night from Pittsburgh.

Memories say it was fifteen minutes before the first pitch when the boy shook him awake. It also says that Satchel asked for five more minutes and then threw a two-hit shutout.

Memories say things like that.

You cut over to Gerard Avenue where a Mickey Mantle home run would have landed if the Stadium's roof hadn't gotten in the way. That's how the memories tell it anyway.

You walk up River Avenue behind the bleachers of the old Yankee Stadium. There will be no more games here, but you keep coming back because this is where your memories are.

You move past the millions that have huddled in the cold and the heat and the rain and sometimes the snow for tickets. The line wraps around the block and down East 161st Street near where a Josh Gibson home run once landed.

Your friend Earl from Harlem carries his father's memory and says that blast may have hit the new Yankee Stadium if it had been across the street back then. Earl says that the new Stadium couldn't have held Gibson any better than the old Stadium. That memory always brings a smile.

You wander down Ruppert Place and away from the new Stadium because it doesn't hold your memories yet.

The players' gate draws you this way. Everyone has walked in and out of those doors and your friend Henry has seen them all. He is at the Stadium every day just like a lot of other people from the neighborhood.

There was a rainy afternoon last year when everyone else left and the cops even took down the barriers, but Henry wouldn't leave because Hideki Matsui was still inside. You both got wet and shook Matsui's hand.

You remember standing there all night when the Yankees won the pennant in 2003 and David Wells came out with a bottle of champagne. He offered up drinks and everyone cupped their hands. The sticky-sweet smell of victory still clings to the scorecard back in your apartment.

You look over at Gate 4A and remember how long this place has been your home. You think about all the wins and the losses too. Every day at the ballpark is a good one, but the pennants and the World Series titles make them even better.

You dig around your memory and try to find the best. There are lots to choose from, but you settle on one from a few years ago.

A boy and his grandfather were waiting in line at Yankee Stadium. The boy was eighteen and unable to buy beer so the grandfather had picked up three bottles at a bodega and slipped them under his coat.

"They won't frisk an old man," he said.

The boy rolled his eyes, but the grandfather got through with the beer.

"Two bottles for me and one for the boy," the grandfather said. "He is young and shouldn't drink too much."

"What are we gonna eat?" the boy asked.

The grandfather pulled a big bag of peanuts from his pocket.

"An old man can get away with anything," the grandfather said.

They found their seats and cheered for all the Yankees, but saved their loudest for Jorge Posada and Bernie Williams.

"We are all from the same island," the grandfather explained. "The Puerto Ricans will always get my best."

Posada and Williams both hit home runs in the game and the grandfather was feeling good.

He started eyeing a lady in low-cut jeans and a skimpy top that was sitting in front of him, and when the Yankees stretched their lead in the eighth inning the grandfather blurted out: "Nice tattoo."

The lady's boyfriend wheeled around and took a swing at the boy. There was a scuffle and the boy defended himself well. The boyfriend and lady were so offended that they left.

"An old man can get away with anything," the grandfather said again.

"Yeah," the boy said.

"It was a good fight," the grandfather said. "And it's been a damn good game."

The boy stared straight ahead, but managed a smile.

The grandfather put an arm around him.

"You're a good boy," he said. "But you gotta protect against the right hook."

They both laughed.

You still see the boy around. He's a man now and can buy beer on his own. His grandfather is gone, but that memory will walk through this neighborhood forever.

Todd Drew died after undergoing surgery for cancer on January 15, 2009, at the age of forty-one. He was a bright and thoughtful voice in the cacophony of the blogosphere. This is Exhibit A.

Contributors' Notes

BRUCE BARCOTT is the author of *The Last Flight of the Scarlet Macaw,* a true-life environmental thriller that was named one of *Library Journal*'s best books of 2008. His feature articles on outdoor adventure and the environment appear in *National Geographic,* the *New York Times Magazine, Outside, Harper's Magazine, On Earth, Backpacker, Runner's World,* and other national publications. Barcott is a frequent contributor to the *New York Times Book Review,* and his short essays can be heard on the syndicated public radio show *Living on Earth.* His previous book, *The Measure of a Mountain: Beauty and Terror on Mount Rainier,* won the Washington Governor's Award and was recently reissued in a tenth anniversary edition. He lives near Seattle with his wife, Claire Dederer, and their two children.

AMBY BURFOOT, formerly the executive editor of *Runner's World,* is now editor at large of *Runner's World* and the author of *The Runner's Guide to the Meaning of Life: What Thirty-Five Years of Running Has Taught Me About Winning, Losing, Happiness, Humility, and the Human Heart.*

BRYAN CURTIS was born in Fort Worth, Texas, in 1977. He was a contributing editor at *PLAY: The New York Times Sports Magazine* for its (blissfully happy) three-year run, and he has also written for *GQ, New York, Slate, The New Republic,* and *Texas Monthly,* where he's a writer at large. He is currently a senior editor at *The Daily Beast.*

During the 1990s, TODD DREW worked for NASCAR in public relations and for *Trackside Magazine* and *Speedway Scene* as a columnist and graphic designer. In 1995 he was listed in the "Notable Sports Writing" in *The Best American Sports Writing.* Most recently Todd was the director of publications at the American Civil Liberties Union for over six years. He blogged about baseball and New York, first at YankeesForJustice.com

(2006–2008) and then for Alex Belth's Bronx Banter (2008). In his own words, he believed in "baseball and an equally free, open, just society for everyone." Todd, at age forty-one, passed away January 15, 2009, from complications after cancer surgery.

DAVID FLEMING is a senior writer for *ESPN: The Magazine* and a columnist for ESPN.com's "Page 2." Before joining ESPN in 2000, Fleming covered the NFL for six seasons as a staff writer at *Sports Illustrated*. He is the author of the memoir *Noah's Rainbow: A Father's Emotional Journey from the Death of His Son to the Birth of His Daughter* and *Breaker Boys: The NFL's Greatest Team and the Stolen 1925 Championship*. A graduate of Miami University in Oxford, Ohio, he and his wife, Kim, and their two daughters live in Davidson, North Carolina.

A former editor at *Rolling Stone* and *Details*, MIKE GUY writes for *Men's Journal, Rolling Stone,* and *Playboy,* among other publications. He lives in Brooklyn and is at work on his first novel.

PATRICK HRUBY is a "Page 2" columnist and occasional contributor to other sections of ESPN.com. A resident of Washington, D.C., he holds degrees from Georgetown and Northwestern and previously wrote about sports for the *Washington Times*. This is his second appearance in *The Best American Sports Writing*.

CHRIS JONES joined *ESPN: The Magazine* in 2008 as a contributing writer. He is also a writer at large for *Esquire* and is working on a book about golf. He lives in Ottawa.

THOMAS LAKE considers himself the third or fourth best storyteller among Robert and Elizabeth Lake's six home-schooled children. His first article was published in the *Evening Times* of Little Falls, New York. It was about a subscriber on his paper route. Lake was cut from two college basketball teams — first at Herkimer County Community College in upstate New York, then at Gordon College, north of Boston. He began his journalism career in 2001 at the *Press-Sentinel*, a twice-weekly in Jesup, Georgia, where his duties included photographing car wrecks and dropping off film at Winn-Dixie. He has since written for the *Salem News* in Massachusetts, the *Florida Times-Union* in Jacksonville, and the *St. Petersburg Times* in Florida, where his story about townsfolk who intentionally shot off their own limbs for insurance money won a first-place award from the American Association of Sunday and Features Editors. He currently writes for *Atlanta Magazine* and lives with his wife, Sara, and their cats, Fox and Finn. "2 on 5" was his first magazine story, and would have been impossible without the intervention of Gary Smith.

MICHAEL LEWIS is the author of *The New New Thing, Liar's Poker, Moneyball, Coach,* and *The Blind Side.* In 2006 he served as guest editor for *The Best American Sports Writing.*

DAVID MCGLYNN is the author of the story collection *The End of the Straight and Narrow;* his stories and essays have appeared in *Alaska Quarterly Review, Image,* the *Missouri Review, Shenandoah,* and other publications. He teaches at Lawrence University in Appleton, Wisconsin, where he is completing a collection of personal essays.

MICHAEL J. MOONEY has been a staff writer since 2007 at *New Times,* a Village Voice Media paper in Fort Lauderdale. He graduated from the University of Texas in 2004 and received his master's degree from the University of North Texas, where he was a Frank W. Mayborn Scholar. His writing has appeared in the *Dallas Morning News, D Magazine,* and *Condé Nast Portfolio.* His story "The Day Kennedy Died" was selected for the 2009 edition of *The Best American Crime Reporting.*

ALAN PRENDERGAST is a staff writer at *Westword* and the author of *The Poison Tree: A True Story of Family Violence and Revenge.* His work has also appeared in *Rolling Stone, Outside,* the *Los Angeles Times Magazine,* and other publications. He lives in Denver and teaches journalism at Colorado College.

STEPHEN RODRICK is a contributing editor for *New York Magazine.* This is his fourth appearance in *The Best American Sports Writing.* He lives in Brooklyn and Los Angeles.

TRACY ROSS is a senior editor at *Backpacker Magazine* and a former editor at *Skiing Magazine.* Her stories, ranging from an exploration of Iran's nascent ski culture to a profile of an autistic seven-year-old living deep in Denali National Park, have been broadcast on Alaska Public Radio and have appeared in several national publications. She lives in the mountains above Boulder, Colorado, and is working on a book-length memoir based on the story that appears in this edition of *The Best American Sports Writing.*

Sports Illustrated senior writer GARY SMITH has appeared in *The Best American Sports Writing* more frequently than any other author — twelve times. He is the author of the anthology *Beyond the Game.*

PAUL SOLOTAROFF is a contributing editor for *Men's Journal* and the author of *The Group* and *The House of Purple Hearts.* This is his fifth appearance in *The Best American Sports Writing.* He lives in Brooklyn.

JOHN SPONG holds a bachelor's degree in history and a JD from the University of Texas at Austin. In 1997, after a brief yet dramatically unfulfilling stint as a civil litigator in Austin, he joined *Texas Monthly* as a factchecker. He became a staff writer in 2002. Spong was named the 2005 Writer of the Year by the City and Regional Magazine Association. He has twice been a finalist for the Texas Institute of Letters O. Henry Award for Magazine Journalism, which he won in 2006 for his story "The Good Book and the Bad Book." His story "King's Ransom" was collected in *Literary Austin,* and his story "Sand Trap" appeared in *Rio Grande.* He has lived in Austin since 1970.

LISA TADDEO is a novelist and frequent contributor to *Esquire* and other magazines. She lives in New York.

MATTHEW TEAGUE is a native of the Mississippi Delta and now lives with his wife, Nicole, and two children in Alabama and Pennsylvania. He has written stories set in places as diverse as Algeria, Sri Lanka, and New Zealand. His work has been included in the anthologies *The Best American Sports Writing, The Best American Travel Writing,* and *The Best American Crime Writing.*

WRIGHT THOMPSON is a senior writer for ESPN.com and *ESPN: The Magazine.* He lives with his wife, Sonia, in Oxford, Mississippi. This is his fourth piece chosen for *The Best American Sports Writing.*

Before joining *Sports Illustrated* in February 1998, senior writer IAN THOMSEN spent six years in Europe as the sports columnist for the *International Herald Tribune,* the world's largest international English-language daily. Since joining *SI,* he has become one of the magazine's top basketball scribes. Thomsen graduated from Northwestern with a journalism degree in 1983, has also worked for the *Boston Globe,* and was a feature writer for *The National.*

A full-time member of the *Sports Illustrated* staff since September 1997, L. JON WERTHEIM received a BA from Yale in 1993 and a JD from the University of Pennsylvania Law School in 1997. He is the author of *Blood in the Cage,* an examination of the rise of mixed martial arts and the culture of Ultimate Fighting. His book *Running the Table* tells the story of pool hustler Kid Delicious. He is also the author of a basketball book, *Transition Game,* and a tennis book, *Venus Envy.* Wertheim has partnered with Jack McCallum, also an *SI* senior writer, to coauthor the novel *Foul Lines.* His work was included in the 2005, 2006, and 2007 editions of *The Best American Sports Writing.*

MIKE WISE has been a sports columnist for the *Washington Post* since 2004. Previously, he worked for ten years at the *New York Times,* where he primarily wrote about the NBA. He has covered five of the past seven Olympiads and fourteen NBA Finals. He has coauthored two books: *Shaq Talks Back,* with Shaquille O'Neal, and *Just Ballin' — The Chaotic Rise of the New York Knicks,* with *New York Daily News* reporter Frank Isola. He is a regular guest on ESPN's *Rome Is Burning,* MSNBC's *Countdown with Keith Olbermann,* and CNN's *Reliable Sources.* He lives in Washington, D.C., with his dog, Talula.

Notable Sports Writing of 2008